AMERICAN SCHOOL ADMINISTRATION

PUBLIC AND CATHOLIC

McGRAW-HILL
CATHOLIC SERIES IN EDUCATION

BERNARD J. KOHLBRENNER, *Consulting Editor*

McCOY · American School Administration

POWER · Education for American Democracy

AMERICAN
SCHOOL
ADMINISTRATION

PUBLIC AND CATHOLIC

RAYMOND F. McCOY

Professor of Education and
Dean of the Graduate School
Xavier University

NEW YORK   TORONTO   LONDON   1961

McGRAW-HILL BOOK COMPANY, INC.

AMERICAN SCHOOL ADMINISTRATION: Public and Catholic

44878

TO MARGE

from her and our youngsters
was borrowed the time
to prepare this book

Foreword

My introduction to the formal study of Catholic education occurred in 1935 when, as a young priest, I was assigned to take courses in the organization and administration of the American parochial school system. Even though all my previous education had taken place in Catholic institutions, there was much I still had to learn about the system as such and considerably more about those important principles which provide the fundamental reasons for its structure, its motivation, and its policies.

During my first two months in graduate school I became acutely aware of what can perhaps best be described as an almost complete absence of any adequate and pertinent literature on the administration of Catholic schools. There was, on the other hand, a wealth of material for all my other courses, particularly those in the history and philosophy of Catholic education. Some practical and real problems, it is true, involving the day-to-day administration and supervision of the Catholic school as an individual unit or as part of a diocesan system, were given limited attention; but on the whole, many larger and equally important aspects of this field had not as yet been described in any publication. To add further to the students' plight, there was no textbook available on Catholic school administration that would at least give students that important sense of order and unity so needed when beginning the study of any complicated and extensive field of knowledge.

Thus it was that I was forced by the sheer lack of a basic literature to read books on public school administration; since there was no dearth of excellent texts on this topic, I read them with great interest, comforted by the thought that they contained much that could be equally applied to Catholic schools. I shall never regret this phase of my self-education, for there have been innumerable opportunities in the years that have since elapsed to apply the techniques and procedures used in the public school system to many of the organizational, administrative, and supervisory problems I have faced in Catholic education. However, when I finished my studies at the university, I knew more about public schools than I did about Catholic education as a system, the area in which I was supposed to become an expert.

I have gone to some length in describing this personal experience because I am sure it will awaken a similar sense of frustration in those who have attempted to grasp the broad picture of the Catholic school administrative setup from the literature currently available. Although many books, articles, and research studies have been published during the past twenty-five years, these are concerned chiefly with particular aspects or phases of some larger part of the total administrative picture. Dr. Raymond F. McCoy's treatment of Catholic school administration here presents for the first time a complete text covering all major areas of this subject. Although it is not his purpose to deal with all these in depth, he does succeed admirably in making available to students the long-awaited and much needed text which will enable them to view and better understand the administration of Catholic schools in the light of the schools' history and philosophy.

Looking back over the years, I would have been delighted if I had had a copy of this book when I first began my studies. What I have learned about Catholic school administration has come to me the hard way, that is, by direct and personal contact with the system over the past quarter of a century. I would find it difficult indeed to summarize and highlight, as this book does so well, the knowledge and insights I have gained through this experience.

I am especially pleased that both public and parochial schools are examined together throughout the text: Although the book gives special attention to the problems of administering Catholic schools, much of the material presented is applicable to the administration of all schools. To quote the author, "There are more similarities between the administration of public schools and the administration of religious-centered or other private schools than there are differences."

There is another important reason why I am pleased that both school systems are included in this book. In recent years contacts and relationships between teachers and administrators in public and Catholic education have greatly increased. More and more they are working closely together in programs of common and mutual interest. I refer here to such matters affecting children as the enforcement of the compulsory education law, health and welfare projects, luncheon and released time programs, bus transportation, and activities sponsored by civil, social, and community agencies. These areas of common interest are found not only on the local but on the state and national levels as well. An understanding and appreciation on the part of public school personnel of the philosophy and principles underlining the structure of Catholic education would do much to ease tensions which may arise from time to time. It is equally true that this same appreciation and awareness of public school administrative policy by Catholic school personnel would likewise help to promote better understanding and cooperation.

Since any school or school system is administered to promote and advance the best interest of the school child, I would ask you who read this book to keep this important principle ever in mind. For if you do this you will succeed in keeping all that you learn in proper focus and in bringing to your future pupils a love for their welfare and a wisdom whereby to achieve it.

Rt. Rev. Msgr. John J. Voight
Secretary of Education
Archdiocese of New York

Editor's Foreword

American School Administration: Public and Catholic by Dr. Raymond F. McCoy is the second volume to appear in the McGraw-Hill Catholic Series in Education. The series began with the publication, in 1958, of *Education for American Democracy* by Dr. Edward J. Power, which was intended to serve as a basic textbook for the beginning course in teacher education. It has served this purpose well and has been adopted as the course textbook in many colleges and universities. Dr. McCoy's book, on the other hand, is addressed primarily to students of the organization and administration of American schools. Its special character is its concern with problems of Catholic school administration. For the first time, students have available in this publication a general and basic treatment of the special aspects of the administration of Catholic schools, along with a consideration of public school administration. This combination makes the present book unique.

Dr. McCoy's book admirably satisfies the requirements established for the Catholic Series in Education. When I wrote the Editor's Foreword to the first book to appear in this series, I stipulated that these would be "substantial books, each written by a person competent both by preparation and experience to do his particular volume. They will take account of contemporary research and deliberation in American education, and their effect on public and private schools." Dr. McCoy's studies and his long experience

xi

in preparing administrative personnel for both public and Catholic schools served him well when he came to write this book. Based on sound principles, it is enriched by its attention to the practical order in which school administrators work through frequent documentation from preferred current practices.

If one might wish for more empirical data on particular aspects of administration than are found here, he would soon discover that such additional data are not now available. But the fundamentals are here, and applications are sufficiently illustrated to enable the administrator to make the adaptations required by the contingencies in his local situation. It may be hoped, also, that the publication of such data as are at hand will stimulate other students of school administration to extend and refine the research that has been done.

The present volume is confidently recommended to those who are searching for a basic textbook in school administration that does justice to both the public and the Catholic schools.

Bernard J. Kohlbrenner
University of Notre Dame

Preface

This book is concerned with the administration of schools in the United States; its unique contribution is intended to be in the emphasis placed on the Catholic school, but since the job of administering schools is much the same irrespective of the type of control, frequent reference is made to other types of schools, public and nonsectarian. Obviously there are more similarities between the administration of public schools and the administration of religious-centered or other private schools than there are differences. Although there is no actual common denominator as such, a body of administrative knowledge and techniques essential to the proper conduct of schools has developed over the years. The author intends to draw on this accumulated knowledge, whether it grows primarily out of the administration of public or of private schools.

Thus, while this book is addressed to the problems of administering Catholic schools, much of the material presented is applicable to the administration of all schools. Indeed, the literature of public school administration is far more extensive than that of Catholic school administration, for the public schools which have become so highly organized in the past century have earlier known on a more massive scale the great problems confronting the school administrator today. These approaches are being studied ever more widely in Catholic schools today by administrators who newly encounter such complex problems as the recruitment of lay teachers and their salary scales, tenure, leaves of absence, retirement, evaluation, promotion, and dismissal.

The text is presented especially for those educators who are or expect to be engaged in the problems of school administration in the elementary or secondary school, either as principals, supervisors, or superintendents. It treats those phases of higher education and the related work of professional organizations which have particular relevance for school administrators.

The book will prove useful, too, to the graduate student as a prerequisite for his research and more intensive speculation. He will be encouraged, the author hopes, to pursue the issues laid before him and to contribute substantially to an ever-growing library of materials on Catholic school administration.

Throughout the book, when differences between public schools and Catholic schools indicate different solutions to the same or similar problems, these differences will be specifically suggested.

No attempt is made here to treat exhaustively the special philosophy of Catholic education which makes it so distinctive; nor is there any special effort to tell in any particular detail of the phenomenal growth of the Catholic school system as the distinctive unit it has become. The problems of administration presented here are those of schools as they have developed in the United States. Included is a basic treatment of the role of the Holy See, canon law, regulations of the Sacred Congregations, and the bishops of the Church in the control of Catholic education. Continuous reference is made to the special studies in education carried on by the graduate and undergraduate schools of Catholic colleges and universities, and to the papers written for the bulletins and proceedings of the National Catholic Educational Association. The bibliography is limited to those works and studies which were considered to be of the most immediate value to the student and the busy school administrator. The author has attempted to take an objective view of controversial issues with the goal of being as helpful as possible in bringing useful information to the school administrator.

Raymond F. McCoy

Contents

xvi   *Contents*

vision, Annual Reports, Communications to the Parents, Parent-Teacher Conferences. School Development Programs. Public Relations in Catholic Schools.

PART ONE

Introduction to Basic Administrative Considerations

1. Basic Administrative Considerations

The first two chapters of this volume are devoted to material introductory to the study of school administration, with particular emphasis on applications to Catholic education. In Chapter 1 are discussed the nature of the administrative job, the art of administration, and the present state of complexity to which administration has generally attained. Chapter 2 is devoted to a general review of the transition of school administration from its early simple state to the complex job it has become.

NATURE OF THE ADMINISTRATIVE JOB

What is administration? As frequently is the case, the more commonly used a term is, the more difficult it is to define. The nature of administration, however, can be considered from three different points of view.

ADMINISTRATION: A SIXFOLD RESPONSIBILITY

School administration may be described as a sixfold responsibility: instruction, administrative operations, pupil personnel services, business management, community relations, and research.

3

Each of these major responsibilities may be broken down into sub-jobs, but every task of the school administrator is logically a subdivision of one of the six.

Figure 1 illustrates this concept of administration as a sixfold responsibility and indicates the breakdown of each into its major components. This approach forms the basis of Part 3 of this book, in which each responsibility is treated in detail. It also provides a conceptual basis for organizing a school system. Of course, in a

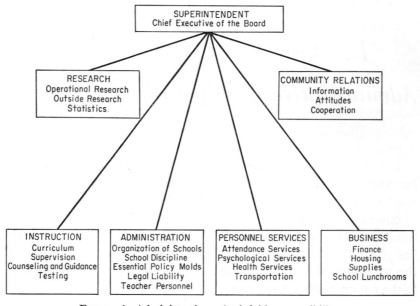

FIGURE 1. Administration: A sixfold responsibility.

small system one person may have to handle all six jobs himself; in a larger school organization each may be delegated to an assistant to the chief executive, whatever title he may bear.

Certain of these six responsibilities are more extensive than others with regard to the number of persons involved in discharging them. As to their relative importance, in one sense instruction is the most important responsibility of the school administrator, for the other five exist only to facilitate instruction. Yet, from another point of view, all are equally important, for if any one of the six is neglected by the administrator his performance is inadequate. As the superintendents of some of the largest school systems in the country have discovered, for example, neglect of the community relations function has nullified genuine instructional progress and has even cost the administrator his job.

ADMINISTRATION: THREE ESSENTIAL ACTIVITIES

A second way of looking at the essential nature of administration is to consider it as activity. There are three essential activities which an administrator must perform in discharging his sixfold responsibility. They are planning, executing, and evaluating. The administrator must plan. Furthermore, he must involve many heads in planning in order that the plans developed may be as sound and as widely accepted as possible.

Once planning has been completed, there must be execution. Plans must be put into effect. When they are put into effect there must be a continuous disposition to evaluate their effectiveness. How well are they working? And if they are not, the cycle begins over again. The school administrator's job may be described as planning, executing, and evaluating activities undertaken to discharge his sixfold responsibility.

ADMINISTRATION: DEVELOPING POLICY MOLDS

A third facet of administration involves developing a policy mold. You may have heard the story of the young man who saw a sign in a supermarket window reading "Help Wanted." He entered the store and spoke to the manager, who said, "It's a real good job, the pay is good, and so are the hours. The surroundings are pleasant." The young man agreed to take the job.

"All right," said the manager. "You see that pile of potatoes over there? Your job is to separate the big potatoes from the little potatoes."

In less than an hour the fellow was back, saying, "I quit!"

"Why?"

"Well, I'll tell you. The pay is good, the surroundings are pleasant, the hours are convenient, but it's making those decisions that's getting me down."

Making those decisions—this also is part of the administrator's job. He feels that there must be a way of separating the big from the little potatoes other than by making a decision for each potato. The first thing needed is some sort of standard. If the young man had simply made a mold by cutting a hole in a board, so that any potato which dropped through it was a little one and any one that did not was a big one, most of the decisions would have been eliminated except one, how big should the hole be?

In the administrative job, this process of formulating a policy mold is one key to success. The wiser the policies formulated, the easier the job will be from then on. This is why the policy mold is basic to successful administration. As policy is developed, the need for decision making is lessened. No longer is it necessary to make an *ad hoc* decision on each question that arises. Of course, there will be times when exceptions to policy have to be made, but if the number of decisions made by an administrator is lessened because wise policies have been established, his job is tremendously lightened.

As the chairman of the board of a large corporation has put it: "An executive has to be right just about all of the time. He is making maybe 100 decisions a day, but if he knows his business he won't have to think about 99 per cent of them. It's that 1 per cent that separates the good executive from the poor one." [1]

OPERATIONAL DEFINITION

School administration, therefore, may be defined as planning, executing, and evaluating those activities undertaken in the discharge of a sixfold responsibility: instruction, administrative operation, pupil personnel services, business management, community relations, and research.

Developing policy molds so as to lessen the number of *ad hoc* decisions to be made is fundamental to administrative efficiency.

ADMINISTRATION AS AN ART

It follows from our operational definition of school administration that there are involved both *what to do* and *how to do it*—the science of administering schools and the art of administering them. Throughout the following chapters considerable attention is de-

[1] From "Defense: The Organization Man," *Time,* Jan. 13, 1958, p. 12.

A SCHOOL ADMINISTRATOR HAS NOTHING TO DO

As everybody knows . . . a School Administrator has practically nothing to do . . . that is . . . except to decide what is to be done . . . to tell somebody to do it . . . to listen to reasons it should not be done . . . why it should be done by somebody else . . . or why it should be done in a different way.

To follow up to see if the thing has been done . . . to discover that it has not been done . . . to inquire why it has not been done . . . to listen to excuses from the person who should have done it . . . to follow up to see if it has been done . . . to discover . . .

That it has been done but done incorrectly . . . to point out how it should have been done . . . to conclude that as long as it has been done it may as well be left as it is . . . to wonder if it is not time to get rid of a person who cannot do a thing correctly . . . to reflect that the person in fault has a wife and seven children and that certainly . . .

No other School Administrator in the world would put up with him another moment . . . and that . . . in all probability any successor would be just as bad and probably worse . . . to consider how much simpler and better the thing would have been done had he done it himself in the first place.

Yes . . . 'tis true . . . a School Administrator has nothing to do.

Author Unknown

voted to the what's of school management since such knowledge is indispensable if the administrator is to be effective.

Reference is frequently made, however, to the equally indispensable element of how to do it—especially in regard to formulating courses of study, improving instruction, developing policy molds, preparing budgets, and maintaining sound community relations. Emphasis on the technique of effective administration is a newer development in the field, one dependent on information slowly drawn in somewhat piecemeal fashion from research in human relations.

So much is the administrator involved with people that administration itself has been defined as "the influencing of one group of human beings, the pupils, to grow toward defined objectives; utilizing a second group of human beings, the teachers, as agents; and operating in a setting of a third group of human beings, the public, variously concerned both with objectives and with means used to achieve them." [2]

The more responsible his position, the more essential to the administrator's success is his ability to work effectively with people—his board of control, assistants, supervisors, principals, teachers, students, parents, and community leaders. Increasingly, the literature of administration is replete with such terms as leadership, democratic administration, group processes, group thinking, committees, communications, identification, and self-realization—all terms drawn somewhat in isolation from the newer behavioral sciences of group dynamics, sociology, social psychology, and anthropology. While research findings in fields dealing with human relations do not easily lend themselves to valid generalizations because of the unique character of each human being, much has already been learned of significance to administrative performance.

THE COOPERATIVE PROGRAM IN EDUCATIONAL ADMINISTRATION

The most comprehensive attempt to learn more about the how to do it aspects of school administration was the Cooperative Program in Educational Administration (CPEA). This nationwide project was sponsored by the W. K. Kellogg Foundation of Battle Creek, Michigan, as a result of the interest and suggestions of the American Association of School Administrators and the National Conference of Professors of Educational Administration. The CPEA was launched in 1950 after the Kellogg Foundation had supported a series of exploratory regional conferences to discover what, if any, national study of school administration was needed. Of these conferences, Moore, in his report on the CPEA, writes:[3]

> The nation had been covered by a series of exploratory conferences. A pattern was running consistently in all of them: There was indeed an urgent need to study the changing nature of public school administration in this country. Community leadership responsibilities had increased at a pace which was alarming to superintendents, most of whom felt inadequately prepared to meet these new respon-

[2] Paul R. Mort and Donald H. Ross, *Principles of School Administration,* McGraw-Hill Book Company, Inc., New York, 1957, p. 248.

[3] Hollis A. Moore, Jr., *Studies in School Administration, A Report on the CPEA,* American Association of School Administrators, Washington, 1957, p. 12.

sibilities. Techniques for maintaining friendly, constructive public relations had been missing, they said, from the preparation they had received in graduate schools across the nation. One phrase was repeated so often in conference after conference that it quickly became a professional cliche. It went something like this: "The people in our communities demand educational leadership from us, but our training has been largely in the managerial aspects of the job."

As a result of the regional conferences, the Kellogg Foundation decided to support a program consisting of grants to regionally selected university centers for research in public school administration. A development committee, representing practicing administrators, advised the foundation on projects to be approved. Over a five-year period, grants of over 3 million dollars were planned for the program.

While results of the five-year program of research studies provide relatively few answers to the problems identified by the preliminary conferences, a review of over 300 CPEA studies of public school administration clearly indicates the following:

1. Personnel relations is a crucial area for the school administrator. One CPEA study of New England school superintendents in the early years of their service showed that 90 per cent of them had encountered critical occurrences in this area. Rated second, and encountered by 54 per cent of the superintendents, were critical experiences in public relations.[4]

2. Administrators need greater understanding of the power structure of their communities, indicating the desirability of more sociological studies of this aspect of community life.

3. Administrators need help in mass communication techniques as well as staff communication techniques.

4. Human relations are improved if groups of people are involved in decision making or policy formulation.

DEMOCRATIC ADMINISTRATION

Although the importance of the human relations aspects of school administration is realized by most authorities in the field, far too frequently the fact that little is actually known has been blithely

---

[4] H. B. Jestin, *Critical Experiences during the Early Years of the Superintendency*, CPEA, Harvard University, Cambridge, 1955.

camouflaged with glib remarks and meaningless verbalism about democratic administration.

Refreshingly different is the comprehensive, analytical approach to this subject presented by Mort and Ross in their *Principles of School Administration.*[5] Their treatment of administration centers around an analysis of fourteen principles of behavior characteristics of Americans. Within this framework, the chapters of their book

> attempt to present the criteria in terms of which decisions are ultimately made by groups in our culture. They attempt to give an awareness of the bases of judgment of the community and of the society of which the community is a part. They seek to provide guidance through the complex maze involved in every decision, in every recommendation to the board of education, so that consideration may be given from the beginning to those factors in terms of which the proposal or practice will eventually stand or fall. In brief, these chapters are an attempt to provide a preview of the crucible in which practices and proposals will be tested. It is proposed that those practices found wanting will not survive, regardless of their initial success, and that those that pass the test will survive the strain of experience.

Since five of the fourteen principles proposed by Mort and Ross are referred to as "highly emotionalized," [6] it would seem to this writer that the school administrator in the United States, public or private, would particularly want to consider carefully whether his handling of people conforms or is at variance with these principles. The first four are:[7]

> *Structural Democracy.* This is the idea that as a general rule control should be placed as close to people affected as it can, that popular sovereignty should be established through provisions of the law, that minimal safeguards should be provided to be sure that the voice of the people is heard even when other considerations may have placed the decision-making power elsewhere.
>
> *Operational Democracy.* Those to whom structure gives power may *behave* in a democratic or undemocratic fashion. To consult with others, to consider the interests and prejudices of those affected by executive decision-making, to respect the dignity of persons of

[5] Mort and Ross, *op. cit.,* p. 22.
[6] *Ibid.,* p. 173.
[7] *Ibid.,* pp. 34–35.

all degrees, to avoid rough-shod riding over the minority, these are counted as aspects of desirable behavior in our cultural setting and are accordingly referred to as "democratic leadership."

Justice. The essential quality in terms of this principle is balance —protection of the individual against the system and the system against the individual; equality before the law, but justice tempered with individual mercy in the verdict; care that the written rules are definite and clear enough so that each may know where he stands, but not so detailed and inflexible that their letter rather than their spirit must be administered.

Equality of Opportunity. This principle demands that each person shall have his chance to reach whatever flowering his inner potential promises. There are times when uniformity of educational service may support this principle, but more often the principle's implementation is to be found in diversity. The equality principle indicates a social commitment to do something extra, "to even things up," for those unfavored by nature.

The fifth highly emotionalized characteristic of American cultural behavior is stability, which according to Mort and Ross "connotes the conservation of the heritage which the race has achieved; the protection of those phases of our inheritance that are considered of lasting value; the protection of those concerned." [8] The authors distinguish sharply between stability and lethargy. The first is conceived of as dynamic; the second, as slow death.

While it is clear that identification of these principles and cultural characteristics assists the school administrator in his relations with the people who possess them, both the process of identification and the use of the results are complicated. A short cut is indicated by Mort and Ross in their discussion of the rationale for using committees in administration. Committees, composed as they are of persons who have the cultural characteristics of their peers, may demonstrate in deliberations the very characteristics of the community which will determine the success or failure of action taken in the matter under consideration. As these authors express it:

> One of the practical merits of working with a varied group of people in developing a program is the opportunity they provide to have the common-sense tests applied by them as the plan evolves. Any

[8] *Ibid.,* p. 227.

group is made up of people who vary in sensitivity to the "meanings" we hold in common. As the group increases in heterogeneity, the more likely will it be that all tests will be applied by them. Conversely, the more the same group of people work together, the more they tend to get their "assumptions" adjusted, the less valuable they become as a gauge of cultural sanctions, whatever other virtues they develop. Here, then, we have an added value for what is known as democratic administration. It is an instrument for applying the cultural sanctions that bypasses the necessity for identifying them.[9]

GENERAL GUIDES

As clearer answers to the how-to-do-it aspects of human relations in school administration are awaited from research workers, the school administrator does have certain principles which are more reliable than his intuition alone.

1. The objective of administrative activity is generally to effect changed human behavior.

2. Appeal to the intellect through presentation of facts, though a *sine qua non,* is in itself usually not enough to change human behavior.

3. Human behavior is generally not changed unless understanding is supplemented by favorable emotional attitudes.

4. Favorable attitudes are frequently developed when groups of people are involved in school decision making.

5. Favorable emotional attitudes may be caught from the school administrator if he is a person who is liked.

6. Administrative decisions will prove most successful if they are made in conformity with cultural attitudes that have already been emotionalized by most people: for example, the cultural concepts of democratic structure, democratic operation, justice, equality of opportunity, and preservation of past values.

7. Representative committees can be useful to administrators since they may reflect cultural reactions to proposals likely to emerge later in the larger group.

In all of his dealings with people, the administrator needs one more characteristic. It is described in the following remarks of

[9] *Ibid.,* p. 24.

Robert M. Hutchins concerning university administration, though it is in no way restricted to that level of school management:[10]

> The pressure of time is so great, the number of people who have to be convinced is so large, interminable discussion of the same subject with the same people is so boring, that the amount of patience a university administrator must have passes the bounds of my imagination to say nothing of those of my temperament. But I have learned at last, or I think I have, that the university president who wants durable action, not just action, must have patience, and have it in this amount.

COMPLEXITY OF ADMINISTRATION

Basic to consideration of school administration is an overview of its present state of complexity. While there are complications arising from other sources, many of today's administrative problems spring from enrollment problems. Table 1 presents a statistical view of enrollment aspects of the American educational enterprise.

COMPLEXITIES ARISING FROM ENROLLMENT

Over the past fifty years the increased percentage of school-age children actually attending schools has brought tremendous difficulties to the school administrator. Today, 98 per cent of the children of elementary school age are to be found in school; and 92 per cent of all high school children of compulsory age are in school.

Fifty years ago, students were in high school because they chose to be. If they chose not to be there, it was a simple matter to be "flunked out." No law required them to be there. Today, however, even a cursory visit to an average high school class reveals students who would much rather be anywhere else than where they are. The increased percentage of children of elementary school age who attend today's schools accounts for many administrative problems, for in this group are the slow-learning youngsters, sometimes only one short step above the idiot level; the hard-of-hearing, the blind, and the crippled; and the emotionally disturbed.

Moderating or administering a high school stage production may present difficult problems. In one city system a high school annually

---

[10] From "The Administrator Reconsidered," remarks by Robert M. Hutchins to the American College of Hospital Administrators, Atlantic City, Sept. 19, 1955.

TABLE 1. THE AMERICAN EDUCATIONAL ENTERPRISE: ENROLLMENTS 1955–1956 AND 1959–1960 SCHOOL YEARS WITH PER CENT OF INCREASE BY LEVEL AND TYPE OF SCHOOL OVER FIVE YEARS—48 STATES AND DISTRICT OF COLUMBIA

Level and type of school	1955–1956		1959–1960		Per cent increase
	Enrollment	Per cent of total	Enrollment	Per cent of total	
Elementary (K–8)					
Public schools	24,290,257	86.2	27,890,000	83.8	14.8
Nonpublic schools	3,886,360	13.8	5,400,000	16.2	38.9
Catholic	3,571,264	12.7	4,962,600	14.9	39.0
Other	315,096	1.1	437,400	1.3	38.8
Total elementary	28,176,617	100.0	33,290,000	100.0	18.1
Secondary (9–12)					
Public schools	6,872,586	89.3	8,100,000	88.5	17.9
Nonpublic schools	823,000	10.7	1,050,000	11.5	27.6
Catholic	704,578	9.2	898,800	9.8	27.6
Other	118,422	1.5	151,200	1.7	27.7
Total secondary	7,695,586	100.0	9,150,000	100.0	18.9
Elementary and secondary					
Public schools	31,162,843	86.9	35,990,000	84.8	15.5
Nonpublic schools	4,709,360	13.1	6,450,000	15.2	37.0
Catholic	4,275,842	11.9	5,861,400	13.8	37.1
Other	433,518	1.2	588,600	1.4	35.8
Total elementary and secondary	35,872,203	100.0	42,440,000	100.0	18.3

TABLE 1. THE AMERICAN EDUCATIONAL ENTERPRISE: ENROLLMENTS 1955–1956 AND 1959–1960 SCHOOL YEARS WITH PER CENT OF INCREASE BY LEVEL AND TYPE OF SCHOOL OVER FIVE YEARS—48 STATES AND DISTRICT OF COLUMBIA (Continued)

Level and type of school	1955–1956		1959–1960		Per cent increase
	Enrollment	Per cent of total	Enrollment	Per cent of total	
Higher education					
Public colleges and universities	1,814,426	58.4	1,972,457	58.6	8.7
Nonpublic	1,291,246	41.6	1,391,801	41.4	5.6
Catholic	255,219	8.2	289,168	8.6	13.3
Other	1,036,027	33.4	1,102,633	32.8	6.4
Total higher education	3,105,672	100.0	3,364,258	100.0	7.7

SOURCES: Elementary and secondary enrollment, 1955–1956: from *Biennial Survey of Education in the United States*, 1955–1956, U.S. Office of Education.
Elementary and secondary enrollment, 1959–1960: estimate of U.S. Office of Education for public and nonpublic schools with breakdown for Catholic and other nonpublic schools interpolated from 1955–1956 distribution of nonpublic enrollments; National Catholic Welfare Conference figures, based on October enrollments, are smaller than U.S. Office estimates.
Higher education enrollments, 1955–1956: based on resident and extension degree students, U.S. Office of Education biennial survey and NCWC statistics.
Higher education enrollments, 1959–1960: based on resident and extension degree students, fall enrollments, U.S. Office of Education and NCWC statistics.

presents a variety show of unusually good quality. One year the manager of a large local theater approached the principal and asked to produce four or five of the acts at his theater during the summer. He did not intend to pay the students but offered a substantial contribution to the school welfare fund. The principal denied the request on the grounds that the school did not exist to facilitate professional appearances. He was immediately faced with vocal parents whose imaginations were caught by images of daughters dancing on the stage of a large local theater. Perhaps in the audience there might be a Hollywood scout! The result was parental excitement and relentless pressure on the school to permit the acts to be staged. It was some time before the school officials could make their point clear: that whatever the parents did to get their children on the commercial stage was their own affair, but that the school would not participate in it.

There are also complex questions involved in maintaining a really fine school orchestra or band. A working policy regarding public appearances must be developed after considering both educational desiderata and the requirements of the musicians' union. When a school musical organization is used in such a way as to make employment of professional musicians less likely, difficulties with the union are more likely. This is particularly true if the school is susceptible, as most schools are, to public pressure. A public school would certainly have to face the problem; and a Catholic school, though perhaps not quite so susceptible to pressure, is in no position to ignore possible charges of being unfair to organized labor.

It is for reasons such as these that administration of high schools is more complicated than administration of elementary schools and that the increased percentage of children to be found in high schools produces complex problems.

The Catholic school administrator shares with the public school administrator all of the complex problems arising from enrollments, and then some; for the trend is, and has been for some time, that an increasing percentage of students in school is to be found in Catholic schools. Statistics on the tidal wave of students are generally alarming, but Catholic schools have been affected more than public schools. That this would be so was clear even before the height of the "war baby" development.

United States Office of Education figures dated 1946 show that, in the previous six years, enrollments and numbers of teachers in private elementary schools, mainly Catholic, increased more rapidly than in public schools. As a matter of fact, in these six years, whereas private schools showed an increased enrollment of 8.2 per cent, public schools in the same years showed a decrease of 8.4 per cent. It was clear, then, that as far back as 1940, an increasing percentage of the children was attending parochial schools.

To put it another way, whereas in 1936 about 10 per cent of the pupils of the country were found in nonpublic elementary and high schools, by 1950 the figure was 12 per cent and by 1960 had surpassed 14 per cent. Freeman reports that between 1940 and 1956 nonpublic schools grew four times faster than public schools. Of the additional children who sought admittance to school in these years, 29 per cent were enrolled in nonpublic schools.[11] This general trend is confirmed in Table 1 and in sampling studies of the U.S. Bureau of the Census. These indicate that private elementary school enrollment rose from 13.4 per cent to 16.1 per cent between 1955 and 1959; high school from 9.8 per cent to 10.9 per cent.

Not all this increased growth is in Catholic schools; other private schools, particularly Lutheran parochial schools, have been increasing in number and size, as have nonsectarian private schools. Yet Catholic schools consistently account for about 90 per cent of nonpublic elementary and secondary school enrollments. In Catholic schools, greater growth has indeed meant greater complexities.

OTHER COMPLEXITIES IN ADMINISTRATION

Financial administration of schools is increasingly complex today. Statistics, which are available for schools, indicate that in just over a century we have progressed from spending around $200,000 a year to an estimated annual outlay of over 20 billion dollars for education.[12] It is simply impossible to spend so much money without complex problems arising. When a large city spends 30 or 40 million dollars each year for current expenses alone, and additional millions for new buildings, it is conducting a big business. Since the public, or certain organized segments of it, is unlikely to contribute the multimillions of dollars needed annually unless assured

[11] Roger A. Freeman, *School Needs in the Decade Ahead,* The Institute for Social Science Research, Washington, 1958.

[12] *Ibid.,* p. 3.

that they are being wisely spent, expenditures are likely to be made with an eye to efficiency.

Additional complexities accompany the many functions newly assumed by or delegated to the schools. As the home and the apprentice system decline in their influence on children, television, the press, and paperback books increase their not completely wholesome impact. The result is that schools have become involved in coordinating extensive athletic programs, particularly interscholastic athletics. Social activities formerly centered in the home are now centered in the schools. Dancing lessons are introduced in the sixth grade, or even in the fifth grade. This leads to complexities!

Laboratories and shops are more complicated and more dangerous than simple classrooms. So, also, are swimming pools and gyms. In fact, the newer plant facilities and equipment are far more difficult to oversee than the older classroom buildings, which, while relatively stark, were decidedly easier to manage.

Questions for Discussion or Investigation

1. Can you think of any administrative tasks which are not logically part of the six major responsibilities outlined for school administrators?

2. Can you think of any activities of a school administrator which are neither planning, executing, nor evaluating?

3. List ten administrative problems (not mentioned in Chapter 1) which are suitable areas for developing policy molds.

4. To what extent can it be validly said that public school administration should be democratic? How can the term be validly applied to Catholic school administration?

5. In what ways is the administration of public schools more complicated than that of Catholic schools; in what ways is the administration of Catholic schools more complicated?

Readings and References

Biennial Survey of Education in the United States (5 chapters printed separately), U.S. Office of Education, 1959.

Campbell, Roal F., and Russell T. Gregg (eds.): *Administrative Behavior in Education,* Harper & Brothers, New York, 1957.

Cooperative Development of Public School Administration in New York State: Modern Practices and Concepts of Staffing Schools, New York State Department of Education, Albany, 1956.

Cooperative Program in Educational Administration: *Decision Making and*

American Values in School Administration, Bureau of Publications, Teachers College, Columbia University, New York, 1954.

Davies, Daniel R.: "Educational Administration at Mid-century," *Teachers College Record,* vol. 54, pp. 125–130, December, 1952.

Dunne, William J.: "Communication—A Problem in Higher Education," *National Catholic Educational Association Bulletin,* vol. 56, no. 1, pp. 175–178, August, 1959.

Fee, Leonard M.: "Staff Participation in Administration," in Michael J. McKeough (ed.), *The Administration of the Catholic Secondary School,* The Catholic University of America Press, Washington, 1948.

Griffiths, Daniel E.: *Human Relations in School Administration,* Appleton-Century-Crofts, Inc., New York, 1956.

Hopkins, L. Thomas: *Interaction: The Democratic Process,* D. C. Heath and Company, Boston, 1941.

Hunt, Harold C., and Paul R. Pierce: *The Practice of School Administration,* Houghton Mifflin Company, Boston, 1958.

McCluskey, Neil G.: "The Dinosaur and the Catholic School," *National Catholic Educational Association Bulletin,* vol. 57, no. 1, pp. 232–238, August, 1960.

Melby, Ernest O.: *Administering Community Education,* Prentice-Hall, Inc., Englewood Cliffs, N.J., 1955.

Moore, Hollis A., Jr.: *Studies in School Administration,* American Association of School Administrators, Washington, 1957.

Mort, Paul R., and Donald H. Ross: *Principles of School Administration,* McGraw-Hill Book Company, Inc., New York, 1957.

Reinert, Paul C.: "Administrative Self-appraisal," *Catholic School Journal,* vol. 59, pp. 65–67, March, 1959.

Report of the Standing Committee, Department of School Superintendents: "The Functions of the Superintendent of the Catholic School," *National Catholic Educational Association Bulletin,* vol. 56, no. 3, February, 1960.

Roy, Robert H.: *The Administrative Process,* Johns Hopkins Press, Baltimore, 1958.

School Board–Superintendent Relationships, Thirty-fourth Yearbook of the American Association of School Administrators, Washington, 1956.

Sears, Jesse B.: *The Nature of the Administrative Process,* McGraw-Hill Book Company, Inc., New York, 1950.

Spaulding, Frank: *School Superintendent in Action in Five Cities,* Richard R. Smith, Publisher, Inc., New York, 1955.

Staff Relations in School Administration, Thirty-third Yearbook of the American Association of School Administrators, Washington, 1955.

Trecher, Harleigh B.: *Group Processes in Administration,* The Women's Press, New York, 1947.

Walton, John: *Administration and Policy-making in Education,* Johns Hopkins Press, Baltimore, 1960.

2. Development
from Administrative Simplicity
to Administrative Complexity

The following paragraphs present a concise picture of the simple organization of early American schools.[1]

The first American schools were most simple and direct in their management. In a land but recently claimed from the wilderness any elaborate organization or control of education was neither possible nor necessary. These early schools, as a result of the sparse settlement of the country, were small and widely separated. They were generally held in the homes of the teachers or in one-room buildings of the crudest sort. The means of school support was at first furnished by tuition fees paid by the parents of each child directly to the teacher, although more and more the schools came to be maintained at least in part by "rates" levied upon the property of the town. Definite grading of the work was unknown and the children were for the most part taught as individuals. Methods of teaching were crude and the equipment was exceedingly primitive and meager. At best it consisted of a few hornbooks, primers, inkhorns,

[1] Frank Pierrepont Graves, *The Administration of American Education,* The Macmillan Company, New York, 1932, pp. 1–2.

quill pens, and sand boxes, together with the ubiquitous ferule or strap. The teacher needed and often had received little training, academic or professional.

The establishment of such a school, the method of its support, and the election and salary of the teacher were at first all determined by direct vote of the citizens at a town meeting or at a session of some church body. Each school district was autonomous and was managed separately, and a state organization was altogether unknown. When the schoolmaster was licensed or supervised at all, these functions were performed by ministers of the locality and neighboring towns, and the teacher was held to be under the immediate control of a town meeting, the selectmen, the ministry, or other existing civic or ecclesiastical group. A special committee for school affairs was only very gradually evolved, and any professional authority higher than the teacher did not begin to appear for nearly two centuries. The schoolmaster was brought into direct touch with his clientele, without the mediation of those agencies which have of late years come to play so important a part in the control of American education,—the board of education and the superintendent of schools.

A CHRONOLOGY OF COMPLEXITY

While it is impossible to establish a date after which educational administration in this country became complicated and before which it was simple, one can with some validity say that before 1820 educational administration was quite simple and thereafter it rapidly became increasingly complex.

BEFORE 1820

Before 1820 there were no really urgent administrative problems in running schools. As a matter of fact, there was not even widespread consciousness of education itself. The chief influence for simplicity at this time was the district-unit system of organizing and controlling schools.

Originally four or five families banded together to support and administer their own school. As more families entered the general area, the school district was generally subdivided into several independent districts, each of which organized its own school as close as possible to the families supporting it. It was this tendency to subdivide school units that led to the district-unit system.

The country in its early years was fortunate to fall into the district-unit system because of its simplicity. However, as life grew increasingly complicated, these little autonomous districts were far too small even to approach administrative efficiency in handling the more complicated problems that developed. Furthermore, the districts naturally developed along lines of super-localism. Had the system continued there would be no reason for a present-day youngster to expect satisfactory placement when transferring from one school to another. Tremendous inequalities of educational opportunity would exist from district to district. Adequate provision for special education could not have been made.

As long as the district-unit system was to obtain in this country, educational administration could never become very complicated. While the system stayed with us for many years after 1820—and we probably still have far too many individually organized public school districts—by that date it was being challenged by three developments.

The first challenge arose from provisions of the national land grants, the first of which was made to Ohio in 1802. Since details of the land grants will be considered later, it will suffice now to mention that grants made to education within the new states, first in the Northwest Territory, necessitated state-wide committees or overseeing bodies for administration of these national land grants. Yet the beginning of any sort of state supervision, even so modest a start, was an inroad on the prior absolute sovereignty of the local district.

The second challenge also came between 1800 and 1820 when some states began passing "permissive laws" allowing local districts to set up schools. The fact that the state passed a law permitting the local district which already had a school to set one up clearly implies that the local districts are far from absolute in their autonomy.

The third challenge became evident around 1800, as at least one city, Providence, Rhode Island, was moving to organize a city school system. By 1820, however, there were no general signs of school systems or of any authority beyond the local district, as Cubberley indicates in the following passage:[2]

> Regardless of the national land grants for education made to the new States, the provisions of the different state constitutions, the beginnings made here and there in the few cities of the time, and the early state laws, we can hardly be said, as a people, to have developed an educational consciousness, outside of New England and New York, before 1820, and in some of the States, especially the South, a state educational consciousness was not awakened until very much later. Even in New England there was a steady decline in education, as the district system became more and more firmly fixed during the first fifty years of our national history. . . .
>
> There were many reasons in our national life for this lack of interest in education among the masses of our people. The simple agricultural life of the time, the homogeneity of the people, the absence of cities, the isolation and independence of the villages, the lack of full manhood suffrage, the want of any economic demand for education. . . . There were but six cities of 8,000 population or over as late as 1810, and even in those, life was far simpler than in a small western village today. There was little need for book learning among the masses of the people to enable them to transact the ordinary business of life. A person who could read and write and cipher in that time was an educated man, while the absence of these arts was not by any means a matter of reproach.

After 1820

After 1820, complexity in educational administration began to set in at an ever-accelerating pace. Just as the greatest single influence for educational simplicity had been the district-unit system, so the greatest single influence in the direction of educational complexity was the Lancasterian school movement. Just before 1800, two gentlemen, Dr. Andrew Bell, an Episcopalian in an English colony in India, and Mr. Joseph Lancaster, an English Quaker, independently conceived similar plans for using monitors to educate children in larger groups than previously believed possible.

Since the ideas of Episcopalians were not in good favor in this

[2] Ellwood P. Cubberley, *Public Education in the United States,* Houghton Mifflin Company, Boston, 1934, pp. 110–111.

country following the Revolutionary War, the monitorial plan that swept the states in the early 1800s was known as the Lancasterian movement, named for Lancaster the Quaker. While many of the ideas of the Lancasterian method were not original, having been included earlier in Jesuit and Ursuline methodology, for example, it was Lancaster who popularized, elaborated, and personally sold the method in the United States.

The first American Lancasterian school was founded in 1806 in New York. The system quickly spread from Massachusetts to Georgia and as far as Cincinnati, Louisville, and Detroit. It was adopted with particular enthusiasm in New York City and Philadelphia. The governors of New York and Pennsylvania recommended to their legislatures the general adoption of the system.

From two hundred to one thousand children could be taught at the same time by one teacher in a properly organized Lancasterian classroom—just short of educational television! The pupils were sorted out and seated by rows in one large classroom with one pupil appointed monitor for ten other pupils. Thus, with two hundred students in a room, there were twenty rows of ten benches to a row, each with a monitor. A thousand children meant about a hundred rows to be supervised.

The teacher taught the monitors, and the monitors, "useful corporals of the teachers regiment," took their rows to "stations" about the wall and proceeded to teach the others what they had just learned from the teacher.[3] The system became quite involved. In a well-organized room there were posts chalked out along the aisles for each monitor. The master monitor was placed at the front of the room, usually at a raised desk, with a long ruler nearby in case of difficulty.

The system was first used only to teach reading and catechism. It was soon extended, however, to include writing, simple arithmetic, and even later, what were then the higher branches of learning.

When the system had developed to the point that monitorial manuals were published, the school operated in such fashion that the child was assigned to a class by a monitor immediately upon admittance to the school. "While he remained, a monitor taught him, together with nine other pupils. When he was absent, one monitor

[3] *Ibid.*, pp. 131–132.

ascertained the fact, and another discovered the reason. A monitor examined him periodically, and when he made progress, a monitor promoted him. A monitor ruled the writing paper. Another had charge of slates and books, and a monitor-general looked after all the other monitors. Every monitor wore a leather ticket, gilded and lettered, 'Monitor of the First Class,' 'Reading Monitor of the Second Class.' . . ." [4]

Why was the Lancasterian system a major influence toward educational complexity? It brought numbers into school, and numbers make for complexity. It fostered the idea that it was possible for people to go to school in large numbers. The manuals for Lancasterian teachers implied teacher preparation. Lastly, there was implied in the system the idea of a large school. It is not too much of a jump of the imagination to proceed from the teacher with ten, twelve, or twenty monitors, all in one room, to the idea of a principal teacher, in an office, and ten, twelve, or twenty assistant teachers separated from one another by partitions. It was in all these ways that the Lancasterian system exerted a great influence on the spread of education, with consequent complexity in administration.

Along with and after the Lancasterian movement came swiftly the following developments in school administration.

In 1817 the first school for deaf mutes was established in this country, the beginning of special education. It was, incidentally, a private school. In 1820 the state of New Jersey first provided free education for pauper children. In 1821 Ohio first authorized taxation for education on a state basis, a significant challenge to the district-unit system. In the same year the first high school was established in Boston. The years 1823 and 1827 mark the foundation of the first private normal schools in the country, the start of formal teacher training. In 1825 cities began to organize public school systems, among them Cincinnati in 1825, Chicago in 1832, and Pittsburgh in 1835. In 1829 the state of Michigan appointed the first Superintendent of Common Schools who had real responsibilities for supervising instruction. In 1837 the first of the state boards of education was organized in Massachusetts. In 1837 Buffalo and Louisville appointed the first city school superintendents. By 1850 the idea of a tax-supported public school had been adopted in every

[4] Quoted by Cubberley, *ibid.,* pp. 133–134.

Northern state. Massachusetts, in 1852, passed the first compulsory attendance law. This established an important precedent, for it is obvious that the compulsory attendance law brought a number of problems to the classroom. It was 1918, however, before all of the states had compulsory attendance laws.

To continue with the development of complexity in education, in 1855 the first kindergarten in the United States was established. This was also a private institution. In 1864 the first supervisor was appointed in Boston. A music supervisor, he was soon followed by supervisors of drawing and writing.

Another point of chronological interest is the development between 1820 and 1860 in the United States of the eight-grade elementary school as the typical school organization. There are two theories concerning its development. The first and more patriotic theory is that the eight-grade elementary school is indigenous to this country and grew up by normal evolutionary processes out of the early colonial primary and writing schools. This theory holds that the eight-grade pattern gradually developed through the combination of the primary school, which was intended for ages 5 to 7½; the writing school, intended for ages 7½ to 10; and the grammar school, intended for ages 10 to 14.

The second theory is that the eight-grade pattern resulted from a trip to Europe by Horace Mann on which he was particularly impressed by the schools of Prussia. Upon his return in 1844, as Commissioner of Education in Massachusetts, Mann devoted his seventh annual report to the graded school system of Prussia. By 1847, the first eight-grade elementary school was established in Quincy, Massachusetts, under the principalship of an enthusiastic follower of Horace Mann.

It would appear, then, that the Horace Mann report was a strong determining influence in forming the eight-grade elementary school. In fact, the buildings in which the original schools were conducted show a strong influence of the German style of school building.

PAROCHIAL SCHOOLS AND THE DEVELOPMENT
OF COMPLEXITY

The items referred to in the development of educational administration to its present state of complexity are found equally in the background of public and Catholic schools. The Lancasterian system, for example, was adopted as the method of instruction in 1818 by St. Peter's School in New York City.[5] But one important item of simplicity merits specific attention.

THE PARISH–DISTRICT UNIT

There is a relationship between the idea of the district-unit system, with both its simplicity and its shortcomings, and the organization of Catholic parochial schools. In the Catholic school system each parochial school has been to a great extent an individual entity, a fact which has militated against anything like the present system-wide organization found in public school administration. It is only in recent times that the office of superintendent of parochial schools has become an office of any stature whatsoever. Even today, the size, scope, and responsibilities of the staff of the superintendent of parochial schools do not begin to compare with those of the staff of a superintendent of public schools when a similar number of schools is involved.

Under the parish system it has been possible, for example, to have a surplus of classrooms in one parish, while in the next there is a shortage. With two different pastors operating the schools and two different religious orders teaching in them, little cooperation between the two schools has been likely.

Because of the strictly parish organization, special education in Catholic schools has not developed to the extent that it has in public schools. If there is a need to conduct a class for slow-learning or for severely maladjusted youngsters in the sixth, seventh, and eighth grades—for example, for girls who are more mature socially than academically—an individual parish school would ordinarily have scarcely enough youngsters of this type to conduct a special class for them. If there were enough such girls in three adjoining parishes, moreover, it would be unusual to organize such a class for the three district school units, for they are headed by independent pastors and probably staffed by three different teaching orders of sisters.

The comparison between the district-unit and the parochial school systems cannot be carried too far, however, since there are reasons for the existence of the one that do not obtain for the other. Basi-

[5] James A. Burns and Bernard J. Kohlbrenner, *A History of Catholic Education in the United States,* Benziger Bros., New York, 1937, p. 79.

cally, the parish school is part of the parish societal unit. The pastor quite normally looks to his school children to perform such auxiliary activities as serving Mass and singing in the choir. In church administration the pastor is traditionally responsible only to his bishop.

In his intensive sociological study of one Catholic parish school, a school which he found generally typical, Fichter describes the administrative pattern of operation as follows:[6]

> From the point of view of authority and function, the teaching personnel of St. Luke's constitutes a relatively "self-contained" unit. The pastor is ultimately responsible to the Bishop for the successful maintenance of the school, but the Bishop does not interfere with the Pastor just as the Pastor does not interfere with the Principal. The formal structural link between the school and the Bishop is the office of the diocesan superintendent of schools, who is a busy Pastor in a distant city. He did not visit St. Luke's during our study, and the extent of his communication was four routine items: the weekly time schedule of subjects, the school year calendar, the uniform report cards, and the list of recommended textbooks. All of these were accepted more as guides, rather than as authoritative directives, by the Pastor and the Principal. Ultimately, all decisions concerning the school were made locally by the Principal with the explicit or implicit approval of the Pastor. . . .
>
> Unlike some of the larger teaching orders of Sisters, the congregation that supplies the Sisters to St. Luke's, has not distributed among its members a formalized manual for teachers. Thus, neither the diocese, through the superintendent of schools, nor the teaching order, through its Mother Provincial, exerts any direct authority over classroom and school procedures at St. Luke's. . . .
>
> St. Luke's faculty belongs to St. Luke's parish. It is dedicated to the task of making good practicing Catholics and exemplary American citizens of our children of the parish.

That there are significant factors operating to preserve the school as a distinctly parish unit rather than an integral part of a highly organized school system is apparent throughout Fichter's study. It is equally evident to the student of Catholic school administration, however, that the increasing strength and professionalization of the office of superintendent of parochial schools is appreciably lessening

---

[6] Joseph H. Fichter, *Parochial School: A Sociological Study,* University of Notre Dame Press, Notre Dame, Ind., 1958, pp. 272–273.

any similarities between parochial school organization and the district-unit system.

BEFORE 1820

In addition to the historical developments toward complexity shared with public schools, the history of Catholic education in the United States supplies a chronology of events unique to the administration of Catholic Schools.

Between 1640 and 1820 were a number of firsts in an era in which relatively few Catholics were to be found in the whole area that has become the United States. It was around 1600 that the first schools within what is now the continental United States were founded by the Spanish Franciscans in Florida and New Mexico. Within the thirteen original colonies, the first Catholic school was established in Maryland in 1640, only five years after the Boston Latin School was founded.

The first religious order of women to teach in the schools of what became the United States were the Ursuline Sisters, who opened a school for girls in New Orleans after arriving from France in 1727. The first parochial Catholic school was St. Mary's School in Philadelphia, a school which was in existence in Philadelphia by 1767, but the tuition-free parish school for boys and girls opened in 1810, at St. Joseph's Parish in Emmitsburg, Maryland, by Mother Seton and her American order, the Sisters of Charity, more fully represents the prototype of today's parochial school. The first Catholic college, Georgetown, was founded in 1789, and the first seminary, that of the Sulpicians in Baltimore, opened in 1791.

1820 TO 1884

The period between 1820 and 1884, however, really provided the historical background for the Catholic educational system as we know it today. It was in these years that Catholic religious leaders concluded that if Catholic youth were to receive a Catholic education in the United States, previously thought possible within the framework of public education, it would have to be in schools supported without public funds. It was after a bitter controversy on this subject in New York City around 1840 that Bishop John Hughes, vigorous proponent of public support for the eight Catholic schools of his diocese, called for parochial schools everywhere; he himself established thirty-eight new schools in his diocese before his death twenty-three years later.

Successive decrees of four councils of Baltimore, one provincial and three plenary councils, reflected the changing attitudes of the hierarchy, that resulted in the present parochial school system. The First Provincial Council of Baltimore (1829) merely judged it "absolutely necessary that schools should be established in which the young may be taught the principles of faith and morality, while being instructed in letters"; but parish schools were not specified. By 1852, the First Plenary Council of Baltimore exhorted the bishops of the United States to establish schools in connection with all the churches of their dioceses and to support them with the revenues of the parish to which the school was attached. The Second Plenary Council of Baltimore (1866) referred to parochial schools as the only remaining remedy in view of the dangers in Catholic children attending public schools. The Third Plenary Council of Baltimore (1884) definitely ordered the erection of a parochial school near each church within two years, unless postponement was allowed for grave reasons by the bishop.

AFTER 1884

From 1884 on, Catholic schools moved toward complexity at an accelerated pace. Diocesan school boards, first instituted on a lasting basis in the Fort Wayne diocese in 1879, were instituted in eight other dioceses by 1900. While the Archdiocese of New York appointed an archdiocesan inspector of schools in 1888, the first superintendent of Catholic schools is credited to Philadelphia in 1894. It was also in Philadelphia that the first central high school for boys was begun in 1890 and three high school centers for girls were begun in 1900.[7] While by 1960, the decree of the Third Plenary Council that elementary schools be founded in all parishes had not yet been completely realized, the 16,996 parishes in the fifty states of the union conducted 10,132 elementary schools. The number varied from 2 in the Diocese of Baker (Oregon) to 416 in the Archdiocese of Chicago. The state of New York with 1,058 had

[7] For further details on the development of Catholic education in the United States, see Burns and Kohlbrenner, *op. cit.*

more Catholic elementary schools than any other. In addition, 1564 diocesan and 869 private Catholic secondary schools were in existence; 267 colleges and universities were in operation; and 537 seminaries and scholasticates were being conducted under Catholic auspices.[8]

As the names of Horace Mann, Henry Barnard, and William T. Harris stand out in the general history of American education, those of three Catholics, all bishops, dominate the history of Catholic education in the United States: Archbishop John Carroll of Baltimore, who lived around the time of the founding of the Republic, and whose zeal for Catholic education led to the establishment of Georgetown College and the first seminary at Baltimore; Archbishop John Hughes of New York, in the second period of Catholic education, who is remembered for his vigorous case for using public funds to support religious schools, and when that battle had been lost, for his devotion to parish schools as the alternative; and Bishop John L. Spalding of Peoria, perhaps the greatest educational figure of them all.

Bishop Spalding's life span (1840–1916) made it possible for him to be termed the leading Catholic educator from the Civil War to World War I. "At a time when the Catholic church was making rapid gains and arousing great antagonism in Protestant circles and among school men, Spalding exerted profound influence on the parochial and higher educational systems of his church . . . his influence also extended to non-Catholic educators."[9]

Bishop Spalding served on the Committee on Schools of the Third Plenary Council of Baltimore and is credited with a key role in formulating educational legislation which committed the Church in America to the parochial school. Himself a scholar-product of Louvain University in Belgium, he worked untiringly from 1884 for the foundation of a similar institution in the United States, an effort which caused him to be considered the "real founder of the Catholic University in Washington."[10] Again, it was in a large measure owing to his efforts that the college for sisters was established in

---

[8] *The Official Catholic Directory 1961*, P. J. Kenedy & Sons, New York, 1961.

[9] Merle Curti, "Bishop Spalding, Catholic Educator," in his *The Social Ideas of American Educators*, Charles Scribner's Sons, New York, 1935, pp. 348–349.

[10] Burns and Kohlbrenner, *op. cit.*, p. 143.

1910 at the Catholic University of America. Under his editorship, textbooks were developed specifically for the Catholic elementary schools of the country.

Of Bishop Spalding, Merle Curti, in his analysis of the social ideas of American educators, writes:[11]

> Brilliant and gifted, a poet, a gentleman of culture and learning, a writer of books on religion, philosophy, sociology, and education, Bishop Spalding as early as 1877 began to advocate what was later known as "Americanism." He contended that the church should with dignity rather than in a combative spirit, enter into the living controversies of the age; should demonstrate that it was not opposed to culture and learning or the new developments in science; and that it should contribute to the literature and culture of the United States, and in short make its influence on American civilization felt.

Questions for Discussion or Investigation

1. Contrast the influence of the district-unit system and the Lancasterian system on the administration of public schools.

2. Discuss the present-day effects of the district-unit system on public school administration. What similarities exist between the district-unit system and Catholic school administration? What differences? Using statistics presented in the *Official Catholic Directory* and the recent *Biennial Survey of Education,* attempt to show that, on the average, Catholic schools are larger or smaller than public schools.

3. Discover why the names of William T. Harris and Bishop John L. Spalding stand out in parallel fashion in the history of public and Catholic school administration, respectively.

Readings and References

Brubacher, J. S.: *A History of the Problems of Education,* McGraw-Hill Book Company, Inc., New York, 1947.

Burns, James A.: *The Catholic School System in the United States,* Benziger Bros., New York, 1908.

———: *The Growth and Development of the Catholic School System in the United States,* Benziger Bros., New York, 1912.

——— and Bernard J. Kohlbrenner: *A History of Catholic Education in the United States,* Benziger Bros., New York, 1937.

Cubberley, Ellwood P.: *Public Education in the United States,* Houghton Mifflin Company, Boston, 1934.

[11] Curti, *op. cit.,* pp. 353–354.

Curti, Merle: "Bishop Spalding, Catholic Educator," in his *The Social Ideas of American Educators,* Charles Scribner's Sons, New York, 1935.

Eby, Frederick, and C. F. Arrowood: *The Development of Modern Education,* Prentice-Hall, Inc., Englewood Cliffs, N.J., 1934.

Encyclopedia of Educational Research, Chester W. Harris (ed.), 3d ed., The Macmillan Company, New York, 1960.

Fichter, Joseph H.: *Parochial School: A Sociological Study,* University of Notre Dame Press, Notre Dame, Ind., 1958.

Graves, Frank Pierrepont: *The Administration of American Education,* The Macmillan Company, New York, 1932.

Good, H. G.: *A History of American Education,* The Macmillan Company, New York, 1956.

Holmes, Pauline: "A Tercentenary History of the Boston Public Latin School, 1635–1935," *Harvard Studies in Education,* vol. 25, Harvard University Press, Cambridge, 1935.

Inglis, Alexander J.: "The Rise of the High School in Massachusetts," *Contributions to Education,* no. 45, Teachers College, Columbia University, New York, 1911.

Johnson, Clifton: *Old-time Schools and School Books,* The Macmillan Company, New York, 1904.

McCluskey, Neil G.: *Catholic Viewpoint on Education,* Hanover House, Garden City, N.Y., 1959.

Martin, George H.: *The Evolution of the Massachusetts Public School System,* D. Appleton & Company, New York, 1894.

Putz, Louis J. (ed.): *The Catholic Church, U.S.A.,* Fides Publishers Association, Chicago, 1956.

Turner, William: "Schools in the United States," in *Catholic Encyclopedia,* vol. 13, pp. 560–562.

PART TWO

The Control of Education

The Church: And first of all education belongs pre-eminently to the Church, by reason of a double title in the supernatural order, conferred exclusively upon her by God Himself: absolutely superior therefore to any other title in the natural order.

The Family: The family therefore holds directly from the Creator the mission and hence the right to educate the offspring, a right inalienable because inseparably joined to the strict obligation, a right anterior to any right whatever of civil society and of the State, and therefore inviolable on the part of any power on earth.

The State: It pertains to the State, in view of the common good, to promote in various ways the education and instruction of youth. It should begin by encouraging and assisting, of its own accord, the initiative and activity of the Church and the family, whose successes in this field have been clearly demonstrated by history and experience. . . . For the State more than another society is provided with the means put at its disposal for the needs of all, and it is only right that it use these means to the advantage of those who have contributed them.

Christian Education of Youth
PIUS XI

3. The Catholic Church and Education

The official position of the Catholic Church on who controls education is clearly presented by Pius XI in his encyclical *Christian Education of Youth*. The control of education, according to this encyclical, is shared by three societal units: the family, civil society, and the Church.

The family, which exists principally to procreate and rear children, has, therefore, the primary right and duty to control the education of its children. This basic principle underlay the words of the Supreme Court of the United States in the Oregon School case:[1] "The child is not the mere creature of the State. Those who nurture him and direct his destiny have the right, coupled with the high duty to recognize and prepare him for additional obligations." The same principle also underlay the following statement from Article 26 of the *Universal Declaration of Human Rights* adopted by the United Nations in 1948: "Parents have a prior right to choose the kind of education that shall be given their children."

Civil society, or government, which exists to promote the common temporal welfare of the citizens of a country, also has legitimate rights and obligations in the control of the education of chil-

[1] *Pierce v. Society of Sisters,* 268 U.S. 510.

37

dren. If government is adequately to promote the common temporal welfare of its citizens, it can legitimately demand that parents include in their provision for education those features which are essential to the well-being of civil society; e.g., formal schooling to such a level and of such quality as is deemed necessary for intelligent citizenship, or perhaps physical education or even military training as they may be considered essential to the defense of the state. Since families themselves are generally inadequate to the task of educating their children to the minimum standards necessary for the common welfare, civil government may well conduct its own schools, not only to satisfy its own minimum educational standards, but also to assist parents in a task which they themselves cannot directly perform in all its complexities.

Had there been no Divine Guidance, had there been no Church founded by God to guide men to their eternal destiny, in short, had there been no supernatural order revealed by Christ, the answer to the question of to whom the control of education belongs would now have been completed—to the parents and to the state as outlined above.

For the Catholic, however, there has been Divine Guidance, there is a supernatural society to which he belongs and through which he learns the will of God, there is a Church founded by Jesus Christ, the Son of God, for the salvation of men's souls. Since the proper education of children is essential to the salvation of souls, a task entrusted by God to His Church, the Church has a right and an obligation to control those phases of education affecting the faith and morals of her members.

Because of the supreme importance of her supernatural mission and because so much of all education impinges on faith and morals, wherever possible the Church makes available to parents schools which provide for the religious education of their children, while at the same time both supplementing the parent's secular educational efforts and satisfying the legitimate requirements of civil society toward civic competency.

According to a survey published in the documentary magazine *Herder Korrespondez*[2] based on data assembled from the *Annuario*

[2] As reported by the Rev. Placid Jordan, O.S.B., in *Catholic Telegraph-Register*, Cincinnati, Ohio, June 14, 1958.

Pontificio, yearbook of the Holy See, and the demographic yearbook of the United Nations for 1957, the Catholic Church was maintaining 157,400 schools, attended by nearly 22 million students. After the United States, in which the largest Catholic school system is maintained, comes France, with 1,330,000 students in 11,356 schools; India, with 1,273,000 students in 6,990 schools; Canada, with 1,080,000 students in 10,240 schools; and the Belgian Congo, with 1,040,000 students in 17,345 schools.

Here in the United States, according to the 1961 *Official Catholic Directory,* the Catholic Church is maintaining 13,294 schools (elementary, secondary, colleges, and universities) with a total enrollment of 5,610,704 students.[3]

The Catholic Church exercises her control over the education of her children through the world-wide organizational structure through which she operates on all matters of concern to her. For the American Catholic, therefore, three sources of Church control of education may be distinguished: the universal control of the Pope and his subordinate policy-making agencies, the local control of the bishop, and the national influence resulting from joint actions of the American hierarchy and the voluntary association of Catholic educators.

THE INTERNATIONAL LEVEL OF CONTROL

All control of the Catholic Church resides in the Pope; thus all control of Catholic schools is in the Pope or flows from him, directly or indirectly. This, of course, is not to say that all problems which arise in running Catholic schools have to be referred to the Pope for decision. For the Pope operates through many executives and policy-making commissions in the direction of Catholic schools. All, however, have authority only as their actions are approved, at least by implication, by the Holy Father himself.

At the international level, or the level of the universal Church, basic policies governing Catholic schools may be found in formal letters issued by the Holy Father himself (commonly in the form of encyclicals or letters addressed to the whole Church); they may be found in canon law, a codified set of 2,414 rules and regulations

[3] *The Official Catholic Directory,* P. J. Kenedy & Sons, New York, 1961.

reissued in 1917; and they may be found in the instructions, decrees, and interpretations of canon law issued by the Roman Curia, the Church's headquarters staff or secretariat.

THE POPE

It is impossible to be a Catholic without believing that in special circumstances, and under certain conditions, the Pope cannot be wrong when he proclaims articles of faith (the doctrine of infallibility). Infallibility implies neither inspiration nor revelation, but Divine assistance preserving him from error when he manifests a declaration concerning the deposit of faith of the universal Church. Only two doctrines have been formally proclaimed in the last 100 years (that of infallibility itself and that of the Assumption of the Virgin Mary). "Actually the 'articles of faith' that must be believed under pain of heresy are few in number." [4]

As heads of the Catholic Church, however, the pontiffs express themselves as teachers in a less formal way—sometimes with and sometimes without the required conditions for infallibility—through allocutions addressed to the world, in audiences with groups of visitors, in short written pronouncements called "bulls," and in encyclicals. "The most impressive way in which a Pope can take a public stand (barring, of course, the infallible definition of dogma) is by means of an Encyclical. This is a letter written to all the faithful." [5] Through encyclicals Church policies are expressed.

In the last 200 years, the popes have issued almost 300 encyclicals on a variety of great questions of their times. In discussing the official position of the Catholic Church on control of education, we have already drawn heavily on the encyclical letter of Pius XI on the *Christian Education of Youth*.

This thirty-eight page statement is the most recent and most comprehensive papal pronouncement on education. In it Pius XI not only treated of the control of education but went on to express himself formally on the nature of the person being educated: the whole man, fallen and redeemed by Christ; man with his disorderly inclinations and his tendencies toward good.

[4] Jean Neuvecelle, *The Vatican*, translated from the French by George Libaire, Criterion Books, New York, 1955, p. 29.
[5] *Ibid.,* p 34.

In this connection the Pontiff points out the grave danger of false naturalism, particularly as regards sex education and coeducation. Regarding the first, he writes: "Far too common is the error of those who with dangerous assurance . . . propagate a so-called sex-education, falsely imagining they can forearm youth against the danger of sensuality by means purely natural, such as a foolhardy initiation and precautionary instruction for all indiscriminately, even in public. . . ." [6] Regarding coeducation, he writes: "False also and harmful to Christian education is the so-called method of 'co-education.' This too, by many of its supporters is founded on naturalism and the denial of original sin. . . ." [7]

After emphasizing the importance of a Christian environment for education in the family and the school, Pius XI concludes with an authoritative statement on the purpose of Christian education from which the following are excerpts: [8]

> The proper and immediate end of Christian education is to cooperate with divine grace in forming the true and perfect Christian, that is, to form Christ Himself in those regenerated by baptism. . . .
>
> For precisely this reason, Christian education takes in the whole aggregate of human life, physical and spiritual, intellectual and moral, individual, domestic, and social, not with a view of reducing it in any way, but in order to elevate, regulate and perfect it, in accordance with the example and teaching of Christ.
>
> Hence the true Christian, product of Christian education, is the supernatural man who thinks, judges and acts constantly and consistently in accordance with right reason illumined by the supernatural light of the example and teaching of Christ; in other words, to use the current term, the true and finished man of character.

CANON LAW

The present Code of Canon Law for governing the Catholic Church was issued on May 27, 1917, becoming effective on May 19, 1918. It is the result of about thirteen years of study and recodification of regulations that had been enacted over nearly 2,000 years of Church history. It consists of 2,414 canons numbered suc-

[6] Pius XI, "Christian Education of Youth," in *Five Great Encyclicals,* The Paulist Press, New York, 1941, p. 56.

[7] *Ibid.,* pp. 56 ff.

[8] *Ibid.,* pp. 64 ff.

cessively and nine documents numbered from I to IX. For a topical outline of the Code, consult Table 2.

Of the 2,414 canons of the Code, twelve are specifically applicable to aspects of Catholic education, although many of the rest are applicable to the administration of Catholic schools as well as to other activities of the Church, e.g., canons covering the administration of Church property or the responsibilities of the bishop.

TABLE 2. TOPICAL PLAN OF THE FIVE BOOKS OF THE CODE

Book I	General rules (Canons 1–86)	
Book II	Persons (Canons 87–725)	
	Part I.	Clerics
	Part II.	Religious
	Part III.	Lay persons
Book III	Things (Canons 726–1551)	
	Part I.	Sacraments
	Part II.	Sacred places and times
	Part III.	Divine worship
	Part IV.	The teaching authority of the Church
	Part V.	Benefices and other noncollegiate ecclesiastical institutions
	Part VI.	Temporal goods of the Church
Book IV	Procedure (Canons 1552–2194)	
	Part I.	Trials
	Part II.	Cases of beatification and canonization
	Part III.	Procedure in certain matters or in applying penalties
Book V	Crimes and penalties (Canons 2195–2414)	
	Part I.	Crimes
	Part II.	Penalties
	Part III.	Penalties for particular crimes

SOURCE: T. Lincoln Bouscaren and Adam C. Ellis, *Canon Law, A Text and Commentary*, 3d rev. ed., The Bruce Publishing Company, Milwaukee, 1957.

Following are twelve canons specifically applicable to phases of Catholic education:[9]

Canon 1113. Religious and Moral Education. Parents are bound by a most serious obligation to provide to the best of their power for the religious and moral as well as for the physical and civil education of their children, and also to provide for their temporal welfare.

[9] Stanislaus Woywood, O.F.M., *A Practical Commentary on the Code of Canon Law,* revised by Callistus Smith, O.F.M., Joseph F. Wagner, Inc., New York, 1957.

Canon 1372. Religious Training. The education of all Catholics from their childhood must be such that not only shall they be taught nothing contrary to the Catholic faith and good morals, but religious and moral training shall occupy the principal place in the curriculum. Not only the parents, as mentioned in Canon 1113, but in addition all those who take their place, have the right and the most serious obligation of providing for the Christian education of the children.

Canon 1373. Religious Instruction in Elementary and Secondary Schools. In every elementary school the children must, according to their age, be instructed in Christian doctrine. The young people who attend the higher schools are to receive a fuller religious training, and the bishops shall see that this training is given by priests conspicuous for their zeal and learning.

Canon 1374. Neutral and Mixed Schools. Catholic children shall not attend non-Catholic or undenominational schools, nor schools that are mixed (that is to say, open also to non-Catholics). The Bishop of the diocese alone has the right, in harmony with the instructions of the Holy See, to decide under what circumstances, and with what safeguards against perversion, the attendance of such schools by Catholic children may be tolerated.

Canon 1375. Right of Church to Establish Schools. The Church has the right to establish schools of every grade—intermediate and higher schools as well as elementary.

Canon 1376. Canonical Erection of Faculty or University. The canonical erection of a Catholic university or faculty is reserved to the Holy See. Even though it is in charge of some religious organization, it must have its statutes approved by the Holy See.

Canon 1377. Academic Degrees. Academic degrees which are recognized in canon law can be conferred only by persons to whom this power has been granted by the Holy See.

Canon 1378. Privileges Attending Degree of Doctorate, etc. Doctors, who have received their degree legitimately, have the right to wear outside of sacred functions a ring with a stone and the doctor's biretta, and in the conferring of the various offices and ecclesiastical benefices the bishop should give preference, all other things being equal, to those who have obtained the doctorate or licentiate.

Canon 1379. Establishment and Support of Catholic Schools. If there are no Catholic elementary or secondary schools, spoken of in Canon 1373, it is the duty especially of the local Ordinaries to see that they shall be established. Likewise, if the public universities are not imbued with the Catholic doctrine and spirit, it is to be desired that a Catholic University be erected in the nation or province. The Catholics should not refuse to aid according to their means in the building and maintenance of Catholic Schools.

Canon 1380. Special Studies for Promising Priests. It is desirable that the local Ordinaries send pious and gifted clerics to the lectures of some university or faculty founded or approved by the Church, in order that they may there pursue especially the studies of philosophy, theology, and canon law, and obtain academic degrees.

Canon 1381. Bishops' Right of Supervision over Schools. The religious teaching of youth in all schools whatsoever is subject to the authority and inspection of the Church. The local Ordinaries have the right and duty to see that nothing is taught or done contrary to faith or morals in any of the schools of their territory. They have, moreover, the right to approve the teachers of religion and the books, and to demand that, in the interest of religion and morals, teachers and books be replaced.

Canon 1382. Right to Visitation. Local Ordinaries have the right, either in person or through others, to visit any schools, oratories, asylums, orphanages, or any other similar institute or house to investigate all matters connected with religious and moral instruction. From this visitation the schools conducted by no religious organization whatsoever are exempted, unless it is a domestic school for the professed members of an exempt organization.

Since the relatively few canons uniquely concerned with education are not lengthy or detailed, further guidance as to their specific implications and implementation is necessary. The Sacred Congregations and the individual bishops each play roles in amplifying individual canons. The process of amplification is illustrated by the development of only one facet of Canon 1374: possible exceptions to the canon requiring attendance at Catholic schools. According to canon lawyers Bouscaren and Ellis, the canon itself plainly intimates that in exceptional cases attendance at other than Catholic schools may be permitted. To the question of under what conditions, they quote the following passage from an instruction of the Congregation of the Holy Office.[10]

[10] T. Lincoln Bouscaren and Adam C. Ellis, *Canon Law, A Text and Commentary,* 3d rev. ed., The Bruce Publishing Company, Milwaukee, 1957, pp. 744 ff.

It will usually be a sufficient reason if there is either no Catholic school at all available, or only one which is inadequate for the suitable education of the children according to their condition. In that case, in order that a public school may be attended with a safe conscience, the danger of perversion which is always more or less connected with its very nature must, by appropriate remedies and safeguards, be rendered remote.

The matter of exceptions was further spelled out by the American bishops in the Third Plenary Council of Baltimore, in which it was specified that the reason for attendance at a non-Catholic school must be approved by the bishop.

CURIA: THE SACRED CONGREGATIONS

The Roman Curia includes eleven Sacred Congregations, which are the administrative and executive arms of the Pope. These eleven, with a brief indication of their functions, are:

1. *The Congregation of the Holy Office*—acts as the guardian of doctrine in faith and morals, with exclusive jurisdiction in marriage cases which involve the Pauline Privilege and dispensations for mixed marriages; and in condemnation of books deemed injurious to faith and morals.

2. *The Consistorial Congregation*—establishes new dioceses and provinces, divides already existing dioceses, and oversees their government; however, it does not have jurisdiction over mission territory subject to the Congregation of the Propagation of the Faith.

3. *The Congregation of the Sacraments*—sets disciplinary regulations concerning the seven sacraments, as distinguished from the doctrinal and ritual aspects of the sacraments.

4. *The Congregation of the Council*—controls discipline of the secular clergy and laity in general, including pastors, pious sodalities, ecclesiastical property, diocesan taxes, councils, and meetings of bishops.

5. *The Congregation of Religious*—has authority over all religious organizations, including their government, discipline, property, and studies. When matters belonging to the jurisdiction of other Congregations are involved, however, they are handled by those Congregations.

6. *The Congregation of the Propagation of the Faith*—has jurisdiction over mission territory and all that concerns the missions,

including societies and seminaries founded exclusively for the missions. Members of religious orders working in mission lands are subject to this Congregation as missionaries, and to the Congregation of Religious as religious.

7. *The Congregation of Sacred Rites*—controls rites and ceremonies of the Latin Church; questions concerning relics and the causes of beatification and canonization are subject to this Congregation.

8. *The Ceremonial Congregation*—determines rank among the cardinals and legates. It is in charge of the ceremonies of the Papal Chapel and Court, the sacred functions performed by cardinals outside the Papal Chapel, and papal protocol.

9. *The Congregation for Extraordinary Affairs*—erects or divides dioceses and appoints bishops in countries where the civil authorities are involved, and conducts general negotiations with civil governments.

10. *The Congregation of Seminaries and Universities*—oversees papal seminaries and universities.

11. *The Congregation for the Oriental Church*—combines responsibilities of the other congregations in matters pertaining to the churches of the Oriental rite.

Each Congregation is presided over by a cardinal prefect unless the Holy Father himself presides. In this case it is directed by a cardinal secretary (Canon 246). The Pope himself is Prefect of the Congregation of the Holy Office, the Consistorial Congregation, and the Congregation for the Oriental Church. Although the congregations are established by canon law and receive power through the law, it must be remembered that this is a delegated power dependent upon approval of the Holy Father.

No one of the eleven congregations has control of Catholic education as its particular province. Over the years at least five congregations have issued instructions concerning aspects of the Church's control of education, most of them interpreting canons of the Code or providing for their observance. For example, the Congregation of the Holy Office has stated under what conditions exceptions may be made to Canon 1374, as indicated earlier. The Congregation of the Propagation of the Faith, the Congregation of Seminaries and Universities, the Congregation of Religious, and the Congregation of the Council have also issued instruction or memoranda on education.

Illustrative of the manner in which the Sacred Congregations participate in the control of Catholic education is the *Instruction on Coeducation,* issued on December 8, 1957, by the Congregation for Religious after five other congregations had been involved in its preparation.

Since this congregation is concerned with supervision of religious orders and since many Catholic schools are conducted by religious orders, it was this administrative organ that the Pope asked to study coeducation—a subject of real significance to Catholic education in this country in view of the fact that a survey of Catholic secondary schools in 1947 revealed that of 2,111 schools, 53.6 per cent were coeducational, 33.6 per cent were for girls, and 12.8 per cent for boys,[11] and that by 1959, no significant changes in these percentages had occurred.

The need for clarification grew out of brief reference to coeducation nearly thirty years previous in the encyclical on *Christian Education of Youth,* in which Pius XI stated, "False also and harmful to Christian Education is the so-called method of 'co-education.' " [12]

Expanding and developing this statement in reference to high school education, the instruction points out that under some circumstances, coeducation can be permitted as the lesser of two evils.[13] For example, to make Catholic high school education unavailable because it would be too expensive to conduct separate schools for boys and girls would be a greater evil.

The instruction suggests coinstitutional housing where possible, that is, providing separate classes for boys and girls within the same school plant. Laboratories and the library, for example, would be used by both at different times. Such an arrangement, in fact, is not considered coeducation.

When coinstitutional housing does not adequately meet the

[11] As reported by Frederick G. Hochwalt, "The Catholic School System in the United States" in Louis J. Putz, C.S.C. (ed.), *The Catholic Church, U.S.A.,* Fides Publishers Association, Chicago, 1956, p. 126.

[12] Pius XI, *op. cit.,* p. 56.

[13] Sacra Congregatio de Religiosio, "Instructio de Iuvenum Utriusque Sexus Promiscua Institutione," *Acta Apostolicae Sedis* 50, pp. 99–103, Feb. 24, 1958.

specific problems facing Catholic school administrators, coeducation itself is permitted as more desirable than terminating the religious education of youth. However, specific precautions are pronounced which include careful selection of teachers, both religious and lay; no intermingling of boys and girls in physical education or athletic activities; seating boys and girls separately; and providing separate class meetings for instruction in the morality of sex or in certain aspects of biology or psychology.

The instruction requires that bishops, in their regular five-year reports to the Holy See, shall account for the functioning of any coeducation within their dioceses and that within a given country, they shall jointly provide norms for determining when, and under what circumstances, coeducation shall be permitted.

The instruction, while indicating a framework of principles and precautions, obviously does not treat of some practical problems which the school administrator may face. For example, in coinstitutional or coeducational high schools, may boys and girls be mixed at the lunch hour? The opinion of one moral theologian on this question is that "Since the present instruction supposes that there can be some association in these schools among the pupils of both sexes, and even refers to such association as having some advantages, it seems to me that a get-together in the lunch hour, properly supervised, would be quite permissible and perhaps even desirable." [14]

THE LOCAL CONTROL OF THE BISHOP

In general, the local control of Catholic education in the United States, as of all other Church concerns, resides in the archbishops and bishops of the 140 archdioceses and dioceses of the country. "They are the successors of the Apostles, and, as the latter had St. Peter as their head, so have the bishops the Roman Pontiff, the successor of St. Peter as their head." [15]

Thus, policies in education set at the international level are carried on, interpreted, and implemented at the local level by the bishops. This relationship between the Pope and the bishops in the govern-

[14] Francis J. Connell, "The Instruction on Coeducation," *American Ecclesiastical Review,* vol. 138, no. 5, p. 291.

[15] Woywood, *op. cit.,* Bk. I, p. 134.

ment of the Church is carried out principally through the Consistorial Congregation which is responsible for making periodic surveys of the management of every non-Oriental diocese. Bishops must make a report to the Consistorial Congregation every five years in reply to a highly detailed questionnaire; and they must periodically report by a personal visit to the Pope and the Prefect of the Consistorial Congregation. The Apostolic Delegate to the United States, located in Washington, also serves as a two-way avenue of communication between the international and local levels of Church control.

Clearly, however, only the most basic policies on education and the most general guidelines are set at the international level. The bishops, by virtue of their high office as successors to the apostles and spiritual brothers of the Pope, have the responsibility for implementing, interpreting, and expanding these basic policies in their geographical territories. In the United States, this responsibility belongs to each cardinal, archbishop, and bishop in his own territory or diocese. Within the diocese, all parish schools, diocesan high schools, and diocesan colleges or universities are completely subject to the bishop's authority.

Within a diocese, however, there may be other Catholic schools conducted by certain "exempt" religious orders. These orders are under the authority of the bishop only in teaching faith and morals. They are subject to the religious superiors of their orders who in turn are subject to the authority of the Pope. This authority is ordinarily exercised through the Congregation of Religious, which bears a similar relationship to the superiors of religious orders as that of the Consistorial Congregation to bishops.

Just as the Pope himself is unable to handle personally all details of the administration of the universal Church and so needs the assistance of the Curia, so too the bishop of a large diocese needs legislative and administrative assistance in discharging his many responsibilities.

Within the dioceses of the United States, considerable differences exist in organizational patterns for developing school policies and practices. There is, of course, no variation in the source of authority, the bishop. Greatest differences exist in the roles of diocesan synods, school boards, superintendents of schools, pastors of parishes, and principals of schools. For a discussion of diocesan school boards and superintendents of schools, the reader is referred to Chapter 6, where these are treated under "Local Units and Education."

Diocesan synods, the source of much basic legislation concerning education, are consultative bodies which by canon law must be convened by the bishop at least every ten years. Diocesan-wide policies and regulations are considered. The bishop presides at the synod, invitations to which must be issued to key diocesan officials. The bishop, however, is the only legislator in the synod, the rest of the members having only an advisory vote.[16] Even though synods are consultative, the real importance of their role in framing educational legislation is shown in the histories of education within dioceses, published and unpublished, which have been submitted as theses for graduate degrees at many universities.

The individual parochial school in the United States is headed by the pastor of the parish who is the agent of his bishop. He is generally responsible for school construction, finance, and staffing. He secures the principal and as many teachers as are available from one of the religious orders of teaching sisters. Ordinarily the principal becomes responsible for administering the instructional program of the schools. Thus it is through the pastor that the educational policies of an individual bishop are implemented in the approximately 10,000 parish elementary schools of the United States.

The actual administration of individual parish elementary schools is described by Fichter, in summarizing the findings of a survey of 433 parochial schools in twenty-nine states, as follows:[17]

> All of the schools are run by local authority with practically no interference from diocesan officials. In more than half (52%) of the schools, the diocesan superintendent of schools did not even visit the school during the year. In twenty-nine per cent of the schools he made only one visit, and in the remaining schools he came from two to five times during the year. In almost seven out of ten (69%) schools, however, the school superintendent provides a list of the textbooks to be used and also sends a recommended time schedule for the subject matter of the classes.

[16] Bouscaren and Ellis, *op. cit.,* p. 176.
[17] Joseph H. Fichter, *Parochial School: A Sociological Study,* University of Notre Dame Press, Notre Dame, Ind., 1958, p. 456.

In only twenty-one per cent of the cases studied does the Pastor himself operate the school. In most of the parochial schools the function of the Pastor seems to be whatever he wants to make it. In ten per cent of the schools he does nothing at all. His most frequently performed role, in seventy-three per cent of the schools, is that of giving out the report cards to the children. In two out of five schools (39%) he teaches religion. In twenty-two per cent of them he acts as ultimate and chief disciplinarian of the pupils. In relatively few instances (7%) does the Pastor visit the classrooms frequently and regularly. There are other isolated activities mentioned in the reports, like judging contests, coaching teams, hearing first Friday confessions.

The Sister Principal, either alone or with one of the parish priests, actually directs the parochial school in more than three-quarters of the cases studied. The full-time Principal, however, is something of a luxury in the parochial school system, existing in only sixteen per cent of the schools. Nine per cent of these schools have part-time Principals, who do some teaching. In the great majority of schools the full-time teaching Principal handles either the eighth grade, or in the smaller schools, the combined seventh and eighth grades. One-fifth of the teaching Principals, however, teach in the lower grades.

NATIONAL INFLUENCE

Just as there are fifty separate public school systems in the fifty states, yet there is an underlying national pattern of public education in the United States, so are there 140 separate Catholic school systems in the 140 dioceses, yet there is an underlying national pattern of Catholic education in the United States. In great measure, this pattern results from the nationwide influence of the American bishops acting jointly through their statements on education; through the Department of Education of the National Catholic Welfare Conference; and through the National Catholic Educational Association.

JOINT STATEMENTS OF THE BISHOPS OF THE UNITED STATES

The national character of Catholic education in the United States is a reflection in part of the joint statements of the bishops which grow out of their annual meetings, held each fall at Washington,

D.C., and from statements of their colleagues representing them on standing committees.

The bishops' annual statements, formerly termed pastoral letters, are intended to express the common viewpoint of all in attendance. As such they have important consequences, though they are not binding on the individual bishop.

Education has received considerable attention in the statements. Since 1919, well over forty significant references to education have been made, ranging from a statement of principles of Catholic education in the bishops' letter of 1919 through statements on education in the depression (1933), Federal aid to education (1944), and the need of religious education for good citizenship (1948).

As an illustration of these joint statements, the five principles of Catholic education enunciated in the 1919 bishops' letter are presented:[18]

> *First:* The right of the child to receive education and the correlative duty of providing it are established on the fact that man has a soul created by God and endowed with capacities which need to be developed, for the good of the individual and the good of society.
>
> *Second:* Since the child is endowed with physical, intellectual, and moral capacities, all these must be developed harmoniously.
>
> *Third:* Since the duties we owe our Creator take precedence of all other duties, moral training must accord the first place to religion, that is, to the knowledge of God and His law, and must cultivate a spirit of obedience to His commands.
>
> *Fourth:* Moral and religious training is most efficacious when it is joined with instructions in other kinds of knowledge.
>
> *Fifth:* An education that unites intellectual, moral, and religious elements is the best training for citizenship.

THE DEPARTMENT OF EDUCATION, NCWC

The National Catholic Welfare Conference (NCWC) is a formal, voluntary organization set up by the bishops to advance the work of the Catholic Church in the United States. Located in its own building at 1312 Massachusetts Avenue, N.W., Washington, D.C., the NCWC grew out of the National Catholic Welfare Council which

[18] Raphael M. Huber, *Our Bishops Speak,* The Bruce Publishing Company, Milwaukee, 1952, pp. 59 ff.

first met in September, 1919, with 92 out of the then 101 bishops in attendance.

The conference serves as a secretariat or headquarters staff for the bishops of this country, providing centralization of services, but not of authority. It is organized into departments which include, besides a department of education, an executive department and departments concerned with immigration, lay organizations (the national councils of Catholic men and women), legal affairs, the Catholic press, social action, and youth.

Expenses of the NCWC, except for those of the Department of Lay Organizations, are met through a yearly budget approved at the annual meeting of bishops. The bishops voluntarily contribute the required funds. Each of the departments, again except for the Department of Lay Organizations, has a bishop as chairman and a director who may be either a priest or a layman.

The Department of Education has four chief functions:[19]

1. To supply information concerning Catholic education to Catholic educators and to the general public

2. To serve as an advisory agency in the development of Catholic schools

3. To act as a connecting agency between Catholic educational activities and governmental agencies

4. To safeguard the interests of Catholic schools

As would be expected, gathering and providing research information relative to Catholic schools; compiling statistical data; maintaining cooperative relationships with governmental agencies, professional organizations, and agencies of all types; and coordinating student exchange are all major activities of the department. In general, the work of the Department of Education, NCWC, resembles the traditional service which the U.S. Office of Education provides for all education in the country—that of a national clearinghouse for problems in the field.

THE NATIONAL CATHOLIC EDUCATIONAL ASSOCIATION

Presently located in the building of the American Council on Education at 1785 Massachusetts Avenue, N.W., Washington, D.C., the National Catholic Educational Association (NCEA) is a national

---

[19] Frederick G. Hochwalt, *op. cit.,* p. 135.

professional organization for Catholic educators serving much the same national function as the National Education Association (NEA) does for professional education in general, that of stimulation and self-improvement.

Except for 1943 and 1945, the NCEA has held annual meetings since 1904. The scope of an NCEA annual meeting is well described as follows:[20]

> Despite rain and fog, delegates from fifty states and many foreign countries gathered in Atlantic City to take part in the fifty-sixth annual convention of the National Catholic Educational Association, March 31–April 3, 1959. More than 10,000 persons filled Convention Hall as they attended the one hundred and twenty-eight sessions and functions which explored the theme of the convention: "Christian Education: Our Commitments, and Our Resources." The delegates not only received information but they also shared their knowledge and experiences in education, thus proving once again that there are two requisites for a successful convention— the people who set it up and the people who participate. In between sessions, the delegates could be found visiting the five hundred and seventy-four exhibits which were located on the main floor of Convention Hall.

The NCEA has seven departments: the College and University Department, the School Superintendents' Department, the Secondary School Department, the Elementary School Department, the Special Education Department, the Major Seminary Department, and the Minor Seminary Department. Departments may have sections within them; for example, a section on teacher education and a Sister Formation section are part of the College and University Department. A vocation section and a Newman Club chaplains' section are unattached to any department.

The College and University Department has established six regional units: Eastern, Middle Western, New England, Northwestern, Southern, and Southwestern. The Secondary School Department has five such regional units. The regional units of these departments regularly conduct their own meetings to permit discussion and study of local problems.[21]

[20] *National Catholic Educational Association Bulletin,* vol. 56, no. 1, p. 11, August, 1959.
[21] Hochwalt, *op. cit.,* p. 123.

The 1958 financial report of the NCEA sheds light on its activities. Its income of about $143,000 was principally from membership fees (51 per cent); convention receipts (35 per cent); and donations (8 per cent). Expenditures of about $150,000 were principally the cost of operating the national office, departmental publications and field expenses, and committee expenses.[22]

The *NCEA Bulletin* is issued quarterly. The August issue regularly carries proceedings of the annual meeting. Since each convention has produced papers and reports of discussions of current problems of Catholic education, the volumes of this issue to date actually constitute a record of Catholic educational thought of the twentieth century. Other NCEA publications include the *College Newsletter, News Notes for the President's Desk,* the *Catholic High School Quarterly Bulletin,* and the *Catholic Education News Digest.* Special newsletters are distributed to the membership as the occasion demands, and special publications, such as the "Directory of Catholic Facilities for Exceptional Children," are issued.

In any discussion of the NCEA, special attention must be called to the Department of School Superintendents whose meetings have had wide influence on the practices in the many Catholic elementary and secondary schools of the country. Meeting twice a year for several days each time, the group has studied the pressing problems involved in administering Catholic elementary and secondary schools. The notable growth in professional attitude since the first dozen diocesan superintendents were appointed between 1888 and 1910 seems in great measure due to their professional organization within the NCEA structure.

Questions for Discussion or Investigation

1. Discuss the philosophical basis for the parents' role in the control of education.

2. What control may the state exert on education? What is the relationship which should exist between the state and the parent in regard to education?

3. Discuss the basis for the Church's role in the control of education.

4. Describe the role of the Pope, canon law, and the Sacred Congregations in the control of Catholic education.

5. On the national scene, two Catholic organizations influence Catholic

[22] *National Catholic Education Association Bulletin, op. cit.,* pp. 439 ff.

education. Distinguish between the Department of Education of the National Catholic Welfare Conference and the National Catholic Educational Association as agencies of such influence.

Readings and References

Boffa, Conrad J.: *Canonical Provisions for Catholic Schools,* Canon Law Studies no. 117, The Catholic University of America Press, Washington, 1939.

Bouscaren, T. Lincoln, and Adam C. Ellis: *Canon Law, A Text and Commentary,* 3d rev. ed., The Bruce Publishing Company, Milwaukee, 1957.

"Christian Education: Our Commitments and Our Resources," *National Catholic Educational Association Bulletin,* vol. 56, no. 1, August, 1959.

Connell, Francis J.: "The Instruction on Coeducation," *American Ecclesiastical Review,* vol. 138, no. 5, pp. 289–293, May, 1958.

Ellis, John Tracy (ed.): *Documents of American Catholic History,* The Bruce Publishing Company, Milwaukee, 1956.

Fichter, Joseph H.: *Parochial School: A Sociological Study,* University of Notre Dame Press, Notre Dame, Ind., 1958.

Guilday, Peter: *The National Pastorals of the American Hierarchy, 1791–1919,* National Catholic Welfare Conference, Washington, 1923.

Huber, Raphael M.: *Our Bishops Speak,* The Bruce Publishing Company, Milwaukee, 1952.

Markham, James J.: *The Sacred Congregation of Seminaries and Universities of Studies,* Canon Law Studies no. 384, The Catholic University of America Press, Washington, 1957.

McCluskey, Neil G.: *Catholic Viewpoint on Education,* Hanover House, Garden City, N.Y., 1959.

Neuvecelle, Jean: *The Vatican,* translated from the French by George Libaire, Criterion Books, New York, 1955.

Pius XI: "Christian Education of Youth," in *Five Great Encyclicals,* The Paulist Press, New York, 1944, pp. 37–75.

Putz, Louis J. (ed.): *The Catholic Church, U.S.A.,* Fides Publishers Association, Chicago, 1956.

Sokolich, Alexander: *Canonical Provisions for Universities and Colleges,* The Catholic University of America Press, Washington, 1956.

Ward, Sister M. Ruth Albert: *Patterns of Administration in Diocesan School Systems,* The Catholic University of America Press, Washington, 1957.

Woywood, Stanislaus: *Canonical Decisions of the Holy See,* Joseph F. Wagner, Inc., New York, 1933.

————: *A Practical Commentary on the Code of Canon Law,* revised by Callistus Smith, Joseph F. Wagner, Inc., New York, 1957.

4. *The Federal Government and Education*

In the United States, the Federal government has always evidenced a strong interest in education. Even before the adoption of the Constitution, when the government was operating under the Articles of Confederation, this interest was demonstrated in some of the provisions of the Northwest Ordinance, a plan for the development of the Northwest Territory. It was this Ordinance which included the often-quoted statement: "Religion, morality, and knowledge being necessary to good government, and the happiness of mankind, schools and the means of education shall forever be encouraged." The Ordinance also reserved portions of each township of the territory for support of schools.

When the Constitution was adopted in 1789, no direct mention of education was made. By implication, the Tenth Amendment to the Constitution reserved education either to the several states themselves or to the people of the states, for the Amendment reads: "The powers not delegated to the United States by the Constitution nor prohibited by it to the States are reserved to the States respectively, or to the people." There has, of course, been a great deal of controversy over interpretation of the "residual powers" clause of the Constitution. Many powers are in the hands of the Federal government that the Founding Fathers never dreamed would reside there. But the basic fact in regard to education is that under the Tenth Amendment, it is reserved to the states or to the people.

That the Constitution made no mention of education was no oversight since the subject was discussed at the Constitutional Convention. Washington, Madison, Pickering, and others wanted to make provision in the Constitution for founding a national university. It was only after much discussion that the idea was dropped.

Nevertheless the influence of the Federal government in education has grown stronger as the years have passed. Its influence has shown itself through Supreme Court decisions and through many legislative enactments.

SUPREME COURT DECISIONS

Over the years, the influence of the Supreme Court on education has been increasingly marked. In the first hundred years following its founding, there were only four decisions on education rendered by the Supreme Court. From 1900 to 1920 there were only three additional decisions. Since 1920, however, there have been over thirty Supreme Court decisions affecting education.

So great has the influence of the Supreme Court on education become that at least one article has been entitled "The Supreme Court as a National School Board." [1] The influence of the Court has been mainly in four areas: the right of independent schools to exist, the "wall of separation" between church and state, racial segregation in schools, and loyalty oaths for school personnel.

THE EXISTENCE OF INDEPENDENT SCHOOLS

Probably the key case relative to the right of nongovernmental schools to exist is the famous Oregon School case. [2]

In 1922, the state of Oregon passed a law which made it compulsory for all children to go to public schools, a law which would have put private schools, religious or secular, out of business. After

[1] Edwin S. Corwin, "The Supreme Court as a National School Board," *Thought,* vol. 23, no. 91, pp. 665–683, December, 1948.

[2] *Pierce v. Society of Sisters,* 268 U.S. 510. For text of this decision, see Appendix A, p. 385.

the District Court of the United States for the District of Oregon had granted preliminary injunctions to a religious order of sisters and a military academy preventing state officers from enforcing the law, an appeal reached the Supreme Court of the United States, where the Oregon law of 1922 was declared unconstitutional. The basis for this decision was that the law deprived teachers, religious orders, and owners of private schools of property without due process, thereby violating the Fourteenth Amendment. The Court then went on to declare:

> We think it entirely plain that the Act of 1922 unreasonably interferes with the liberty of parents and guardians to direct the upbringing and education of children under their control. As often heretofore pointed out, rights guaranteed by the Constitution may not be abridged by legislation which has no reasonable relation to some purpose within the competency of the State. The fundamental theory of liberty upon which all governments in this Union repose excludes any general power of the State to standardize its children by forcing them to accept instruction from public teachers only. The child is not the mere creature of the State. Those who nurture him and direct his destiny have the right, coupled with the high duty to recognize and prepare him for additional obligations.

The importance of this decision to the right of the independent school to exist is obvious. It should be noted how closely the point of view in this quotation resembles that later expressed by Pius XI in his encyclical *Christian Education of Youth*. While stress is given to the basic right of parents to choose education for their children, to direct their upbringing, and to be concerned with matters which go beyond and are above the interest that civil society has in education, there is nothing in this decision that diminishes the state's legitimate right to insist on minimum standards so that an adequate education is provided for all children of the state.

Several other cases have had bearing on the right of independent schools to exist. One of them, the earliest decision of the Supreme Court concerned with education, was the famous Dartmouth College case in which it was held that when the state had given a charter to a private college, such a charter was a contract and could not be revoked by the state without the consent of those to whom the charter had been issued.[3] This decision was made when Dartmouth, Harvard, Yale, and similar institutions were in danger of being forcibly made state colleges and universities. The preservation of their right to exist has had strong implications for private education.

Also bolstering this right to existence was the Nebraska case.[4] As a reaction to the anti-German emotionalism of World War I, Nebraska passed a state law prohibiting the teaching of foreign languages to pupils not only in public elementary schools, but in private elementary schools as well. Therefore, parents could no longer choose whether a child would learn German or French in school. No foreign language could be taught.

In a 1923 decision, the Supreme Court declared this Nebraska law unconstitutional. The right of the private school to teach what it wanted to teach, as long as it taught also what the state required it to teach, had been again maintained, although it is important to note that the Court actually based its decision on property rights and decided that the Nebraska law unreasonably deprived foreign language teachers of their means of livelihood.

THE "WALL OF SEPARATION"

The second direction in which the Supreme Court has influenced education has been with respect to the concept of the "wall of separation" between church and state.

The first case of the Supreme Court affecting this matter was the Indian Affairs case of 1908.[5] In this case the Supreme Court sustained the policy of the United States Office of Indian Affairs in using funds publicly appropriated in furtherance of an Indian treaty as well as some Indian trust funds to obtain the education of children by contract with Catholic schools. While the decision of the Court was based on the fact that the funds practically belonged to the Indians not the government, the view of the Court in this case is

[3] "But the Constitution of the United States has imposed this additional limitation, that the legislature of a state, shall pass no act impairing the obligation of contract." *Trustees of Dartmouth College v. Woodward,* 4 Wheat. 518 U.S. 1819. For text of this decision, see Appendix A, p. 389.

[4] *Meyer v. State of Nebraska,* 262 U.S. 390. For text of this decision, see Appendix A, p. 390.

[5] *Quick Bear v. Leupp,* 210 U.S. 50. For text of this decision, see Appendix A, p. 395.

an interesting contrast to that of most state constitutions which prevent the use of public funds in schools controlled by religious organizations, a stand which to date the Federal government has not taken.

Pertinent to the meaning of the wall of separation are two other cases: the Louisiana Textbook case[6] and the New Jersey School Bus case.[7] In the first, the Supreme Court sustained the validity of a state law which provided free textbooks to children in private schools, including religious schools. In other words, the Supreme Court declared that if a state wishes to furnish to religious schools the same free textbooks as are furnished to other schools, it may do so. In the New Jersey case, the Court found constitutional a state law making it possible for local school districts to transport children to parochial schools on the same basis as children attending public schools.

Two other cases are especially pertinent to the wall-of-separation concept: the first, the Illinois Released Time case,[8] and the second, the New York Released Time case.[9]

The Illinois case was concerned with the released time program of religious instruction in Champaign, Illinois, where the school system made it possible for children to take religious instruction in school, with the school providing the necessary forms for parents to indicate whether the child was to receive religious instruction and if so, whether such instruction should be with a Catholic priest, a Jewish rabbi, or a Protestant minister.

One youngster named McCollum, the child of professed atheists, wanted to take no religious instruction. This was quite all right, except that everyone else was taking instruction and the child was alleged to have suffered extreme embarrassment by having to stay in his regular classroom while the other children were released for their religious instruction. Because of this embarrassment, his mother brought suit. The decision which resulted appeared to put the

[6] *Cochran v. Louisiana State Board of Education,* 281 U.S. 370. For text of this decision, see Appendix A, p. 397.

[7] *Everson v. Board of Education,* 330 U.S. 1. For text of this decision, see Appendix A, p. 399.

[8] *McCollum v. Board of Education,* 333 U.S. 203. For text of this decision, see Appendix A, p. 405.

[9] *Zorach v. Clauson,* 343 U.S. 306. For text of this decision, see Appendix A, p. 408.

Supreme Court on the side of an absolute cleavage between religion and education while ruling unconstitutional the Champaign, Illinois, plan for religious instruction in an 8 to 1 decision.

Something seems to have happened in the thinking of some of the Justices of the Court between the decision in the Illinois case (1948) and that rendered four years later in the New York case, for in a 6 to 3 decision the New York program was held constitutional. While the difference between the two decisions centered around whether or not governmental coercion was involved in the two programs, in the New York case the Court deserted the absolute wall-of-separation stand it took in the earlier decision, as the majority decision included the following quotation:

> The First Amendment within the scope of its coverage permits no exception; the prohibition is absolute. The First Amendment, however, does not say that in every and all respects there shall be a separation of Church and State. Rather, it studiously defines the main, the specific ways, in which there shall be no concert or union or dependency one on the other. That is the common sense of the matter. Otherwise the state and religion would be aliens to each other—hostile, suspicious, and even unfriendly. Churches could not be required to pay even property taxes. Municipalities would not be permitted to render police or fire protection to religious groups. Policemen who helped parishioners into their places of worship would violate the Constitution. Prayers in our legislative halls; the appeals to the Almighty in the messages of the Chief Executive; the proclamation making Thanksgiving Day a holiday; "so help me God" in our courtroom oaths—these and all other references to the Almighty that run through our laws, our public rituals, our cere-monies would be flouting the First Amendment. A fastidious atheist or agnostic could even object to the supplication with which the Court opens each session "God save the United States and this Honorable Court.

In summary, what do these five cases say about the "wall of sep-aration between church and state" in regard to education? From the maze of legal terminology involving affirmations and dissents, these generalizations seem clearly valid: there shall be no establish-ment of religion; but this does not mean an absolute wall of separa-tion between religion and state schools. There shall be no governmental coercing of children to take any religious instructions. Certain services to children are basically just that—services to children rendered primarily for their safety, health, or education. They are intended to aid children, not religion, in the same way that the GI bills were designed to aid veterans, not the religious school they might choose to attend.

RACIAL SEGREGATION IN SCHOOLS

The story of the Supreme Court's influence on racial segregation in schools, in its broad outlines, is one of chipping away at the doctrine of "separate but equal facilities" until in 1954 the Court declared that racial segregation in public schools is unconstitutional.

The doctrine that racial segregation was constitutional as long as equal educational opportunities were offered all races (without much examination of whether or not such facilities were really equal) was firmly established in 1896 by the Court's decision in *Plessy v. Ferguson* (136 U.S. 537), a case involving segregation in a railroad Pullman car, but by implication applying to busses, places of amusement, hotels, restaurants, and schools. The doctrine was the basis for a 1927 decision which ruled constitutional Mississippi's action in assigning a native-born child of Chinese descent, Gong Lum, to schools maintained for colored people (275 U.S. 78).

One of the first instances in which the Court narrowed its concept of separate but equal facilities came in a Missouri case.[10] In this case it was held that Missouri's willingness to pay a Negro student's tuition to an out-of-state law school while denying him admission to its own state law school was not providing equal facilities for him.

The erosion of the separate-but-equal principle was speeded up as Justice Jackson, in an opinion on an Oklahoma Law School case (332 U.S. 631), evidenced concern that the equality of facilities provided be real, not "legal fiction." In the Sweatt and McLaurin cases, both decided in June, 1950, the definition of equal was substantially sharpened. The Sweatt case[11] resulted in a decision that a law school provided by the state of Texas for Negroes must actually

[10] *Missouri ex rel. Gaines v. Canada,* 305 U.S. 337. For text of this decision, see Appendix A, p. 412.

[11] *Sweatt v. Painter,* 339 U.S. 629. For text of this decision, see Appendix A, p. 414.

be equal in faculty qualifications, library, and other facilities. More than that, the Court held:

> The law school to which Texas is willing to admit petitioner excludes from its student body members of the racial groups which number 85% of the population of the State and include most of the lawyers, witnesses, jurors, judges and other officials with whom petitioner will inevitably be dealing when he becomes a member of the Texas Bar. With such a substantial and significant segment of society excluded, we cannot conclude that the education offered petitioner is substantially equal to that which he would receive if admitted to the University of Texas Law School. . . .

In the *McLaurin Case*[12] it was unanimously held that when a Negro graduate student is admitted to a state university, he must be treated as any other student, with no racial restrictions applied by university regulations.

In the segregated school systems cases of 1954, five of them decided in historic decisions on May 17, the Supreme Court flatly rejected the entire separate-but-equal doctrine as far as public education goes. The Court went on to say in one of these, the Kansas case,[13] that separate, equal facilities do not in fact provide equal protection of the law as required by the Fourteenth Amendment; and that separation on the basis of race in itself is discrimination. The decision quoted an earlier finding of a Kansas court as follows:

> Segregation of white and colored children in public schools has a detrimental effect upon the colored children. The impact is greater when it has the sanction of the law; for the policy of separating the races is usually interpreted as denoting the inferiority of the Negro group. A sense of inferiority affects the motivation of a child to learn. Segregation with the sanction of law, therefore, has a tendency to retard the educational and mental development of Negro children and to deprive them of some of the benefits they would receive in a racial[ly] integrated school system.

A year later the Court ordered that all segregation in public schools must be removed under supervision of the Federal district

---

[12] *McLaurin v. Oklahoma State Regents,* 339 U.S. 637. For text of this decision, see Appendix A, p. 416.

[13] *Brown v. Board of Education of Topeka,* 347 U.S. 483. For text of this decision, see Appendix A, p. 417.

courts which were to require of school authorities such progress as is reasonable in the face of problems of "administration, school plant, transportation, personnel, revision of school districts, local laws and regulations."

Some criticism from those who favor the Court's decision on the segregated systems cases has centered around the extent to which the current climate of social opinion seemed to have influenced the decision. Such critics point out that something more stable than the results of public opinion polls or the opinions of experts in the social sciences must provide the legal bases for Supreme Court decisions; witness: the Salute to the Flag cases.

SALUTE TO THE FLAG CASES

Two cases concerning the compulsory salute to the flag in schools also serve to illustrate the danger of using the climate of social opinion, rather than natural law concepts, as a basis for Supreme Court decisions.

In the 1940 Pennsylvania case (310 U.S. 586), the facts were these. The children of a Jehovah Witness refused to conform to a school district regulation that each child participate daily in the flag salute or be expelled from public school. The children were expelled although they had been brought up conscientiously to believe that such a gesture of respect for the flag was forbidden by command of Scripture. The regulation in question has to be seen in the climate of the emotion-laden days immediately before the United States entered World War II: the national awakening to the danger of war, the peace-time draft, "Bundles for Britain," "America First," and the emphasis on national defense. The Court in its decision on this first case saw the issue in these words:

> A grave responsibility confronts this Court whenever in course of litigation it must reconcile the conflicting claims of liberty and authority. But when the liberty invoked is liberty of conscience, and the authority is authority to safeguard the nation's fellowship, judicial conscience is put to its severest test. Of such a nature is the present controversy.

It decided the controversy in favor of authority and found the compulsory flag salute regulation constitutional after considerable discussion which included statements on the flag as a symbol of our national unity, transcending all internal differences, and on the wisdom of training children in patriotic impulses.

Three years later in the West Virginia case (319 U.S. 624), also involving a conflict between a Jehovah Witness and a compulsory flag salute law, the previous decision was flatly reversed, and the decision went to the right of the individual rather than to authority to safeguard the nation's fellowship.

> If there is any fixed star in our constitutional constellation, it is that no official, high or petty, can prescribe what shall be orthodox in politics, nationalism, religion, or other matters of opinion or force citizens to confess by word or act their faith therein. If there are any circumstances which permit an exception, they do not now occur to us.
>
> We think the action of the local authorities in compelling the flag salute and pledge transcends constitutional limitations on their power and invades the sphere of intellect and spirit which it is the purpose of the First Amendment to our Constitution to reserve from all official control.

LOYALTY OATHS FOR TEACHERS

Up to 1958, the Supreme Court heard four cases concerning requirements of state authorities that public employees, including teachers, be required to take loyalty oaths. These oaths generally included a statement that the teacher never belonged to the Communist Party or any front organization affiliated with it, or to any organization officially listed as subversive. The oath, once signed, permitted authorities to discharge teachers proved to have perjured themselves.

In three of the cases, involving a Los Angeles, a New York state, and a Maryland oath, the Supreme Court indicated that it was constitutional for state agencies to demand that teachers affirm their loyalty to the United States and swear that they had never belonged knowingly to any organization advocating the violent overthrow of the present form of government. Oklahoma, however, passed a law prescribing a loyalty oath for public employees, making it possible to dismiss teachers who had unknowingly belonged to a subversive organization. The Court distinguished this case (344 U.S. 183) from the previous three involving loyalty oaths in these words:

> Yet under the Oklahoma Act, the fact of association alone determines disloyalty and disqualification; it matters not whether association existed innocently or knowingly. To thus inhibit individual freedom of movement is to stifle the flow of democratic expression and controversy at one of its chief sources. . . . Indiscriminate classification of innocent with knowing activity must fall as an assertion of arbitrary power. The oath offends due process. . . .

FEDERAL LEGISLATION

While up to 1961 there was no comprehensive program of direct aid to education on a national basis, with national coordination, the United States government has aided education substantially through an impressive number of legislative acts which, on a piecemeal basis have represented a substantial contribution, directly or indirectly, to education in the United States.

LAND GRANTS

The aid which the Federal government has given to education from land grants took its origin in one of the troublesome questions solved when the country was operating under the Articles of Confederation. The varying and conflicting claims of the thirteen original colonies to much of the then "Western" lands were settled when the Congress of the Confederation persuaded the original states to give up their claims in favor of the Federal government which would adopt the territory as national domain and use any profits derived for the benefit of all the states. Through this agreement and subsequent land acquisitions, the Federal government became the owner of extensive lands.

A standard method of surveying the public domain, adopted in the Ordinance of 1785, provided for dividing the lands into townships 6 miles square and in turn, subdividing the townships into 36 sections, each 1 mile square and numbered from 1 to 36 according to its position in the township. This Ordinance further provided that

1787?

"there shall be reserved the lot No. 16 of every township for the maintenance of public schools within the said township."

Nothing was done to implement this last provision of the Ordinance of 1785 until after the adoption of the Constitution which gave Congress the right to dispose of the national domain. The act enabling Ohio to become a state in 1802 contained the provision reserving section 16 "to the inhabitants thereof" for schools in return for the state's agreement not to tax land sold from the public domain for four years. Acts enabling the creation of later states gave the reserved lands to the states rather than to the townships directly. This development involved an encroachment on the autonomy of the district system previously mentioned.

Enabling acts creating subsequent states followed this general pattern of reserving lands for education, although in all states admitted to the Union after California in 1850, both sections 16 and 36 were reserved for schools.

Through the "Seminary Acts," the Congress further provided that two whole townships be set aside for seminaries of higher learning, providing a basic endowment for subsequent state universities. Further aid to higher education came through the Morrill Act of 1862, which provided that 30,000 acres of public lands be allocated to the states for every senator and representative of the state in 1860 or at the time of its admission, if subsequent to 1860. Ninety per cent of the proceeds from the sale of these lands was to be used to endow at least one college in which agriculture, mechanical arts, and military science were taught, although other subjects were not excluded. The colleges receiving this endowment generally became the agricultural and mechanical colleges of the state. It is interesting to note that in at least one state, New York, this money was allocated to a private, sectarian institution, Cornell.

The national domain was the basis for additional substantial aid to schools, because the states chose to use for schools funds made available to them by the Federal government. In this way state schools benefited from the proceeds from the sale of salt lands which had been turned over to the states; proceeds from the 500,000 acres of land given to the states in 1841 for "internal improvements"; and proceeds from the sale of swamp lands given to some fifteen states. Schools in the states were also major beneficiaries from the distribution of Federal surpluses of 1836 and 1841, surpluses arising from sale of national land. Incidentally, under the provisions of the Distribution Act of 1841, schools would probably still be receiving this indirect aid, but there has been no government surplus since. Provision was also made for 20 per cent of the profits from Federal forestry reserves to go to schools and roads within the states where the reserves are located.

Allotments of Federal lands in aid of schools potentially represented tremendous financial help. All told, an area of 145 million acres, almost two hundred times the size of the state of Rhode Island, was granted for common schools alone. By 1860 the advantages of the sizable gifts made earlier had been in great measure dissipated through what, from today's viewpoint at least, was mismanagement.

It should be remembered that the general pattern established by the land grant program was to allocate lands to the states for use for schools as they wished. Little Federal control accompanied the gifts. Some of the Federal aid, on the decision of the states involved, went to private denominational colleges. Some small lands went to Catholic schools for Indians.

OTHER FEDERAL LEGISLATIVE AID

In addition to the Federal aid to schools through land grants, the national government has evidenced considerable interest in education and has aided schools through a variety of legislative actions over the years. The number of such acts and the cost of such aid have increased substantially in recent years, reaching a high point in 1948–1949 with the expenditure of over 3½ billion dollars for veterans' education, and declining to close to 1½ billion dollars in 1952–1953, after which total expenditures of the Federal government for education began again to rise.

Some of this aid to education has been direct, as in the case of vocational education; much has been incidental to some other purpose of the government, as in the case of considerable aid extended incidental to the relief expenditures in the depression years of the 1930s. Following are some of the ways in which education has benefited by legislative action, directly or indirectly.

Vocational Education. In addition to the First Morrill Act of 1862, subsequent actions of Congress in support of vocational education amounted to an annual expenditure of nearly 41 million dollars by 1959. Chief among these measures are the Second Morrill Act of 1890, providing for an annual grant of funds to support instruction in agriculture and mechanical arts; the Smith-Lever Act of 1914, providing funds for agriculture, trades, industries, and home economics, as well as for training teachers in these subjects; and the Smith-Hughes Act of 1917 and the George-Dean Act of 1936, which added education for distributive occupations. Throughout these and other acts pertinent to vocational education has emerged a general pattern, which includes:[14]

1. Allotment of funds to the states on the basis of a formula serving as a measure of the relative needs of the states with relation to each program

2. Matching of at least part of the funds by the states

3. Advanced approval of state plans for the use of Federal money to make sure that such plans are in agreement with the purposes of the Federal act

4. Federal advisory service to assist in the development of the program

5. Federal supervision and audit of state expenditure of Federal funds

Special Education Project. Another category of Federal aid to education is concerned with what we might think of as special education projects. The Federal government has supported since their founding the American Printing House for the Blind and the Columbia Institute for the Deaf, both private institutions. It makes major contributions to the support of Howard University, a private university for Negroes. Since 1920, through state agencies, the Federal government has had extensive provisions for rehabilitating the physically disabled. This program provides for physical examinations, necessary medical treatment, psychiatric treatment, and individual counseling and training.

Aid Incidental to Relief Activities. The Federal government has indirectly aided education through relief activities carried on during the depression years of the 1930s. At that time a number of Federal agencies, created primarily for relief purposes, substantially aided

[14] *Program of the Federal Government Affecting Children and Youth,* U.S. Office of Education, 1951, p. 11.

the work of schools. The Civilian Conservation Corps (CCC) became in part a relief to school personnel, as young people of high school and early college age were able to substitute clean, wholesome employment at reforestation, supplemented by educational programs, for school activities less congenial for them. The Works Projects Administration (WPA) in conjunction with the Public Works Administration (PWA) and the Federal Emergency Relief Administration (FERA) used funds to help build schools; to promote vocational, avocational, and nursery education; and to develop education for leisure time, home and family living, and public affairs. It even put unemployed artists to work on building models, dioramas, and other visual aids. The National Youth Administration (NYA) paid students to do work around high schools and colleges in assisting teachers, working in the library, and cleaning up the grounds. The Reconstruction Finance Corporation (RFC) helped finance new school buildings through long-range, easy payment loans.

Aid Incidental to Defense Activities. In conjunction with promoting the national defense, the Federal government maintains its service academies: the Military Academy, the Naval Academy, the Air Force Academy, the Coast Guard Academy, and the Maritime Academy. For personnel of the armed forces, United States Armed Forces Institute (USAFI) operates a comprehensive educational program with courses given for credit through the Institute itself or by extension or correspondence with accredited universities. Special training programs carried on either within the military services' own schools or by assignment of personnel to universities are becoming ever more widely available to service personnel.

The extensive education of veterans following World War II and the Korean action, through Public Laws 16 and 346 and through the Korean GI Bill, incidentally aided the institutions which the veterans chose to attend to the extent of several billions of dollars a year at the height of these programs.

Aid, related to defense activities, has also come through the surplus property which was made available to schools as part of the government's surplus property disposal program. Schools have first call on surplus property released by the Department of Defense, the Atomic Energy Commission, and other Federal agencies. Whole buildings, electronic equipment, laboratory equipment, and such items as chairs, typewriters, desks, and calculators have been made available to public and private schools free except for the costs of warehousing and transportation. Surplus property valued at 363 million dollars was turned over to schools in 1959.

Further related to defense activities is the aid which has come to many areas in building new schools under Public Law 815. This has occurred where the national defense has made such an impact on a community that it cannot handle the building of its own schools. When an atomic plant is built near a small community, for example, it becomes necessary for the Federal government to assist in the building of schools in the area so that the children of plant employees may receive an education. Federal aid is particularly necessary when defense installations are on government property not taxable by the state in which it is located; yet the children of employees living in the community must be educated. Under Public Law 874, the Federal government compensates a local school district from 50 to 100 per cent of its local share of the cost of educating children whose parents work or live on Federal tax-exempt property. Appropriations in 1959 for these two programs totaled nearly 181 million dollars.

It is in the category of aid incidental to defense activities that the post-Sputnik proposals to emphasize the development of mathematicians and natural scientists fall, since these proposals are directed at out-performing Russia in the realm of technological warfare. In this category falls the National Science Foundation's program for improving instruction in science and mathematics at all levels of schools, including supporting teacher in-service institutes and other provisions for improving teaching and research. Chief among the legislative measures in this category, however, is the National Defense Education Act of 1958.[15]

The National Defense Education Act of 1958. "To strengthen the national defense and to encourage and assist in the expansion and improvement of educational programs to meet critical national needs; and for other purposes. *Be it enacted. . . .*" So begins Public Law 85–864, the National Defense Education Act of 1958. Though it was passed as a defense measure in the climate of national concern

[15] For text of the National Defense Education Act of 1958, see Appendix B.

after Russia's successful launching of Sputnik, it is significant in that it is closest to comprehensive Federal aid to education of any legislation in the country's history up to 1961.

It is comprehensive in that it is concerned with aspects of elementary, secondary, and collegiate education; it is comprehensive in that it affects both public and private educational institutions; it is comprehensive in that the term national defense encompasses activities that both more and less directly contribute to this end, yet circumvents the difficulties which beset frank "aid to education" proposals. The urgencies of national defense made it desirable to propose solutions without too much concern for even so controversial a subject as aid to religiously-operated schools.

Thus, this act is a rather comprehensive aid to education bills as written, and it became even more so as administered. For example, there were twenty-three National Defense Fellowships for the graduate study of classics approved for 1960–1961 under the act.

The act provides 90 per cent of the money needed to establish loan funds in institutions of higher education for college students, with special consideration given to superior students desiring to teach and to superior students in science, mathematics, engineering, or a modern foreign language; it provides financial assistance for strengthening science, mathematics, and modern foreign language instruction through equipment and expanded supervisory services; it provides for 1,500 National Defense Fellowships, paying doctoral students $2,000 to $2,400 per year, plus $400 per dependent, as well as paying up to $2,500 per student to the college or university involved; it provides for assisting state educational authorities to establish and maintain programs of testing, guidance, and counseling and for paying colleges for conducting, and students for attending counseling and guidance-training institutes; it provides money for establishing language and area-study centers, for conducting research projects designed to improve instruction in foreign languages, and for paying colleges for conducting, and students for attending, language institutes; it provides for research in educational television and audio-visual media to help states improve public education or help universities improve their use of these media; it provides for assisting states to improve their on-going vocational education programs; it provides for the National Science Foundation to establish a science information service, including indexing, abstracting, translating, and disseminating scientific information.

For these purposes, the act authorized expenditures in the three years from 1959 to 1961 of approximately 182, 220, and 235 million dollars respectively. However, actual appropriations in 1959 totaled about 115 million dollars; and requested appropriations for 1960 and 1961 were in the neighborhood of 167 and 171 million dollars. Thus for the three years, Congressional appropriations seem likely to be around 30 per cent less than the amounts authorized in the act.

Of significance from the point of view of Catholic education and Federal aid proposals is a noteworthy inconsistency in regard to the use of Federal funds for private and religious schools. Student loan funds are available to public or private schools; however, forgiveness of 50 per cent of loans is available only to students who teach in public schools after graduation. National Defense Fellowships are made available to all types if interested. To strengthen science, mathematics, and foreign language teaching, grants are made to state agencies, but loans are made to nonprofit private elementary or secondary schools; when it comes to guidance, counseling, and testing, however, Federal funds are made directly payable to private schools for testing, but nothing for guidance or counseling.

National Defense Education Act Amendments of 1961. By the spring of 1961, as the 1958 Act approached expiration, bills were introduced in both the House and the Senate under sponsorship of the Kennedy Administration to extend and improve the provisions of the original act. All titles of the original act were retained in the new bills; but most provisions, including contemplated expenditures, were considerably broadened. As controversy grew over general aid to education bills, also proposed by President Kennedy as discussed later in this chapter, the National Defense Education Act Amendments of 1961 became, strategically, the safety measure on which proponents of Federal aid could fall back if the principal aid bills failed. For example, whereas the original act provided for strengthening the teaching of science, mathematics, and modern foreign languages for defense purposes, new proposals were made to add physical fitness, English, and social studies as subjects critical to the national purposes. Strategically the Amendments of 1961 became linked in another way to President Kennedy's general assistance to education proposals. As aid to private schools, including religious schools, became highly controversial once more, it became clear that any aid to religious schools would come only through possible extension of the Defense Education Act. Thus proposals of Catholic bishops for government loans to aid construction of private school facilities were scheduled to receive serious consideration in the context of aiding the teaching of those subjects deemed critical to the national defense. Facilities used for teaching religion would be specifically excluded from loan aid.

When addressing themselves specifically to the Administration's proposed amendments to the act before Senate subcommittee hearings, representatives of the National Catholic Welfare Conference asked for removal of those provisions of the original act which placed children and teachers in private schools at a relative disadvantage. Stressing that the purposes of the national defense should be realized irrespective of the school involved, the following four changes in the Act of 1958 were urged:

1. That teachers in all schools benefit from the forgiveness feature of the loan program as provided for public school teachers (Title II).

2. That personnel in all schools be equally encouraged to attend NDEA institutes by receiving stipends as provided for public school teachers (Title V and Title VI).

3. That students in all schools receive the same benefits from grants for equipment, teaching materials, and minor remodeling of facilities needed for teaching science, mathematics, modern languages, and other subjects deemed by Congress to be critical to the national defense (Title III).

4. That students in all schools receive the same counseling and encouragement to make the most of their talents in the national interest, just as all receive the benefits of the same provisions for testing (Title V).

These became the basic issues as the Congress moved to act on the National Defense Education Act Amendments of 1961.

Education for International Understanding. Since World War I the United States government has demonstrated interest in the development of international understanding at home and abroad. Between World Wars I and II, most of the activities of the government for this purpose centered around Latin America and the work of the Pan American Union, now the Organization of American States. Money was provided for the exchange of two graduate students with each Latin American country and to support the in-service training of Latin American government workers by bringing them to see how government functions in this country. The exchange of professors and specialists was also provided, as was the setting up of cultural libraries in South American countries.

Since the beginnings of the United Nations Educational, Scientific, and Cultural Organization (UNESCO) in 1946, the State Department has broadened its activities in this area through active participation, with most of the other countries of the world, in UNESCO activities designed to improve education throughout the world and to foster world-wide cooperation among educators, scientists, and cultural groups. Exchange of teachers, technicians, and students has been tremendously increased since the pre-World War II days.

On its own it has fostered many of the same objectives as the UNESCO program through the Fulbright Scholarship program for the exchange of teachers, students, and scholars; and the Information Exchange Act which enabled foreigners to visit the United States for additional technical training to use in the development of their own countries.

School Lunch Program. The Department of Agriculture has administered the National School Lunch Act, passed in 1946, "to safeguard the health and well-being of the Nation's children and to encourage the domestic consumption of nutritious agricultural commodities and other food . . ." Obviously, aid to schools is again an indirect result of the program; nevertheless, as is clearly indicated in Chapter 19, where the management of school food services is discussed in detail, the aid to schools, both public and parochial, is sizable.

The program is basically designed to be operated through the states with the Federal money allocated to the states under a formula contained in the act. Since matching funds from within a state are required, where state constitutional provisions prevent the distribution of state monies to religious schools, regional offices are set up for administering the program directly with such schools. Under the act, cash reimbursement is provided up to certain maxima for approved lunches served to children of high school age or under; certain minimum nutritional requirements must be met; lunches must be served free or at a reduced price to children unable to pay the full price; and the program must be maintained on a nonprofit basis. Commodities purchased under surplus removal programs are made available to school lunchrooms.

Library of Congress. Reference to the activities of the Federal government in aiding education must include the significant role played by the Library of Congress in the scholarship of the nation. The extent of its own collection of books which are available to scholars throughout the country and its continuing contribution to the proper indexing and cataloguing of books in libraries throughout the nation make it of fundamental value to education in the United States.

EXECUTIVE ACTIVITIES

While of course it is impossible to isolate executive activity from the legislative which authorizes and sustains it, two types of Federal activity on behalf of education are particularly associated with the executive branch of the national government: that of the U.S. Office of Education and that of presidential committees and conferences.

THE U.S. OFFICE OF EDUCATION

The United States Office of Education is a part of the executive branch of the national government. It is headed by a Commissioner of Education responsible to the Secretary of Health, Education, and Welfare (see Figure 2). Its role in education in the United States is described in the following words of Commissioner Derthich in 1959:[16]

> The Office of Education recognizes that the schools belong to the people, that their strength is derived from the people; it respects the independent organization and operation of public and private school systems and within its power tries to safeguard their freedom and

[16] *Handbook,* U.S. Office of Education, 1960, pp. 7–8.

independence. Furthermore, the Office recognizes that, if the schools are to serve the diverse interests and needs of the people, the people

U.S. DEPARTMENT OF HEALTH, EDUCATION, AND WELFARE

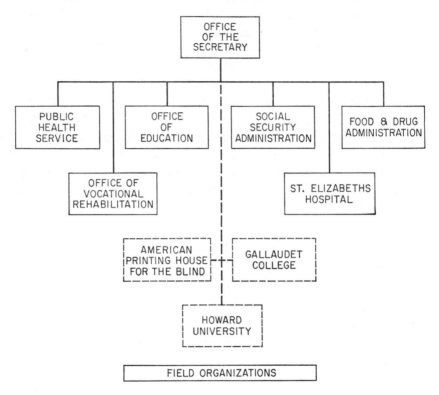

FIGURE 2. The organization of the U.S. Department of Health, Education, and Welfare. SOURCE: *Handbook,* U.S. Office of Education, 1960.

directly concerned must determine their procedures, their policies, and their curriculums.

Realizing these facts, the Office seeks to provide national leadership without domination and assistance without interference; to fill gaps in information and services; to stimulate ideas and action.

The Office seeks to encourage citizen understanding of, and responsibility for, education; to focus attention on the value of education to the individual and the Nation; to promote agreement among educators and laymen on common goals; and through research and the publication of research findings, to make accurate information available to all.

In carrying out its programs, the Office goal is to work in partnership with individuals and groups who are trying to improve American education. It therefore cooperates closely with other Government agencies, the States and Territories, professional groups and institutions, citizen groups and individuals, and international agencies. Its strength and the quality of its service depend in large measure on cooperative effort.

The Office carries on its work through publishing its research findings, studies, and survey reports; through participating in con-

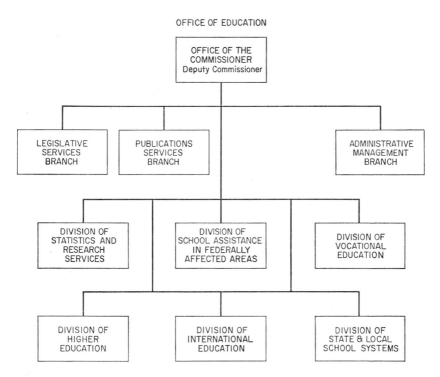

FIGURE 3. The organization of the U.S. Office of Education. SOURCE: *Handbook,* U.S. Office of Education, 1960.

ferences; through speaking and writing; through consultation and field work; through contracting with colleges, universities, and state departments of education to conduct research; and through administering grant funds as stipulated by the Congress. It seeks to serve education and to have its services accepted on the basis of merit.

Under the general direction of the Commissioner of Education and his deputy, activities are carried out through six program divisions (see Figure 3). Each is headed by an assistant Commissioner:

Division of School Assistance in Federally Affected Areas
Division of Higher Education
Division of International Education
Division of State and Local School Systems
Division of Vocational Education
Division of Statistics and Research Services

Auxiliary services are carried on in independently organized offices responsible to the Commissioner: Administrative Management, Publications Services, and Legislative Services.

PRESIDENTIAL COMMITTEES AND CONFERENCES

Two executive techniques which have proved helpful over the years, particularly in focusing the attention of the country on outstanding problems and expert opinion on the steps which ought to be taken in their solution, are the appointment of *ad hoc* presidential committees and the convening of White House conferences.

President Herbert Hoover's national Advisory Committee on Education (1929 to 1931) and President Franklin D. Roosevelt's Advisory Committee on Education (1936 to 1938) are illustrative of presidential committees which issued influential reports. Both reports dealt with the fundamental question of desirable relations between the Federal government and education within the states. The appointment of a Committee on Education Beyond the High School by President Eisenhower, at a time when a tidal wave of college students threatened to inundate existing institutions, served to awaken the public to the gravity of the problem and to present to them considered recommendations for solving it.

Serving somewhat the same ends as presidential committees, but perhaps more effective in calling problems to the attention of the public and less effective in the weight to be given to the recommendations which emerge from them, are White House Conferences, two recent examples of which are the 1960 White House Conference on Children and Youth and the White House Conference on Education.

The latter was especially noteworthy for the extent of its success in publicizing the outstanding problems facing elementary and secondary education in 1955. Since the Conference held in Washington had been preceded by fifty-three state and territorial "State White House Conferences," which were themselves preceded by some 3,600 local community "Little White House Conferences," the breadth of formal citizen discussion on the following six topics was perhaps unparalleled in the history of this, or any, country:

1. What should our schools accomplish?

2. In what ways can we organize our school systems more efficiently and economically?

3. What are our school building needs?

4. How can we get enough good teachers and keep them?

5. How can we finance our schools; how can we build and operate them?

6. How can we obtain a continuing public interest in education?

While the results of all this discussion with its attendant publicity throughout the country are impossible to measure, there are few local school administrators who question that citizen interest in the problems of schools was significantly stimulated and that school problems, especially financial problems, became a bit easier to solve because of the White House Conference on Education.

COMPREHENSIVE PROPOSALS FOR FEDERAL AID
TO EDUCATION

Post-World War II proposals for comprehensive Federal programs to aid elementary and secondary education have been generally aimed either at supplying funds for current expenses of running schools in the states or at school construction costs. Both types of proposal are based on the fact that the wealth of the nation is unequally distributed among the fifty states. Depending on the particular measure of wealth used, some variation in conclusion emerges from basic research, but in general about one-third of the states are found above average in their ability to pay for schools and about two-thirds below average. For example, Research Division figures of the National Education Association[17] indicate seventeen states above the average in annual income payments per child of school age (5 to 17) in 1954. Nevada, Connecticut, Delaware, New York, and New Jersey lead with income payments of over $11,000 per child. Mississippi, Arkansas, South Carolina, and Alabama rank lowest with $3,018 to $3,917 per child.

Equally significant to these proposals is the concept of "effort," which is measured in the same report as the per cent of income payments represented by current expenditures for education in the states. On this basis, the three lowest-ranking states in effort expended on behalf of education are all among the eight wealthiest states. Conversely, among the states exerting above-average effort on behalf of schools, with a few notable exceptions, are to be found most of the poorer states, whose school systems are generally considered qualitatively inferior.

FEDERAL AID FOR CURRENT EXPENSES

The years immediately after World War II saw bills introduced into Congress to aid the states in meeting school costs; saw these bills progress through the Senate, then die in committee in the House of Representatives. The pattern of such bills as the Hill-Taft-Thomas bill of 1946 was to guarantee a fixed amount of money per child of educable age in each state, determine the average effort needed to reach this amount, and then supply from Federal funds the difference between the amount reached by average effort (e.g., spending 1.1 per cent of income payments on schools) and the amount to be guaranteed providing the state in question exerted above-average effort (e.g., spending 2.5 per cent of income payments on schools).

The bills all failed of enactment because of opposition from a variety of sources. The combined opposition, however, barely prevented passage of the bills. Its main sources were:

1. *Persons fearing Federal control.* Considerable opposition came

[17] *National Education Association News,* vol. 11, no. 3, Feb. 1, 1957.

from those who saw a danger of Federal control accompanying Federal funds, in accordance with a general administrative maxim: whence comes money comes some measure of control. Their arguments became stronger when proponents of this kind of Federal aid added a set amount per child—$5, in one proposal—to be distributed to all states whether they needed it or not. The provision was designed to gain legislative support from the wealthier states, on the shortsighted grounds that their representatives had "gotten something for the people at home"; actually it extended the possibilities of control to all the states instead of only to those qualifying for aid on a need-and-effort basis.

2. *Persons interested in Catholic schools.* While individuals interested in Catholic schools frequently proved sympathetic to solving the problems behind these postwar aid to education bills, a provision which was not incorporated in their final form and several provisions that remained in them ultimately caused strong opposition from those interested in Catholic as well as public education. Catholic educators, with the long-range aim of having an acceptable pattern established for Federal aid, if *any* pattern was to be set, insisted that in the initial comprehensive aid to education program, at least a token amount should be earmarked for services to children, irrespective of what school they attended. This was in line with the reasoning of the Supreme Court in the Louisiana Textbook and New Jersey School Bus cases, as well as the recommendations of the 1936 President's Advisory Committee on Education. When opposition to this assistance by those committed to an extreme wall of separation between Federal funds and religious schools made such a provision impossible, those interested in Catholic schools preferred that no bill be passed if services to children in parochial schools were not included; the advocates of the bills in their final form, on the other hand, preferred no bill to one which did provide for such services.

Catholic educators also registered objections to provisions of aid bills which allocated money to the states on "children of educable age" basis, thus reimbursing the states for children being educated in parochial schools, without cost to the state.

3. *The economy-minded.* As with any proposal involving large expenditures of money, considerable opposition came from those

who opposed additional Federal expenditures at the time and from those seeking a balanced budget. The Hill-Taft-Thomas bill envisaged initial expenditures of from 150 to 250 million dollars a year.

FEDERAL AID FOR SCHOOL CONSTRUCTION

As any move for Federal aid to the states for current educational expenses in the late 1940s became hopelessly stalemated by the combination of opposing forces and as the most aggravated problems facing many states came from the necessity of providing school plants to house the tremendously increased school population, Federal aid proposals began to center increasingly around the school construction problem in the 1950s.

In January, 1957, after the platforms of both major political parties in the 1956 elections had included aid to education planks, President Eisenhower sent a special message to Congress urging help to the states in solving their problems of school construction. Specifically, he urged Congress to enact legislation to provide:

1. Federal grants to the states for school construction, at the rate of 325 million dollars a year for four years, or a total of 1.3 billion dollars.

2. Authorization to spend 750 million dollars over the four-year period for Federal purchase of local school-construction bonds if school districts could not market them at reasonable interest rates. These loan funds would have been made available to the states on the basis of school-age population. The state educational agency was to determine the priority of local school districts for Federal loans based on their relative need for financial aid in construction of school facilities.

3. Advances to help provide reserves for bonds issued by state school-financing agencies. This would facilitate the issuance of these bonds to finance schools which would be rented from the Federal government and eventually owned by local school districts.

4. Matching-grants to states totaling 20 million dollars to strengthen state and local school construction programs.

These new proposals for aid to states in building schools, being more in the nature of emergency aid, drew opposition from the same sources as had the proposals of the 1940s, but in different proportions. While some opposition came from persons fearing an overly strong Federal government and some from persons desirous of aid for constructing religious schools, it was from the economy-minded in both parties that major opposition came; and these bills became hopelessly entangled in the civil rights strife as proponents and opponents of antisegregation provisions made passage of any bill impossible.

STATUS OF FEDERAL AID IN THE EARLY 1960s

The election in 1960 of John F. Kennedy, the first Catholic to become President, brought the Federal aid issue to the forefront. Upon taking office, in keeping with campaign promises, he speedily proposed a program of aid to colleges and universities, public and private; and a separate program for public elementary and secondary schools which was incorporated in legislative bills entitled "School Assistance Act of 1961."

As proposed, the Assistance Act would authorize a three-year program of Federal grants to states to assist them "to construct urgently needed public elementary and secondary school facilities, to employ needed additional public school teachers and pay them adequate salaries, and to undertake special projects directed to special or unique educational problems or opportunities." A further purpose envisioned "that inequalities of educational opportunities within and between States will be substantially reduced."

Through an approach similar to previous proposals, the amount of aid per pupil in each state would be dependent on income per pupil in the state compared to average income per pupil throughout the nation. Each state, however, would receive a minimum of $15 per pupil in public schools. Subsequent amendments as the bill passed the Senate changed the basis for payment from pupils in public schools to pupils of educable age within a state and permitted the aid to be spent for any educational purpose, not merely for construction or teacher salaries.

President Kennedy's clear statement that he considered aid to religious schools as unconstitutional aroused immediate opposition from those who had consistently fought over the years for the principle that if Federal aid to schools should come, some aid to religious schools—if only a token—must be included. The issues were widely publicized, debated, and discussed; and although bitter emotions flared on occasion, the issues seem to this observer to have received more reasonable discussion than previously. The Catholic bishops, through the archbishop-chairman of the administrative board of the National Catholic Welfare Conference, called for loans for construction of private school facilities in any Federal aid to education program.

As the maneuvering developed in the first half of 1961, it became clear that if any Federal aid to religious schools were to be provided, it would not be as part of a general aid bill, but part of an extended National Defense Education Act (discussed earlier in this chapter).

The proposals of the Catholic bishops for government loans were partially incorporated as changes to the Administration's Defense Education Act Amendments of 1961. Provisions were inserted for long-term loans to private schools for constructing buildings or facilities to improve instructions in subjects deemed critical to the national defense—science, mathematics, foreign languages, and physical fitness.

Administration strategists fought to have the aid to public schools passed before the National Defense Education Act Amendments of 1961 were debated, leaving any decisions on the parochial school question to later action, if any. The strategists for aid to parochial schools, however, fought to have the defense amendments, with loans and other aid to private schools included, acted upon before, or simultaneously with, the general aid bills.

Administration strategy prevailed in the Senate which passed the general aid bill before acting on the defense amendments. In the House, however, not enough votes could be mustered in the Rules Committee to report the general aid bill out for action before the Defense Act Amendments bill was cleared for action.

Thus by mid-1961, it was impossible to predict the final disposition of the Kennedy Administration's Educational Assistance Act of 1961 or of the National Defense Education Amendments with which it was linked. The bill, as a number of its predecessors, was in difficulty in the House of Representatives. Opponents and proponents remained much the same: those who feared Federal control of education would result, the economy-minded, and those who favored civil rights provisions in any program adopted. Proponents of Catholic schools showed no enthusiasm for Federal funds to help the salaries of public school teachers, a development which could only make the position of private schools less favorable in the competition for qualified teachers who might teach in either system; and they flatly opposed any program specifically limited to public schools.

GENERAL OBSERVATIONS ABOUT FEDERAL AID

Several observations about Federal aid to education in the states ought, in the opinion of the author, to be made here:

1. The markedly unequal distribution of our national wealth among the fifty states of the Union makes it unrealistic to expect the poorer states to bring their schools up to nationally accepted standards out of their own resources.

2. As a general principle, no responsibility should be transferred to a higher unit of government if it can be handled on a local level. This means that if aid is needed in certain states, as may be indicated by the statistics on distribution of wealth and effort exerted, it should be limited to those states and not extended to all. In the words of the chairman of the Subcommittee on Education of the Committee for Economic Development:[18]

> The national interest in good schools everywhere and the national interest in a decentralized school system are not irreconcilable. The combination of these two interests calls for the assumption of an important but limited responsibility by the Federal government. This is a residual responsibility. It is to provide support to the extent necessary in situations where the decentralized system cannot provide good schools. And the support should be reserved for cases where the deficiency is clear.

3. When a situation necessitates Federal aid, the author would suggest it be on a temporary, emergency basis; meanwhile, efforts should be made to help the economic development of the states through activities in areas less likely to lead to a school system sub-

servient to a strong president as permanent subsidation of education might do.

4. Since the economic conditions which necessitate Federal aid to education apply throughout the areas affected to public and parochial schools equally, any aid devised should include provision for services to students in parochial schools.

5. Any attempt to equalize educational opportunities is less effective when areas are reimbursed for educating children whose cost they do not defray. Thus average daily attendance or average daily membership are better bases for aid than "children of educable age" who do not become the responsibility of the public school.

Questions for Discussion or Investigation

1. To what extent is it valid to consider the Supreme Court as a national board of education?

2. How high a wall of separation between civil government and religious education has the Supreme Court of the United States erected?

3. Catholic school administrators, though approving the decision in the New Jersey Bus case, found in the decision of this and the Illinois Released Time case cause for grave concern; this concern was considerably relieved by the decision in the New York Released Time case. Can you discover, from reading the full decisions in Appendix A, what justification there is for (*a*) the increased concern and (*b*) the feeling of some relief?

4. To what extent can it be said that Federal legislation aiding education has been directed to public education alone and to what extent has it included religious schools?

5. The Civilian Conservation Corps (CCC) has been said by some school officials to be one relief agency of the 1930s which should have been continued through today. Do you think so? Why?

6. After consulting details of the National Defense Education Act in 1958 in Appendix B, do you consider it really a defense act or an act in aid to education? Document your answer.

7. Through library research, document the proposition that the wealth of the United States is unevenly distributed among the states of the Union.

8. If you were a Catholic school administrator, what would your own attitude be toward Federal aid to schools?

9. What was the eventual outcome of the controversies over the School Assistance Act of 1961? Of the National Defense Education Amendments of 1961?

[18] Ralph Lazarus, *We Can Have Better Schools,* Committee for Economic Development, New York, 1960, p. 13.

Readings and References

Allen, Hollis P.: *The Federal Government and Education,* McGraw-Hill Book Company, Inc., New York, 1950.

Axt, Richard G.: *The Federal Government and Financing Higher Education,* Columbia University Press, New York, 1952.

Carlson, Theodora: *Guide to the National Defense Education Act of 1958,* U.S. Office of Education Circular 553, 1959.

Corwin, Edward S.: "The Supreme Court as National School Board," *Thought,* vol. 23, no. 91, pp. 665–683, December, 1948.

Federal Relations to Education: Report of the National Advisory Committee on Education, 2 vols., 1931.

Gordis, Robert and others: *Religion and the Schools,* The Fund for the Republic, New York, 1959.

Grieder, Calvin, and William Everett Rosenstengel: *Public School Administration,* The Ronald Press Company, New York, 1954.

Hale, Dawson: *Federal Control of Education,* Teachers College, Columbia University, 1955.

Handbook, U.S. Office of Education, 1960.

Higher Education for American Democracy, 6 vols., President's Commission on Higher Education, 1947.

McCluskey, Neil G.: *Catholic Viewpoint on Education,* Hanover House, Garden City, N.Y., 1959.

Munse, Albert R., and Edna D. Booker: *Federal Funds for Education, 1956–57 and 1957–58,* U.S. Office of Education Bulletin 1959, no. 2, 1959.

Oregon School Cases (complete record), The Belvedere Press, Baltimore, 1925.

Report of the Committee, Advisory Committee on Education: 1938.

Russell, James E.: *Federal Activities in Higher Education after the Second World War,* King's Crown Press, New York, 1951.

Sanford, Charles W., and others: *The Schools and National Security,* McGraw-Hill Book Company, Inc., New York, 1951.

Spurlock, Clark: *Education and the Supreme Court,* University of Illinois Press, Urbana, Ill., 1955.

Taylor, Howard C.: *The Educational Significance of the Early Federal Land Ordinance,* Bureau of Publications, Teachers College, Columbia University, New York, 1922.

Wahlquist, John T., and others: *The Administration of Public Education,* The Ronald Press Company, New York, 1952.

Kitkowiak, Stanislau B.: *Limitations Imposed upon the Rights and Powers of Respective States over Education by the United States Supreme Court,* The Catholic University of America Press, Washington, 1942.

5. *The States and Education*

The state is the political unit to which is basically delegated that control of education in the United States which properly belongs to civil society. Thus there are fifty systems of education in this country—one for each state. They have in common only the constitutional principles defined by the Supreme Court of the land, general American educational traditions, the nationwide influence of professional educational organizations, and the extensive literature of the field which is disseminated without regard to state lines. Owing to these influences, the similarities between the systems in the individual states are so great that in fact, if not technically, we do have an American system of schools.

Court decisions in nearly all states have clearly indicated that the state, not the local school district, is the governmental unit responsible for education. Local school districts are held to be agents of the state, existing only on sufferance of the state, to perform those educational tasks delegated to them by the state. Unequivocal are the words of a Tennessee decision to this point: "The public school system is a matter of state, and not local concern, and the establishment, maintenance, and control of the public schools is a

90

legislative function. To promote the public schools, the state, through the legislature, may levy taxes directly, or the state, having as it does full control over its agencies, the counties, may authorize them to levy a tax, or may by statute require them to levy a tax for the establishment and maintenance of public schools. . . ." [1]

Two general principles govern the legal framework within which the states operate: state legislatures have absolute powers unless limited by Federal and state constitutional provisions; and the control of education is in no way inherent in local government, except as legislatures choose to make it so.

THE DEVELOPING ROLE OF THE STATE

In general, this preeminence of the state in relation to local school districts is as it should be, whether considered from an economic, social, or political viewpoint.

While there is great disparity in the distribution of wealth among the fifty states, there has been even greater disparity in the distribution of wealth within individual states. For example, in 1953 one-third of the children of Ohio lived in sections of the state where over one-half the wealth was located; thus two-thirds lived in districts where less than one-half the wealth was available to support their education. In 1955, the Ohio School Survey reported that the richest local district had one hundred and seventy times the ability to pay as the poorest, with a $225,000 tax valuation per pupil compared to $1,500 per pupil in the poorest. The proportion of valuable industrial property on the tax duplicate and the value of residential property in a district vary so widely that something larger than the local district must serve as the basic economic unit for the support of education.

Sociological research on population mobility clearly leads to the conclusion that concern for the scope of educational opportunities given children must extend beyond the bounds of the local school district. In large cities it is not unusual that as much as 25 per cent of the population has moved in from neighboring geographic areas. This percentage contributes disproportionately to the number of arrests, relief cases, and other grave municipal problems.

[1] *Tennessee v. Meador,* 284 S.W. (Tenn.) 890.

While state boundaries may on occasion rather arbitrarily separate geographic unities, such as St. Louis, Missouri, and East St. Louis, Illinois, each state is a political unity large enough to accomplish some sociologically desirable standardization of educational opportunities, with sufficient diversity among them to make a national socialistic approach unlikely. Thus politically, economically, and sociologically, the state is large enough to achieve a considerable measure of efficiency, but not so large or self-sufficient a governmental unit as to lead to anything like Federal standardization of education.

While the state should by logic and law be the basic unit, its real position over the years has been far different from its theoretical position. As the district-unit system became firmly entrenched throughout the country in the early 1800s, local districts were practically autonomous in the conduct of schools. It is only in the last fifty years that the state has attained anything like the position to which it is entitled by logic and law. It has reached its present position through a process of recalling its powers, a process which in a sense began with the early permissive laws, which, when passed by the states, permitted local districts to run schools even though they already had been doing just that. The process continued as the post-colonial states adopted constitutional clauses accepting responsibility for education, though not as broadly as Indiana did with its 1816 provision that: "It shall be the duty of the General Assembly, as soon as circumstances will permit, to provide by law for a general system of education, ascending in a regular graduation from township schools to a state university, wherein tuition shall be gratis, and equally open to all."

Despite tremendous progress in lessening the number of small public school districts in the last thirty years, there are still far too many of them in most states. Between 1932 and 1958 the number of public school districts had declined from 127,530 to 48,036, a decline of 62.3 per cent. In 1958, however, it could still be written that 52 per cent of all operating school districts each employed 9 or fewer teachers; that in 1956 the average staff for rural elementary schools was 3.7 and for rural secondary schools 8.7; and that in 1956 more than one-third of all of the public school districts in the

United States averaged 15 or fewer pupils in their classes, while half of these small districts did not operate any schools.[2]

The success of the state in recalling its powers has been in direct proportion to its success in consolidating the far too many small school districts into larger, more efficient local units. Consolidation, wherever it occurs, breaks the super-localism which fights it bitterly. After the first break in absolute local control occurs, transfer of control to larger units, even to the state itself, is made easier.

Actually, consolidation seldom occurs without a violent battle, even though reason, experience, and economics indicate that consolidation of very small units has usually meant broader curricular opportunities, better teaching salaries, better teachers, and frequently less expense, even when the costs of these improvements and the cost of transporting the children are included. Research has indicated, for example, that a public school of 200 pupils can be run at about one-third the expense of twenty schools with ten pupils each, and all the other advantages of a larger school are made possible at the same time.[3]

Nevertheless, telling blows, loaded with emotional connotations, can be struck by those opposing consolidation of schools. Village patriots can stir up a tremendous fuss over closing the local school to which, it is alleged, local dignitaries owe their present successes; local pride can be easily injured at the thought of losing a school to a rival village down the road; impassioned and appealing speeches can be made on the advantages of children getting a good, warm, home-cooked meal served with loving care.

Because of the popular appeal of arguments against consolidation, historically the state has had to force it; and it has had one effective lever to use: money. As the support of public schools has shifted from an almost complete dependence on real estate taxes, which in a sense never leave the local community, to state-wide income or sales taxes, which go from the local communities to the state for redistribution to the local subdivision after elements of control have

[2] Walter H. Gaumnitz, *Small Schools Are Growing Larger,* U.S. Office of Education Circular 601, 1959.

[3] H. A. Dawson, *Satisfactory Local School Units,* Field Study 7, George Peabody College for Teachers, Nashville, Tenn., 1934.

been added, the state could and did refuse to support schools or districts too small for efficiency.

Over the last sixty years, the percentage of public school support coming directly from state sources, as opposed to local sources, has risen from 17 per cent in 1920 to about 40 per cent in the 1950s. (See Table 3 for a twenty-six year record of this development.) When a school district depends upon the state for nearly half of its

TABLE 3. TOTAL REVENUE RECEIPTS OF PUBLIC SCHOOL SYSTEMS, AND PERCENTAGE DISTRIBUTION, BY SOURCE: CONTINENTAL UNITED STATES, 1929–1930 TO 1955–1956

| | Revenue receipts | | | | | |
| | | | Percentage from: | | | |
Year	Total amounts (thousands)	Total per cent	Federal	State	Inter-mediate (county, etc.)	Local and other*
1	2	3	4	5	6	7
1929–1930	$2,088,557	100.0	0.4	16.9	10.4	72.3
1931–1932	2,068,029	100.0	.4	19.8	8.8	71.0
1933–1934	1,810,652	100.0	1.2	23.4	9.3	66.1
1935–1936	1,971,402	100.0	.5	29.3	7.1	63.1
1937–1938	2,222,885	100.0	1.2	29.5	6.5	62.8
1939–1940	2,260,527	100.0	1.7	30.3	6.7	61.3
1941–1942	2,416,580	100.0	1.4	31.5	6.2	60.9
1943–1944	2,604,322	100.0	1.4	33.0	5.6	60.0
1945–1946	3,059,845	100.0	1.4	34.7	6.0	57.9
1947–1948	4,311,534	100.0	2.8	38.9	5.3	53.0
1949–1950	5,437,044	100.0	2.9	39.8	6.0	51.3
1951–1952	6,423,816	100.0	3.5	38.6	6.0	51.8
1953–1954	7,866,852	100.0	4.5	37.4	3.1	55.0
1955–1956	9,686,677	100.0	4.6	39.5	1.8	54.1

* Other receipts, which include gifts, and tuition and transportation fees from patrons, accounted for 0.2 of 1 per cent of total revenue receipts in 1955–1956.
NOTE: Because of rounding, detail may not add to totals.
SOURCE: *Biennial Survey of Education in the United States*, 1955–1956, U.S. Office of Education, chap. 1.

income, or for over half as was true of fourteen states in 1956, obviously it is mandatory that state manuals of regulations be carefully read and followed lest a major share of the support of its schools be lost by noncompliance.[4] Thus it has been that distribution of state money has been the avenue by which the state has managed to approach the position it should logically and legally occupy.

The refusal of local communities to relinquish control of education to state authorities, even in the face of powerful financial pressures, is itself impressive evidence of an American phenomenon which has been a valuable element in the control of education and which, in its best aspects, should remain a strong factor: the tradition of localism in education, described by Mort, Reusser, and Polley as follows:[5]

> Traditionally we have opposed doing things by government that we could do as individuals; we have opposed doing things by state government that we could do by local government; we have opposed doing things by the federal government that we could do fairly well by state government. *We are biased toward keeping the control close to the people.* It is of interest that this bias has shown up so clearly in that most intimate of governmental forms—the school system. Apart from highways there is no aspect of government that so nearly reaches all the people. In addition, it deals with matters which are of intimate personal concern to the public—the education of children. Here, whatever may have been our sampling of remote government accepted purely for efficiency's sake, we have sought to maintain control close to the people.

In addition to the entrenched position of small local districts, the state has had several other major obstacles to overcome before reaching its present relatively influential status. Two of these are related: arriving at a satisfactory pattern for the state administration of education and securing adequate chief state school officers.

---

[4] It should be noted that New Hampshire and Nebraska stand out for the low percentage of state support to local districts. In 1955–1956, New Hampshire contributed 5.5 per cent; Nebraska, 6.5 per cent from permanent funds and endowments. At the other extreme were Delaware and South Carolina with 83.7 per cent and 74.5 per cent, respectively.

[5] Paul R. Mort and others, *Public School Finance,* 3d ed., McGraw-Hill Book Company, Inc., 1960, p. 26.

STATE ORGANIZATION FOR EDUCATION

STATE BOARDS OF EDUCATION

Political scientists and educators have tended to differ sharply over how education ought to be organized at the state level. Generally speaking, political scientists have felt that education is one of the areas of which the governor is the chief executive. Accordingly they recommend that education should be the function of a state department administered by a director who is a member of the governor's cabinet, as are the heads of other major executive departments. As such, he is accountable to the governor and through him to the political party which he represents; the party is, of course, accountable to the public.

On the other hand, professional educators tend to insist that since education is the state's most extensive responsibility, it should be separated from the ordinary executive functions of the governor. Further, education should be beyond any control of political parties. They support the idea of a state board of education, modeled after local boards, responsible for developing policy and for hiring its own chief executive. Board members, it is maintained, should be elected on a nonpartisan basis. In effect, they argue that state government should have four distinct branches instead of the traditional three: legislative, executive, judicial, and (fourth) educational.

Developments in some states indicate that a pattern which has worked reasonably well at local levels need not work so well when transferred to the state level. Some of the difficulties stem from the very size of the state unit. Whereas nonpartisan election of board members in a closely-knit community is possible, at the state level the absence of party responsibility leaves little opportunity for public control of its most extensive state operation. In the absence of control by the general public, control by the only organized groups interested in education, those of professional educators, becomes more likely.

The manner in which not only control, but also influence, of educational developments can pass from the public to professional educators can be seen from the following lines of influence discernible in one state: state board of education members are elected from congressional districts in the state on a nonpartisan basis (with the electorate generally unaware of who represents them on the board, since only the leaders of professional teacher organizations seem to care who wins this nonsalaried position); the state board employs a superintendent of public instruction as its chief state school officer; the superintendent is a member of the Council of Chief State School Officers; the Council of Chief State School Officers has influenced the organizing and control of the National Council for the Accreditation of Teacher Education; the National Council for the Accreditation of Teacher Education enforces standards in colleges and universities of a state through the influence of the Chief State School Officers, whose agency, to a great extent, it has been and whose recommendations, to a great extent, influence decisions of the State Board regarding certification. The college or university which might attempt to vary from NCATE standards has no place to turn. On whom will it attempt to exert its influence? With the accrediting agency it dare not be unorthodox; and there is no one else in the organizational picture who has any impelling reason to be concerned. An appeal to the general public can hardly be effective.

Yet nonpartisan state board members, elected for long, staggered terms, may prove not only immune to the passing whims of the public they represent, as planned, but also sometimes independent of any popular control whatever—even being immune to the control of the professional educators whose Frankenstein's monster they have sometimes turned out to be.

Clearly, both patterns of state organization for education—that of the executive department under the governor as advanced by the political scientists, and that of the state board as advanced by the professional educators—have advantages. Recent trends, however, have been toward state boards of education with responsibility for hiring their own chief state school officer. While by 1958 forty-four of the forty-eight states had school boards, many of them actually represented compromises between the two points of view. Of these, fifteen select their own chief state school officer. In most of these states members are appointed by the governor for terms of about six years, although in one of these, Maine, five of the ten members are appointed, one by each of the following organizations: Maine

Municipal Association; Maine Superintendents Association; Maine Congress of Parents and Teachers; Maine Teachers Association; and the presidents of liberal arts and teachers' colleges of the state. In one state, members are appointed by the state legislature; in another the governor's appointees must be approved by the state legislature; in two they are elected on nonpartisan ballots; and in one they are elected on a party ballot.

CHIEF STATE SCHOOL OFFICERS

The second difficulty faced by most states as they have sought to assume a position of preeminence in education has been that of securing good state leadership. Far too frequently chief state school officers have been political appointees or elected office-seekers of little professional standing. In general, the salary paid the chief school officer by many states has been far overshadowed by salaries paid to superintendents of medium-sized or large city school systems or to college presidents and deans within the state. Thus, in the past, the state superintendent of instruction has usually been a man of considerably less prestige and security than many other educators in the state, some of them theoretically his subordinates. This difficulty is more easily corrected when education is separated from the other state functions under a state board; the board is usually empowered to employ a chief executive at a more adequate salary than that paid to heads of other state departments, such as safety, health, or highways.

All states have a chief state school officer, but this is almost the only generalization that can be made about this official. He is called by such titles as superintendent of public instruction, commissioner of education, superintendent of education, director of education, and superintendent of schools. As we have seen, he may be responsible to the governor or to a state board of education. He is usually appointed, but he may be elected. His duties and the scope of his responsibilities vary from state to state.

He administers a department of education that is responsible for carrying out state educational policies set by the state constitution and legislative enactments. In the process, he may enact administrative regulations which have the force of law, or he may merely recommend such regulations to a state board which enacts them.

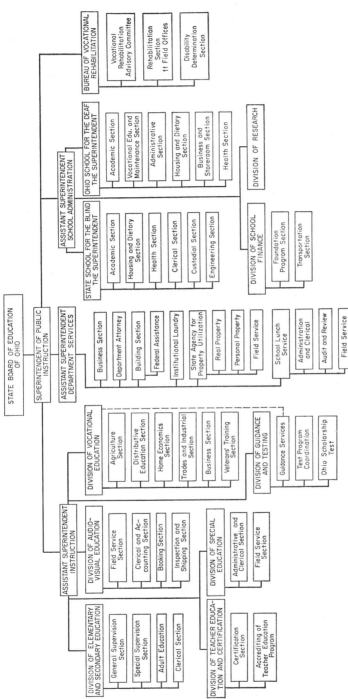

FIGURE 4. Organizational chart of the State Department of Education of Ohio.

The extent and complexity of his department will depend upon the scope of responsibilities assigned to him. He will usually have responsibilities for elementary and secondary education within the state; he may or may not have responsibilities for state universities or colleges; he may or may not have responsibilities touching private colleges and universities (other than responsibilities for teacher preparation and certification, which he almost certainly does have); he may or may not have responsibilities for libraries, schools for the handicapped, or even censorship of movies. Figure 4 is an organizational chart of one state department of education; it indicates the complexity of organization developed to enable the state to discharge its responsibilities to public and private education within the state.

STATE FUNCTIONS AND PUBLIC SCHOOLS

In his study of the state's functions in education, Beach describes them in such general terms as protecting the lives and health of its children and youth; guaranteeing safety and economy in the use of educational funds; ensuring efficiency in management of the educational enterprise; providing a framework for the instructional program which would assure a basic minimum in both scope and quality; and ensuring an educated citizenry.[6]

While there are variations among the states as to the approaches they take in discharging their responsibilities, a major state function, and one that as seen above frequently proves the key to many state regulatory powers, has been sharing the cost of schools with local school districts. This is usually carried out through a school foundation program.

SCHOOL FOUNDATION PROGRAMS

The state's role in sharing with local school districts the cost of public schools is generally extended through state foundation programs intended to be an undergirding to the financial structure of local districts, some of which are grossly unable to support adequate schools. In the process, all school districts usually emerge with some

[6] Fred F. Beach, *The Functions of State Departments of Education,* U.S. Office of Education Misc. 12, 1950, p. 8.

aid, although the poorer or hardship districts receive proportionately more.

Certain features are common to most state foundation programs, features similar to those incorporated in the bills designed to provide Federal aid for current expenses (see Chapter 4): a guaranteed amount of state aid is set; a standard of average effort, expressed in tax rates for local districts, is decided upon; the state pays the difference between the amount raised by average effort locally and the guaranteed figure; and a flat minimum amount is paid by the state, even though the wealthier local district, with average effort, raises more than the guaranteed amount.

Until the last few years, state foundation programs were simply organized to provide financial aid along these lines, leaving to the local district most of the decisions as to how to spend the state moneys received. Since 1950, newer foundation programs have been adopted to provide considerably more and detailed stipulations as to how the money must be spent.

A typical example is Ohio's change from the older to the newer type of foundation program, adopted in 1955. Under the old Ohio foundation program, the guaranteed amount was $137.50 for every elementary school pupil and $160 for every high school pupil in average daily membership in a public school of approved size. There was a flat distribution of $60 and $70 per child, with any additional aid, up to the guarantee, dependent on the wealth of the district. How the school district spent its money was left to local decision providing only that state law was not violated.

Under the new Ohio program, the guarantee is in terms of classroom units of a specified size. The amount of state aid which a local district now receives is determined by the size of class it maintains; the amount of salary paid its teachers; the level of training and experience possessed by the teachers employed; the actual employment of allowed administrators and supervisors and the salaries paid them. Received also are an amount per classroom unit for operating expenses and an amount for transportation of pupils calculated on a detailed formula involving conditions of roads, length of trips, etc. Clearly the change to the newer method of determining the guaranteed foundation program necessitates tremendously more detailed administrative conformity to state administrative standards than the old flat guarantee of $137.50 or $160 per year per child in average daily membership. It substantially lessens the room for local administrative discretion.

OTHER STATE FUNCTIONS

The state has played a traditionally increasing role in setting minimum standards for teachers: their qualifications, training, certification, minimum salaries, tenure, retirement, and oaths of allegiance. Compulsory attendance has been a state concern, although enforcement responsibilities have been delegated to the local districts. Related to compulsory attendance has been the state's responsibility for approving schools as meeting minimum state requirements. This has involved both setting standards and inspection. State legislation has generally included prescriptions for teaching certain subjects in the curriculum—typically, the history and geography of the state, the English language, and the evils of alcohol and narcotics.

State departments of education must generally approve budgets adopted by local school districts for their operation. State auditors are given authority to certify the legality of expenditures made by local public school units. Ordinarily, school sites and building plans for public schools must be approved at the state level. All matters concerning transportation of pupils to schools—including standards for school bus drivers, safety standards for busses, and most of the expenses involved—tend to be controlled at the state level.

The impact of Federal legislation in aid of education has had a noticeable effect on the expansion of state functions and staff, since Federal assistance to public schools is almost uniformly channeled through state offices. Relatively recent additions of state offices and staff for handling Federal distribution of surplus property, the national school lunch and school milk programs, and the vocational rehabilitation education programs are typical of this expansion. Provisions of the National Defense Education Act of 1958 have also tended to result in increased staff and prestige to state departments of education, particularly in the areas of counseling, guidance, testing, and the supervision of science, foreign language, and mathematics study.

There are two educational leadership functions which the states can perform for local districts without risking charges of overcentralization of authority: providing research services—assembling the facts on which greater local educational opportunities can be based; and providing advisory services—assisting local districts by making expert advice available to them on technical aspects of finance, building construction, transportation, and legal questions. While states are generally doing something along both of these lines, more and better research and advisory service is needed at the state level.

THE STATE AND RELIGIOUS EDUCATION

It is extremely difficult to make valid generalizations regarding the relationship of the state to religious education once one passes from the level of the Supreme Court of the United States to the level of the state where the individual constitution, legislation, and court decisions actually determine the situation within each state.

Generally speaking, the individual states have more vigilantly erected a wall of separation between public education and religious education than has the Federal government. While Federal legislation has never specifically excluded the possibility of direct financial aid to religious education, the states, particularly since the Civil War, have generally done so.

Yet in regard to the tax-exempt status of schools conducted under religious auspices, McCluskey could write:[7]

> One traditional way that the American governments have acknowledged the importance of religion as a beneficent factor in civic life is the tax exemption of educational, literary, and charitable institutions under church sponsorship. . . . So natural is this that some states to this day have never bothered writing an explicit statute to cover the status of tax-exempt institutions.
>
> The constitutions of thirty-six states, however, do contain explicit provisions under which the property of nonpublic schools can be freed from taxation. Eight other states—Iowa, Maine, Maryland, Massachusetts, Michigan, New Hampshire, Rhode Island, and Vermont—have provisions in their constitutions calling for the encour-

[7] Neil G. McCluskey, *Catholic Viewpoint on Education,* Hanover House, Garden City, N.Y., 1959, pp. 148–149.

agement of education. Several states—like Michigan, North Carolina, Ohio, and Nebraska—have based tax exemption on these
well-known words of the Northwest Territorial Ordinance of 1787:
"Religion, morality and knowledge being necessary to good government and the happiness of mankind, schools and the means of
education shall forever be encouraged." New Hampshire and Massachusetts courts have upheld the granting of tax exemptions to
nonpublic schools under constitutional provisions of this type. Tax
exemptions may be provided by statute for certain classes of
nonpublic schools without contravening the constitutions of Connecticut, Mississippi, Oregon, and Utah.

Some states, however, have constitutional provisions preventing
the use of public money for sectarian education. More provide that
public *school* funds may not be so used.

Nevertheless, in about half of the states transportation of parochial school pupils is permitted and in nine states free textbooks are
available to children in religious schools, more liberally in some
than others. In other states, court decisions have led to opposite
practices.

Where states do provide transportation and free textbooks for
parochial school pupils, the reasoning of the courts is usually that
such provisions are in keeping with the principle that benefits extended by the state to its citizens should be extended without regard
to their religious beliefs. This point of view is an extension of the
no-religious-test clause of the United States Constitution and serves
to counterbalance the concept of separation of church and state.

In view of the specific constitutional provisions or the legislation
in many states forbidding use of school moneys in aid of sectarian
education, the extent to which state courts will go to provide welfare
aid for children attending religious schools depends on the specific
wording of legislative enactments. If these measures envisage administration by departments other than the state department of education, less difficulty is likely. For example, where the health department is charged with providing health services to children or where
the safety department is charged with providing for pupil transportation, no involvement of school money results. Even where such
money is involved, however, as McCluskey points out, the courts
will consider such questions as: Is the benefit to the school direct

or indirect? Is it basic or supplementary? Is it personal or institutional? Is it economic or social? [8]

The question of employing members of religious orders as public school teachers has been a thorny one. In some states this has been viewed as indirectly teaching religion, especially when religious garb is worn, and therefore, it is prohibited on constitutional grounds. In others, it has been ruled constitutional. When specific legislation has been passed to forbid teachers wearing religious garb, rulings of state courts have generally indicated that such laws were constitutional and did not constitute a religious test for the teachers involved.

State money to Catholic orphanages or schools for delinquent children has on occasion been held permissible on the grounds that these institutions were not schools in the usual sense. Renting religious-school buildings for use as public schools when religious instruction was not being given has generally been approved by the courts. Conversely, state courts have generally held that church use of public school buildings when school is not in session does not involve aid to religious education.[9]

Despite varying practices within individual states, several principles stand out as fundamental to the relationship of religious schools to states. First, religious schools exist because of rights which states are powerless to change, as affirmed by the United States Supreme Court decision in the Oregon School case. Second, religious schools must carry out the legitimate demands of the state in educating the children who live within its borders.

However, each state is found to differ in what it considers legitimate minimum demands to be made from the private and religious schools. Practices vary from a virtually laissez-faire attitude to detailed prescriptions. Even when regulations among states are similar, enforcement may be relatively rigorous in one and almost absent in another.

Catholic schools are most frequently affected by state regulations concerning accreditation; enforcement of compulsory education, including minimum length of the school year; inclusion of American

[8] *Ibid.*, p. 157. For a penetrating discussion of the question of governmental aid to nonpublic education, see chap. 7.

[9] For a detailed discussion of some specific state cases, see *The State and Sectarian Education,* National Education Association, Research Bulletin 34, no. 4, Washington, December, 1956.

history and government in the curriculum; compliance with fire drill regulations; compliance with state school building codes; and compliance with immunization and vaccination regulations.

Teachers in Catholic schools may or may not need state teaching certificates. In at least one state, they are not issued certificates; this seems to be the effect of a department of education regulation which prescribes student teaching in a public school as a condition of state certification. An increasing number of states, however, are bringing about state certification of all teachers and principals by making it a requirement for school accreditation.

In general, the professional kit of the religious school administrator must include an up-to-date copy of his state's educational code, a tool which will also assist him in dealing with the widely heard, but frequently unfounded remark, "There's a state law which provides. . . ."

As states continue the present trend to more detailed prescriptions of standards on such matters as subjects to be taught, time allotments, specific course requirements for teacher training, use of central school libraries rather than classroom libraries, details of methodology, and length of high school class periods, the theoretical right of religious schools to exist could, in practice, disappear. Administrators of religious schools must be alert to the necessity for enthusiastically carrying out the minimum standards of state educational authorities; but they must be equally alert to the necessity for exerting leadership so that state standards are, in fact, kept minimum.

Questions for Discussion or Investigation

1. In what respects may it be justifiably said that the state is only now achieving the position in control of education to which it is legally entitled? What limits to its role exist or ought to exist?

2. Is there a state board of education in your state? How is it chosen? What are its responsibilities? Does it seem to function between the extremes of sensitivity to popular whim and independence of popular control?

3. What are the specific curricular provisions for all schools in your state? Are they a result of state legislative action directly or are they administrative regulations?

4. What, if any, constitutional provision does your state have covering the relation of the state to religious education? Does the regulation cover state

money or state school money? Are there any such provisions in the school code of your state? What is the status of the "child benefit" theory in your state?

Readings and References

The Administrative Handbook for the Schools of Indiana, Department of Public Instruction Bulletin 200, Indianapolis, 1948.

Anderson, William: *The Nation and the States, Rivals or Partners?* University of Minnesota Press, Minneapolis, 1955.

Beach, Fred F.: *The Functions of State Departments of Education,* U.S. Office of Education Misc. 12, 1950.

———— and Robert F. Will: *The State and Education,* U.S. Office of Education Misc. 23, 1955.

————: *The State and Nonpublic Schools,* U.S. Office of Education Misc. 28, 1958.

Biennial Survey of Education in the United States 1954–56, 6 chaps. printed separately, U.S. Office of Education, 1959.

Chase, Francis S., and Edgar L. Morphet: *The Forty-eight State School Systems,* Council of State Governments, Chicago, 1949.

Edwards, Newton: *The Courts and the Public Schools,* rev. ed., University of Chicago Press, Chicago, 1955.

Gaumnitz, Walter H.: *Small Schools Are Growing Larger,* U.S. Office of Education Circular 601, 1959.

Keesecker, Ward W.: *State Boards of Education and Chief State School Officers,* U.S. Office of Education Bulletin 1958, no. 12, 1950.

McCluskey, Neil G.: *Catholic Viewpoint on Education,* Hanover House, Garden City, N.Y., 1959.

Mort, Paul R., and others: *Public School Finance,* 3d ed., McGraw-Hill Book Company, Inc., New York, 1960.

Remmlein, Madaline Kinter: *The Law of Local Public School Administration,* McGraw-Hill Book Company, Inc., New York, 1953.

The State and Sectarian Education, National Education Association, Research Bulletin 34, no. 4, Washington, December, 1956.

Thurston, Lee M., and William M. Roe: *State School Administration,* Harper & Brothers, New York, 1957.

Veles, Nelson E., and Ray L. Hamon: *State School Plant Services,* U.S. Office of Education Misc. 26, 1956.

Wahlquist, John T., and others: *The Administration of Public Education,* The Ronald Press Company, New York, 1952.

6. *The Local Unit and Education*

THE LOCAL PUBLIC SCHOOL DISTRICT

Although in practice the state is rapidly assuming more and more of the power in educational administration to which it is legally entitled, much of the actual conduct of public schools is handled through the local districts which have traditionally been so powerful throughout the United States. Local districts are known variously throughout the country as county or parish (Louisiana) school districts, city school districts, town or township districts, or just local school districts.

In Ohio, for example, the county school districts are an intermediate unit between the state and smaller local school districts. All cities, however, are exempt from county supervision and are directly responsible to the state in educational matters. School districts are separate political entities from the political subdivisions whose names they bear; thus a city school district may or may not have the same boundaries as the city from which it takes its name. The Ohio situation is reasonably typical of that in most states. West Virginia and Florida, however, are examples of county-unit states in which there are no smaller subdivisions exempted from county supervision. The parish school organization of Louisiana is close to the county-unit system. On the other hand, the New England states have no county school districts. Rhode Island, for example, has thirty-five city or town superintendents, one of whom jointly handles a two-town union; but in the older states there is no unincorporated land, for one town or city immediately adjoins the next, as do counties in the West.

THE SCHOOL BOARD IN LOCAL DISTRICTS

Over the years, as the local school districts have been playing the key governmental role in running public schools, a number of principles for their effective organization have become evident, mainly as a result of past mistakes. These principles are concerned with the organization of local boards of education and the role of the local superintendent of schools. Many of the same principles are equally applicable to public and Catholic school districts.

1. *Boards of education should be small.* Depending on the size of the local school district, five or seven members have come to be considered the best size for school boards. Inefficiency resulted from the unwieldiness of boards of education around the turn of the century when, for example, Milwaukee had thirty-six members; Philadelphia, thirty-seven; and Brooklyn had forty-five general members and three for each school in the city.

2. *Board members should represent the district as a whole, not some subdistrict or ward.* Again around the turn of the century, Cincinnati with thirty board members, each representing a ward, was typical of other city school board organizations. The logrolling, so likely to result when members represent a subdistrict, made it clear that whole-district representation tends toward wiser board action. Today the preponderance of city school board members represent school districts as a whole.

3. *Board members should be elected on a nonpartisan basis.* Schools should not be part of the political maneuvering which is so usually associated with city governmental administration, nor should they provide a tempting plum to persons interested in patronage or more powerful political organization, as frequently has happened in the not-too-distant past. Accordingly, whereas formerly board members were generally appointed by the mayor, the city council, or

judges, today they are generally elected by popular vote on a non-partisan ballot. It is still possible to elect demagogues or persons who look to incidental publicity as a step toward election to a salary-paying office. Yet the nonpartisan ballot, in an area small enough that men can be known for what they are, increases the likelihood of securing genuinely public-spirited citizens as board members. When the nonpartisan ballot is used in a large city, one danger should be mentioned; self-appointed committees with high-sounding titles, through endorsement of certain candidates, may achieve control of the schools without even the measure of responsibility to the public which party accountability gives.

4. *Board members should be chosen for at least a four-year term and the terms staggered so that all members do not come up for election at the same time.* The one- or two-year terms of fifty to one hundred years ago were far too short to be helpful today. The problems of determining policy for a multimillion-dollar-a-year business, as running the schools of many local districts is, are so complex that with a short term, the member is up for reelection before he has learned enough about the problems of schools to have been of any help. Staggered terms prevent sudden, complete turnover in response to transient public whims—without making drastic change impossible—since a complete turnover could be accomplished in four years.

5. *Board of education members should generally act as a committee of the whole, with no standing committees and few* ad hoc *committees.* Once again, around the turn of the century, it was the practice of boards to organize standing committees which really administered aspects of the school programs. One board had seventy standing committees. With the smaller size of boards today, it is easy for them to operate as committees of the whole while background research is done by members of the professional staffs of the schools.

6. *The job of the board of education is fourfold: (1) policy formation, (2) approval of administrative detail, (3) evaluation of policies and practices, (4) selection of a superintendent.* In today's complicated school situation, the fourth of these, selecting a superintendent, is vital if the board is to represent the people adequately in discharging the duties delegated to it by the state.

THE SUPERINTENDENT OF PUBLIC SCHOOLS

In public school administration, it is axiomatic that a board of education needs a chief executive to whom is delegated all responsibility for the administration of schools; this job is so extensive today that it can be safely entrusted only to an experienced and specially trained professional man in whom the board has genuine confidence. Once the board loses confidence in its executive, once it can no longer feel that his recommendations to it are sound and should be approved, it is time for a new executive. A board of education, or the board of control of any educational venture including college and university boards of trustees, is primarily a negative check on the recommendations of its chief executive and must be so convinced of the probable soundness of his recommendations as to grant to them a prima-facie status. Anything else means delay and mistakes by inexpert board members as they "learn by doing" in areas for which they are paying for expert research, analysis, and opinions.

This is not to say that boards must be rubber stamps. Usual procedure at well-conducted board meetings is for the chief executive to present a report including policy recommendations and recommendations concerning administrative details which must have board approval. Acceptance of the report, except for items to which individual board members object, is then moved. After acceptance of the rest of the report, the exceptions are then discussed, further explanations sought, and the recommended action either approved, disapproved, or modified by the board.

This kind of board-superintendent relationship, like the principles concerning board organization indicated above, has developed as a means for operating schools efficiently while preserving necessary control over professional administrators and has developed only after other approaches were tried and found inadequate. In the past, boards tried having two coordinate chief executives—a superintendent of instruction and a business manager—only to find the interrelationship of their responsibilities such that one or the other must become subordinate. When the business manager was placed over the superintendent, it soon became clear that a mistake had been made, for business management is really a service to instruction, which is primary. Formerly, school boards employed nonprofessional superintendents—lawyers, former board members, college professors of any subjects, and former businessmen—but with little success.

Today it is obvious that specific training, even to the earned doctorate in school administration, and wide experience in all phases of the administrative job are necessary if these budgets of many millions of dollars are to be well administered in the best educational interests of children.

THE DIOCESE IN CATHOLIC SCHOOL ADMINISTRATION

If the state is to discharge its responsibility as a civil society for the education of its citizens for their common temporal welfare, Catholic education, as well as all private education, must play a role similar to that of the local public school district in maintaining the standards set for education by the state. The roles differ in that, in accordance with the decision in the Oregon case, the Catholic schools exist, not on sufferance of the state, but by a right which follows necessarily from the natural right of parents to choose the kind of education which their children shall have.

The diocese, therefore, bears a similar relationship to the state as the local school district in matters of public educational responsibilities, though in a few concerns—notably in child accounting and enforcement of compulsory attendance laws—it is frequently responsible directly to the local public school district.

A Catholic diocese is a geographical area headed by its ordinary (cardinal, archbishop, or bishop), set up by the Holy See for the administration of Church concerns within that area. For convenience, we are using the term bishop throughout this book as though it were synonymous with the term ordinary of a diocese, since most ordinaries carry the title of bishop. In 1961, there were 140 dioceses in the United States, most of them large enough to be sound administrative units for school administration; this figure contrasts with the nearly 50,000 local units for administering public schools.

The bishop of a diocese, as a successor to the apostles, is the chief teacher of his diocese. As such, he is ultimately responsible for all diocesan schools within his geographical jurisdiction, and within the limits set by canon law, he has varying degrees of control over private Catholic schools operated by religious orders within his diocese.[1] Traditionally, the pastor of an individual parish is the responsible administrator of the parochial school in that parish. This is the basis for our previous comparison of the organization of parish schools in the United States with the district-unit system in public school administration.

In the United States the extensive and increasingly technical aspects of administering Catholic schools—aspects which the bishops, with their complex duties in the whole spectrum of church administration, could not directly handle and aspects with which individual pastors, with similar broad responsibilities, could not be expected to cope without professional assistance—have caused the institution of two intermediate agencies: the diocesan school board and the diocesan superintendent of schools. The resemblance in title, and increasingly in function, between these two institutions and their counterparts in public education is clear. Yet the differences are basic and must not be overlooked.

The most basic difference follows from the fact that the control of public education is fundamentally in the public itself, but control of diocesan education is fundamentally in the bishop by virtue of his divine office as chief teacher. Consequently, boards of education and their relationships to the superintendents of public schools are established by law; but in Catholic schools, boards of education and their relationships to the superintendents of Catholic schools nowhere figure in canon law; they are the creations of individual bishops in response to the needs of schools. As a result, both institutions are what the individual bishops make them. Their functions are precisely what the bishop may delegate to them.

Nevertheless, the influence of both has been increasing in the past thirty years in response to the growing complexity of problems facing Catholic schools. And increasingly, the role and interrelationships of the diocesan school board come closer to the pattern found

[1] See chap. 3 for Canons 1381 and 1382 for bishops' right of supervision and right of visitation in regard to religious instruction. For a discussion of possible exemption from visitation arising from privileged status claimed by certain religious who conduct private Catholic schools, see T. Lincoln Bouscaren and Adam C. Ellis, *Canon Law, A Text and Commentary,* 3d rev. ed., The Bruce Publishing Company, Milwaukee, 1957, p. 748.

most successful in public school administration—with always one exception, however; the power of enacting policy for Catholic schools remains with the bishop himself.

Within this general framework of historical fact and basic principles, it is now possible to examine the present status of the diocesan school board and the superintendent of diocesan schools, and to discuss desirable future developments in regard to both institutions.

THE DIOCESAN SCHOOL BOARD

A 1960 report of the Superintendents' Standing Committee on the Function and Status of the Diocesan Superintendency of Schools, Department of School Superintendents of the National Catholic Educational Association, gives the following description of the diocesan board of education as it is generally found:[2]

> In most dioceses a board is appointed by the bishop to advise the Superintendent of Schools and to work together with him in formulating programs and policies subject to the final approval of the bishop. Usually the Superintendent is the executive officer of this board. Membership on the board varies considerably throughout the country, but the most common pattern is that the board is made up of clergymen and ranges from six to fifteen members. Such boards are made up of members of the diocesan clergy representing various interests in the diocese. They are men of experience in both parish or diocesan work and sometimes educators in their own right.
>
> Such boards are usually consultative in nature. They are not administrative boards. Therefore, they assist the Superintendent of Schools by studying with him various educational problems and they help him formulate the programs and policies which are in the best interest of the diocese. In almost every instance the bishop is the honorary chairman of this board and meets with the members in order to give direction and authority to the many decisions which must be made.

That the diocesan school board operates in rudimentary fashion in some dioceses is indicated by one investigator who in a 1954 study reported that "Of nineteen dioceses reporting diocesan boards

[2] Report of the Standing Committee, Department of School Superintendents; "The Functions of the Superintendent of Catholic Schools." *National Catholic Educational Association Bulletin,* vol. 56, no. 3, p. 22, February, 1960.

of education concerned with high schools there are seven in which diocesan superintendents are board members. In one instance the bishop is chairman of the board and in four instances the vicar general is chairman. One board includes a member designated as director of secondary education. Each of these arrangements serves to confuse the function of enactment and execution and vice versa." [3]

Further insight into the present status of Catholic school boards is gained from the findings of a 1957 study of administrative patterns in diocesan school systems: [4]

> Some boards exist which have little or no contact with the superintendent, however, and serve as a consultative group to the Ordinary with most of their time, if not all, taken up with matters of finance. Other boards are concerned with school building and expansion programs, frequently requesting enrollment figures and estimates from the superintendent's office, but more usually not related to his office in any other way. . . .
>
> Of the boards which do sit formally to hear the superintendent's report annually or to consider his recommendations and to make approvals or rejections of these, the usual pattern reveals the Bishop as ex officio chairman, presiding, and the superintendent as the executive secretary. In some few dioceses, the Bishop identifies himself as active and presiding chairman of the board, participating broadly in policy-making. On the whole, the concept that the school board represents the Bishop's authority in education is a less well-developed one than is the concept of his being represented by the superintendent of schools. . . .
>
> A common number of meetings for active boards is four each year, while the more formal groups meet only once a year, as do the boards with lay members.

Whereas the functions of policy formation and enactment are both included in the responsibilities of public school boards of control, a distinction between the two is essential for effective organization of a diocesan school board, or for that matter, of boards of control in general. Policy formation may be the function of the

[3] John P. Breheny, "Diocesan Administration of Catholic Secondary Education in the United States: Its Status—With a Design for the Future," doctor's thesis, Harvard University, 1954, pp. 112–113.

[4] Sister M. Ruth Albert Ward, *Patterns of Administration in Diocesan School Systems,* The Catholic University of America Press, Washington, 1957, pp. 90–92.

board. Policy enactment is the function of the bishop (or the religious superior in private Catholic institutions).

Breheny, writing to the point that neither those who are charged with enactment of policy, nor those who are responsible for its execution should have membership on the diocesan board of education, says:[5]

> It has been pointed out that the enactment of diocesan policy for education is rightfully the responsibility of the bishop and also of his vicar general, unless the bishop shall determine otherwise. Indeed, it has been recommended that the bishop reserve this responsibility to himself. Obviously, by the very fact that the bishop is responsible for the declaration of policy, he will also play an important role in its formation. However, the diocesan board will be better able to fulfill its function, that of bringing to bear various lay [nonprofessional] points of view on the issues under consideration, if the bishop is not a board member. To a degree this will be true also as regards the vicar general and other diocesan officials. The authority vested in them may tend to bring about a situation in which as board members they will unwittingly dominate the thinking and decisions of the board. There will be ample opportunity for the bishop to participate in shaping policies once the recommendations of the board have been received. If he so chooses the bishop may accompany his decisions with a declaration of the reasons for his stand which may serve as a guide to the board in giving further consideration to the matter in question or in considering related matters in the future.
>
> Similarly, the chief education officer of the diocese has no place on the diocesan board of education. As an official charged with the execution of diocesan policy for education he should be a specialist, trained and experienced in the administration of schools. He is in a position to submit plans for the conduct of Catholic education within the diocese for consideration by the board and enactment by the bishop. He should act as a professional advisor both to the bishop and to the board, but his membership on the board itself will serve no purpose and will destroy its lay [nonprofessional] character. If he is a member of the board on a par with others, his proposals may not receive the consideration which is their due, coming from a professional educator, or on the other hand the weight of his opinions may be exaggerated to a point where he will

[5] Breheny, *op. cit.*, pp. 113–115.

dominate the action of the board. An unhealthy identification of proposals with the personality of the education officer will be avoided if he is in a position to act in a positive and impersonal fashion, placing his plans before the board, giving them the benefit of his counsel and awaiting their recommendations, rather than defending them within the board group as another member.

Once the basic distinction between policy formulation (by the board) and policy enactment (by the bishop) is made, it makes remarkably little difference whether one begins with ultimate control by the bishop, as in Catholic local school districts, or with ultimate control by the people, as in the local public school district; the principles of effective organization will be the same: There should be a board of education. The board should be relatively small—five or seven members. Board members should represent the diocese as a whole, not a subdistrict. In the diocese, the board will be appointed by the bishop for whom they will be formulating policy. Board members should serve staggered terms which are long enough to get the members thoroughly immersed in the complicated problems of school administration. Board members should act as a committee of the whole, without standing committees. Duties of the board should consist of (1) policy formulation, (2) approval of administrative detail, (3) evaluation of policies and practices, and (4) recommendation for appointment of a professional superintendent who shall be their executive officer.

Some dioceses exhibit a tendency to fragment the total responsibility for diocesan schools by limiting the scope of school boards (and superintendents) to parish elementary schools. Separate school boards have historically been organized for diocesan high schools, sometimes one for each centralized high school. Another school board for a diocesan college may be in operation. While a case may be made for a separate board of control for the diocesan college, the common problems of elementary and secondary school management, the desirability of curriculum integration, the necessity for skilled business services, the waste of effort involved in separately developing policies that are equally applicable to both levels—all these indicate that policy formulation for diocesan elementary and secondary education should be unified under one board of education.

Whether or not the diocesan school board includes lay members is not of the essence of effective Catholic school administration. Several school boards have recently been reorganized in large dioceses to provide for lay representation, as well as for representation by members of religious communities operating schools within the diocese. A case for including laymen has been made by Ryan, who attempts to show "that the time is ripe to give the laity a greater measure of responsibility in Catholic education on the elementary and secondary levels." [6] Certainly there are significant psychological advantages to be realized by involving laymen on diocesan boards of education.

The use of laymen on a board of education in order to secure inexpensive assistance in solving administrative problems is likely to result in confusion of the function of the board and the function of the superintendent. The organization of advisory councils to the superintendent himself would seem the appropriate vehicle by which to involve the particular skills, judgments, and services of professional men and business executives in the solution of administrative problems within their areas of expertness.

THE DIOCESAN SUPERINTENDENT OF SCHOOLS

In every diocese in the United States, a priest is assigned to the position of superintendent of schools. This may be his title, or he may be called secretary for education or secretary of the school board. His functions are those assigned him by his bishop. While assignments of responsibility vary tremendously in scope and depth, they may include elementary schools, secondary schools, diocesan colleges and universities, schools providing special educational facilities, and institutional schools. The role of the Catholic school superintendent has been described as follows:[7]

1. *The superintendent is the delegate of his bishop in education.* "He is directly responsible to the bishop for such programs under his charge."

2. *The superintendent is the chief executive officer of the diocesan school system.* "The Superintendent acts to advise and assist the pas-

[6] Carl J. Ryan, "Ghosts of Trusteeism," *Homiletic and Pastoral Review,* vol. 57, pp. 705–714, May, 1957.

[7] The Report of the Standing Committee, *op. cit.,* pp. 21 ff.

tor in the discharge of his educational duties and serves as a consultant in providing solutions to local problems."

3. *The superintendent is responsible for external public relations of the diocesan school systems.* He maintains contact with civil authorities and professional organizations.

4. *The superintendent is an educator.* "It is his responsibility to develop and promote the instructional program. . . . The Superintendent undertakes from time to time critical research work. . . . It is often necessary for the Superintendent to establish specific requirements, to provide for the fulfillment of any state requirements which refer to Catholic school personnel, to set up certification procedures, or to initiate teacher training schools."

5. *The superintendent is the chief supervisor of education.* "Most Superintendents appoint either community or diocesan supervisors to make regular visitations to each classroom in the diocese or to each educational unit under his charge."

6. *The superintendent evaluates the educational program.* "Very often this is achieved through a testing program which is intended to measure the achievement of children in various subjects."

7. *The superintendent is the interpreter of the Catholic school program.* "The Superintendent must interpret the school program and policies to his own personnel and . . . bring to the general community a knowledge and understanding of the Catholic school."

8. *The superintendent has responsibilities for new school buildings.* "In this role the Superintendent becomes a partner with community planners, architects, contractors, pastors, and religious superiors. . . . the Superintendent is often a member of the building commission of the diocese or a building committee established by the bishop to study new projects in the diocese."

The above description of the status of the diocesan school superintendent from the report of the superintendents' own standing committee indicates quite a different role, in many respects, from the concept of a strong superintendent under a board of control, as advocated by most professional school administrators.

In even sharper contrast are the observations of one experienced Catholic school superintendent who in the following observations underscores two differences between the public and Catholic school superintendency, differences which have far-reaching results. The first is a difference in authority and the second, a difference in financial control of schools:[8]

> For example, when a public school system sets the calendar for the school year, no individual principal would dare to declare a free day on his own responsibility. Any persistent ignoring or violation of a school regulation could lead to dismissal and the administrator would have the law on his side. On the other hand, many of the regulations governing parochial schools are the regulations of the bishop, or school board, and are not civil law. As a result, for example, a pastor of a parish school might grant a few extra days a year, or ignore other school regulations, and there is not much the superintendent can do about it.
>
> It is true that if a certain pastor would persistently and flagrantly ignore diocesan school regulations to the point where the school was seriously affected, the bishop would undoubtedly step in. On the other hand, a prudent school superintendent would not report to his bishop every violation of a school regulation that came to his notice. Neither would the bishop, as a good administrator, take cognizance of every such violation. The Catholic school authorities depend on the good will of pastors, principals, and teachers in following out diocesan school regulations. . . .
>
> In the public school system the same authority that makes the regulations also controls the purse strings. When the public school board of education makes regulations and requirements, it must also provide the necessary finances to carry out its regulations. In the Catholic school system it is different. The regulations are made by the bishop, either directly or through the diocesan school board, or superintendent, but the pastor has to raise the money. Thus a pastor could, if he wanted to, use as an excuse for not complying with many school regulations the fact that the parish cannot afford it. This could apply to overcrowded classrooms—the parish cannot afford to build or hire more teachers; employing untrained lay teachers —the parish cannot afford to pay the salary a trained teacher would expect.
>
> This is an argument the school superintendent usually cannot answer. Ordinarily he does not have direct and accurate knowledge of parish finances. Probably he could obtain such information from the chancery office. But what good would it do? Unless it was a very

[8] Carl J. Ryan, "Parochial Schools Rest on Good Will," *Catholic Educator,* vol. 26, pp. 493–494, April, 1956.

serious matter he would not take it to the bishop—nor would a bishop want to have all such cases brought to him for action.

A further obstacle to effective functioning of Catholic school superintendents is a frequent absence of suitable financial arrangements to meet necessary overhead expenses. Levies on parish elementary schools—seldom on high schools—are sometimes made. Special collections for this purpose are sometimes held in all parishes. And sometimes support of the superintendent's office depends on commercial arrangements. Breheny found that in three dioceses, support of the office came from the sale of textbooks, workbooks, and courses of study.[9]

While there are significant obstacles to a strengthened position of the superintendent in diocesan administration, these are steadily being overcome in response to the increased complexity of the problems demanding solution—such as those concerning the greater use of lay teaching. The chief forces leading in this direction, however, are external to Catholic education itself; such developments as the increasing tendency of states to deal with Catholic schools through the diocesan superintendent's office, the tendency of states to apply accrediting procedures to private as well as public schools, and the desirability of participation in the Federal School Lunch Program have strengthened the superintendent's position.

THE PASTOR-PRINCIPAL RELATIONSHIPS

Enough has been said of diocesan school systems to indicate that a key to the future development of Catholic school systems is the role of the pastor and the relationships which exist between him and the superintendent of schools and between him and the principal of the school.

One nationwide study finds at least three patterns of interrelationships in operation today.[10] In the most common, the pastor is in full charge of the parochial school. In a second, the pastor remains the administrative head of the school, but he delegates most of his school administrative duties to the school principal, perhaps assigning the assistant pastor to teach religion. In a third type, administrative regulations or evolving practices specify certain administrative

[9] Breheny, *op. cit.*, pp. 135–136.
[10] Ward, *op. cit.*, pp. 118–121.

responsibilities for the pastor and certain others for the principal. The pastor may be given responsibility for supervising religious education in the school; providing funds for maintenance and operation of the school; providing teachers for the school, especially religious teachers; providing adequate school plant; or some combination of these functions. In these matters he may deal directly with the bishop. There may also be a diocesan regulation which specifies, however, that he is in no way to control the remaining administrative functions, leaving these to the principal to carry out in relationship with the superintendent.

The first pattern, the oldest and still most widely found, was the only pattern envisioned in the educational legislation of the Councils of Baltimore from which the parish school system developed. The second and third patterns, the future organizational patterns of diocesan administration, have found their impetus in problems most urgently demanding professional solution at higher than the parish level, including lay teacher personnel problems, curriculum planning, testing, textbook adoptions, purchasing procedures, relations with state departments of education, the meeting of standards for state accreditation, and even participation in the Federal School Lunch Program.

SUMMARY—ORGANIZATION OF DIOCESAN SCHOOLS

Undoubtedly, Catholic school systems owe much of their present success to priest-superintendents who have increased the stature of their positions by frequently heroic efforts in the face of administrative patterns needing further refinement and development; nor is there any doubt that the professional activities of the Department of School Superintendents of the National Catholic Educational Association have facilitated the solution of many problems that have vexed individual administrators. But neither is there any doubt that the complexity of the educational problems immediately ahead will necessitate further refinement and development of diocesan administrative patterns to include:

1. Clear recognition that while enactment of policy in school matters rests with the bishop, the school board must be developed as the policy-formulation agency of the diocesan school system

2. Clarification of the role of the superintendent as chief executive of the board

3. Provision of adequate financial arrangements for a suitable central office staff

4. Further integration of both elementary and secondary schools into a school system through the avenue of effective leadership from a central office

The older pattern, characterized by a pastor supreme under the bishop in educational matters, can too frequently result in an autonomy exercised with more vigor and self-assurance than professional knowledge. In such extremes it too closely resembles the district-unit system which so long plagued public education.

It is precisely to this point that McCluskey addresses these remarks:[11]

> The parochial school as an independent, parish-controlled and parish-financed operation is an anachronism. For the greater good all parochial schools should become diocesan schools. This will mean, of course, that pastors will have to yield control over their schools. We speak loosely of a Catholic school "system," but only a few dioceses approach education systematically. . . .
>
> Take the planning of schools. A central planning board would allocate schools and priorities in building, would pass on additions, consolidations and suppressions of schools. Special schools would be located at strategic points in the diocese. In these schools the exceptional children would at long last get their full due. There would be special schools and staffs for the mentally retarded and physically handicapped. There would be a special diocesan transportation provision for the handicapped who attend regular schools. College preparatory schools, terminal schools, pre-professional, and technical schools would likewise be centrally located for patronage by youngsters of the entire area or diocese.

Yet as a stronger board–chief-executive pattern of organization obtains more widely, care must be taken by the board to avoid a mistake frequently made in Catholic institutions, mainly colleges and universities, where this pattern has been attempted. It is the

[11] Neil G. McCluskey, "The Dinosaur and the Catholic School," *National Catholic Educational Association Bulletin*, vol. 57, no. 1, p. 235, August, 1960.

failure of board members to understand the "negative check" role which they must play and the prima facie status to be accorded the recommendations of their chief executive as developed through his staff. As a result, ill-fated attempts at administration by committee have been frequent; or valuable time has been wasted on routine recommendations which should have been approved *pro forma.* But both of these also happen in many local public school districts.

Questions for Discussion or Investigation

1. At the local level, nonpartisan election of school board members is recommended; yet for the state level, this method is not recommended. Why might a recommendation be good at one level and undesirable at another?

2. The unitary concept of administration under a chief education officer is recommended as desirable administrative procedure. This has not been universally achieved in public education. How is it sometimes violated? Nor has it been generally attained in Catholic school administration. Why not?

3. Construct a basic administrative chart for Catholic schools. Indicate flow of authority and briefly describe the function of positions shown. Bear in mind desirable principles of school administration. Note for discussion any difficulties you encounter.

4. Do the same for a private Catholic high school conducted in a diocese by a religious order. Footnote this chart with your recommendations for board-of-control membership. Again note for discussion any difficulties encountered.

5. Why should staff members of a school organization not be members of its board of control?

Readings and References

The American School Superintendency, Thirtieth Yearbook of the American Association of School Administrators, Washington, 1952.

Bouscaren, T. Lincoln, and Adam C. Ellis: *Canon Law, A Text and Commentary,* 3d rev. ed., The Bruce Publishing Company, Milwaukee, 1957.

Breheny, John P.: "Diocesan Administration of Catholic Secondary Education in the United States: Its Status—With a Design for the Future," doctor's thesis, Harvard University, 1954.

Cooper, Shirley, and C. O. Fitzwater: *County School Administration,* Harper & Brothers, New York, 1953.

Grieder, Calvin, and William Everett Rosenstengel: *Public School Administration,* The Ronald Press Company, New York, 1954.

Legal Status of the School Superintendent, National Education Association, Research Bulletin, vol. 29, no. 3, October, 1951.

McCluskey, Neil G.: "The Dinosaur and the Catholic School," *National Catholic Educational Association Bulletin,* vol. 57, no. 1, pp. 232–238, August, 1960.

Moore, Hollis A., Jr.: *Studies in School Administration,* American Association of School Administrators, Washington, 1957.

Mort, Paul R., and Donald H. Ross: *Principles of School Administration,* McGraw-Hill Book Company, Inc., New York, 1957.

"Parochial Schools Rest on Good Will," *Catholic Educator,* vol. 26, pp. 493–494, April, 1956.

Pittinger, John C.: *The School Board Member,* McGraw-Hill Book Company, Inc., New York, 1951.

Professional Administrators for America's Schools, Thirty-eighth Yearbook of the American Association of School Administrators, Washington, 1960.

Profile of the School Superintendent, American Association of School Administrators, Washington, 1960.

Reeves, Charles E.: *School Boards: Their Status, Functions, and Activities,* Prentice-Hall, Inc., Englewood Cliffs, N.J., 1954.

Report of the Standing Committee, Department of School Superintendents: "The Functions of the Superintendent of Catholic Schools," *National Catholic Educational Association Bulletin,* vol. 41, no. 3, February, 1960.

Ryan, Carl J.: "Ghosts of Trusteeism," *Homiletic and Pastoral Review,* vol. 57, pp. 705–714, May, 1957.

School Board–Superintendent Relationships, Thirty-fourth Yearbook of the American Association of School Administrators, Washington, 1956.

Spaulding, Frank: *School Superintendent in Action in Five Cities,* Richard R. Smith, Publisher, Inc., New York, 1955.

Voelker, John M.: *The Diocesan Superintendent of Schools,* The Catholic University of America Press, Washington, 1935.

Ward, Sister M. Ruth Albert: *Patterns of Administration in Diocesan School Systems,* The Catholic University of America Press, Washington, 1957.

PART THREE

Administration—
A Sixfold Responsibility

INSTRUCTION

ADMINISTRATIVE OPERATION

PERSONNEL SERVICES

BUSINESS MANAGEMENT

COMMUNITY RELATIONS

RESEARCH

7. *Instruction:*
The Curriculum

Basic to the instructional responsibilities of the school administrator is the curriculum of his school—those experiences offered to children under the guidance of the classroom teacher. Despite efforts of some educators to classify organized opportunities offered to students outside class hours as curricular or cocurricular, the term extracurricular remains in general use.

The use of the words "those experiences offered to children" implies some selection of the experiences to comprise the curriculum. Actually experiences included will change considerably from time to time as the child's environment changes. On the other hand, certain elements of the curriculum designed to develop what are frequently referred to as the eternal verities will change not at all. Changes in the curriculum, therefore, will arise from the rapidly changing world in which we live; but unchanging human nature supplies a stable factor in the school curriculum.

THE CHANGES IN CURRICULAR EMPHASES

The past seventy years of American education have been marked by pronounced shifts of emphasis in curricular theory and practice.

129

These changed emphases are first noticed in the professional literature of the field, from which they swiftly find their way into teacher training institutions around the country. As more and more teachers are educated under the influence of a new approach to education, practices in conformity to the theory are adopted by teaching staffs, first in the elementary schools where teacher turnover is swiftest. Some years after the theory has been widely promulgated, it may become the predominant practice at both elementary and secondary levels. At about that time a new curricular emphasis may be the preoccupation of the theorists.

Over the years, the major shifts in curricular emphasis in the United States may be described in terms of successive major eras: the subject-matter era, the psychologized subject-matter era, the child-centered era, and the society-centered era. Dates for such eras, of course, can be but approximations, since historical movements can be described only in sweeping generalizations to which there are many exceptions. The lag between theory and practice, a lag so great that older teachers may seem to have been completely unaffected by any theory subsequent to their graduation from college, complicates fixing dates. Furthermore, there is something unreal about describing an era in terms of its theoretical extremes when fortunately, teacher resistance keeps practice nearer the middle ground.

Nevertheless, it is both useful and valid to consider the periods of major curricular emphasis in this country as follows:

> Up to 1890—Subject-matter era
> 1890 to 1910—Psychologized subject-matter era
> 1910 to 1930—Child-centered era
> 1930 to present—Society-centered era

SUBJECT-MATTER ERA

Up to around 1890, curricular thinking centered about what should be taught in schools. Knowledge of subject matter was the major prerequisite for the teacher. Generally speaking, the textbook was the lone instructional tool; teacher assignment and student memorization and recitation constituted standard instructional procedure.

Typical of the texts used is the following passage from Mitchell's *New School Geography,* published in 1868:[1]

93. What are Zones?
    Zones are belts or divisions of the Earth's surface, lying parallel to the Equator. The word *Zone* is from the Greek, and means a *belt* or *girdle.*
94. By what lines are the Zones formed?
    Zones are formed by the Tropics and the Polar Circles.
95. How many Zones are there?
    There are five Zones: the Torrid Zone, the North and South Temperate Zones, and the North and South Frigid Zones. *Torrid* means *hot* or *parched; frigid* means *cold* or *frozen.*
96. Where is the North Frigid Zone?
    The North Frigid Zone lies between the North Pole and the Arctic Circle.
97. Where is the South Frigid Zone?
    The South Frigid Zone lies between the South Pole and the Antarctic Circle.
98. Where is the North Temperate Zone?
    The North Temperate Zone lies between the Tropic of Cancer and the Arctic Circle.
99. Where is the South Temperate Zone?
    The South Temperate Zone lies between the Tropic of Capricorn and the Antarctic Circle.

PSYCHOLOGIZED SUBJECT-MATTER ERA

Between 1890 and 1910, the influence of the educational reformers of Europe, many of them psychologists, was prominent in American educational literature as educationists began applying to teaching theory the lessons learned from the new field of psychology. The rapidly developing normal school movement spread the theories of Froebel, Spencer, and especially Herbart.

Between 1889 and 1897, influential professional books were published, such as *Essentials of Methods* by Charles De Garmo in 1889, *General Method* by Charles A. McMurry in 1892, and *Method in Recitation* by Frank McMurry in 1897. Of great influence in spread-

[1] As reported by Strayer, Frasier, and Armentrout in *Principles of Teaching,* American Book Company, New York, 1936, p. 89.

ing Herbartian teaching methods was the National Herbart Society, founded in 1892.

This was the period when psychologically oriented plans for effective teaching of subject matter were couched in such terms as apperceptive mass, correlation, recitation, culture-epoch theory, and lesson planning. Teaching method became almost synonymous with the five Herbartian steps for organizing the daily lesson: preparation, presentation, comparison, generalization, and application.

CHILD-CENTERED ERA

By 1910 the dominance of psychologized plans for effective teaching of subject matter was challenged by increasing emphasis on the child—his individual differences, his interests, his aptitudes, his "inherent goodness." As the group testing movement developed startling evidence of the range of differences among children, the role of the individual child became so important in the educative process that educational experts and followers alike could and did seriously remind each other that they "taught children, not subject matter." In the early 1930s, the emphasis on the individual child had become so great that one teachers college student said, with considerable justification, that whenever he was in doubt about the answer to any examination question in a professional course, he wrote a good paragraph on individual differences, which got him by nicely.

With the lag between theory and practice, it was in the late thirties before one large city school system fought the "battle of scope and sequence" in its curriculum revision program. Many teachers, principals, and supervisors were firmly convinced that individual differences were great enough that a course of study could not describe the scope of any subject at any elementary school grade level; nor could any grade allocations be given for teaching fractions, for example, or teaching long division with decimals. Rather it was held that the curriculum must emerge from the classroom as the children's interests and capabilities were individually revealed to the teacher. This was the era of Indian and Mexican units in any or all grades of some schools.

Just as the growth of the testing movement led to extreme emphasis on individual differences represented by the planless curriculum, so the spread of a Rousseau-like conception of human nature led to other facets of the child-centered era. Educational psychologists increasingly popularized the sentimental concept that the child was "naturally good" and bound to get better if only his environment did not interfere with his natural goodness. Accordingly, if the teacher taught well enough, the child had to learn. Repression of the child's nature was frowned on. External disciplinary measures were unthinkable. Self-expression, whether in writing, spatter painting, or nonconformist acts, was encouraged on principle. Projects, activities, the omnipresent frieze, and the "hum of industry in the classroom" all fitted the general laissez-faire social climate of the post-World War I years.

Society-centered Era

By 1930, radical changes in the world were leading in the direction of greater state socialism. The influence of Hitler and Mussolini, and the influence of communism with its own brand of national socialism, were being felt far beyond the boundaries of Germany, Italy, and Russia. Here in the United States, the Depression brought with it the necessity for much more social planning than had previously been known. During the New Deal years, banks, industries, wages, hours, and investments were all regulated in an effort to recover from the Depression. We and the world were moving consistently in the direction of national planning in accordance with the needs of society.

Shortly after 1930, it became clear to many educational theorists that the rugged individualism and self-expression of the child-centered era did not adequately meet the needs of society. Curriculum experts began to emphasize society with a capital "S." The emphasis was not on civil society, not on religious society, not on the society of the family, not on a society for savings and loans, but on some nebulous and overriding concept called *society*. A corollary to such a premise as *society* is overemphasis on educating youngsters to meet its needs.

As we neared World War II and entered it, the theorists who held that schools must meet the needs of society were reinforced by those who claimed that far too many products of the child-centered years were of little use to the armed services, because the young people did not know enough arithmetic or science, for example, to help the country win a scientific and technological war.

One of the most succinct descriptions of the creed of the society-centered curriculum expert is to be found in Caswell and Foshay, *Education in the Elementary School*:[2]

> The curriculum should be organized so that direct attention is centered on the problems and needs of broad social significance and of immediate concern to children. . . . It is perfectly clear that our society supports schools because of the belief that they make a direct contribution to the perpetuation and improvement of our democratic way of life. . . . With the increasingly complex problems that we face in the future it becomes evident that the program of the school must bear more directly on the problems of our times if a significant contribution to their solution is to be made. No longer is mere literacy adequate; no longer will the study of Indians and Eskimos suffice. If we are to save our soil and use our coal and oil and forests wisely; if we are to extend individual rights guaranteed by democracy to minority groups; if we are to protect our government from subversive acts; if we are to have an adequate diet; if we are to protect life on our highways; if we are to meet the multitude of problems which our country faces, instruction in the schools must deal with these matters and the curriculum must be so organized as to call them to direct attention. Chance cannot be relied upon to achieve this important end.

GENERAL OBSERVATIONS

As previously noted, no review of the shifting curricular emphasis of the past seventy years is real if a shift is described only by the absurdities to which extremists brought it and if the description neglects that which was desirable, valid, and necessary in the changes. For theories are not likely to find widespread acceptance unless they promise, at least partially, substantial improvement over the *status quo*. So it was with each of the major curricular changes described. The subject-matter era wisely stressed the something to be taught; in so far as it neglected appropriate methodology, individual differences, or the needs of children, a change was needed. The psychologized subject-matter years soundly emphasized the necessity of

[2] Hollis L. Caswell and A. Wellesley Foshay, *Education in the Elementary School*, 3d ed., American Book Company, New York, 1957, pp. 272–273.

organizing the lesson so that learning would be fostered; in so far as it led to automatic application of teaching formulas, it reached an indefensible extreme. The child-centered era substantially contributed to teacher awareness of the sharp differences in ability and interests of children and of the importance of student motivation and attitude in learning; in so far as interests and motivation became ends in themselves or in so far as this period led to a sentimental view of the goodness of human nature, absurdities resulted. In turn, the society-centered view began as a necessary check to the excesses of the child-centered period; in so far as uncritical advocates tended to make schools mere instruments of society as expressed in the will of the majority, they betrayed a vital aspect of the American heritage.

THE PURPOSES OF SCHOOLS TODAY

By the 1950s, two sharply different answers to the question, what are schools for, were evident in the general literature of the field. The first answer was a natural development from the extreme emphasis on the needs of children and the needs of society prevalent in the preceding child-centered and society-centered eras; the second is a reaction to the extremes of both periods and is characterized by an emphasis on intellectual development as primary among the purposes of schools.

THE FIRST ANSWER: DIRECTLY MEETING NEEDS

The first approach to the purposes of schools, and by far the predominant one among theorists, uses interchangeably the terms *objectives of education* and *objectives of schools*. The approach is best illustrated by the growing list of objectives of education widely disseminated and memorized throughout the first half of this century. Outstanding among them is the 1918 list of "Cardinal Principles of Education" of the Commission on the Reorganization of Secondary Education: health, command of the fundamental processes, worthy home membership, vocational efficiency, citizenship, worthy use of leisure, and ethical character.

After many lists of lesser fame published in the intervening years, there came the purposes of education listed in the Educational Policies Commission's *Education for All American Youth,* which in 1944 stated the objectives of high schools as these ten imperative needs of youth:[3]

1. All youth need to develop salable skills and those understandings and attitudes that make the worker an intelligent and productive participant in economic life. To this end, most youth need supervised work experience as well as education in the skills and knowledge of their occupations.

2. All youth need to develop and maintain good health and physical fitness.

3. All youth need to understand the rights and duties of the citizen of a democratic society, and to be diligent and competent in the performance of their obligations as members of the community and citizens of the state and nation.

4. All youth need to understand the significance of the family for the individual and society and the conditions conducive to successful family life.

5. All youth need to know how to purchase and use goods and services intelligently, understanding both the values received by the consumer and the economic consequences of their acts.

6. All youth need to understand the methods of science, the influence of science on human life, and the main scientific facts concerning the nature of the world and of man.

7. All youth need opportunities to develop their capacities to appreciate beauty in literature, art, music, and nature.

8. All youth need to be able to use their leisure time well and to budget it wisely, balancing activities that yield satisfactions to the individual with those that are socially useful.

9. All youth need to develop respect for other persons, to grow in their insight into ethical values and principles, and to be able to live and work cooperatively with others.

10. All youth need to grow in their ability to think rationally, to express their thoughts clearly, and to read and listen with understanding.

Last, but not fewest, come the objectives of life-adjustment education. Here we find spelled out in considerably more detail the necessity of adjusting youth to all the specific problems met by them.

[3] Educational Policies Commission, *Education for All American Youth: A Further Look,* National Education Association, Washington, 1952, p. 216.

New lists of objectives are stated in terms of problem areas and present-day problems. One such list gives forty-five new problem areas. The National Commission on Life Adjustment Education discusses these areas and objectives in the light of eight major headings, with room for breakdown into many others. For example, Harl R. Douglas suggests that one of these eight, health, might be broken down into the following thirteen problem areas:[4]

1. How to adjust personal abilities and ambitions.
2. How to succeed without bragging and to fail without making excuses.
3. How to determine a well-balanced diet.
4. How to develop good health habits.
5. How to understand the functioning of the body and its care.
6. How to avoid disease and combat it.
7. How to render first aid in emergencies.
8. How to conserve human resources.
9. How to develop big muscles and endurance.
10. How to develop grace and poise.
11. How to maintain good personal hygiene.
12. How to maintain public health in the community.
13. How to control and enjoy one's emotions.

If the same is done in the other objective areas, the result is a list of over 100 objectives. As the list grows, it has been suggested that footnotes and "horizontal articulation" may be necessary—somewhat of an understatement.

There are three things to note about these lists of objectives. One, they are getting longer, much longer; two, thinking and the tools of thought are sinking from the number two spot to the number ten spot—and right out of some lists; and three, all these objectives are assumed to be equally important in the job of the schools.

The Second Answer: Intellectual Development

The second point of view is in some ways an older point of view and is one which is gathering momentum and much new support. Its adherents maintain that two different questions are confused in the first answer: what is the nature of the educational job, and what

[4] Harl R. Douglas (ed.), *Education for Life Adjustment—Its Meaning and Implementation,* The Ronald Press Company, New York, 1950, pp. 60–61.

is the unique or special job of schools? They admit that seven, ten, or fifteen general objectives may be listed as the objectives of education; but they maintain that schools are not organized to do the whole job of education. While schools should help out as much as possible in realizing the objectives of education, such help should not be at the expense of their unique job, the job for which they are chiefly responsible and uniquely fitted—the intellectual development of students.

Arthur Bestor of the University of Illinois stated this point of view before the American Historical Association in 1953 with these words:[5]

> The idea that the school must undertake to meet every need that some other agency is failing to meet is a preposterous delusion that can wreck the educational system without contributing anything to the salvation of society. . . . The responsibility which the school may not sacrifice to any other aim, however worthy, is its responsibility for providing intellectual training.

The conflict in point of view as to the job of the schools is between the prevailing group of theorists who believe that the school should train children to adjust to the specific problems of today and the minority of the theorists, becoming more vocal, who believe that schools help children most by doing what the schools alone can do, developing the knowledge, intellectual tools, and thinking habits needed to solve the problems of tomorrow as well as today. To state the issue specifically, do we train children to fill out their income tax returns today on today's forms with today's tables and percentages; or do we educate them to read, compute, and think so that they may fill out today's, next year's, and even those blanks as yet undevised?

THE IMPLICATION OF THESE ANSWERS

The first answer, which considers the purposes of education and of schools as coextensive, soon leads to an overcrowded curriculum in which one need may be considered as vital as another. This approach so scatters the efforts of the schools that nothing specific may result and all integrative influence may be lost. It is with this viewpoint that one teacher could seriously write about a junior high

[5] As reported in *Time,* Jan. 5, 1953, p. 52.

school course, entitled *Homemaking Education for Boys and Girls,* in the following terms:[6]

> The boy, as well as the girl in junior-high school needs to grow in his understanding and practices of successful family living. . . .
>
> The supervisor . . . conceived the idea that an upper division home-making class, open to both boys and girls, would fill the need to develop wholesome, friendly attitudes toward members of the opposite sex. . . .
>
> There is also a pie-baking project (very popular with both pupils and parents) when each pupil has the opportunity to bake a large pie to take home to his family. The pupils take a trip to a large bakery, dairy, or the farmers' market. . . .
>
> Each class plans the food with the teacher's help, decides which teachers and administrators to invite, learns about invitations and then writes them, and then finally prepares, serves, and eats (a most important part) the food. . . .
>
> Soon after the organization of the class we discovered a need among the pupils for instruction in social dancing. . . . We started having dance classes every Friday during the class period. You don't have to be an Arthur Murray to teach dancing. A simple two-step, a waltz step, and finally a simple jitterbug step is enough.
>
> To help pupils learn what to say, to wear, how to act at social gatherings, we discuss manners and etiquette as they apply to the junior-high school pupils. Since we find that how to make and acknowledge introductions bothers most teen-agers, we practice making introductions with members of the group acting as parents, teacher, boy-friends, or girl-friends. . . .
>
> We at Horace Mann feel this class fills a definite need in the junior-high school curriculum.

The second answer leads to a considerably more manageable curriculum. If the view obtains that the unique purpose of the school is the intellectual development of the youngster, then certain curriculum experiences become more basic than others. Intellectual development of this kind means skills in the tools of the intellect and knowledge in areas in which facts and understanding are necessary if children are to fill their roles as individuals and citizens successfully.

[6] Winifred T. Snyder, "Homemaking Education for Boys and Girls," *California Journal of Secondary Education,* vol. 27, pp. 139–141, March, 1952.

Thus, language arts is essential to the curriculum, since reading the thoughts of others, expressing one's own thoughts precisely, and knowing the meaning of words (the labels we ordinarily use in thinking and learning), are indispensable to intellectual development. Social studies, science (at least at the high school level), literature, and a pervasive emphasis on sound thinking also receive priority in this approach to the curriculum.

On the other hand, specific vocational training, consumer education, driver training, social dancing, and wholesome boy-girl relationships are examples of areas to which the school can give, at most, general support but not an equal curricular weight. Religion, which the religious parent considers the most important of all areas, can in the public school receive only the most general support and must be left to the home and church almost exclusively.

One caution should be expressed here. To accept intellectual development as the unique role of the schools should not mean a return to older methodologies. The interests of children, the necessity for maneuvering them into a felt need for what is to be learned in school, and the importance of developing an informed citizen-voter must still be stressed if the purposes of the schools are to be realized and the curriculum is to be effective.

THE PURPOSE OF CATHOLIC SCHOOLS

Catholic schools exist in this country because public education is unable to include among the fields of knowledge the most important of all, religion; for upon the individual's knowledge of religion and discharge of his responsibilities to God depends the salvation of his immortal soul—man's ultimate purpose in living.

The clarity of the Church's religious and philosophical principles has generally kept Catholic education in this country from the excesses associated with the child-centered and society-centered eras in curriculum development. Obviously the Church, which so positively stands for the doctrines of the fall of man, his susceptibility to inordinate desires as represented by the capital sins, and his redemption, is not likely to indulge in the excesses flowing from a Rousseau-like concept of man as naturally good and likely to get better if only the influence of bad teaching is removed. Nor with its doctrine of the intrinsic worth of each man, based on his creation as an individual in the image and likeness of God, is it likely to emphasize man's responsibilities to society to the point where his individuality is lost.

Furthermore, the philosophical position that each man is responsible for following the dictates of his "right reason" places emphasis on intellectual development as a basis for moral actions.

This is not to say, however, that Catholic educational theory has been unaffected by the general curricular emphasis given to meeting directly the needs of children or of society; or that some Catholic educators have not confused the purposes of education with the purposes of schools. They have.

Statements on the purpose of Catholic schools, wherever they are found, generally find their beginning and end in such famed quotations from the encyclical of Pope Pius XI on Christian Education as the following:[7]

> The purpose and immediate end of Christian education is to cooperate with divine grace in forming the true and perfect Christian. . . .
>
> For precisely this reason Christian education takes the whole aggregate of human life, physical and spiritual, intellectual and moral, individual, domestic, and social, not with a view of reducing it in any way, but in order to elevate, regulate and perfect it, in accordance with the example and teaching of Christ.
>
> Hence the true Christian, product of Christian education, is the supernatural man who thinks, judges, and acts constantly and consistently in accordance with right reason illuminated by the supernatural light of the example and teaching of Christ; in other words, to use the current term, the true and finished man of character.

Notice that the encyclical is concerned in general with Christian education. Nowhere is there an attempt to discuss the specific or unique role of the school in Catholic education.

Yet, in keeping with the predominating approach of literature on curriculum in recent years, it is not uncommon for Catholic educators to commit the same mistake as other experts in failing to deter-

[7] Pius XI, "Christian Education of Youth," in *Five Great Encyclicals,* The Paulist Press, New York, 1941.

mine the role of the Catholic school in Christian education. That failure is likely to lead to a church school with an overcrowded curriculum ranging over the needs of the "whole man" met by public education, plus the religious needs met in religious schools. For Catholic education has had its Christian life-adjustment movement, as witness the following excerpt from the printed philosophy and objectives of one high school:

> Since the study of our objectives has proved that certain experiences will be common to all, whereas others will pertain to specialized groups, we have decided to abolish all the class distinctions caused by parallel courses and introduce a system of general and specialized subject fields. The subjects termed "general" are those which answer the needs of all students and which all students pursue. They include religion, English, social studies, fine arts, physical education, mathematics, and home making. Religion, English, and social studies are full-time subjects throughout the four years. In addition to these, in order to establish in the minds of the students a realization of the purpose of each living thing in God's creative plan, a respect for life in general and of family life in particular, a study of biology, we feel, is also necessary for every student. Moreover, since the home is the basic unit of society, all should have definite training in home making. Thus, a carefully planned course in home making to be pursued by both boys and girls for at least two periods a week throughout the four years has been given a prominent place in the curriculum. This differs from the home-making course as understood by most schools in that it is not elective nor a substitute for other courses, but a part of each student's program carefully planned to assist him in meeting the responsibilities of life. This course, moreover, since it includes manual arts, fine arts, and training for leadership in parish and civic groups, has the additional value of teaching the student certain hobbies and skills so necessary in the recreational phase of his life adjustment.

And from the same source:

MATHEMATICS IN THE CURRICULUM

The student's relationship with God, his fellowmen, and himself is fostered by the study of mathematics in aiding him to develop definite understandings, attitudes, and skills in the five major areas in which his life will be spent.

The Objectives Are Obtained by:

1. An appreciation and respect for truth, law, order, authority
2. Preparation for the solution of life's problems

The Means Used, Especially for Algebra, Are:

1. Mechanics
2. Reasoned problems

The Goals Attained Are:

1. Responsibility
2. Respect for authority
3. Mental alertness
4. Self-reliance
5. Self-control

The student learns to recognize, realize, resolve upon life's problems through his study of mathematics.

One question immediately comes to mind. What happened to the distinctive contribution of mathematics to the curriculum?

Despite these extreme examples of Catholic educators following prevailing opinion among curriculum authorities, it is fair to say that most Catholic schools have not succumbed to the lure of over-extended statements of purpose which would surely result if the purpose of Christian education was equated with the purpose of schools. Actually, the Catholic school curriculum has tended to lag behind the advance guard who advocated violent curriculum changes, and so the schools have not laid themselves open to criticism on these grounds. In fact more criticism has been made, and with reason, on the grounds that Catholic schools have been inadequately influenced by valid advances dictated by environmental changes; e.g., schools have held too rigidly to the complexities of formal grammar; or they have overstressed the importance of Latin when many of the reasons for its inclusion are long since gone. Further criticism has come on the grounds that Catholic schools, in revulsion at the extremes of the child-centered and society-centered eras, have frequently failed to incorporate in their curriculum the valid changes those eras so dramatically offered, such as proper concern for interests of children and the needs of society if instructional programs are to be effective.

Yet the alert Catholic elementary schools of the United States have been profoundly influenced by the monumental three-volume work of the Commission on American Citizenship of the Catholic University of America entitled *Guiding Growth in Christian Social Living.* These volumes do represent concern for both the interests of children and the needs of society. They are discussed more fully later in this chapter.

THE COURSE OF STUDY

The principal instrument of the curriculum, after the teacher himself, is the course of study. It is a guide to teachers which defines the instructional job at a particular level or grade, or in a particular subject-matter area. Thus, for example, a school should have available a course of study for the primary or intermediate grades, for the fifth grade, or for high school English.

The development of suitable courses of study is the administrator's major instructional responsibility. The nature of the courses of study and the manner in which they are developed will to a large extent determine the effectiveness of a school system's curriculum.

The necessity for these guides for teachers arises from the fact that most schools form part of a school system. The term "system" implies an organization of curricular experiences offered children so that a similar approach is used and so that if children move from school to school, grade placement can be made. A course of study presupposes that there is scope and sequence in curriculum planning.

The existence of these guides for teachers clearly indicates that a school rejects the extreme concept that individual differences in ability among children are so great that curriculum can be developed in a given classroom only after exploring the interests and needs of particular children. Common interests and needs of children in a particular classroom, it is assumed, provide a general basis for organizing the class. A school must involve some measure of group instruction and some conviction that certain educational experiences are desirable for most members of any class.

Contents of a Course of Study

Prior to the introduction of the course of study, teachers "taught the textbook." One of the things which the progressive eras in American education made obvious is that the use of the textbook alone is a highly inadequate approach to teaching a subject. As the course-of-study approach to curriculum planning has become more general, so has the concept of what should be included in such a course of study come to include the following:

1. *Purposes of the school.* Courses of study for all levels or subject areas of a school should begin with a statement of the philosophy or purpose of the school involved. This common answer to the question of why the school exists provides the basis for the next section of the course.

2. *Particular contribution of the subject (or level or grade) in realizing the purpose of the school.* The curriculum of the school will be solidly based only as this question is answered: what is the role of this subject in realizing the distinctive purpose of the school?

3. *List of major understandings, skills, or attitudes around which instructional units are to be organized.* Since instruction today tends to be organized in major instructional units lasting anywhere from several days to several months, with understandings, attitudes, or skills as the overriding objectives or unitary forces of each, to outline major objectives in the light of the specific purpose of the course is the next step.

4. *Sample units.* The course of study should present several fully developed units to illustrate ways of achieving objectives. Thus desirable methodology is suggested, but not prescribed.

5. *Suggested instructional materials for each unit.* A good course of study suggests to the teacher a wealth of teaching materials which might be used effectively in realizing the objective of each unit. Appropriate references to sections of the textbooks can be made. Reference materials from supplementary books, library materials, current pamphlets, or brochures may be listed with the places where they may be obtained. Appropriate films, filmstrips, and recordings, together with their sources and cost, should be included. Thus the teacher is given rich resources to use in planning the year's instructional experiences for children.

6. *Suggested techniques for evaluation of learning.* Techniques for testing the results of teaching, sources of ready-made tests suitable for use, and other instruments for evaluating the effectiveness of a given unit or the course as a whole are suggested in the modern course of study.

DEVELOPING A COURSE OF STUDY

Actually, the value of a course of study to the instructional program of the school is determined in great measure by the manner in which it is developed. Frequently in the past an expert was hired to produce a really top-flight course of study. The result was then distributed to the schools and found its way to some shelf, unread and unused. Thus, if the course of study was an end in itself, the project was a success.

Today the common approach is to form a committee of teachers and to assign them to prepare a course of study. The result of many committee meetings in which many teachers participate may not be a course of study quite as fine as that developed by an expert, but it will have one great advantage over that produced by an expert. When it is completed and distributed to the schools for use, there will be a large number of teachers who already are familiar with its contents, who have some pride of ownership in the results, and who will be likely to start to use it. After all, a course of study is designed for use.

There are, of course, other advantages to having the course of study prepared by teachers. Teachers do have good ideas on how to make units work. In the course of many years, some of them have independently discovered valuable source material for use in units, source material of which other teachers are unaware. In the committee meetings, teachers learn from sharing ideas with each other at the same time as a course of study is being developed.

However, the development of the curriculum does not have to be an either-or proposition: produced either by an expert or by the teachers. There is a way of combining the advantages of both methods in the development of a course of study. A curriculum committee representative of the teachers and principals who will use the curriculum is appointed for the task. An expert, who might be a supervisor or an outside individual hired specifically to assist in the curriculum development, is assigned to the committee, not as its chairman or chief, but as a sort of secretary, consultant, or coordinator. His job is that of stimulating the thinking of committee members. This expert, drawing on his knowledge of the field, may suggest publications or research studies pertinent to proposals under discussion. Along the same lines, he may suggest ways in which similar problems were handled by committees in other systems. Thus this expert, through his minor position, leads the committee as far as possible in the direction where his expertness has led him. His effectiveness will be in direct proportion to the extent that he can convince committee members of the validity of his ideas through such techniques as discussion, stimulation, and pertinent reading. The resulting course of study may not be as excellent as the ideas of the expert, nor will it represent the mediocrity into which the teachers may have sunk. It will be somewhere in between, and its biggest asset is that it will probably be used.

The committee approach does, of course, involve a great deal of work on the part of the expert—much more than if he wrote the course himself. Long hours of work will precede the selection of committee members, and many more hours before each meeting will be spent in preparation of tentative statements, advance discussion with individual committee members, and persuasion to avoid undesirable directions.

Today, large school systems frequently mention with satisfaction that hundreds of teachers in a given year have been working on curriculum development programs. Their satisfaction is justified by the principle fundamental to the new field of group dynamics: the more people are involved in a project and feel some pride in its development, the more effective it is likely to be.

GUIDING GROWTH IN CHRISTIAN SOCIAL LIVING

In regard to both the purposes of Catholic elementary schools and the implementation of these purposes in courses of study and specially prepared textbooks, the three volumes of *Guiding Growth in Christian Social Living*[8] published by the Commission on American Citizenship of the Catholic University of America in 1944–1946 have had widespread national influence on Catholic elementary schools.

The elementary curriculum presented in these volumes takes its

[8] Sister Mary Joan and Sister Mary Nona, *Guiding Growth in Christian Social Living: A Curriculum for the Elementary School*, 3 vols., The Catholic University of America Press, Washington, 1944–1946.

origin from the response of the American bishops to the instruction of Pope Pius XI, contained in an apostolic letter addressed to them on September 21, 1938, to draw up for the people of the United States a constructive social program of education based on Christian principles. For this purpose the Commission on American Citizenship of the Catholic University of America was organized. Under the auspices of the commission were developed and presented three significant contributions to the curriculum of Catholic elementary schools. The first was a statement of Christian principles to guide curriculum development in Catholic schools, entitled *Better Men for Better Times*;[9] the second was the elementary curriculum itself, *Guiding Growth in Christian Social Living*; and the third was a series of textbooks specifically designed to help implement these curricular provisions, the *Faith and Freedom Literary Readers*.[10]

The three volumes of the curriculum itself are devoted respectively to grades 1, 2, and 3; grades 4, 5, and 6; and grades 7 and 8. They are marked by a uniform statement of basic purposes, logically extended to specific objectives and further developed to outline general unit content. Suggested activities, teaching materials, and evaluative techniques are included, as are unit outlines and statements on the interrelationship of curricular and extracurricular activities.

While highly organized so as to indicate the contribution of major subject areas to the growth of children in social living, the curriculum was in no way intended to be prescriptive. Rather was it offered to the Catholic elementary schools of the country for adaptation to their needs. The authors of the volumes state:[11]

> It is suggestive, flexible, and broad enough for the construction of more detailed courses of study from its general plan. It should be helpful to diocesan educators in the building of their own curricula and separate courses of study in subject-matter areas. The teacher training institutions of dioceses and religious congregations will find it helpful for giving young teachers a broad yet compre-

[9] Commission on American Citizenship of the Catholic University of America, *Better Men for Better Times*, The Catholic University of America Press, Washington, 1943.

[10] *Faith and Freedom Literary Readers*, published for The Catholic University of America Press by Ginn and Company, Boston, 1942–1949.

[11] Sister Mary Joan and Sister Mary Nona, *op. cit.*, Preface.

hensive view of the elementary school program. While the curriculum is offered principally to the teachers in our schools, it may be helpful also to pastors, parents, recreational directors, and others who share responsibility for the guidance of children.

That the hopes of the commission and the authors have been realized in significant measure is indicated by references to the curriculum in the administrative handbooks of a number of diocesan school systems, of which the following excerpt is typical:[12]

The Courses of Study constructed for the elementary schools of the Diocese are based on the curriculum content of the three volumes entitled GUIDING GROWTH IN CHRISTIAN SOCIAL LIVING. Every school is expected to possess these volumes in its professional library. All teachers, both religious and lay, are urged to familiarize themselves with the philosophy and objectives contained therein.

SOME CURRICULUM PROBLEMS—THINKING THEM THROUGH

The whole area of curriculum, including the purpose of the school, the role of a given subject-matter area in the school program, and the selection of appropriate methodology, needs careful thinking through by school staffs if sound answers to the problems involved are to be forthcoming and if children are to be educated according to a consistent, defensible educational plan.

Influencing events and writings of the sixties have been the orbiting of Russian sputniks; the writings or speeches of Arthur E. Bestor, Jr., Admiral Hyman Rickover, Mortimer Smith, Rudolph Flesch, Paul Woodring, and James Conant, among many; and the flood of articles published in popular magazines with national circulation or in influential newspapers, such as the series of articles by John Chamberlain in *The Wall Street Journal* early in 1960, subsequently reprinted under the title *Problems in Education: Where Do We Go from Here?* All these, rightly or wrongly, have had at least one result; more than ever before the American people are intensely

[12] *Handbook of Regulations for the Elementary and Secondary Schools of the Diocese of Syracuse,* Diocese of Syracuse, Office of the Superintendent of Schools, Syracuse, 1957, p. 29.

interested in, and are vigorously questioning, the instructional policies of their schools.

The critical review of American education, which seems certain to continue through the 1960s, will be led either by professional school administrators and their staffs along reasonable, pedagogically sound paths, or by popular pressures which will impel American education and educators along paths which, tragically, will bypass all the professional knowledge that years of research and practice have developed. In the professional leadership needed as American education continues to be reevaluated, however, there is little room for the shallow, anti-intellectual approach characteristic of so many educational reformers of the recent past; nor is there much room for the uncritical return to a remote past for methods and procedures which were discarded for the good reason that something was wrong with them!

Because intelligent analysis and consistent response to basic instructional questions are so important, answers to some provocative instructional questions are sketched in the following paragraphs more as illustrations and stimuli to the thinking of the administrator than as definitive answers.

Illustration A: Social Studies in Catholic Schools

Answering the question of what ought to be the role of the social studies in Catholic schools involves answering three questions in order.

1. *Why Catholic schools?* The answer is a twofold one: Catholic schools share with the family, church, civil society, and all community educative agencies in the total education of the child—morally, intellectually, and physically—so that he may save his immortal soul. While sharing in the total job of education, the schools accept specific and unique responsibility for the intellectual development of the child. This intellectual development encompasses the major areas of knowledge—religious knowledge, language arts, social studies, natural science—and must stress the major intellectual tools of sound thinking habits, reading, writing, and arithmetic.

Thus the Catholic school shares in an important way in developing a good practicing Catholic, but the school is specifically responsible for the child's intellectual development, giving proper emphasis to religious knowledge.

2. *Why social studies?* Social studies, like religion, language arts, and natural sciences, is a major area of knowledge which has a fundamental role to play in the intellectual development of the child. As an area of knowledge it is concerned primarily with understanding the relationships between man and his physical and social environments. Thus social studies includes geography, political science, sociology, and economics: geography, the relationship between man and his natural environment; political science, between man and governmental organizations; sociology, between man and fellow man in nongovernmental societies; and economics, between man and fellow man in the production, distribution, and consumption of worldly goods. The study of each of these subdivisions of the social studies—man and his environment, man and government, man and his societies, and man and his material needs—demands a study of man's past experiences which have influenced his present and give some clues to his future. This study is history. Materials from all of these disciplines—geography, history, political science, economics, and sociology—make up the social studies.

3. *Why Catholic social studies?* Social studies is an important area of knowledge in all schools, Catholic and public. What is the difference? The facts of geography, history, political science, sociology, and economics are the same wherever social studies is taught. It is in the all-important frame of reference that the chief difference is found. Catholic social studies begin and end in God—the creator and sustainer of all man's political, social, and economic activities, past, present, and future. A social studies program which fails to keep within the focus of religious knowledge is not Catholic social studies. A program which fails to suggest social studies activities related to Christian social principles is not Catholic social studies. A program which ignores the Church's role in the community, local or world, is not Catholic social studies.

ILLUSTRATION B: METHODOLOGY IN SOCIAL STUDIES

Obviously, there is no single method to be used in teaching social studies. Yet methodology should bear a relationship to the purposes of a given subject area. Are these objectives chiefly, though not exclusively, to be realized by a methodology appropriate for learning facts, by a methodogoly appropriate for developing understandings, or a methodology appropriate for developing appreciation?

If, as indicated in the paragraphs above, social studies has as its primary contribution the development of understanding, then it has not been taught adequately unless understanding is developed. Therefore, the principal methodology for teaching social studies must promote student thinking, since without thinking there can be no understanding. Insight must be fostered; patterns and configurations must be perceived. Intellectual abstraction and reflective thinking in problem situations are essential. No amount of drill or no amount of attitude development can be expected to realize the unique contribution of social studies to the education of a man, though these methods may contribute to important but subordinate goals of social-studies instruction—to knowing facts or to liking the subject.

ILLUSTRATION C: METHODOLOGY IN TEACHING LITERATURE

If the author's conception of the purpose of teaching literature is valid, there is probably no area in which teachers are generally less successful. Literature is taught to develop in students a responsiveness to an author's conception of some phase of life. As an artist, the author arranges his words in an art form, using imaginative and emotional appeal to convey his concepts.

The student in the literature class needs increasing understanding of the art form: the poem, the short story, the essay, or the novel; he must mature in his understanding of the imagery and emotional appeal of the artist; he must understand the artist's thoughts. So understanding is important and the methodology leading to reflective thinking, as in the social studies, is important.

But the essential element of appreciation is not understanding alone; therefore, the principal methodology is not the same as that for the social studies. The distinguishing element of appreciation is the favorable response of the student. The student must come to like the literary selection. He must develop a favorable emotional attitude towards it. Literature—along with the other fine arts in the school curriculum, music and art—must first of all be liked by the students.

Attitudes have been described as understandings touched by feelings, pleasant or unpleasant. What then is the appropriate methodology for developing favorable attitudes? This is a more difficult question than how skills or even understandings are developed, or how facts are taught. Less is known about it. These things we do know, however: *first,* if the teacher does not try to develop a favorable emotional response, it will not come; *second,* if the teacher merely teaches to develop knowledge about literature, the emotional response does not ordinarily come; *third,* favorable emotional attitudes are frequently caught, not taught, so the teacher of literature must himself engender favorable student emotions by his own likable personality and his own enthusiasm for the literature he is teaching; *fourth,* the teacher must select literary materials which can be liked by students in his classes; and *fifth,* he must carefully nurture the development of the student's understanding of literature in such a way that emphasis on knowledge does not outstrip the student's capacity to like it.

If at the end of a literature unit, most pupils do not like the poems or short stories or novels or essays taught, the teaching has failed, for a favorable emotional attitude is a *sine qua non* among the results of the teaching of any fine art. With it, there can be successful teaching; without it, there can be no success.

ILLUSTRATION D: FORMAL GRAMMAR

A recurring question in curriculum development is, how much should formal grammar be emphasized in schools? Since formal grammar is merely a tool in achieving correct written and oral expression in English, the more basic questions seem to be, what is correct expression? And how is it developed?

Correct Expression. By aiming at an unrealistically high level of correct expression, the school can so scatter its efforts that nothing substantial may be accomplished. A reasonable standard of correctness, one attainable by most youth during their years in school, seems more profitable in the long run. Such a standard involves aiming at the colloquial level of correctness, that which is considered correct among educated persons in informal conversation. The adoption of such a realistic goal concentrates attention on fundamentals: eliminating illiterate mistakes (not worrying about split infinitives or distinctions between shall and will); punctuating the kinds of thoughts the students are likely to express (not drilling on identifying compound-complex sentences); eliminating run-ons or fragments pawned off as sentences (not teaching elliptical sentences); or stressing proper reference of "-ing" words (not drilling on participles or distinguishing between participles and gerunds). A reasonable standard of correctness will help remove the typical student's impression that speaking or writing correctly is so impossibly complicated that he is bound to make mistakes and that he might as well go ahead and make them!

Developing Correct Expression. Correct expression consists in habits—a totality of individual habitual expressions. If there is anything in the field of education which is known for certain, it is how habitual responses are formed. Indisputably, habitual responses are the result principally of repetition or drill—practice on the response desired. While understanding has some role to play in habit formation, as does favorable student attitude, the thorough understanding of the science of grammar, as manifested by the complicated techniques of sentence diagraming, is hardly the appropriate technique for habit formation.

Drill only on the responses desired; overlearn; use understanding only as it contributes directly to the desired effect; drill in as pleasant a manner as possible. These are among the things certainly known about forming habitual responses.

Where does this leave formal grammar? For most classes in elementary school or high school, it is left with only those elements which are directly useful in developing the desired habits. It is left with only the relatively few terms essential to intelligent and orderly discussion of correctness in expression.

Application to Correct Punctuation. As usually taught and as most texts still are written, punctuation is needlessly difficult, replete with complex terminology and statements more exact than legal documents, with exceptions more complicated than the original rule, and so involved that all but English teachers fear to venture. Almost endless drill is necessary for the comprehension of such terms as "appositive," "parenthetical," "phrase," and "clause." The distinction between restrictive and nonrestrictive clauses is just too profound, perhaps, for most of the high school population of today.

After all the drill needed to understand the rule, more is required to memorize it, while still more is necessary properly to apply it. Yet all that is needed is this simple generalization: words thrown in a sentence—that is, not needed for the sense—are separated from the rest of the sentence by commas. After this is understood, there remains only practice until a habit is formed.

Another simple, time-saving concept is that long introductory remarks are followed by commas. This eliminates the need for the familiar old rules covering the use of the comma after introductory subordinate clauses (except noun clauses used as the subject and object of sentences), after long introductory participial phrases, and after long introductory prepositional constructions. This concept, furthermore, does not postulate tedious and difficult drill on the distinction between clauses and phrases; subordinate and principal clauses; noun, adjective, and adverbial clauses; or participial and prepositional constructions.

The writer's examination of the field of punctuation, with a view to securing the smallest and simplest group of concepts satisfying the needs of the ordinary high school student in his written expression, resulted in the following principles of punctuation.

Do not use a punctuation mark unless for one of the following reasons:

1. Long introductory remarks are followed by commas.

2. Before a conjunction in compound sentences, commas are used.

3. Items in series are separated from one another by commas.

4. Words thrown in are separated from the rest of the sentence by commas.

5. Names of persons addressed are separated from the rest of the sentence by commas.

6. Words omitted in a sentence are replaced by a comma.

7. A person's quoted words are separated from the rest of the sentence by commas and quotation marks.

8. An apostrophe is used to show possession or contraction.

9. When there is no conjunction in compound sentences, a semicolon is used.

10. A colon is used to show that a long list or something bulky is to follow.

It should be noted that the only remnants of the complicated terminology formerly involved in punctuation are "compound sentence" and "conjunction," neither of them particularly difficult to comprehend.

Once the field of punctuation has been reduced to minimum essentials, it is easily presented psychologically. An overview of the whole field can be given in half an hour. No longer will punctuation seem to the average high school student to be discouragingly complex and disorganized; it is a limited, definite, and unified body of material which he can master as an organized whole. Mastery then comes with practice.

CONTROVERSIAL ISSUES IN THE CURRICULUM

Only a small part of the total instructional program of a school involves teaching about so-called controversial issues. Most of this is confined to the high school program. Yet from the administrative viewpoint, there is always the possibility of an explosion rocking the school and community over a teacher's handling of some controversial issue in the classroom. Since the force of such an explosion has been known to blow both teachers and administrators right out of their jobs, advance consideration of the problem should result in the adoption of a system-wide policy regarding handling controversial issues in a school. The policy adopted must be based in sound curricular principles and be so defensible that it can be used as a shield for the teacher or administrator who conforms to it; yet it must not be so loose as to shield the teacher who may abuse his relationship to his students by propagandizing his own prejudices.

An issue may be defined as controversial when some of the possible solutions to it run counter to the emotional attitudes of a section of the public from which the school draws its support. If that section of the public belongs to an active propaganda organization, the danger is obviously greater. Questions involving race relations meet this definition of controversial issues in many parts of the country; issues involved in the politics of electioneering are also controversial; in some areas and at varying times since its foundation, the United Nations has been a controversial issue; so have some of the attempts to rout Communists from government, radio, or television. In a public school, issues bearing on the religious beliefs of the children are always ready to burst forth.

A commonly held fallacy, particularly among non-Catholics, is that controversial issues are a problem only to public school personnel—that there are no controversial issues among Catholics. Actually the only difference is that religious principles and certain primary philosophical principles are eliminated from controversy in Catholic schools. Otherwise, the handling of other controversial issues is as delicate a matter as in public schools.

Some provisions suggested for a policy regarding controversial issues in the school curriculum are:

1. Where the study of a controversial issue follows naturally from curricular activity or is a specific part of a course of study, it should be studied as a matter of educational policy.

2. The study of such an issue should be handled as a systematic problem-solving exercise.

3. The role of the teacher is not to indoctrinate, but to guide the student through the usual problem-solving activities: defining the problem, exploring what is already known, formulating a hypothesis, collecting and organizing new information, evaluating the information, drawing valid conclusions from the data, and testing hypotheses.

When such provisions as these are met by a reasonably prudent teacher, controversial issues are generally handled without flare-up, to the obvious educational profit of the students. Should there be controversy, the teacher must have firm administrative backing or the freedom of children to learn is imperiled. Conversely, no backing can be expected by the teacher who violates the curriculum policy on handling controversial issues.

Questions for Discussion or Investigation

1. How do you think future educational historians will characterize the present era as they trace the development of the curriculum of American schools. Why?

2. The movement for life-adjustment education which was launched in the post-World War II years came to a sudden halt. Why were the years immediately after the war propitious for the launching? What factors brought the movement rather abruptly to a halt?

3. Critically evaluate the curricular implications of a book listed under *Readings and References* by one of the following authors: Aikin, Conant, Joan, Smith, Ward, Woodring.

4. In the light of your conception of the purpose of schools, state with precision the contribution to that purpose, if any, which you expect from behind-the-wheel driver education, physical education, arithmetic, or music.

5. Compare the role of the course of study with that of the textbook in instruction.

6. Cite specific illustrations to show that philosophy has curricular implications.

7. What are some of the controversial issues which come up in teaching a subject in high school or a grade in elementary school?

Readings and References

Aikin, W. M.: *The Story of the Eight Year Study,* Harper & Brothers, New York, 1942.

American School Curriculum, Thirty-first Yearbook of the American Association of School Administrators, Washington, 1953.

Bayles, Ernest E.: "Present Status of Educational Theory in the United States," *School and Society,* vol. 87, no. 2145, pp. 5–8, Jan. 17, 1959.

Burton, William H., and others: *Education for Effective Thinking,* Appleton-Century-Crofts, Inc., New York, 1960.

Chamberlain, John: *Problems in Education: Where Do We Go from Here?* A bound collection of articles previously published in *The Wall Street Journal,* New York, 1960.

Commission on American Citizenship of the Catholic University of America: *Better Men for Better Times,* The Catholic University of America Press, Washington, 1943.

Conant, James B.: *The American High School Today,* McGraw-Hill Book Company, Inc., New York, 1959.

Department of Education, The Catholic University of America: *Criteria for Evaluation of the Catholic Elementary Schools,* 2d rev. ed., The Catholic University of America Press, Washington, 1949.

Fitzgerald, J. A., and P. G. Fitzgerald: *Methods and Curricula in Elementary Education,* The Bruce Publishing Company, Milwaukee, 1955.

Flaherty, James L.: *A Study of the Effect of Operational Factors on Secondary School Instruction,* The Catholic University of America Press, Washington, 1952.

Gwynn, J. Minor: *Curriculum Principles and Social Trends,* 3d ed., The Macmillan Company, New York, 1960.

Jameson, Marshall C., and William V. Hicks: *Elementary School Curriculum,* American Book Company, New York, 1960.

Joan, Sister Mary, and Sister Mary Nona (eds.): *Guiding Growth in Chris-*

tian Social Living, 3 vols., The Catholic University of America Press, Washington, 1944–1946.

Kaiser, Sister Laurina: *Concept and Function of the Catholic Elementary School,* The Catholic University of America Press, Washington, 1953.

Leonard, J. Paul: *Developing the Secondary School Curriculum,* rev. ed., Holt, Rinehart and Winston, Inc., New York, 1953.

McManus, William E.: "Building the Curriculum," *National Catholic Educational Association Bulletin,* vol. 45, no. 3, pp. 17–28, February, 1949.

Nona, Sister Mary: *Philosophy of the Curriculum of the Catholic Elementary School,* The Catholic University of America Press, Washington, 1954.

O'Connell, Laurence J.: *Are Catholic Schools Progressive?* B. Herder Book Company, St. Louis, 1946.

Pritzkau, Philo T.: *Dynamics of Curriculum Improvement,* Prentice-Hall, Inc., Englewood Cliffs, N.J., 1959.

Rucker, W. Ray: *Curriculum Development in the Elementary School,* Harper & Brothers, New York, 1960.

Smith, Mortimer: *And Madly Teach,* Henry Regnery Company, Chicago, 1949.

Spiers, Edward: *The Central Catholic High School,* The Catholic University of America Press, Washington, 1951.

Ward, Leo R.: *New Life in Catholic Schools,* B. Herder Book Company, St. Louis, 1958.

Woodring, Paul: *A Fourth of a Nation,* McGraw-Hill Book Company, Inc., New York, 1957.

————: *Let's Talk Sense about Our Schools,* McGraw-Hill Book Company, Inc., 1953.

8 . Instruction:

Supervision

Defined broadly as the improvement of instruction, supervision, always an important part of the instructional function of the school administrator, becomes increasingly important when the supply of fully trained teachers is inadequate to meet the demands of swiftly growing schools.

The broad view of school supervision as the improvement of instruction just about makes it coextensive with the whole instructional job, including curriculum development, system-wide appraisal services, and counseling of the usual child. However, these three specific aspects of the total instructional activity are generally treated apart from supervision itself. This chapter, therefore, is concerned with the nature of supervisory activity, which is pertinent to the whole instructional responsibility of the administrator, and with supervisory techniques other than those specific to curriculum development, appraisal, and counseling.

It should be remembered that supervisory responsibility in a school system, if that system is large enough, is usually shared by persons called supervisors and principals; of course in a small

160

system, one person may be responsible not only for all supervisory activity but for all other administrative functions as well.

THE NATURE OF SUPERVISORY ACTIVITY

Much has been written about authoritative supervision and democratic supervision, the net result of which is to confuse the basic issue with "color" words involving strong emotional reactions. The fundamental concern of the administrator is actually with effective supervision.

The supervisor is primarily concerned with changing persons, whether he starts with authority to order changes or with no authority at all. His task is to change people so that the person changed does not merely grudgingly conform on the surface when he feels himself under observation, but so that he changes his practices out of a developed intellectual conviction that a new course of action is a better one. Thus the object of the supervisor in dealing with teachers is to bring about changes in a teacher, just as the teacher's success or failure depends upon the changes effected in children. While there are obvious differences between the role of the teacher with children and that of the supervisor with teachers, there are similarities. Both must bring about changes in knowledge, attitude, or skills. The supervisor's task is generally the more difficult, however, since he is working against the fixed opinions, emotional attitudes, and behavior patterns of adults.

No one is an expert on how one adult can change another. Individuals are so complex and react so differently that no detailed prescriptions for effective supervisory activity can be made. Experience has taught us certain general principles by which supervisory activity must be carried on if it is to succeed.

1. *The supervisor helps.* This means that the success or failure of the supervisor in discharging his responsibilities will rest primarily on how helpful he is to the teacher. The helpful person has certain personality characteristics; not among these is an authoritarian manner in ordering the teacher to do one thing or another. Rather, the supervisor, diagnosing a teacher's problem, offers help. If this is done properly and the help is useful, most teachers will welcome it.

2. *The supervisor persuades.* This means that the success or failure of the supervisor in changing the actions of the teacher will depend upon how successfully, through conversation and persuasion, he can put across the ideas he proposes. The supervisor who persuades may well cause the teacher to change because he has realized the importance of making that change. On the other hand, the supervisor who orders instead of persuades might get grudging acceptance, but only while the supervisor is in the immediate area.

3. *The supervisor knows.* This means that a supervisor ought to be an expert in a wider sense than is meant in describing an expert as a "person from out of town." The supervisor should know well the schools, the purposes of schools, the curricular trends, and the specific devices for helping the teacher.

4. *The supervisor leads.* This is in contrast to driving. It is from the knowledge of the supervisor, which ought to be in advance of that of most teachers, that suggestions come which may well result in the development of a better teacher. The process is the same as that by which the supervisor or the expert leads in curriculum development. The supervisor may never get the exact results desired, but he leads and causes change in the right direction.

5. *The supervisor is liked.* There is nothing in the nature of being a supervisor which should contribute to feelings of resentment or general dislike of the supervisor by the teacher. There is no reason why a supervisor with an adequate personality and a certain amount of intelligence and acuity in dealing with human beings should not be thought of as a likable, friendly, helpful person. If the general impression is anything else, it is time for a change of supervisors, since the supervisory job will not be done adequately.

The supervisory job, therefore, involves the concepts of helping, persuading, knowing as an expert knows, leading, and being well liked.

SUPERVISORY TECHNIQUES

Whatever the titles of staff members who have responsibility for the improvement of teaching performance, a range of supervisory techniques is available for carrying out this function. Basic to the supervisor's work are the observation of the teacher at work and the individual conference which follows. In addition, certain techniques are available to the supervisor for use with teachers, individually or in groups.

THE SUPERVISORY OBSERVATION AND CONFERENCE

Each supervisor, in accordance with his own personality, will develop his own art of observing teachers at work and conducting a follow-up conference. Accordingly, it is not possible to advance any one formula which will be effective for all. Certain do's and don't's can be stated with some absoluteness, however.

Regarding the observation of teaching, it is realized that some measure of artificiality is introduced by the mere presence of an adult other than the teacher in the classroom. However, frequent supervisory visits tend to make their occurrence more of a normal event. The principal who unobtrusively drops in on classes regularly, even daily in smaller schools, without any formal recognition of his presence by pupils or teachers prepares the way for his own more extended supervisory visits, as well as for the observations of the outside supervisor. Casual acceptance of the comings and goings of the principal or assistant principal is essential if the observation of instruction is to be reasonably valid. Clearly, the supervisor must remain with one teacher long enough to get a true picture of the teaching situation. Any actual note taking by the supervisor while in the classroom will probably interfere with the normalcy of the teacher's performance. In some cases it will petrify the teacher, even a good teacher.

To date, mechanical aids such as recording machines and two-way communication sets have usually proved ineffective, except for such limited uses as with the teacher whose voice or presentation is lifeless. Closed-circuit television with a receiver in the principal's office, suggested as a method of observing teaching, might have some possibilities; although the attitude of the professional teacher to "spying" on her work, even if the installation were feasible economically, would probably limit its usefulness, because the supervisor must be concerned first of all with establishing proper rapport with the teacher to be helped.

The supervisor who comes from a central office will need to prepare for the observation by reviewing personnel records of the teachers to be observed. The teacher's background, reports of earlier observations indicating strengths and weaknesses, and suggestions made should be studied in advance.

Immediately after the observation, the supervisor should make his notes on the strengths and weaknesses of the teacher with a view to an individual conference later in the day. Specific suggestions for helping the teacher should be prepared. The success of the conference itself will depend on the success of the supervisor in selling his ideas in such a way that will make them accepted voluntarily by the teacher. Pleasant conversation, establishing rapport, and discussing good features before concentrating on aspects which should be improved comprise a pattern many supervisors follow in the conference. The nondirective techniques of the professional counselor are highly successful if used by the skilled supervisor.

INDIVIDUAL TECHNIQUES

The supervisor has available a group of techniques from which to select in helping the teacher individually. Among them are the following:

Interschool Visitation. Some administrative provision for days which a teacher may use for interschool visitation makes possible one of the most valuable techniques the supervisor can use. In a public school system where this provision is in effect, the board of education hires a substitute to replace the teacher while he visits other schools and classes one or two days a year. While this is not often possible in parochial school systems, sometimes each school is permitted to close for this purpose one or two days during the year; for if visitation results in better teaching, it is worth the loss of the days.

To be effective, teacher visitation ought to be suggested by the supervisor with care for the weak points of the teacher who is visiting and the strong points of the one visited. For example, if a teacher has difficulty in motivating a tenth-grade English class on ballads, he may be encouraged to visit a teacher who is markedly successful in this regard.

The simple fact that there is a policy providing for intervisitation will not automatically give maximum results. Caution is needed lest teachers use their visitation days to augment vacation trips out of town while spending only a minimum of time actually visiting classes. Where the visit is not being made by a specific teacher for a specific purpose, it ought to be made in a variety of schools over a period of years. Thus a parochial school teacher who occasionally visits a public school and the public school teacher who occasionally visits a parochial school may each benefit from their observations.

Professional Reading. Another technique available to the supervisor is to stimulate the professional reading of the teacher along desirable lines. Most of the problems faced by teachers are not unique, and the supervisor should know where help can be found in the literature of the field. By suggesting the right article or the right book, the supervisor might well start a teacher toward the solution of some of his problems.

University Courses. Again, the expert knowledge of the supervisor of the availability of an appropriate university course or workshop may be helpful to a teacher with a weakness in a particular area of work. The teacher with classroom problems centering around remedial reading problems, for example, may find answers in a good university course or clinic. Science, mathematics, and modern language teachers are increasingly finding government-sponsored institutes available to assist them in up-dating their knowledge and techniques, sometimes at no cost to themselves and sometimes with expenses more than defrayed.

Teacher Self-evaluation. Another technique available to the supervisor is the use of teacher self-evaluation procedures purely as a basis for discussion of the teacher's strong and weak characteristics and without regard to such administrative concerns as retention, promotion, or dismissal. Strictly for their own self-improvement, the teachers of a school system may draw up their own self-evaluation scale emphasizing those characteristics considered essential in light of the system's statement of purpose. The benefits to those participating in formulating such a scale may more than justify the undertaking.

GROUP TECHNIQUES

Some supervisory activity is appropriately carried on with groups of teachers through in-service educational programs. Service on curriculum committees, as previously discussed, on textbook committees, or on committees working on other aspects of the conduct of schools all are likely to lead to improved teaching performance.

Teacher Institute and Meetings. The teacher institute, prior to the opening of the school year, is widely used to set an instructional emphasis for the school year. Frequently, such institutes are two- or three-day workshops at which attendance is compulsory, with the teachers being paid as though they were teaching. In large systems where two to three thousand teachers may be in attendance, such an institute sometimes takes on the characteristics of a national professional convention with its general sessions, discussion groups, and keynote speech, as well as its discussion leaders, resource persons, and recorders.

Meetings of the faculty of an individual school or meetings of teachers of certain grades or subject areas, if handled well, may also provide the supervisor with a vehicle for stimulating better teaching performance.

Demonstration teaching by the supervisor or one of the key teachers at such meetings still has possibilities, although current films on teaching problems and methods may prove even more useful and effective. Either is a modern improvement on Henry Barnard's troupe of one teacher and twelve children which traveled Connecticut in the early 1800s to show teachers how to teach.

Professional Library. The professional library for teachers provides another device for teacher improvement. A school system will need to maintain a library of textbooks, supplementary books, and courses of study developed in other schools for the use of those interested in these avenues to improved instruction. In individual schools, the principal may maintain in his office or in teacher lounges current professional periodicals and books, the use of which he may consciously stimulate, even if only by making them available.

Salary and Certification Requirements. Group supervisory techniques may be embodied both in the salary policies of school systems and in the certification requirements of states. Both may require teachers to return to university study periodically to qualify either for salary increments or for higher levels of certification.

This "refresher approach" is spreading to professions other than teaching. It is further illustrated by forward-looking policies on leaves of absence, such as the sabbatical leave provisions common to college and university supervisory programs.

Supervisory Bulletins. Under a variety of titles such as "Better Teaching," "Improved Teaching," "News Notes for Teachers," or "Successful Practices," school systems publish periodicals designed to help the teacher in the performance of his responsibilities. Such bulletins, mimeographed or printed, provide a clearing house for instructional information within a system. Curriculum developments are reported; unusual but promising practices are reported; and new sources of instructional materials are described as they are uncovered.

SUPERVISION IN CATHOLIC SCHOOLS

While most of the above observations on the theory and techniques of supervision are goals equally appropriate to public and Catholic education, it is fair to say that little resembling the typical organization for the improvement of teaching in the large public school system exists in the typical diocesan school system. Neither a comparable number of supervisors, nor equal clarity of organizational responsibility, nor the same degree of integration of supervisors within the administrative framework is generally found.

The explanation for the differences grows out of a different basic organizational structure historically characteristic of diocesan school systems. The pastor, responsible rather completely for his parish school, traditionally made arrangements with the superior of a religious order to supply the principal and teachers for his school from the members of the order. The order appointed the principal and assigned teachers to the school. It was completely responsible for their training and supplied community supervision both for the religious development of the individuals assigned and for their professional improvement. The order may have had one, several, or many schools within any particular diocese.

What exists today ordinarily represents an intermediate stage between this complete supervisory responsibility of an order for schools staffed by its members and the much more highly integrated diocesan organization of supervisors responsible to, and controlled by, the chief executive of the school system. The progress made along the line of development from the traditional to the theoretically desirable supervisory organization in any given diocese is the result of a series of compromises forced by the conflict between the traditional and the problems of finances; of the necessity for additional lay teachers; and of the urgency of system-wide curriculum planning, course-of-study development, testing, and other instructional concerns which transcend the individual parish lines. At the high school level, diocesan-wide supervision of teaching has been markedly less frequent than at the elementary school level.

Two facts have greatly impeded the full development of desirable supervisory activity in Catholic schools: shortage of money and shortage of teachers. As Catholic parents have struggled to give adequate support to their parish schools, money has but rarely been made available for adequate administrative overhead, including diocesan supervisory staff and the secretarial assistance needed to free principals for more supervisory functions. Further impeding supervision is the fact that securing teachers for the ever-increasing number of classrooms is so basic a task that the promotion of teachers to supervisory activities seems considerably less urgent; the same relative lack of urgency has hampered the appointment of nonteaching principals, positions essential to strong supervisory programs.

Three general patterns of diocesan organization for supervision can be found throughout the country: the program which depends completely on supervision from religious communities staffing the schools; the program which depends on diocesan supervisors; and the program which combines these two.

USING COMMUNITY SUPERVISORS

Some dioceses depend exclusively on supervisors appointed by a religious order of sisters to handle both diocesan and community supervision in the schools staffed by the given religious order. Under such circumstances, the superintendent is not in a position to control who will be assigned or for how long. The primary loyalty of the community supervisor is normally toward the religious order to which she belongs, not to the diocesan program. Yet diocesan superintendents depending on community supervisors are developing techniques for involving them more and more in the diocesan educational program. The use of community supervisors exclusively, but combined with increasing involvement with the superintendent and his staff, is the pattern in operation in the Archdiocese of New York. Financing supervision is left to the various religious superiors. Supervisory duties suggested are: to visit every school staffed by members of the community at least once a school year; to forward to the superintendent a complete report of the visitation within ten days on a form provided by the superintendent's office; to visit each class, inspect written work, examine the pupils orally or by written tests, and examine student records and teacher lesson plans; to make certain that diocesan policies are being observed; to confer with the whole faculty as a group; and to confer, on request, with the superintendent on administrative matters, curricular developments, and related problems.

The general status of the supervisor is described in the New York *Administrative Manual for the Elementary Schools* as follows:[1]

> The supervisor is the person appointed by his religious superior to act as the liaison between the community and the schools on the one hand, and the schools and the Superintendent's Office on the other. He is the master-teacher who visits the schools, assists the classroom teachers in their work and interprets to the members of the school staffs new projects as they evolve. In addition, he works in cooperation with the Superintendent of Schools advising him on new programs and in turn helps to interpret these programs to the schools.

Using Diocesan Supervisors

Other superintendents employ supervisors specifically to carry forward the instructional program within the diocese. While arrangements to employ a given sister are usually made with a mother superior, who still controls the assignment and its length, the diocesan supervisor is, as it were, detached from community responsibilities in the performance of her job. She may supervise some schools

[1] *Administrative Manual for the Elementary Schools,* Archdiocese of New York, Superintendent of Schools, New York, 1956, pp. 30–31.

staffed by her own order and some staffed by other orders; there would, perhaps, be advantages if she supervised no schools staffed by her own order. In any case, other individuals carry on the tasks of general community supervisors, including all matters of the religious development of the individual sister, priest, or brother.

Under this system, religious teachers in a Catholic school are the recipients of supervisory activity both from the school system in which they teach and from the religious order which controls their assignment, their training, and their promotion (within standards set by local school administrators). For this reason a clear conception of the responsibilities of each set of supervisors must be formulated if the danger of subjecting the individual teacher to divergent professional influences is to be minimized. A division of responsibility generally occurs along these lines:

1. To the community supervisor belongs the responsibility for developing a good professional teacher regardless of the school system to which he or she may be assigned.

2. To the diocesan supervisor belongs the responsibility for developing a teacher who carries on well the instructional policies of the school system.

Clearly on occasion a fine line of distinction may be involved. That this theoretical division has worked out well in many dioceses is owing to two factors: the genuine cooperative activity of all concerned in a task for which their lives are given and the relatively underdeveloped status of many diocesan supervisory programs. As the second changes, some strain may be placed on the first.

Using Both

A combination of the two basic patterns for diocesan administration was found by Ward in some dioceses, though relatively few. In these systems, diocesan supervisors were employed and their activities paid for by the diocese. Yet in diocesan planning, community supervisors with responsibilities within the diocese are involved through formal meetings which seek a meeting of the minds that will result in the diocesan program becoming the program also of the community supervisors. The dioceses attempting this mixture of the two basic patterns report an enthusiasm for the constructive results achieved.[2]

GENERAL STATUS OF DIOCESAN SUPERVISION

In dioceses which have made substantial strides toward effective supervision of teaching, the following four characteristics, some of them indicating problems for solution, are outlined in Ward's study:[3]

1. Supervisors are charged "to feel out" the teachers' problems and bring them into the superintendent for conference and finally for remedy through some process.

2. Superintendent's program depends greatly upon the major religious superiors' choice of supervisor. In the event that the supervisor is to be diocesan, the superintendent acts to get the "right" person for the job, although in most cases, he is still unable to secure such appointments with absolute surety. Practice commonly found is a rotation plan by which the teaching communities most active in the diocese appoint a supervisor to serve the diocese in that capacity for three or five years, relinquishing the work at the end of that time to another community.

3. Because the rotating plan of supervisory staffing telescopes the supervisor's efforts into the year or two assigned, superintendents tend to plan within that span of time, too. However, since not all the personnel is changed simultaneously, they must frequently accommodate their program to a new supervisor who must, of course, be oriented to her functions too.

4. Supervisory-centered programs tend to be remedial working upon the results of the diocesan testing program as the primary and fundamental ingredient of next year's supervisory program for the schools. Learning or teaching poorly accomplished this year becomes the focal point of the supervisory plan next year.

SUPERVISION IN PRIVATE CATHOLIC SCHOOLS

As indicated in Chapter 3, along with diocesan elementary and secondary schools, there exists in the Catholic school enterprise in the United States an extensive system of private schools, mainly high

[2] Sister M. Ruth Albert Ward, *Patterns of Administration in Diocesan School Systems,* The Catholic University of America Press, Washington, 1957, p. 94.
[3] *Ibid.,* p. 100.

schools. Only 4.6 per cent of the Catholic elementary schools of the country are private; but 35 per cent of the high schools, enrolling 38 per cent of the youth in Catholic high schools, are private. These schools are appropriately referred to as private because they are privately controlled and financed by the religious order which owns and operates them; and they have been generally free from diocesan supervision except in regard to the teaching of religion, over which the bishop is given certain control by canon law, a control usually exercised through his educational representatives. Even in regard to the teaching of religion, however, a few religious orders claim the privilege of exemption.[4]

While details of nomenclature may vary from order to order, generally the line of control for private Catholic schools is from the head of the school (principal, president, rector, or superior) to the superior of a province (a geographical area); from the provincial head to the mother general or father general, who heads the order; and from the general to the Sacred Congregation of Religious, an administrative department of the Curia which represents the Pope.

Individual religious orders have their own constitutions and traditions which are reflected in the kinds of schools they operate and the kind of supervisory influences they feel. Illustrative of the organization which exists in private Catholic schools, though not necessarily typical, is that which exists within the schools of the Society of Jesus (Jesuits), an order with a distinguished history and strong traditions. Each of the ten Jesuit provinces of the United States has a province prefect of studies or educational director, responsible to his provincial for improving the educational program of the schools of the province. For the high schools or colleges, or both, which are his responsibility, his duties include development of provincial-wide curricular programs and courses of study, testing programs, and other supervisory activities. The latter include regular observation of teachers, supervisory conferences, development of supervisory bulletins, initiation of instructional policy formulation at the province level, and recommendation of instructional policies to the chief administrative officer, the provincial of the province.

In turn, he and the other provincial educational directors com-

---

[4] See T. Lincoln Bouscaren and Adam C. Ellis, *Canon Law, A Text and Commentary,* 3d rev. ed., The Bruce Publishing Company, Milwaukee, 1957, p. 748.

prise the executive commitee of the Jesuit Educational Association, the administrative board of which is composed of the provincials of all provinces of this country. The Jesuit Educational Association itself, with offices and staff in New York, exerts supervisory influence on the Jesuit schools of the country through research projects; activities of standing commissions; special studies of timely problems by *ad hoc* committees; an annual national conference of administrators of Jesuit schools for the joint examination of areas for improving instruction; and publications cooperatively developed, such as an administrative manual for high school administrators or suggested statutes for colleges or universities.

It is through avenues such as those employed by the Society of Jesus for its schools that supervisory activity in the private Catholic schools of the country has been brought to a more advanced level, especially in the high school, than that generally found in diocesan high schools, except as the latter are turned over completely to a religious order with its own developed supervisory program.

From the standpoint of a unified diocesan supervisory program, however, at least one student of Catholic secondary school administration envisions some problems ahead as diocesan administrative patterns continue to develop. Breheny states:[5]

> In order that educational leadership and service will be supplied which will be realistically related to sectional and local needs, and the totality of those needs, and effectively correlated with the requirements and efforts of civil agencies, it would seem that both, together with some measure of control, must come from the diocese, and must be extended to all schools.

Expanding on this observation, he continues:[6]

> All things being considered it would seem that the diocese should be permitted a control of minimum standards in health, safety and education where schools are immediately controlled by religious of papal rank, exempt and non-exempt, to be enforced by means of visitation and referral to superiors in the case of non-exempt insti-

[5] John P. Breheny, "Diocesan Administration of Catholic Secondary Education in the United States: Its Status—With a Design for the Future," doctor's thesis, Harvard University, 1954, p. 88.

[6] *Ibid.*, pp. 89–90.

tutes and by means short of visitation in the case of those that are exempt. The responsibility in which the bishop is held by Catholics and by the public at large for the temporal welfare of those intrusted to the care of recognized Catholic institutions within his diocese, a responsibility not without basis in the natural law, would seem to offer grounds for some supervision of such schools even in matters others than these relating to religious education and faith and morals. The supervision need not be extensive. The means by which it is exercised should be in accord with the spirit and purpose of existing legislation. Thus, the suggestion that in the case of schools of exempt religious minimum standards should be enforced not through visitation, but rather by means of required reports concerning program, staff, building and enrollments, with referral to the superiors of the institutes concerned. If this would necessitate some adjustment in the provisions of Canon Law, then such may be in order.

THE IMPACT OF THE LAY TEACHER ON SUPERVISION

The increasing percentage of lay teachers in Catholic schools portends a sharply different approach to supervisory activity if the faculty as a whole and the school as a whole are to be improved. Formerly, with the Catholic school staffed only by religious teachers who lived together in the convent or community home, faculty meetings and supervisory programs occurred as a part of community living. Clearly that day is past for the Catholic school now that over 30 per cent of even Catholic elementary school teachers are lay. The advent of lay faculty members means that all the supervisory activity described as desirable will have to move out of community quarters into the school itself, if religious and lay teacher alike are to be welded into an efficient, unified school staff.

Questions for Discussion or Investigation

1. Why is it theoretically valid to say that a person with managerial authority is handicapped in discharging supervisory responsibilities?

2. What advantages does the principal enjoy in his supervisory activities compared with those enjoyed by a supervisor from a central office? What disadvantages?

3. While all individual and group supervisory techniques are a part of a balanced program, which one technique in each category strikes you as particularly helpful? Why?

4. If you are on the staff of a Catholic school, how is supervision carried on? Through what organizational pattern? What next steps do you see as desirable developments in the program for improving teaching?

5. What particular supervisory emphases do you see as desirable in your own school situation?

6. Construct a teacher self-evaluation form for use either by elementary school teachers or by secondary school teachers.

Readings and References

Adams, Harold P., and Frank G. Dickey: *Basic Principles of Supervision,* American Book Company, New York, 1953.

Bartky, John A.: *Supervision as Human Relations,* D. C. Heath and Company, Boston, 1953.

Beecher, Dwight E.: *The Evaluation of Teaching,* Syracuse University Press, Syracuse, 1955.

Boardman, Charles W., and others: *Democratic Supervision in Secondary Schools,* Houghton Mifflin Company, Boston, 1953.

Breheny, John P.: "Diocesan Administration of Catholic Secondary Education in the United States: Its Status—With a Design for the Future," doctor's thesis, Harvard University, 1954.

Briggs, Thomas H., and Joseph Justman: *Improving Instruction through Supervisors,* The Macmillan Company, New York, 1952.

Burton, William H., and Leo J. Brueckner: *Supervision, A Social Process,* 3d ed., Appleton-Century-Crofts, Inc., New York, 1955.

Elsbree, Willard S., and Harold J. McNally: *Elementary School Administration and Supervision,* 2d ed., American Book Company, New York, 1959.

Hammock, Robert C., and Ralph S. Owings: *Supervisory Instruction in Secondary Schools,* McGraw-Hill Book Company, Inc., New York, 1955.

Kyte, George C.: *The Principal at Work,* rev. ed., Ginn & Company, Boston, 1952.

McNerney, Chester T.: *Educational Supervision,* McGraw-Hill Book Company, Inc., New York, 1951.

Reeder, Edwin H.: *Supervision in the Elementary School,* Houghton Mifflin Company, Boston, 1953.

Richardine, Sister Mary: "What Public Schools Are Doing for In-service Professional Growth," *National Catholic Educational Association Bulletin,* vol. 56, no. 2, pp. 7–16, November, 1959.

Spears, Harold: *Improving the Supervision of Instruction,* Prentice-Hall, Inc., Englewood, Cliffs, N.J., 1953.

Staff Relations in School Administration, Thirty-third Yearbook of the American Association of School Administrators, Washington, 1955.

The Superintendent as Instructional Leader, Thirty-fifth Yearbook of the American Association of School Administrators, Washington, 1957.

Ward, Sister M. Ruth Albert: *Patterns of Administration in Diocesan School Systems,* The Catholic University of America Press, Washington, 1957.

Wiles, Kimball: *Teaching for Better Schools,* Prentice-Hall, Inc., Englewood Cliffs, N.J., 1953.

9. *Instruction:*
Testing

A well-conceived testing program for a school system, no matter how large or small the school organization may be, is essential if the administration is to discharge adequately its instructional responsibilities. Someone more expert than the typical teacher or principal ought to be made responsible for adequate emphasis on testing in the total instructional program of schools. Known variously by such titles as supervisor of testing services or supervisor of appraisal services, this staff member is charged with responsibility for planning a system-wide testing program in contrast to the evaluation of achievement which each teacher will carry out as a part of his instructional procedures. Even the teacher with his own classroom testing problems may receive professional advice from the system's expert in this field.

Instructional testing programs will generally be limited to group testing. Individual testing, as needed in the diagnosis of severe problem cases, is more properly considered a pupil-personnel service and logically is organized as such, rather than as a part of the instructional program available to the usual student.

THE PURPOSE OF A SYSTEM-WIDE TESTING
PROGRAM

A well-planned system-wide testing program will serve a variety of purposes, all related to the over-all aim of making the instructional program of the schools as effective as possible. It provides basic information about the children who are to be taught; it supplies a basis for determining needed curricular changes; it serves to check on the effectiveness of the instructional approaches outlined in courses of study; and it furnishes general information on the effectiveness of an individual school teaching staff or, on occasion, the effectiveness of a given teacher.

1. *Testing for basic information about children.* Because a school is fundamentally an organization for group instruction, the school organizer and the individual teacher must know enough about the children of a school to group them so that they will profit from the learning experiences they are to receive. Testing readiness, especially reading readiness; testing intelligence or academic aptitude; and testing vocational interests and aptitude all contribute to the effective placement of children in instructional groups.

2. *Testing to determine curricular changes.* Since school personnel, like most people, frequently become habituated to teaching certain material according to a plan which changes little from year to year, a specifically designed test will frequently give those responsible for curriculum planning dramatic illustrations of the need for change. For example, one system, which accepts responsibility for developing an awareness of some of the great problems facing the United States today and in the years immediately ahead, met resistance from history teachers when a suggestion that "Problems of American Democracy" be introduced in grade 12 instead of the traditional "American History," which would be moved to grade 11. A major allegation of the American history teachers was that the scope of the new course was already handled by them. After agreement by a committee as to what were some of the outstanding national problems with which the high school graduate ought to be familiar, a test was specifically designed to discover their awareness of such issues as the protective tariff, the role of government in la-

bor-management relations, and the organization of the United Nations. Results demonstrated vividly enough to convince all but the most die-hard that, as had been suspected, the American history teacher was running out of class time somewhere between the Spanish-American War and World War I.

3. *Testing the effectiveness of instructional programs.* We have already seen some of the extreme directions which curriculum planning has taken over the past sixty years in the United States. As an individual school system moves too far in one direction or not far enough in another, the administration of achievement tests, particularly in the basic tools of reading, vocabulary, spelling, and arithmetic indicate marked deviations from national norms. Such tests raise the question: why the deviations? Where the answer is not supplied by similar deviation in IQ or aptitude tests, course-of-study inadequacies may be indicated.

4. *Testing the effectiveness of the teacher.* Sometimes deviations from norms, national or city-wide, permit of only one explanation: ineffective teaching, either in one classroom or in a whole school. While extreme caution should be used before determining upon this explanation, there is no doubt that expert analysis of standardized test results sometimes clearly indicates teacher responsibility. Part of the expertness of the supervisor of testing service will be demonstrated by the delicacy with which such results are conveyed to the teacher or faculty concerned, so that constructive action rather than resentment follows.

One major caution needs underlining here. While some purpose can be served by standardized tests in the tool subjects where there is general agreement around the country about expected results, administering nationally or regionally standardized tests in such fields as social studies or English literature may produce unfortunate teaching results.

In these fields, courses of study may vary so much and creative teaching efforts may lead to such different emphases from system to system or from teacher to teacher that nationally standardized tests produced to evaluate the average instructional program may give distorted results and tempt the teachers to teach for the exams, no matter how inappropriate some of the test sections seem.

A test geared to local courses of study which deviate from the average approach must be constructed locally. System-wide norms must replace national norms as a basis for evaluation. Perhaps this construction of locally made tests is the greatest single reason for the establishment of system-wide expert testing services, for far too frequently curricular advances and real creative teaching have been constrained by the necessity for using only state, regional, or national tests prepared to appraise what persons outside the system think ought to be tested. The ready-made test then replaces the course of study in specifying course essentials.

This has been the general situation when expert testing services have not been available within a system, such as in most Catholic schools and in public school systems, other than the largest, where only ready-made tests are available.

A MINIMUM SYSTEM-WIDE TESTING PROGRAM

A minimum system-wide testing program should include testing for IQ or reading readiness by the end of the kindergarten year in anticipation of group placement problems in grade 1. Otherwise the testing should be done in the first few days of the first grade. Intelligence testing should be provided before each major step in the pupil's progress through school: at the end of grade 3, when he is about to leave the primary unit; at the end of grade 6 or grade 8, before entering junior or senior high school; and early in grade 12, when results will be important to counseling the student about future educational or vocational programs. Retests should, of course, be made whenever the teacher questions the accuracy of the results obtained.

System-wide achievement tests with national norms should be given in a regularly planned cycle to provide as comprehensive a picture of achievement as is financially feasible. Nationally standardized tests in at least reading and arithmetic should be given to all children in grade 3 and again before they leave the elementary school. Spelling and vocabulary tests also may be included. In the other curriculum areas, ready-made or locally constructed tests should be given according to whether the former adequately correlate with local course-of-study provisions.

At the high school level, interest and personality inventories should be administered as part of the vocational guidance program.

As special needs of a school system dictate or as the success of particular curricular emphases are to be evaluated, additional tests will be given.

THE ROLE OF THE EXPERT IN TESTING

Throughout the whole program of system-wide appraisal, the need for expert coordination is demonstrable. Tests must be selected, ordered, packaged, distributed, administered, collected, and summarized. Sometimes machine grading in a central testing office is called for. Sometimes detailed directions for teacher scoring and summarizing must be drawn up. Follow-up studies must be made if the test results are to be presented intelligibly to teachers, administrators, or the public. If the results are to help improve instruction in the classrooms, teachers and principals must be informed and even educated as to the significance of test findings. All these are the responsibilities of a supervisor of appraisal services in a large administrative unit. In a small system, they must be assigned to someone, perhaps a teacher, who will develop more expertness in this specialized field than the usual teacher or principal.

A particularly valuable contribution of the supervisor of testing services and his staff is made as they acquire adequate information on "typical school populations" to make valid small-sample testing possible as a less cumbersome method of conducting special testing projects.

The most fundamental value of the professional testing expert to a school system, however, may well lie in the assistance given in avoiding testing pitfalls, for these are numerous. While standardized tests are extremely valuable tools when properly used, they easily become decidedly unfair or equally extremely harmful when they are misused. There is a strong relationship between the success of a testing program and the advanced planning which has gone into it. The program must be understood in advance by the school staff, the pupils themselves, and their parents if the students are to be motivated so as to perform at their best without undue strain. Testing has to be scheduled wisely during the school year to avoid excessive disruption of administrative routines or teacher frustration. The latest techniques to facilitate scoring and summarizing test results must be incorporated into the program. These are described by McLaughlin as follows:[1]

> Below grade four, pupils mark their answers in test booklets which therefore can be used only once. In grade four and above, however, it is possible for the school to purchase, for many kinds of tests, a reusable test booklet and an expendable separate answer sheet—which diminishes the overall cost of a testing program. If a new test is printed in a reusable booklet form, a separate answer sheet must be designed that can be scored quickly by hand or machine. A scoring key must also be planned, prepared, and punched to fit the answer sheet.
>
> For schools in which the teachers must score the tests, several types of self-scoring answer sheets have been developed. One type consists of tamper-proof double sheets with a carbon sealed between. When the sheets are separated, it is easy to count the correct answers. A similar type is prepared with chemically treated paper which will clearly record the correct answer or indicate the incorrect answer which was chosen. In another type of test pupils use a pin to punch holes through several thicknesses of paper.
>
> Some large schools or county systems rent test-scoring machines which will score properly marked answer sheets at the rate of over 200 an hour—and thus release teacher time for more profitable tasks than counting dots or marks. These machines can also indicate how many pupils in a class choose each answer for each question. Such information aids the teacher in locating class deficiencies.
>
> One of the most recent developments in the test-scoring field is an answer card which can be scored and punched with a new machine and then sorted on standard machines. Some large-scale programs now use machines which simultaneously "read" the name of the pupil and score all tests of a battery—at the rate of 5,000 papers an hour.

PROFESSIONAL TESTING SERVICES BY CONTRACT

Despite the need for a skilled professional staff with adequate facilities for coordinating system-wide testing, the fact remains that financial considerations have made this type of service unavailable to most smaller public school systems and to most Catholic schools.

[1] Kenneth F. McLaughlin, "How Is a Test Built?" in *Understanding Testing,* U.S. Office of Education, OE-25003, 1960, pp. 4–7.

For those school systems which have been unable to develop their own professional testing services, other possibilities for securing many of the same advantages, without as much overhead cost, now exist:

1. Except for the curricular areas in which distinctive local programs have been developed, schools may contract for organized system-wide testing programs with a nationwide testing service which will assist in planning programs, in supplying testing materials, in providing machine scoring, and in reporting the results in a form agreed upon by the system and the service. Science Research Associates, Inc. (SRA) is one such national organization with professional testing services available to school systems and individual schools on a contract basis.

2. Contracts with neighboring university testing bureaus can be made for providing some of the same services or even for developing local tests, properly standardized, for those subjects in which unique curricular features are found.

3. Schools may increase their participation in state testing programs while avoiding the danger that the state testing program will stifle curriculum improvements.

4. Fullest advantage may be taken of Title V of the National Defense Education Act of 1958.[2] Title V specifically authorizes assistance to states for testing in secondary schools under state-developed plans. Although its primary purpose is to identify able students, this necessarily involves testing all students. In states where laws permit testing of nonpublic school youth, Catholic schools may participate in the over-all state program. In states which prohibit the use of state funds for nonpublic schools, special contracts for assistance in testing may be made by Catholic schools with the United Sates Commissioner of Education to secure reimbursement for expenses of up to $1 per year for each high school student tested.

TESTING IN CATHOLIC SCHOOLS

In her national study of administrative patterns in diocesan schools, Ward found:[3]

[2] For Title V of the National Defense Education Act of 1958, see Appendix B.
[3] Sister M. Ruth Albert Ward, *Patterns of Administration in Diocesan School Systems,* The Catholic University of America Press, Washington, 1957, p. 153.

Superintendents reported that, lacking personnel to supervise by personal visitation often enough to see that effective teaching and learning situations prevail, they are forced into putting into testing more faith than it deserves as a tool for measuring the value of their program of education. They rather report that by a cursory glance at the test results showing pupil achievements of last year, they have the nucleus for next year's program. It was not at all unusual to learn that this procedure produces the supervisory program.

Regarding some negative effects of diocesan testing, the same author found that some superintendents were suspicious of commercial tests, although they judged diocesan tests to be less reliable and less validly constructed; they felt that teachers too often were tempted to teach for the test outcomes or were vitiating the entire program by "practicing" with old tests as their guide; they showed concern that pupils come to over-value memorized facts and information gathered for performance on tests; and they believed the expense of standardizing diocesan tests or diocesan norms to be prohibitive.

In a study of Catholic high schools by a questionnaire which included two questions on testing, Stack found that 294 of 1,000 Catholic high schools cooperating in the study had a testing bureau. Since no definition of what constituted a testing bureau was included, it would seem likely that a broad definition was used by some responding schools. In answer to a request to name the three most frequently used tests in their testing program, 257 schools named none; 51 schools named only one test; 210 schools named two tests; and 482 schools, as requested, named three.[4] Table 4 indicates the types of tests reported by the participating schools.

In general, private Catholic schools within a diocese participate in diocesan testing programs, although they may not report their scores to the diocesan school office, except for their scores on religion tests; administering and reporting results on these tests may be mandatory in a given diocese. There seems to be some inconsistency between the emphasis given to testing in many Catholic schools as reported by Ward and the absence of skilled testing services as indicated by Stack. Promise of continued improvement in the

[4] Philip Lawrence Stack, *A National Study of the Guidance Services in the Catholic Secondary Schools,* The Catholic University of America Press, Washington, 1958, pp. 64–65.

whole testing area, however, is to be seen in the noticeable increase among dioceses in use of outside professional testing programs, such as that of SRA, and in the advantage taken in some dioceses of the financial assistance to their own testing programs offered by the Defense Education Act.

TABLE 4. TYPES OF TESTS MOST FREQUENTLY USED BY THE CATHOLIC SECONDARY SCHOOLS.

Types of tests	Number of times mentioned	Percentage times mentioned	Different tests mentioned
Intelligence	1,067	55.56	25
Interest	221	11.51	6
Achievement	168	8.75	18
Reading	143	7.45	15
Aptitude	86	4.48	17
Educational	54	2.81	14
Personality	27	1.47	8
Screening	13	0.68	6
Prognostic	12	0.63	5
Diagnostic	7	0.36	3
Religion	2	0.10	2
Other	119	6.20	
Total	1,919	100.00	119

Number of schools responding: 775
Number of schools no response: 225
SOURCE: Philip Lawrence Stack, *A National Study of the Guidance Services in the Catholic Secondary Schools,* The Catholic University of America Press, Washington, 1958, p. 65.

Questions for Discussion or Investigation

1. How is your own school system organized for group testing of students? List the stronger features of the program. List the weaker features. Be prepared to discuss both.

2. Precisely what can be accomplished by system-wide testing that cannot be accomplished by the individual teacher?

3. Discuss under what circumstances, if any, testing could indicate that a given school is doing a poor instructional job in a given subject. Discuss the same question in regard to pinpointing poor teaching by an individual teacher.

4. What pitfalls are to be avoided in system-wide testing?

5. To what extent do you believe that every teacher should have information on the mental age and IQ of his students at his desk?

Readings and References

Adams, Georgia Sachs, and Theodore L. Torerson: *Measurement and Evaluation for the Secondary School Teacher,* Holt, Rinehart and Winston, Inc., New York, 1956.

Ahmann, J. Stanley, and Marvin D. Glock: *Evaluating Pupil Growth,* Allyn and Bacon, Inc., Englewood Cliffs, N.J., 1960.

Anastasi, Anne: *Psychological Testing,* The Macmillan Company, New York, 1954.

Cronbach, Lee J.: *Essentials of Psychological Testing,* 2d ed., Harper & Brothers, New York, 1960.

Durost, Walter N.: "What Constitutes a Minimal Testing Program for Elementary and Junior High School," *Test Service Notebook Number 1,* rev. ed., Division of Test Research and Service, Harcourt, Brace & World, Inc., New York, 1956.

Froehlick, Clifford P., and others: *Guidance Testing,* Science Research Associates, Inc., Chicago, 1948.

Garrett, Henry E.: *Testing for Teachers,* American Book Company, New York, 1959.

Green, Harry A., and others: *Measurement and Evaluation in the Elementary School,* 2d ed., Longmans, Green & Co., Inc., New York, 1953.

Jordan, Arthur M.: *Measurement in Education,* McGraw-Hill Book Company, Inc., New York, 1953.

McLaughlin, Kenneth F. (ed.): *Understanding Testing,* U.S. Office of Education, OE-25003, 1960.

Noll, Victor H.: *Introduction to Educational Measurement,* Houghton Mifflin Company, Boston, 1957.

Remmers, H. H., and N. L. Gage: *Educational Measurement and Evaluation,* Harper & Brothers, New York, 1955.

Ross, C. C., and J. C. Stanley: *Measurement in Today's Schools,* 3d ed., Prentice-Hall, Inc., Englewood Cliffs, N.J., 1954.

Segal, David, and others: *An Approach to Individual Analysis in Educational and Vocational Guidance,* U.S. Office of Education Bulletin 1959, no. 1, 1959.

Stack, Philip Lawrence: *A National Study of the Guidance Services in the Catholic Secondary Schools,* The Catholic University of America Press, Washington, 1958.

Thorndike, Robert L., and Elizabeth Hagen: *Measurement and Evaluation in Psychology and Education,* John Wiley & Sons, Inc., New York, 1955.

Traxler, Arthur E., and others: *Introduction to Testing and the Use of Test Results in Public Schools,* Harper & Brothers, New York, 1953.

Wrightstone, J. W., and others: *Evaluation in Modern Education,* American Book Company, New York, 1956.

10. *Instruction: Counseling and Guidance*

In the conduct of schools two kinds of counseling become essential. One is the counseling of the usual, or ordinary, student. This is a part of the instructional program, and it is designed to help the ordinary student derive the greatest possible benefit from the school program. The other is the kind of detailed individual counseling and guidance needed for the severe problem case. This latter type of guidance will be discussed as an aspect of pupil personnel services.

Counseling and guidance services as part of the instructional program of schools have been receiving increased emphasis in school administration in recent years, particularly as a result of two 1958 developments having wide impact on American education: the Conant report on *The American High School Today* and the National Defense Education Act.

In the Conant report, the first recommendation for improving public secondary education is the following:[1]

[1] James B. Conant, *The American High School Today,* McGraw-Hill Book Company, Inc., New York, 1959, pp. 44–45.

In a satisfactory school system the counseling should start in the elementary school, and there should be good articulation between the counseling in the junior and senior high schools if the pattern is 6–3–3 or between the counseling in the elementary school and the high school if the system is organized on an 8–4 basis. There should be one full-time counselor (or guidance officer) for every two hundred fifty to three hundred pupils in the high school. The counselors should have had experience as teachers but should be devoting virtually full time to the counseling work; they should be familiar with the use of tests and measurements of the aptitudes and achievement of pupils. The function of the counselor is not to supplant the parents but to supplement parental advice to a youngster. To this end, the counselor should be in close touch with the parent as well as the pupil. Through consultation, an attempt should be made each year to work out an elective program for the student which corresponds to the student's interest and ability as determined by tests of scholastic aptitude, the recorded achievement as measured by grades in courses, and by teachers' estimates. The counselors should be sympathetic to the elective programs which develop marketable skills; they should also understand the program for the slow readers and be ready to cooperate with the teachers of this group of students.

Title V of the National Defense Education Act of 1958 [2] provides that a state will receive Federal funds for

. . . a program of guidance and counseling in the public secondary schools of such State (A) to advise students of courses of study best suited to their ability, aptitudes, and skills, and (B) to encourage students with outstanding aptitudes and ability to complete their secondary school education, take the necessary courses for admission to institutions of higher education, and enter such institutions.

The same title further provides for financing counseling and guidance training institutes conducted by institutions of higher education "to improve the qualifications of personnel engaged in counseling and guidance of students in secondary schools, or teachers in such schools preparing to engage in such counseling and guidance."

[2] For Title V of the National Defense Education Act of 1958, see Appendix B.

THE SCOPE OF THE COUNSELING SERVICE

Counseling helps pupils get the most out of the school program by providing educational, vocational, and personal guidance; by isolating student problems which demand more detailed treatment; and by liaison with community service agencies concerning student problems.

One object of counseling activities in school is to help the youngster pursue the best courses or the best school opportunities for his particular abilities and desires. Thus, counselors provide assistance in choosing courses, selecting individual subjects, and obtaining scholarships for the student's future education in college, especially when financial help is needed. This last has become a major emphasis of counseling today. If the school does not have a good counseling program, the record of scholarships obtained is generally much lower than it could be.

A second counseling activity is guidance concerning employment: first, guiding the youngsters into jobs and vocational areas where there are jobs and for which the youngsters' talents are suited; and second, guiding youngsters away from too early employment. This is a particularly serious problem when jobs are plentiful; many youngsters seek employment before they have reached the maximum development of their talents as further schooling might have developed them.

A third objective of counseling service in schools is to provide students with personal guidance, particularly when the school situation provides an opportunity which, if not seized immediately, could be permanently lost. In any gathering of hundreds or sometimes thousands of young people in large schools, there will be many whose schoolwork is seriously disrupted by personal problems. These young people will frequently turn to someone at school for help. This is particularly true when personal problems arise from broken families or a generally unhappy family life. It is this kind of personal help that counselors in schools must supply if young people are to profit from the school program. Thus, the school counselor may have to supplement parents and pastors in the area of personal guidance.

Though the counselor may suspect a serious personal or educational maladjustment, perhaps evidenced by failure to perform in keeping with ability, complete diagnosis and treatment are beyond the instructional responsibility of the school. The problems with which the school counselor is concerned frequently lead to other agencies for their solution. The child and his parents may be referred to a psychological clinic maintained by the schools themselves or perhaps maintained as a separate diocesan service. It is the counselor, for example, who knows what social agencies there are in the community which would provide the corrective glasses needed by a youngster whose family cannot pay for them. During the Depression of the 1930s, there were many children whose absence from school was directly traceable to the lack of shoes. Again, the school counselor may discover the need and, with his knowledge of the community and his social service background, guide the youngster and his parents to the proper social agency for assistance.

Thus, the counseling service of the school, organized to help children get the most out of their instructional program, provides educational, vocational, and personal guidance; discovers abnormalities needing special treatment by others; and cooperates with other social agencies in the solution of the problems of children.

ORGANIZATION FOR COUNSELING

Counseling as a part of the instructional program is generally carried on both by professional counselors and by principals and teachers. Few schools have been able to employ the number of professional counselors necessary for them to meet the guidance needs of all students; and it seems educationally unsound for teachers or principals, who are frequently "on the spot" when guidance opportunities present themselves, to refer to a counselor a problem which they may handle more expeditiously and more effectively.

THE PROFESSIONAL COUNSELOR

Counseling and guidance are not synonymous terms. Guidance is the broader. In a technical sense, counseling is only one element in a guidance program which may also include analysis of the student to help him obtain facts about himself from test results, cumulative records, and other means of identifying potentialities and interests;

supplying him with facts about educational and vocational opportunities and requirements; orienting him to the school program and its relationship to those same educational and vocational opportunities; assisting him in job or further educational placement; and following up the student to see how his plans worked out and how well the school's program served him after leaving.

Yet, since what is everyone's job usually becomes no one's, it is the professional counselor who dramatizes and personifies guidance in the typical American high school. It can ordinarily be safely generalized that the school with a professional counselor can have a good guidance program; the school without one will not.

The professional counselor is a person who has had specific training for the job. This training ought to include acquaintance with the techniques of counseling; knowledge of group testing, especially aptitude, interest, and personality tests; understanding of what can be done with individual testing; some knowledge of psychology, normal and abnormal; and some knowledge of community organization. In general, of course, the counselor must be the kind of person who is capable of establishing the rapport with young people so indispensable to success in helping them.

The professional counselor will carry on a variety of activities. Since it is rarely possible to maintain a sufficient number of counselors on the staff for them to do all the guidance and counseling required, it is important that the professional counselor advise, furnish information, and in general, stimulate principal and teachers to do a major share of the school counseling. He is, therefore, the expert on the faculty who does much of the work himself, but who is also responsible for helping the rest of the teachers and the administration give adequate emphasis to this phase of instructional activity.

Table 5 presents a specific listing of counseling activities over five years in a large, typically organized city school system. The system had the equivalent of thirty-three full-time counselors and a supervisor of counseling to carry on its service.

Under the organizational plan that prevails in this system, one or two professional counselors are assigned to the faculty of the individual school, depending on its size. There is one supervisor of counselors assigned to the downtown office with responsibility for the improvement of the counseling job done by the professional counselor. Therefore, each counselor, like a teacher, is responsible to the school principal and receives expert assistance in the performance of his job from a central office supervisor in the same way that a teacher of chemistry might from a science supervisor.

A different kind of organization for counseling—more intensive and more expensive—is illustrated by a smaller school system with sufficient financial resources to finance a more elaborate program. Here the high school counselor is assigned to the children of one

TABLE 5. ACTIVITIES OF COUNSELORS: 1954–1958

Activity	1953–1954	1954–1955	1955–1956	1956–1957	1957–1958
Obtaining occupational and educational information (days)	143	142	142	212	227
Periods of teaching in guidance classes	274	273	256	473	604
Individual pupils counseled	12,527	14,712	12,091	13,190	13,559
Brief contacts with individual pupils	100,095	119,916	176,220	187,930	186,069
Group conferences with pupils	587	621	755	781	834
Trips for pupils arranged by counselor	412	543	735	488	472
Contacts with school and social agencies regarding pupils	7,265	7,857	8,092	11,387	11,416
Conferences with principals	4,149	4,048	5,073	5,212	6,308
Conferences with teachers regarding classes	274	314	374	398	302
Contacts with parents	14,855	16,467	17,111	19,510	20,744
Speeches made	87	92	103	131	119
Meetings attended	484	579	379	472	413

eight-grade elementary school. She begins her contacts with them while they are in grade school and follows the same children through their four years in high school, with educational, vocational, and where needed, personal guidance. This approach makes possible detailed information as to the academic background of those counseled; actual acquaintance with the child's home situation—an acquaintance which becomes more intimate as brothers and sisters come along; and a more detailed knowledge of the neighborhood and associations of the child than is generally possessed by high school counselors. In this system, both counselors and homeroom teachers must regularly visit the homes of those counseled.

How many counselors does a given secondary school need? The

answer to this question obviously depends on many factors, such as how much emphasis is given to group guidance by the teaching staff? How much assistance does the counselor get from a centralized testing program? How homogeneous is the student body? And how much does the community value good counseling services for their young people?

Some approaches to answering this question, however, are supplied by Froehlich in *Guidance Services in Schools:*[3]

> When schools think about the number of hours of staff time which should be assigned to the guidance program, the work load a counselor can handle is an important factor. Usually the load is calculated in terms of numbers of pupils to be served. Frequently the load is stated as a ratio of pupils per full-time counselor. Thus, a commonly accepted ratio of 500:1 indicates 500 pupils are enrolled and 1 counselor is employed. For convenience, some state supervisors of guidance services have stated the ratio in terms of pupils and daily periods that a staff member is available for guidance purposes. Thus, the ratio 100:1 means that for every 100 pupils a counselor is assigned guidance duties for 1 period daily. A school with 200 pupils enrolled would assign some staff member 2 periods each day for guidance work. In actual practice this ratio has been found to provide insufficient time. A much more satisfactory ratio is 50:1. This means that a counselor would be employed full time in a school enrolling 300 pupils. The Twenty-fourth Yearbook of the American Association of School Administrators [1946] recommends a pupil-counselor ratio of 250:1.

One general caution about the assignment of responsibility for counseling service in a school should be expressed: the counselor and the school disciplinarian should ordinarily not be the same person. This would be better expressed as an absolute principle rather than a caution were it not for the relatively rare school disciplinarians whose skill and manner are such that they can enforce disciplinary regulations without interfering more than momentarily with their generally pleasant student relations. Related to this caution is another: the principal of a high school must resist the understandable, but nevertheless pernicious, temptation to use the counselor

[3] Clifford P. Froehlich, *Guidance Services in Schools,* McGraw-Hill Book Company, Inc., New York, 1958, p. 58.

to get clerical and mechanical work done, particularly in connection with attendance and tardiness, or to use the counselor as a substitute teacher.

THE PRINCIPAL AND TEACHERS AS COUNSELORS

Clearly the principal has to be a counselor. Even when there are more skilled staff members available, many of the duties of the principal or his assistant in dealing with youngsters will involve counseling. So too, must the teacher be a counselor and guide, since frequently the teacher, who may not be professionally trained in guidance techniques, is the person who has the kind of individual relationship with the child necessary for effective counseling. Consequently, it is with the teacher that the child chooses to discuss his problems.

In the typical high school situation, homeroom teachers are often assigned responsibility for handling group guidance aspects of counseling, especially for presenting occupational or job opportunities. Assistance from the counselor may include basic information, supplementary activity with individual cases too complicated for the teacher, and arrangement of group meetings with persons experienced in the major lines of vocational activity open to youth. In relation to the homeroom teacher, the professional counselor serves in the dual capacity of supervisor of counseling and resource person to the homeroom teacher. Increasingly, high schools are making schedule provisions for greater contact between homeroom teacher and secondary school student, sometimes by scheduling a longer homeroom period once a week and assigning group guidance responsibilities to this teacher. Provisions for assisting the teacher may include a curriculum guide, not unlike a course of study, with resource materials resembling a textbook.

Student interest, group discussion, and student reports are characteristics of the program in group guidance. The skilled teacher generally finds no need for grading, examinations, or formal lectures in carrying on this program. He will find need for resource material, both that found in books and that supplied by the professional counselor.

FACILITIES FOR COUNSELING

If the counselor is to perform satisfactorily his important instructional task, he must be able to count on the administrators of his school to provide him with the necessary facilities and materials. He must have a suitable office. He must have records to use as a source

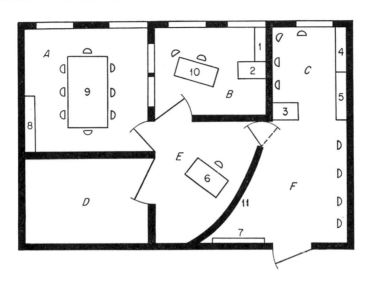

Key to Rooms	Key to Equipment
(*A*) Conference room, testing room for groups, etc.	(1) Bookshelf
(*B*) Counselor's office	(2) Filing cabinet with lock
(*C*) Browsing space for information materials, or another counselor's office, or work space for clerical assistants	(3) Filing cabinet for information of loose-leaf variety
(*D*) Storage space, or counselor's office, or work space	(4) and (5) Shelves and display rack for information materials
(*E*) Space for receptionist (student assistant)	(6) Desk or table for receptionist
(*F*) Waiting room	(7) Bulletin board
	(8) Storage cabinet for tests, etc.
	(9) Conference table or work space for testing
	(10) Counselor's desk, small or medium
	(11) Counter-high partition

FIGURE 5. Adaptation of a standard classroom into facilities for guidance services. SOURCE: Edward C. Roeber, Glenn E. Smith, and Clifford E. Erickson, *Organization and Administration of Guidance Services,* McGraw-Hill Book Company, Inc., New York, 1955.

of information on students. He must have certain materials for his information-giving responsibilities. He may need a receptionist— perhaps a student serving on a regular schedule related to his study periods.

THE COUNSELOR'S OFFICE

Without privacy, there can be no real counseling. Accordingly the school administrator is expected to provide a private office for the counselor. Ideally such an office should be partitioned to provide an inner office large enough for a desk, several comfortable chairs, a filing cabinet or two with locks, and a bookcase. An outer office should provide for a receptionist's desk, a waiting-room area with chairs, and display facilities for educational and vocational materials of interest to the students.

Since the space for counseling facilities frequently comes from adapting a former classroom to these purposes, Figure 5 provides a suggested floor plan for a converted classroom. While any private office is better than none, a strong case can be made for a location close to the office and school records. Other considerations, however, include distance from the noise centers of the school and accessibility to pupils, parents, and teachers. The general furnishings and décor of the counselor's office will ordinarily be similar to those of administrative offices in a given school building with one exception: conscious attention must be given to making the counselor's office conducive to establishing the rapport with the student which is so essential to successful counseling.

STUDENT RECORDS

The administration of a school must provide adequate records if the counselor is to do his job well. The cumulative-record card or folder is an essential tool of the counselor. Ideally, it is the record of a large number of test results, personal-social data, and school achievement. It should follow the student throughout his elementary and secondary school program as far as is administratively feasible, at least as long as he is in the same school system. Some schools feel that it should show information about the student's activities for five years after he leaves school, though this may be questioned as somewhat impractical and somewhat beyond the high school's responsibility and financial resources.

The following seven items should be included in every set of school records:[4]

1. Autobiography, including family background, home, and neighborhood environment

2. Health history, including physical and medical examination data

3. Standardized test results

4. School marks

5. Anecdotal items

6. Participation in extracurricular activities

7. Work experience

Cumulative records with this information included must be accessible not only to the school counselor, but also to all members of the school's staff whose responsibilities involve individual diagnosis: the teacher, the attendance officer, the school health officials.

Besides cumulative records, administration will have to make adequate budgetary provision for the counselor's own records and interview forms, for testing kits, for suitable educational and occupational reference and resource material, and for mimeographing facilities.

DISTINCTIVE ASPECTS OF GUIDANCE IN CATHOLIC SCHOOLS

In most respects the basic design for proper counseling and guidance services in both public and Catholic schools is the same. As is true in some other phases of school administration, however, financial considerations and shortage of professional personnel have generally limited the extent of formal guidance programs in Catholic high schools to the level of smaller, less well-financed public school systems. This is indicated by some of the findings of Stack in his 1958 study of guidance services in Catholic high schools. This investigator concludes that emphasis on group guidance activities, rather than individual guidance, was reflected in the data; Catholic

[4] See Royce E. Brewster, "The Cumulative Record," *Understanding Testing,* U.S. Office of Education, OE-25003, 1960, pp. 14–15.

high schools were inclined to utilize faculty members in incidental guidance rather than trained personnel; a weakness found was the lack of organization of guidance services under a director-coordinator; and over a period of eight or ten years, very few, if any, significant increases in the guidance procedures were noted in Catholic high schools.[5]

Nevertheless, Catholic high schools do have at least four great resources of a guidance nature in which they have advantage over public schools. A considerable percentage of their staffs is composed of priests whose extensive training is designed to make them professionals in personal guidance or of religious brothers and sisters whose training makes them, at the very least, exceptionally knowledgeable in this same area and whose lives provide example and inspiration of a high order to their students. The religiously oriented curriculum provides knowledge which is fundamental to personal guidance. The religious activities of a typical Catholic high school—such as the three-day spiritual retreat, regular confession, Mass and Holy Communion as a student body, Catholic Youth Organization activities —are all unique to guidance activities in a Catholic school. And perhaps partly owing to a common framework of basic theological and philosophical principles, excellent teaching materials for group guidance have been developed in all areas—educational, vocational, and personal. These special resources cannot easily be overvalued; but neither do they constitute a complete guidance program as some Catholic school administrators have been known to rationalize them. For example, they cannot compensate for the absence of trained counselors to coordinate a guidance program and to do the skilled individual educational and vocational counseling which is essential. Yet they constitute guidance strengths distinctive to religious schools.

A special word should be said of some of the excellent group guidance materials developed for use by the homeroom teacher in the Catholic high school, for Stack's report clearly indicates that much of the guidance in Catholic high schools depends on the

[5] Philip Lawrence Stack, *A National Study of the Guidance Services in the Catholic Secondary Schools,* The Catholic University of America Press, Washington, 1958.

homeroom teacher. In the opinion of this author, the Insight Series[6] provides comprehensive and significant teaching aids for group guidance in Catholic schools. The series, together with the highly professional teaching manuals developed for it, should help improve the group guidance program in Catholic schools at a time when the Defense Education Act provides considerable financial aid to public schools in developing their total counseling services but relatively little aid to private school counseling programs. Catholic schools will have to rely heavily on group programs to provide increased guidance opportunities for their students in the years immediately ahead.

Questions for Discussion or Investigation

1. Distinguish between guidance and counseling.
2. After consulting some of the professional literature on counseling, be prepared to discuss the directive and non-directive approaches to counseling.
3. Why can it be said that not all guidance and counseling problems should be turned over by a teacher to a professional counselor?
4. Do you agree that the school which does not have a professional counselor will not have a good guidance program?
5. Some few Catholic school administrators have claimed that the priest-chaplain is adequate to handle counseling problems in a Catholic high school. To what extent may this be true? To what extent is it wishful thinking?
6. After consulting the National Defense Education Act of 1958 (Appendix B), compare the aid provided for counseling programs in public and private schools.

Readings and References

Arbuckle, D. S.: *Guidance and Counseling in the Classroom,* Allyn and Bacon, Inc., Englewood Cliffs, N.J., 1957.

Bennett, Margaret E.: *Guidance in Groups: A Resource Book for Teachers, Counselors, and Administrators,* McGraw-Hill Book Company, Inc., New York, 1955.

Berdie, R. F. (ed.): *Concepts and Programs of Counseling,* University of Minnesota Press, Minneapolis, 1951.

Custer, Sister Violet Marie: *An Evaluative Study of the Guidance Program*

---

[6] The Insight Series, 4 vols. with teaching manuals, Harcourt, Brace & World, Inc., New York: *It's Your Life,* 1957; *It's Your Education,* 1959; *It's Your Personality,* 1960; *It's Your Future,* forthcoming.

in the Archdiocesan High Schools of Saint Louis, The Catholic University of America Press, Washington, 1955.

Cribbin, James J.: *Teacher's Handbook for It's Your Life,* The Insight Series, Harcourt, Brace & World, Inc., New York, 1958.

Crow, Lester D., and Alice Crow: *An Introduction to Guidance,* American Book Company, New York, 1951.

Edward, Sister M.: "Occupational Guidance," *The Catholic School Journal,* vol. 52, no. 10, pp. 317–318, December, 1952.

Erickson, C. E.: *A Practical Handbook for School Counselors,* The Ronald Press Company, New York, 1949.

Farwell, Gail F., and Herman J. Peters (eds.): *Guidance Readings for Counselors,* Rand McNally & Company, Chicago, 1960.

Froehlich, Clifford P.: *Guidance Services in Schools,* McGraw-Hill Book Company, Inc., New York, 1958.

Gordon, I. J.: *The Teacher as a Guidance Worker,* Harper & Brothers, New York, 1956.

Harris, Philip (ed.): "Readings for Catholic Counselors," *The Catholic Counselor,* 1958.

————: "Using Homeroom for Guidance in Personality Development," *Catholic Educational Review,* vol. 57, no. 2, pp. 97–105, February, 1959.

Hunt, Herold C., and Paul R. Pierce: *The Practice of School Administration,* Houghton Mifflin Company, Boston, 1958.

Janet, Sr. Mary, S.C.: *Catholic Secondary Education—A National Survey,* Department of Education, National Catholic Welfare Conference, Washington, 1949.

Jones, Arthur J.: *Principles of Guidance and Pupil Personnel Work,* 4th ed., McGraw-Hill Book Company, New York, 1951.

Julius, Brother: "Some Guidance Needs of High School Seniors," *Personnel and Guidance Journal,* vol. 32, pp. 460–463, April, 1954.

Keltner, J. W.: *Group Discussion Processes,* Longmans, Green & Co., Inc., New York, 1957.

Leonard, E. A.: "Counseling in Catholic Secondary Schools," *Catholic Educational Review,* vol. 43, pp. 280–284, May, 1946.

McDaniel, Henry B.: *Guidance in the Modern School,* Holt, Rinehart and Winston, Inc., New York, 1958.

Martinson, William D.: *Educational and Vocational Planning,* Scott, Foresman and Company, Chicago, 1959.

Peters, Herman J., and Gail F. Farwell: *Guidance: A Developmental Approach,* Rand McNally & Company, Chicago, 1959.

Philip, Brother Arthur: "Vocational Guidance by the Classroom Teacher," *National Catholic Educational Association Bulletin,* vol. 52, no. 1, pp. 378–381, August, 1955.

Robinson, Frances P.: *Principles and Procedures in Student Counseling,* Harper & Brothers, New York, 1950.

Roeber, Edward C., and others: *Organization and Administration of Guidance Services,* McGraw-Hill Book Company, Inc., New York, 1955.

Ross, Vivian: *Handbook for Homeroom Guidance,* The Macmillan Company, New York, 1954.

Stack, Philip Lawrence: *A National Study of the Guidance Services in the Catholic Secondary Schools,* The Catholic University of America Press, Washington, 1958.

Warters, Jane: *High School Personnel Work Today,* McGraw-Hill Book Company, Inc., New York, 1956.

Willey, Roy D., and Dean C. Andres: *Modern Methods and Techniques in Guidance,* Harper & Brothers, New York, 1955.

11. *Administrative Operation: School Organization*

Since the school is basically an institution for bringing the instructional program to children in groups, adequate operation of schools begins in consideration of school organization. The school administrator's professional knowledge of organization must cover changing concepts of the American educational ladder; classroom organizational patterns; homogeneous grouping, acceleration, and promotion practices; school and class size; and relations with accrediting agencies.

THE AMERICAN EDUCATIONAL LADDER

Traditionally, of course, the American school system has consisted of an eight-grade elementary school with a four-year high school followed by a four-year college. Professional schools and graduate studies have been at the summit. Despite the emergence of the junior high school movement, which grew out of dissatisfaction with the length of the educational program in the United States and the lack of progress made in grades 7 and 8 as they were organized, the 8–4 pattern is still the most typical elementary-secondary school pattern in the United States. Practically all the Catholic schools of the country are organized in this way, and between 40 and 50 per cent of the public high schools of the country are of the regular four-year type. Although by 1952 the 8–4 organizational plan was still the most widely used single plan, over half of the public schools had been reorganized to some other plan—6–3–3, 6–2–4, or 6–6 being the most common.

As long as the enthusiasm of the original organizational reformers influenced it, the rapid growth of the junior high school movement in the 1920s was due to a desire to provide a new school unit with a specific role to play distinct from that of the elementary or secondary school. Subsequent events have clearly indicated that continued acceptance of the junior high school has been more the result of space pressures than any well-conceived educational values associated with it. This too is the implication of the following statement issued by the United States Office of Education in 1955:[1]

> If more room was needed in the elementary school, all or part of Grade 6 was sent to the junior high school; when the high school was crowded, all or part of Grade 10 was sent to the junior high school "catch-all." When the junior high school was found to be "bursting its seams," 7th graders might be sent back to the elementary school or 9th graders to the senior high school. The point is that the junior high school, instead of being given a definite place in its own right having specific educational purposes affecting young adolescents which neither the elementary nor the senior high school could serve as well, was not taken with sufficient seriousness to become a fully distinctive institution.

In fact an earlier report of the U.S. Office of Education on elementary school organization indicated little drive for school reorganization in fifty-two city school systems except when space problems would be expediently met by building junior high schools.[2] Some cities were reported to be shifting the seventh or eighth grades back to elementary schools, and where changes in organization were contemplated, they were in the direction of making the junior high

[1] Walter H. Gaumnitz and others, *Junior High School Facts,* U.S. Office of Education Misc. 21, 1955, pp. 4–5.

[2] Effie G. Bathurst and others, *14 Questions on Elementary School Organization,* U.S. Office of Education Pamphlet 105, 1948.

more like the elementary schools with one teacher responsible for most of the day's instruction of a single class.

Thus, while the junior high school reorganization is increasingly with us, there is little to suggest that it has really changed the American educational ladder in any basic sense.

The addition of the kindergarten before grade 1 in most public school systems and the increasing prevalence of the two-year junior college at the end of the twelfth grade are other twentieth century variations in school organizational patterns which have found wide acceptance in public education, though both are seldom part of a Catholic school system. As the kindergarten, usually meeting half-days, has been increasingly accepted as a part of public education, it has become an integral part of primary education, frequently being given the role of specifically preparing the child for the first grade through emphasis on readiness programs, particularly reading readiness. The junior college, the recent growth of which is phenomenal, particularly in the West, has come to serve two purposes: terminal technical education for nonprofessional occupations and replacement of the first two years of liberal arts college work. With the increasing shortage of space in regularly established colleges, an expansion of the public junior college to handle more and more of the college general education program seems likely, although in many areas the question as to whether the junior college shall be organized within the present college-university framework or within the public school system remains to be answered.

Clearly evident is a tendency to consider the kindergarten–grade 3 segment of elementary education as a separate organizational entity devoted principally to developing reading, preparatory to entering the upper-elementary level. A study made by the U.S. Office of Education covering practices in late 1958 shows 18 per cent of public elementary schools using some form of a primary unit organization. Another 13 per cent indicated the possibility of future adoption of this plan of reorganization.

The ungraded primary plan for the first three years of schooling (grades 1 to 3) was adopted in 1953 by the archdiocesan schools of St. Louis. The *National Catholic Educational Association Bulletin* of November, 1960, carried a report on the operation of the St.

Louis ungraded primary unit, including details of curriculum reorganization and an evaluation of the plan. Two results of the St. Louis plan, which stresses intra-room and inter-room flexibility, developmental teaching, and organization based on levels of performance, are cited as higher reading achievement by children entering the fourth grade and more children working up to their ability level.

A survey of developments in vocational education throughout the country has made it apparent that there is a shift away from the separately organized vocational high school in the direction of including vocational education in the comprehensive high school program.

Vocational education originally grew in this country in separate high schools which tended to be organized for the training of adolescents in a particular branch of vocational activity: mechanical, automotive, building-trades, electrical, or sewing-trades high schools.

These high schools tended to be so organized that their programs contained only courses directly contributing to the vocational proficiency of the youngster. In a typical electrical high school, for example, one-half of the day would be spent in shops, and the other half in shop mathematics and shop-English—whatever that is—with little of a general nature in the program other than perhaps civics, which might be required along with some American history.

As the Depression, which began in 1929, gained a hold on the country, persons trained so specifically were somewhat lost when no jobs were available in their fields. Studies indicated that as our American economy and manufacturing processes became more complicated, people were fired or released from their jobs, not so much because they were unable to perform the work, but because of personality clashes with their fellow employees or employers. In addition, the work week has been amazingly shortened since 1930. People, then, have had increased opportunity to do things other than talk shop English and practice shop arithmetic. Therefore, emphasis has swung from vocational training for specific jobs to a broader concept of vocational education which includes general education as found in the comprehensive high school, with increasing emphasis through the high school years on shop vocational training or actual work experience under school auspices.

Thus it is thought desirable to include the same kinds of musical, dramatic, or sports activities found in the usual secondary school. The point is that the organization of the separate vocational high school seems to be disappearing from the American scene. It is being replaced by the comprehensive high school approach, with emphasis in the early years on general education. General education perhaps decreases but never disappears as the student progresses through the four years of high school; and as it decreases there is an increasing amount of time devoted to vocational training.

A promising development in school reorganization—slow but persistent—is apparent in the literature of Catholic education and in experimental practice in some Catholic schools, particularly those of the Cleveland diocese. Growing out of a 1942 National Catholic Educational Association Committee on Reorganization of the School System and continuing with a *Second Report of Progress— 1947,* impetus to the reorganization plan has been slowly gathered, with every likelihood that pressing financial problems of Catholic schools in the years just ahead as well as general educational concern with "educational locksteps" will accelerate acceptance of its major features.

Basically, it is a 6–4–4 organizational plan for the average student: six-year elementary, four-year high school, and four-year college education. Thus for those able to do it, two years of schooling would be saved. For the other students, the Cleveland plan provides for a review-preview grade at the end of the primary unit and another at the end of the elementary six years, thus making an eight-year elementary program available for the slower children. It should be noted that skipping grades is not part of the program, since the curriculum is organized into primary and upper-elementary divisions. As more time is needed by slower children, the extra years are provided. Here this plan differs from the old Cambridge multi-track plan.

Since it was introduced to two Cleveland Catholic schools in 1946 and extended to other parochial schools in Cleveland since then, the plan has had extensive trial in one city. An evaluation of results of the plan after some years of experience with its operation should make a major contribution either to extending the program or to abandoning it. At one time Kansas City's seven-grade parochial elementary schools were another evidence of the growing interest in school reorganization in Catholic educational circles; so is the Latin high school approach which involves accepting specially selected youngsters after their sixth grade to do the work of the usual six years in four years of high school.

Should an evaluation of the Cleveland plan be favorable, it is likely that some of its features may influence public school organizational patterns, particularly as all educators are giving increased attention to greater flexibility of organization to provide more adequately for the gifted child; financial advantages to eliminating any needless schooling for a sizable group of students are, of course, always attractive.

CLASSROOM ORGANIZATIONAL PATTERNS

Two extreme approaches to organizing the individual classrooms are possible to the administrator. The self-contained classroom, almost universal through the primary grades, has one teacher teaching the same group of children all subjects in the same room all day. Departmentalization, which organizes the school so that a specialist teaches his own subject to different groups of children, is found with increasing frequency as one moves up through the grades, until it is as universally used in high schools as size of school and staff qualifications permit. In between the two extremes, modifications are found until the one approach merges into the other.

Generally speaking, the self-contained classroom organization has been ideally suited to the primary grades where little children need the stability of constant guidance by one teacher who can come to know their individual aptitudes and problems well, and where the depth of knowledge or technique needed to meet their needs is not too great for the average teacher to encompass. Neither is there any controversy about the suitability of departmentalization at the high school level, for it is difficult for any one teacher to be competent to the extent required by mature students in divergent areas such as chemistry, art, music, English, foreign language, and the many vocational areas of the curriculum.

Nor is there any advantage to either the self-contained classroom or the departmentalized organization from the viewpoint of operational efficiency. Both involve one teacher with an average-size class using one room for the entire school day. With departmentalization, however, much more scheduling is involved if this norm of maximum operational efficiency is to be reached.

The area of controversy in regard to plan of classroom organization lies mainly in the grades between the third and the first year of senior high school. The self-contained idea involves maximum operational efficiency (one teacher, one class, and one room); it solves the need of the child to belong somewhere without adjusting to different teaching personalities and different classrooms, and it permits a teacher to develop more intensive knowledge of the individual characteristics of his students. The ordinary teacher, however, may not be able to teach such subjects as physical education, art, or music equally satisfactorily, especially to children gifted in these areas. This is especially true if the teacher is old, color-blind, or tone-deaf. Consequently, various modifications of the self-contained idea are used. The simplest and least expensive is to have two teachers whose weak areas complement each other exchange classes; for example, one handles the art in both classes while the color-blind teacher teaches an academic area to the first teacher's class. This eliminates only the gross incompetencies, however.

The next step is to hire special teachers for art, music, physical education, or industrial arts, teachers who are supplementary to the regular teaching staff and who probably teach their specialty in enough schools to give them a full teaching week. Such itinerant teachers need facilities: a gym, a music room, an art room, a home economics room, or a shop. Now for each class of, say, 30 pupils we have the time of one teacher plus perhaps another fourth of a teacher's time (the total of the time of the several special teachers depending on the length of the period allotted to each special subject); and we have these pupils using their own room fully and four other classrooms part time. If there are 16 classes involved, the special-teacher–special-room feature departs from the standard of maximum operational efficiency by the cost of four teachers and five special rooms. This may mean an extra annual cost of $25,000 to $28,000 per year for the 16 classes and thousands of dollars in capital outlay for the rooms.

To get around the difficulties involved in the self-contained classroom approach, some administrators may turn to a departmental approach which is equally efficient as far as teacher costs and room usage go. The special subjects can be taught by specialists in special rooms while the academic subjects are taught in regular classrooms, but certain undesirable features show up. The student's education at the elementary level becomes too compartmentalized; he is the responsibility of no one teacher; he must adjust to many teaching personalities; and his learning experiences are unlikely to be integrated. To obviate these difficulties, some administrators have turned to a modification of extreme departmentalization known as the modified platoon plan of elementary school organization.

The original platoon school, popularized in the early 1900s as the Gary Plan, provided that the school day be divided into two equal halves; the classrooms into two kinds, academic and special subject; and the children of one grade into two sections or platoons. While platoon 1 was in the regular classroom for half the school day learning the fundamental subjects with a single teacher, platoon 2 was distributed around the special classrooms with special teachers for art, music, home economics, manual arts, gym, library, and auditorium. Note that if the system was to work at maximum efficiency, platoon 2 had to have as many special teachers and rooms as there were academic teachers, no more and no less. Further, every special class had to be as long as any other special class with half of the day divided equally among the special subjects. Maximum efficiency in use of teachers and rooms was secured, but only by subordinating curricular planning to a mechanical organizational pattern.

A modified platoon organization as used in a few of the larger city systems today is an improvement over its prototype in that special classes like "library" or "auditorium" are not invented to balance the platoons. Instead, some of the fundamental subjects, such as arithmetic and science, are moved to the special-subject half of the schedule to bring the two sections into better balance. Thus language arts and social studies taught by one teacher are balanced by arithmetic, science or health, gym, music, art, and practical arts for both boys and girls—to avoid difficulties in scheduling boys in industrial arts and girls in home economics. Administrative efficiency is maintained if the school organizer solves the intricate puzzle of balancing the platoons while maintaining proper time allotments to the special subjects, but frequently this is accomplished at the expense of instructional desiderata. For example, to ensure that each faculty member is employed full time with a schedule that is fully assigned, some strange teaching combinations may be necessary for which the teacher is no more competent than the tone-deaf teacher of the self-contained classroom in teaching music. Perhaps what is needed is a teacher who can teach music and practical arts or physical education and art; these bizarre combinations are too often found by the school organizer. That they are found at all arouses suspicion that administrative efficiency may have caused instructional inadequacies.

Of the two approaches, the complete self-contained pattern is simpler and, as practiced, is more educationally sound than the modified platoon system. Where finances permit, a modified self-contained organization with special teachers in special rooms— sometimes called resource teachers in resource rooms—is the ideal. The modified platoon owed much of its revival to depression conditions which necessitated doing away with itinerant special teachers in some systems. The revived platoon system simply made it possible to continue their employment at less expense, without regard to the educational rationalizations used in justification of the system.

HOMOGENEOUS GROUPING, ACCELERATION, AND PROMOTION PRACTICES

All three of these items of concern to school administrators have one thing in common. Much that is sentimental and unrealistic has been widely disseminated in professional circles about each. The policy which the administrator accepts in regard to each of them must ultimately be based on the answer given to the basic instructional question: what is the unique purpose of schools?

HOMOGENEOUS GROUPING

Homogeneous grouping in the pre-World War II era of sentimental concepts of democracy was widely attacked as undemocratic and a denial of the principle of human equality. Since schools exist for group instruction, it is logical that the more homogeneous the group, the more manageable the instructional job of the teacher; and if schools are to make their unique contribution to education in intellectual matters, efforts to group students according to measures of intellectual aptitude—other things being equal—are well directed.

In a school which has two or three classes at a given grade level, the easiest grouping for the administrator is on an alphabetic basis. No explanations to parents are needed about why the child upstairs was assigned to the best class while their own wound up in the slowest group. No one need persuade teachers of the importance of their assignment to slower classes. No unkind remarks will be made by one child to another. The classes are effortlessly organized to accomplish conveniently mediocre results. If problems of slow learners obtrude themselves, the administrator will be forced to organize classes for these students, undoubtedly; the gifted students, however, will probably come to no one's attention as they ease along without obvious difficulties and with their potentialities dissipated by years of average performance.

Identification of students with unusual abilities poses problems, of course. Tests do not always measure perfectly what they are supposed to measure; attitudes and physical conditions sometimes interfere with the accuracy of test results. Teachers' grades vary in their validity from class to class and school to school. Likewise, there are the nonperformers and the late bloomers. While there is much to be said for all these obstacles to adequate identification of unusual students, they still constitute no excuse for doing nothing about the problem; and generally speaking, in self-righteously viewing possible imperfections of possible actions, too many school administrators are doing nothing for the gifted child other than to speak glowingly of enrichment attempts within the classrooms.

Generally these enrichment attempts involve class assignments and projects differentiated according to the ability of each student in the class. While this is administratively the easiest device to claim to be doing, the future to this approach gives no greater promise than past accomplishment. It has met with only limited success because it depends upon a type of teacher that is rare: a teacher with boundless energy, tremendous talent for running multi-ringed circuses, knowledge approaching omniscience, and a capacity for getting along without sleep. Sentimentalists to the contrary, there are not many such teachers.

A national survey of practices and policies in elementary school administration by Stuart E. Dean of the U.S. Office of Education reveals that by January, 1959, children were grouped heterogeneously in 72.1 per cent of the public schools in grades 1 through 6 and in 60 per cent of the public schools in grades 7 and 8. The same survey indicated, however, the likelihood of future increases in homogeneous grouping on all grade levels, a development in keeping with post-Sputnik reexamination of educational policies.

ACCELERATION

Early admission to school and procedures for accelerating progress through school both fell into disuse as the extremes of the child-centered era led educators to inordinate concern about possible social inferiorities and maladjustments.

While no child should be admitted to grade 1 prior to being ready for the instructional program offered, first under the child-centered influences and more recently under pressures of large enrollments a chronological age of six by the beginning day of school has increasingly become a minimum requirement. Several observations seem pertinent. The concept of individual differences is negated when such an absolute rule is enforced. Relief from enrollment pressures gained by enforcing the six-year requirement is at best only a one-year relief, since the following year a full year's contingent of six-year-olds must be admitted. A third observation is this: in the city system in which the author entered grade 1, the usual age for admission was five by the opening day of school. No studies are available as to the failures that resulted, but certainly the student of average ability seemed to progress as well as the average six-year-olds do in the same system today.

Considerable emphasis is currently being given to experimental plans for accelerating gifted youngsters in larger numbers than formerly thought possible. Initiated primarily to stimulate the gifted students of high school and college age to intellectual performance in keeping with their academic abilities, the plans are being conducted in accordance with highest research standards. They include the Advanced Placement and Early Admission to College programs.

Both have been dramatized and formalized and are being studied with Ford Foundation moneys. Both have been tried less spectacularly but for more years by other colleges and universities. Neither was adopted by many Catholic institutions until widely accepted elsewhere. Both are aimed at eliminating the overlapping of high school and college work for those who do not need the repetition. Both depend on cooperative work between high schools and colleges in identifying the exceptional youths while they still are in high school.

The Advanced Placement Program. This program involves students taking courses in high school designed to be college equivalents, taking College Entrance Examination Board Tests, and receiving either college credit for the work from the college entered or at least advanced placement in college.

The Cincinnati public high schools participate in this program. At the Walnut Hills School, for example, the exceptional student may take math through calculus. It is taught by specially selected teachers in accordance with outlines constructed by committees of cooperating university and high school faculties. On completing this course and satisfactorily completing the College Entrance Examination Board Test, the student receives advanced standing either with or without college credit from one or another of the thirty-four colleges participating in the plan. The practice of actually awarding college credit is growing and enables the student to finish college early. Even if the college does not actually award the credits, the student is placed in sophomore courses in his freshman year, thus enabling him to take more advanced work even though he may still have the normal number of college credits to earn. In addition to math, other subjects which can be taken in high schools under this program include English, chemistry, physics, biology, Latin, and French.

Administratively, there is no reason why a college interested in an advanced placement program cannot work out similar arrangements with one or more feeder high schools without formally participating in the College Board program. A school can construct and use its own exams. It can determine the subject or subjects it will allow the student to take. It can grant its own credit or merely advanced standing, although the first would seem to supply external motivation to the participating high school students. Many Catholic colleges and universities would have been in a far better position to work out such a program early in the movement than geographically scattered institutions under separate control, since sometimes the same religious order may control the university and also one or more feeder high schools.

Early Admission Program. Like the Advanced Placement program, the Early Admission program depends on identification of talented youngsters in high school and is an attempt to eliminate duplication of high school and college subject matter. Certain youths of high academic ability have been taken into the freshman year at colleges and universities after their sophomore or junior year of high school. Thus the universities challenge these younger students to work in keeping with their abilities. Results reported to date indicate these youngsters do better academically in college than those of similar ability who complete high school before entering. They also do at least as well in social and extracurricular activities, except for interscholastic athletics.

PROMOTION PRACTICES

In the operation of a school system, perhaps no operational area presents as complicated a problem as the one involved in promotional policies. Extreme alternatives are: shall student promotion be automatic from year to year or shall promotion be based upon the achievement of minimum grade standards? While few administrators will wish to see either extreme adopted, the desired mean is difficult to determine in specific terms.

Leading toward automatic promotion are many facts concerning pupil failures gathered since this matter first became an object of research shortly after 1900. Among the more pertinent findings, it is found that children who repeat a grade generally do no better the second year; children who are advanced learn more by the end of the following year than comparable children who repeat the grade; factors other than achievement frequently influence teachers' decisions on failures, as evidenced by an undue proportion of boys who are failed; children who fail grades tend to compensate by behavior associated with delinquency; children who repeat grades find little stimulation to learn from using the same texts under the same teacher; the problems of children sometimes clear up as sudden insights are received, making repetition of a grade a waste of time when the insight would have come in the next grade just as well. For a thorough analysis of studies leading to these conclusions, the student is referred to Caswell and Foshay.[3]

On the other hand, tending toward promotion policies based on achievement of grade standards is the concept of the school as uniquely set up to contribute to the intellectual advance of youngsters. This concept is identified by concern with what happens to the character of the youth who slides by without performance, concern with the expanding range of individual differences at higher levels after students have progressed according to age, and concern about the value of high school graduation if everyone gets through.

In attempting to find a defensible ground somewhere between extremes of promotion policies, yet giving adequate weight to the research conclusions mentioned above, the individual school system should make prudent application of the following general principle: the teacher must demonstrate that repetition of a grade by a particular child is likely to be profitable to that child because of the particular circumstance involved.

It is realized that the application of this principle is closer to the extreme of automatic promotion than to the opposite extreme; that the administration will have to provide many special classes for the gifted, for the slow learners, for those needing remedial work, and for other types of problem children who need adjusted curricula; and that these classes will have to be provided right through high school.

SCHOOL AND CLASS SIZE

SCHOOL SIZE

The size of schools varies widely from locality to locality according to boundaries of school districts controlling them or the size of the parishes involved. This fact has caused considerable interest by school administration experts in the question: is there a best size for an elementary or high school?

[3] Hollis L. Caswell and A. Wellesley Foshay, *Education in the Elementary School*, 3d ed., American Book Company, New York, 1957, chap. 13.

Much research related to this problem has been carried on, mainly from the cost-efficiency viewpoint. A review of results leads to the following general conclusions: (1) generally speaking, larger school units are more economical to operate, more efficient, and can offer greater educational opportunities; (2) this is even more true of high schools than elementary schools; (3) an enrollment of around 800 students constitutes a desirable minimum size; (4) general operating expenses decrease with the size of the plant; and (5) the expense of construction generally rises in direct proportion to the number of students to be accommodated.

While a number of authorities in school administration can be cited as a basis for the above general conclusions, the following quotations from one of the earlier works in this field are still true. From *Public School Plant Program* by Arthur B. Moehlman are taken the following excerpts:[4]

> In general, the number of buildings for each type of school should be as few as possible. Since it is questionable whether a school of less than 800 membership is economical with regard both to instruction and to administration, the board of education must early determine the area from which each unit is expected to draw. . . .
>
> The administrative and operating staff requirements are practically the same for buildings of 800 capacity as for buildings of 1,200 capacity. It is therefore obvious that the administrative cost, or "overhead," will tend to be larger in the smaller units. The erection of a series of small units will also have direct bearing upon the future operation cost. On the other hand there is no available evidence that instructional efficiency decreases with the size of the school. In fact, the opposite is nearer the truth. The presence of larger units of children in each age-group permits greater flexibility in grading and promotion than is possible in the smaller units. Progressive administrative opinion appears to favor increasing the size of the school in order to make possible a greater efficiency and adjustment of the curriculum to the needs of the individual. . . .
>
> The factor of size for administration and classification purpose and for use of special facilities and equipment, makes it necessary to determine definitely upon the minimum size of the school unit. The lower and upper limits of economical organization are accepted

[4] Rand McNally & Company, Chicago, 1929, pp. 36, 133, and 135–136, respectively.

as ranging from 800 to 2,100. The Detroit instructional program, which is quite typical of those used in the larger cities, showed that the most efficient use of rooms, equipment, and specialized personnel appeared to be reached with a 2,100 membership. Any extension beyond that point, to be economical, must again advance by large units. The next economical unit above 2,100 will be 2,900. With respect to the lower limit, the conception of a junior high school in terms of an ultimate capacity of less than 800 must result in a curtailment of physical facilities and a development of duplicate facilities to secure efficiency of operation.

The above considerations regarding school size and efficiency of operation are equally applicable to public and parochial schools, though the parish school organization tends to keep parochial schools smaller than public schools. For example, in one large city, 68 public elementary schools averaged 700 pupils each in 1955–1956, whereas in the same city 60 parochial schools averaged 330 pupils each in the same year.

That school size continues to be a problem at the high school level in public schools is indicated in a 1958 report of the American Association of School Administrators.[5] This report found that of the 23,746 public high schools of the country, 13,142 enrolled less than 200 pupils; 7,117 enrolled less than 100 pupils; and 2,720 enrolled less than 50 pupils. In high schools of less than 200 pupils it is clear that the eight teachers or so will have all they can do to provide a basic program without providing advanced or accelerated programs for gifted pupils, remedial work for slow learners, or programs to meet special interests or develop unique abilities of their students.

CLASS SIZE

The question of the effect of class size upon the learning of children has taken on new significance as the wave of postwar children is having its impact on schools. The question is doubly important in Catholic school administration, where in some localities the strain on facilities is even greater than in neighboring public

---

[5] *The Point of Beginning: The Local School District,* American Association of School Administrators, Progress Report of the Commission on School District Reorganization, Washington, 1958.

schools. In the same metropolitan area referred to above, public elementary schools maintained an average class size in 1955–1956 (exclusive of special schools and classes) of 32.1. The corresponding parochial school system was struggling to maintain an average class size of about 44. Only 4 per cent of the public school classes enrolled 40 or more students; in the parochial system, 66 per cent of its classes enrolled 40 or more students.

Much research has been done on the influence of class size on the learning of children, with generally unexpected results. The net results of many research studies were appropriately described by one author as the "enigma of class size." [6] Freeman, in his study, refers to dozens of studies on class size and states that findings more often showed academic achievement to be higher in larger classes.[7]

Thus, the preponderance of research results, notwithstanding the opinions of nearly all teachers and principals to the contrary, fails to substantiate the claim that children learn more academically in smaller classes when small classes are considered those enrolling up to twenty-four pupils and large classes those with twenty-five to fifty pupils. Recent studies made of college class size, such as those at Miami (Ohio) University, generally indicate that as far as is measurable, students in large college classes perform as well as matched students in smaller classes. Of course, if the defense of smaller classes rests on the intangible results of education, no objective measures are possible by the very definition of intangible.

One explanation for the relative superiority of the larger class is that teachers seem to rise to the challenges presented; conversely, they may ease their efforts unconsciously when numbers do not force them to maximum performance. Another explanation given is that teaching approaches in smaller classes are often not changed to take advantage of greater opportunities for class discussion. In any case, none of the studies measures the relative state of teacher exhaustion at the end of a day of managing a class of fifty or the effect of such workouts on teacher life expectancy!

There must be exceptions to the generalization that large classes

---

[6] Ellsworth Tompkins, "Enigma of Class Size," an article made available by the U.S. Office of Education, 1948.

[7] Roger A. Freeman, *School Needs in the Decade Ahead,* The Institute for Social Science Research, Washington, 1958, p. 81.

are as effective as small classes. Size of classroom certainly will limit the number of pupils who can be taught in it; where there is no room for movement by students in a classroom (to a library table, to a committee work situation, or to prepare for a dramatization), instructional approaches must be limited. Furthermore, it is inconceivable that a first-grade class of seventy will be as successful as one of twenty, everything else being equal. Classes in some subject-matter fields would also be less affected by class size than others. Certain teaching methods are more effective in smaller classes than larger.

Perhaps the most accurate statement of the enigma of class size is that it does not seem to affect learning in those areas where learning can be measured. There are limits, however, to the amount of efforts which the conscientious teacher can be expected to make year after year in a teaching situation.

With the crowded conditions obtaining in many diocesan elementary schools around the country, the question of which grades should be sacrificed first—if a given Catholic school cannot accommodate all students—is rapidly becoming less academic. Some persons who have given consideration to this problem feel that the higher the grade level, the more essential it is that the distinctively Catholic features be included in the educational programs. On the other hand, others maintain that "as the twig is bent. . . ." Accordingly, they feel that the early grades are essential to Catholic formation.

Strictly from the professional educator's viewpoint, and accepting intellectual development as the school's unique purpose, it would seem that if any one grade, other than kindergarten, must be sacrificed, the first grade offers the best possibilities for economy. With beginning reading as its chief function, it is in the first grade that smaller classes, with individual attention to the difficulties of beginning students, are most desirable. Most public schools do provide smaller classes. Thus, if a class size of thirty in this critical year is to be maintained, a teacher is saved for each class of thirty children transferred to public schools. At the upper level of elementary school, class size (as has been indicated) is less critical.

One Catholic educational leader, addressing himself to this problem before the 57th Annual Meeting of the National Catholic Educational Association, stated:[8]

> If we are forced to abandon a section of formal Catholic schooling, it ought to be the first six grades. To achieve maximum results Catholic education should start with the 7th grade or junior high school, continue through senior high school and include the 13th and 14th grades or junior college. A network of junior colleges under diocesan and religious-order directions would mean that many tens of thousands of Catholic young men and women, at a critical stage of intellectual maturation, would have at least some access to what few of them will ever discover elsewhere—the documents of philosophical and theological treasures of Christian humanism, as well as the great Catholic social thought. This is no small gain.

The Handbook of Regulations for the Archdiocese of Cincinnati prescribes the following procedures when an elementary school cannot accept all who apply for admission to the first grade:

A. When it is impossible to accommodate all applicants for the first grade in classes of 50 or less, the school shall either:
1. Divide the classes if teachers are available;
2. Operate on half-day sessions if additional teachers are not available;
3. Use the facilities of a neighboring parish school, if available.
B. In those parishes where bus transportation makes half-day sessions impossible, recourse shall be had to the School Office for a solution to the problem.
C. Where half-day sessions are necessary, the following rule shall hold: if the same teacher is to teach both morning and afternoon sessions, the sessions shall be three hours in length. If different teachers are to teach both morning and afternoon sessions, the length of these sessions shall be four hours. Half-day sessions should not be adopted in the lower classes unless it can be foreseen that all the children enrolled can be accommodated in the upper classes.
D. Kindergartens should not be maintained in any school which cannot accommodate all children who wish to enroll in grades one to eight.
E. Over-crowded conditions or half-day sessions constitute suffi-

[8] Neil G. McCluskey, "The Dinosaur and the Catholic School," *National Catholic Educational Association Bulletin,* vol. 57, no. 1, p. 237, August, 1960.

cient reason for the pastor to grant to parents permission to send their children to a public school, provided they give the usual promise of sending their children to religious instruction.

F. Wherever a considerable number of children (20 or more) are enrolled in public schools, a period of summer vacation school must be provided by the parish and the parents of such children have the obligation of sending their children.

RELATIONS WITH ACCREDITING AGENCIES

At the high school and college level the question of joining, or maintaining membership in, one of the voluntary accrediting agencies is of considerable importance. The five regional associations of secondary schools and colleges, which cover all of the states except California in their respective territories, are the New England, Middle States, Southern, North Central, and Western associations. The state university in California has carried on accreditation there.

Initiated to help colleges and universities smooth the entrance of graduates of better high schools into college, the regional accrediting agencies have expanded their work to include establishing approved lists of colleges and universities which have met standards for members. Over the years these agencies have made genuine efforts and real progress in establishing evaluation criteria which are more qualitative than quantitative. Flexibility in application of criteria is attempted by having an institution state its purposes. In the light of its own conception of its purposes, it is then evaluated.

The contributions of accrediting agencies to educational progress have been considerable. Generally speaking, they have succeeded in raising the quality of performance of institutions, particularly smaller institutions, seeking accreditation. The institutional self-survey, which has come to be a first step in preparing for an inspection by representatives of the association, generally means improvement of the institution, no matter what the decision on accreditation. National cooperative studies of standards have resulted in more qualitative and fewer mechanical quantitative standards being used. This is even more true for college than high school criteria.

As a whole, accrediting agencies have raised the professional tone of institutions seeking membership. With regular reexamination of member institutions becoming a general policy of these agencies, their influence will be felt even more widely as long-time member institutions, which were relatively unaffected by periodic statistical reports on a few significant items, may well be impelled toward changes as their procedures and policies come up for their own and the agency's evaluation.

Since accreditation agencies are voluntary private associations, previous court decisions indicate that no appeal to courts of their decisions to admit or drop an institution from membership is likely to serve any useful purpose. Yet, loss of prestige to institutions dropped from membership is so great, particularly at the college level, that those charged with operation of member institutions actually have lost some freedom of action, as is equally true for members of most voluntary associations.

Although they subscribe to the general view of evaluating an institution in the light of its own philosophy, some accrediting agencies for schools and departments—especially at the college and university level—have insisted on specific standards which reflect a particular point of view, not necessarily that of the school being evaluated. On occasion these standards have become so rigid as to prevent the genuine progress which comes from variety; or so expensive as to be possible only in wealthier schools; or so arbitrary as to create suspicion that monopoly in restraint of competition is a major goal. Considerable relief to the college administrator harassed by the specific requirements of many special interest groups is promised by the developing influence of the National Commission on Accrediting.

The advantages to joining the major regional accrediting agencies, to which age has brought the wisdom to appreciate and encourage institutional diversity and experimentation, clearly outweigh any disadvantages. The case for seeking national accreditation by agencies with more restricted curricular interests is much less strong.

Questions for Discussion or Investigation

1. Contrast the completely self-contained plan of elementary school organization with the modified platoon system; list advantages and disadvan-

tages for grades 4 and 5 and grades 7 and 8. Is there any difference in the suitability of the two plans at these levels?

2. What advantages or disadvantages do you find in the "primary unit" concept of school organization?

3. Based on your experience, would you say that the Cleveland plan of elementary school organization is a desirable development?

4. Does one's concept of the purpose of schools affect his answer to the question of whether classes should be grouped homogeneously?

5. Discuss: If a college awards advanced standing to students, should it also award equivalent college credits?

6. In the light of desirable promotion practices, should several types of high school diplomas be awarded?

7. Under what possible circumstances could a public or private high school of about 150 students be justified? Does it make any difference to the justification whether the school is public or private?

8. Carefully study at least two research studies on the effect of class size. Prepare an evaluation of each.

9. Analyze changes in the 1960 edition of *Evaluative Criteria* produced by the National Study of Secondary School Evaluation compared with the 1950 or earlier editions produced by the Cooperative Study of Secondary School Standards. Do the changes seem to reflect significant modifications in educational philosophy? Specify.

Readings and References

Administration: Procedures and School Practices for the Academically Talented Student in the Secondary School, National Education Association, Washington, 1960.

Bathurst, Effie G., and others: *14 Questions on Elementary School Organization,* U.S. Office of Education Pamphlet 105, 1948.

Bridging the Gap between School and College, Fund for the Advancement of Education, New York, 1953.

Caswell, Hollis L., and A. Wellesley Foshay: *Education in the Elementary School,* 2d ed., American Book Company, New York, 1957.

Coffield, William H.: "A Longitudinal Study of the Effects of Non-promotion on Educational Achievement in Elementary Schools," doctoral thesis, State University of Iowa, 1954.

Conant, James B.: *The American High School Today,* McGraw-Hill Book Company, Inc., New York, 1959.

————: *Recommendations for Education in the Junior High School Years,* Educational Testing Service, Princeton, N.J., 1960.

Cunningham, William F.: "Rebuilding Our American School Structure," *National Catholic Educational Association Bulletin,* vol. 52, no. 3, pp. 7–17, February, 1956.

————: *The Pivotal Problems of Education,* The Macmillan Company, New York, 1940.

Dean, Stuart E.: *Elementary School Administration and Organization, a National Survey of Practices and Policies,* U.S. Office of Education Bulletin 1960, no. 11, OE-23006, 1960.

Elsbree, Willard S., and Harold J. McNally: *Elementary School Administration and Supervision,* 2d ed., American Book Company, New York, 1959.

Freeman, Roger A.: *School Needs in the Decade Ahead,* The Institute for Social Science Research, Washington, 1958.

Gaumnitz, Walter H.: *Small Schools Are Growing Larger,* U.S. Office of Education Circular 601, 1959.

————, and others: *Junior High School Facts,* U.S. Office of Education Misc. 21, 1955.

Goodlad, John I.: "Research and Theory Regarding Promotion and Non-promotion," *Elementary School Journal,* vol. 53, no. 3, pp. 150–155, November, 1952.

Gruhn, William T., and Harl R. Douglas: *The Modern Junior High School,* 2d ed., The Ronald Press Company, 1956.

Hagman, Harlan L.: *Administration of Elementary Schools,* McGraw-Hill Book Company, Inc., New York, 1956.

Hoflich, James E.: "The Ungraded Primary," *National Catholic Educational Association Bulletin,* vol. 57, no. 2, pp. 8–25, November, 1960.

Hunt, De Witt: *Work Experience Education Programs in American Secondary Schools,* U.S. Office of Education Bulletin 1957, no. 5, 1957.

The Identification and Education of the Academically Talented Student in the American Secondary School, National Education Association, Conference Report, 1958.

Moehlman, Arthur B.: *Public School Plant Program,* Rand McNally & Company, Chicago, 1929.

Morrison, D. G., and S. V. Martorana: *The 2-Year Community College, an Annotated List of Studies and Surveys,* U.S. Office of Education Bulletin 1958, no. 14, 1958.

National Study of Secondary School Evaluation: *Evaluative Criteria—1960 Edition,* American Council on Education, Washington, 1960.

Reeder, Ward G.: *The Fundamentals of Public School Administration,* The Macmillan Company, New York, 1958.

They Went to College Early, Fund for the Advancement of Education, New York, 1957.

Tompkins, Ellsworth: "Enigma of Class Size," made available by the U.S. Office of Education, 1948.

12. *Administrative Operation: School Discipline*

The proper management of children is a problem for administrators and teachers alike. While the success of a principal or teacher will not be guaranteed by his ability to manage the children in a school or class, it certainly is true that maintaining good discipline is a *sine qua non*. The principal must not only be able to handle children effectively himself; he must also be able to help teachers do the same, for there is no more tragic figure than the teacher who, though unable to maintain discipline, remains in the profession year after year. By October of each year, he is grimly holding on until the next year, when it is fondly hoped a good class will come along. But to such teachers a "good" class never comes.

Basic attitudes toward discipline in school should flow directly from one's philosophical or theological principles about the nature of man. Fundamentally, three views are possible:

1. *Man is naturally bad and must be protected from himself.* This view of the nature of man, typical of the early Puritan attitude, is held today by few educators. When it was held, detailed rules of conduct supplemented by frequent and severe punishments were common. The teacher and principal took on many of the characteristics of the old-fashioned jailer.

225

2. *Man is naturally good and bound to get better if freed from unfortunate environmental influences.* This view of man thoroughly infiltrated most educational literature of the child-centered era. Teach well, remove restraints, permit self-expression, and there will be no discipline problems, say advocates of this view. The doctrine, an outgrowth of the Rousseau concept of the nature of man, spread hand in hand with the progressive education doctrines of the pre-World War II era. More than any other single factor, it was responsible for the widely held picture that teachers' college courses and professional educational literature were unrealistic.

3. *Man has natural tendencies toward good and also has within him certain disorderly tendencies.* The latter include pride, envy, sloth, covetousness, anger, lust, and gluttony, to revert to the terminology of the seven capital sins. This view of man's nature as a mixture of good and bad is basic in the theological doctrines of original sin and the Redemption. From the view that man has tendencies to both good and bad with the power to choose one or the other comes a dual conclusion: that good teaching minimizes disciplinary difficulties and that as long as children are children there will be disturbances in the school which must be skillfully handled. Thus two approaches to good discipline are indicated: the indirect approach, appealing to the child's better nature; and the direct approach, restraining his lower nature. The two together comprise a realistic method of effectively managing children.

THE INDIRECT APPROACH TO DISCIPLINE

The indirect approach to discipline consists in teaching so effectively that disciplinary disturbances will be relatively few. Progressive education movements, to the excesses of which we have previously taken sharp exception, have made effective contributions to the teacher in minimizing disciplinary difficulties through the indirect approach. Without developing a treatise on the methodology of good teaching, it is possible to point to the essential elements of the indirect approach to discipline as follows:

1. *Use the interests of children.* A child who is interested in what is going on in the classroom is not likely to be a discipline case.

Capitalizing on children's interests can help tremendously in motivating the child to learn. All studies of children's interests indicate that phenomena of science or nature rank first: why does it rain or snow, how do plants grow, how does the water system work? Language arts skills, for example, are more likely to be developed around such subject matter than through prepared exercises involving nothing interesting to a class.

2. *Maneuver the child into a felt need for a specific learning activity.* Unfortunately not everything which children need to learn can be made to interest them even by the genius-teacher. Time spent in motivating the child to want to learn is time spent in making disciplinary problems less likely. Obviously, appealing to adult needs is ineffective with the child who can not even look ahead to the results of a bad report or failing a course. Such an approach has as little appeal to most children as a recital of the advantages of a classical education.

3. *Follow the instincts of children where possible.* Whether they call them instincts, motives, or drives, psychologists generally confirm the layman's impression that children do have certain innate tendencies. When these are used by the teacher or principal—and not all of them can be—disciplinary problems are lessened. For example, children need physical activity; accordingly the teacher or school which fails to provide some physical activity in the school day is increasing the likelihood of misbehavior. Children tend to enjoy collecting things (the acquisitive instinct); teachers may capitalize on this through encouraging collection of science specimens or scrapbooks to further instructional objectives. Children like to talk; a principal who decrees that there will be no talking in the school lunchroom is needlessly running counter to the nature of children and building up enforcement problems.

4. *Create an air of fun in the classroom.* While all learning activity may not be pleasant, the teacher who can create the general attitude that being in his room is pleasant is building up a store of good will which will carry him over the less interesting instructional activities with less danger of behavior problems. An air of fun in the classroom and genuine respect for the teacher are not mutually exclusive.

THE DIRECT APPROACH TO DISCIPLINE

No matter how effective the teacher, there will be disciplinary infractions arising from the disorderly tendencies in the child's nature. Irrespective of how favorable the learning situation created, certain youngsters on certain days will choose not to conform. This calls for a direct approach which might be described as the direct imposition of the personality of the teacher upon the malefactor.

Since some teachers and principals are completely successful when direct disciplinary action is called for and some are equally complete failures, what makes the difference? What is the indispensable characteristic of the effective disciplinarian? First, however, a word as to what it is not:

It Is Not Physical Size. College football all-stars have sometimes been notoriously unable to maintain classroom discipline, while a relatively puny physical lightweight is never out of control of the same class a few minutes later.

It Is Not Being a Man Rather than a Woman. In one city junior high school, police squad cars arrived each day at three o'clock to drive two men teachers a mile or two away from school to where their cars were parked, thus giving them a start on the students for their own protection. At the same time, on the same faculty, there were several ninety-pound women teachers who never had disciplinary troubles with the same students.

It Is Not Keeping Youngsters after School. Observation confirms that the teachers who keep youngsters after school most frequently have no more luck maintaining discipline after school hours than they had during school, which is to be expected after all.

It Is Not Willingness to Use the Paddle. In one school known to the author, the football coach taught English to several classes of eighth-grade boys. After some disciplinary disturbances he began to keep a paddle in the classroom. The first day he paddled one boy; the second, several youngsters. As more and more were paddled it became a badge of merit to have been paddled by the former college all-star tackle, since the boys well knew that he could not really injure them.

It Is Not Organizing a "Jug." When a "jug" or special room is set up for keeping youngsters after school, usually with all teachers taking turns as jailer, it soon becomes apparent that the good teach-

> Let him [the teacher] therefore adopt a parental attitude to his pupils, and regard himself as the representative of those who have committed their children to his charge. Let him be free from vice himself and refuse to tolerate it in others. Let him be strict but not austere, genial but not too familiar: for austerity will make him unpopular, while familiarity breeds contempt. Let his discourse continually turn on what is good and honourable; the more he admonishes, the less he will have to punish. He must control his temper without, however, shutting his eyes to faults requiring correction: his instruction must be free from affectation, his industry great, his demands on his class continuous, but not extravagant. He must be ready to answer questions and to put them unasked to those who sit silent. In praising the recitations of his pupils he must be neither grudging nor over-generous: the former quality will give them a distaste for work, while the latter will produce a complacent self-satisfaction. In correcting faults he must avoid sarcasm and above all abuse: for teachers whose rebukes seem to imply positive dislike discourage industry. He should declaim daily himself and, what is more, without stint, that his class may take his utterances home with them. For however many models for imitation he may give them from the authors they are reading, it will still be found that fuller nourishment is provided by the living voice, as we call it, more especially when it proceeds from the teacher himself, who, if his pupils are rightly instructed, should be the object of their affection and respect. And it is scarcely possible to say how much more readily we imitate those whom we like.
>
> —*Quintilian*[1]

[1] *Quintilian,* translated by H. E. Butler, G. P. Putnam's Sons, New York, 1920, p. 213.

ers seldom need or use it; the poor teachers fill it up with no noticeable good effects.

It Is Not the Severity of Punishments Meted Out. The usual approach of the teacher who is inept at disciplinary matters is to increase the severity of the punishments meted out. "Copy pages 234,

235, and 236." "Why?" "And pages 237, 238, and 239." "What did *I* do?" "And pages. . . ." This is the way the sequence goes, but as the students see the impossibility of adequate performance, behavior remains unaffected.

It Is Not Sending Youngsters Out of the Room. If the youngsters are sent outside the door, others will want the same privilege. Because teachers who have to send youngsters to the principal invariably have to send too many, and because the principals do not care to maintain discipline for the teacher, this practice more frequently results in the dismissal of the teacher at the end of the year rather than in improved discipline.

The essence of the good disciplinarian's success in his dramatic technique, his acting ability. Without it, physical size, sex, keeping youngsters after school, corporal punishment, severity of punishments, sending children to the principal, or "jugs" are all completely ineffective; with dramatic technique, they are all almost unnecessary. It is not what is done, but how it is done: a lowered but distinct voice; a sudden shift in voice; a difficult-to-answer question; a dramatic pause; a raised voice; an eye which suddenly becomes fixed on the disturber of the peace. All these may enter into the dramatic technique of a teacher.

There are of course some other important considerations for good discipline. Make as few rules as possible, since there is no sense in creating needless enforcement problems. Enforce these rules assiduously, especially against the first transgressors, since the first apparently harmless violations of essential rules have a way of snowballing. Always deal with an individual, never a whole class; in the interests of both justice and efficiency it is better to determine the individual responsible than to challenge, much less punish, a whole class. Lastly, the disciplinarian should always *act:* act disturbed; act as if the incident, which really seems trivial to the teacher, is of transcending importance; and act emotionally disturbed, taking care never to get really emotionally involved in the handling of misbehavior. For it is when the teacher participates in an emotional interaction with the child that he is likely to make an unwise statement or take an imprudent step; or as someone has observed, "If the teacher is dog-tired at the end of each day, maybe it is because he has been barking all day."

THE SCHOOL ADMINISTRATOR AND DISCIPLINE

In helping teachers develop as effective classroom managers, the principal must himself understand the general considerations discussed above. Good disciplinarians can be developed; dramatic technique can be learned. In handling the disciplinary cases which will inevitably be referred to him, of course, the dramatic techniques of the principal himself will be severely strained, at least in the first months of his tenure. The non-classroom disciplinary tone of the school will ordinarily be the result of many dramatically handled individual cases. These many separate jobs of acting by the principal should create the general impression among the students that, nice as the principal ordinarily is and fair as he always is, it is uncomfortable to deal with him when you are in the wrong.

In the light of what is known about effective discipline, the school administrator, whether in a large or a one-school system, will find it necessary to develop some regulations governing disciplinary activities of the staff. These will especially be needed in matters concerning detention of pupils, corporal punishment, suspension, expulsion, or exclusion of students from school, and specifying types of punishment not permitted. Sample policies covering these items are presented below.

DETENTION OF PUPILS[2]

No pupil shall be detained as punishment during the noon recess. Reasonable detention at the close of the school day is not forbidden, but such detention shall not exceed 30 minutes for elementary school pupils or 45 minutes for high school pupils. In case a child in an elementary school is detained at the end of the day, the parents shall be notified in advance. A child who is transported in a school bus shall not be made to miss the bus by reason of such detention, except with the permission of the parents.

Comment. It is clear from the phraseology used ("is not forbidden") and the restrictions set (advance notification of parents, time

---

[2] *Rules and Regulations,* Cincinnati Board of Education, 1955.

limits, and children who ride busses) that the use of detention is not encouraged under this policy. Moreover, for the weak teacher detention is generally ineffective, since there is little reason to think such a teacher will handle students any better after school hours than during them. For the strong teacher, who uses detention only sparingly, the above policy is not too restrictive. The handbooks of several diocesan school systems discuss detention along the lines of the following quotation from the *Handbook of School Policies and Practices* of the Diocese of Rochester: "Detention after school should be used rarely and it should never be prolonged beyond fifteen minutes. It is never permitted to detain pupils of the Primary Grades after school hours. Such detention usually penalizes an older brother or sister who must wait for the detained child." The *Administrative Manual for the Archdiocese of New York* states: "The detention of an entire class is to be deplored."

CORPORAL PUNISHMENT[3]

Except in most unusual circumstances, corporal punishment shall be used only as a last resort after other corrective measures have been used without success. Whenever possible, the parents shall be advised in advance of the decision to administer such punishment and the reasons therefor.

The decision to administer corporal punishment shall be made by the principal after consultation with the teachers or other staff members familiar with the case.

When such punishment is administered, the following rules shall be observed:

a. The punishment shall be administered by the principal, or by some member of the professional staff designated by him. In case the responsibility is delegated by the principal, there shall be a separate and distinct delegation for each instance of corporal punishment.

b. The punishment shall be administered by striking the pupil across the buttocks with the palm of the hand or a broad paddle, and in no other manner.

c. The administration of corporal punishment shall be witnessed by at least one other member of the staff.

d. Corporal punishment shall not be administered with malice

---

[3] *Ibid.*

toward the pupil, nor at a time when the person administering the punishment is angered or impassioned, nor shall the nature or amount of punishment be unreasonable or of such nature as to leave permanent marks or permanent ill effects.

e. The principal shall file a report on the proper blank in the office of the assistant superintendent in charge of the department of administration after each and every instance of corporal punishment.

A teacher may use physical force against a pupil without advance approval by the principal, when, because of unusual circumstances, immediate action is essential for self-defense, for the preservation of sufficient order to permit instruction to proceed, or for the protection of other persons or of property of the board of education. In every such case, the teacher shall within 24 hours make a report to the principal setting forth the circumstances and the nature of the action taken.

Comment. A policy like the one above is clearly not designed to foster wide use of corporal punishment, yet the possibility of using it remains a vague threat, where such is useful. The specific restrictions outlined serve the useful purpose of protecting the teacher: the principal must make the decision; parents shall generally be notified in advance; a paddle (not a club) shall be used. Furthermore, the presence of a witness and the necessity for a report serve to help the legal case of a teacher or principal tried for assault or sued for damages, neither an unlikely outcome of corporal punishment. Once more it can be said that the good teacher seldom needs to use corporal punishment; and for the poor teacher, it is ineffectual and possibly expensive, emotionally and perhaps even financially. It is for these reasons that some states, some public school systems, and some dioceses specifically forbid any type of corporal punishment. In dioceses where corporal punishment may be permitted, regulations specify that the approval of the pastor must first be secured.

Suspension, Expulsion, and Exclusion of Pupils from Public School[4]

Suspension or expulsion of pupils shall be made in accordance with Section 3313.66 of the Ohio General Code, Revised, which states: "No pupil shall be suspended from school by a superintend-

[4] *Ibid.*

ent or teacher except for such time as is necessary to convene the board of education, nor shall one be expelled except by a majority vote of the full membership of such board, and after the parent or guardian of the offending pupil has been notified of the proposed expulsion, and permitted to be heard against it. No pupil shall be suspended or expelled from any school beyond the current term thereof."

Exclusion from school, for a period not to exceed three days, shall be used as a means of discipline only for serious offenses against the welfare of the school or for gross violation of the rules of the schools, and only in cases where other forms of discipline are not likely to be sufficiently effective. Such exclusion shall be effected only with the approval of the principal who shall immediately notify the child's parent of the action and the reasons therefor in writing; he shall also immediately notify the appropriate attendance center by telephone and send a copy of the letter to the supervisor of the attendance center.

Comment. The restrictions of a policy such as this make it difficult to think of suspension, expulsion, and exclusion of children from public schools as possible disciplinary measures. Teachers and principals are left with one real weapon, their dramatic technique!

EXPULSION OF PUPILS FROM CATHOLIC SCHOOLS[5]

The expulsion of a child from a Catholic school is a serious matter, and should be invoked only as a last resort. The fact that a child presents a behavior problem is not in itself a sufficient reason for expelling the child. An effort must be made to find the cause of the trouble. The social worker, the physician, the psychologist, and the psychiatrist can be of assistance in determining the cause of misbehavior. Frequently the cause is one which can be removed and the behavior problem solved. In such cases expulsion will not solve the problem, but may only aggravate it by removing the child from the influence of a Catholic school environment.

Every case of expulsion is an admission that even with religion in our program, we are unable to correct the trouble. Nevertheless, cases arise when expulsion is justified. While it is not possible to enumerate all cases that would arise in this connection, two general conditions may be laid down.

[5] *Handbook of Regulations for the Schools of the Archdiocese of Cincinnati,* 1957.

A. Delinquency and immorality that would warrant commitment to a correctional institution, or would constitute a definite menace to the morale of the school.

B. Incorrigibility, and persistent irregular attendance.

Before a pupil may be expelled from school the parents must be notified. The parents should be asked to call at the school. Every effort should be made to enlist the cooperation of the parents in order to save the child and avoid invoking the extreme penalty of expulsion.

It is the responsibility of any non-public school to notify the public school authorities whenever a pupil is dropped from its enrollment for any reason. In Cincinnati the name of an expelled pupil must be listed as a *withdrawal* on the census report sent to the Board of Education. All cases in which no legal reason is given for the withdrawal are referred immediately by the Census Department to the proper Attendance Department for investigation, so that school-placement may be made as soon as possible. . . .

The dropping of a pupil from high school for inability to do the type of work offered in the Catholic high school is not to be regarded as expulsion. Authority to proceed in such cases rests with the principal.

Comment. While exclusion from school (with resulting transfer to public schools) is more possible for the Catholic school administrator than for the public school administrator, as pointed out above, each instance is an admission that even with religious guidance, the school could not solve the problem. Action which results in placing the child in a school where the help of religion is not available is indeed a last resort to be used only when the administrator and teacher have given up all hope. In keeping with this point of view, the manual of the Diocese of Bellville, Illinois, concerning expulsion, reads: "Grave reason is always necessary to justify expelling a child from our parochial schools. Lack of academic achievement or effort should never be considered a reason for dismissal. Moral delinquency alone is considered sufficient reason for expelling a child, and then only when such delinquency is a bad influence on other children. The purpose of our Catholic schools should not be to weed out pupils, but rather to change or modify undesirable behavior."

DISAPPROVED DISCIPLINARY MEASURES[6]

The following disciplinary measures are forbidden: (1) corporal punishment including shaking and slapping; (2) language which is sarcastic or calculated to bring ridicule on the pupil, his parents, his background, etc.; (3) sending pupils outside the room, to the coat room, a lower class, the corridor, to their home, etc., where instruction is missed and supervision is absent; (4) using specifically religious actions (e.g., kneeling in church) or important class assignments as punitive measures; (5) bizarre and unusual punishments; (6) withholding or altering rightfully earned academic marks; (7) fines where no destruction of property is involved.

Comment. A number of diocesan handbooks have rules covering disapproved disciplinary measures or indiscreet punishments such as the above. Regarding sarcasm, the Rochester diocesan handbook reads: "Sarcasm is likewise to be avoided, as doing irreparable harm and accomplishing nothing." A regulation forbidding the use of religious actions or class assignments as punitive measures is, of course, based on the likelihood of transferring emotional reactions to punishment to areas where favorable attitudes are particularly important.

Questions for Discussion or Investigation

1. Is discipline more of a problem in schools today than it was about twenty years ago? Can you locate any evidence, one way or another, on this question?

2. On the basis of reading and investigation, prepare a precise description of Rousseau's concept of the nature of man.

3. Be prepared to present three instances of dramatic technique other than those referred to in this chapter—techniques which you have used, observed, or consider likely to be effective as a part of the direct approach to maintaining sound discipline.

4. Are there disciplinary measures which you feel should be expressly forbidden by policy within a school or school system in addition to the seven cited from the manual of the Archdiocese of San Francisco? Are there any of these seven which you feel should not have been included?

Readings and References

Addicott, Irwin O.: *Constructive Classroom Control,* Howard Chandler, Publisher, San Francisco, 1958.

[6] *Administrative Handbook,* Archdiocese of San Francisco, 1956.

Brothers of the Christian Schools in the New York Province: *A Teacher's Guide,* La Salle Bureau, New York, 1959.

Chamberlain, John: *Problems in Education: Where Do We Go from Here?* A bound collection of articles previously published in The Wall Street Journal, New York, 1960.

Charitas, Sister Mary: *Purposive Classroom Management,* Holt, Rinehart and Winston, Inc., New York, 1953.

Cutts, Norma E., and Nicholas Moseley: *Teaching the Disorderly Pupil in the Elementary and Secondary School,* Longmans, Green & Co., Inc., New York, 1957.

Hymes, James L., Jr.: *Behavior and Misbehavior,* Prentice-Hall, Inc., Englewood Cliffs, N.J., 1955.

Ojeman, Ralph H.: *Personality Adjustment of Individual Children,* National Education Association, What Research Says to the Teacher series, no. 5, Washington, 1954.

Sibbing, Paul A.: "Evaluating School Discipline in 1952," *National Catholic Educational Association Bulletin,* vol. 48, no. 3, February, 1952.

Stack, Philip Lawrence: *A National Study of the Guidance Services in the Catholic Secondary Schools,* The Catholic University of America Press, Washington, 1958.

Teacher Opinion on Pupil Behavior, 1955–56, National Education Association Research Bulletin 34, vol. 2, April, 1956.

13. *Administrative Operation:*
Essential Policy Molds

Developing policy molds to lessen the number of *ad hoc* decisions which administrators must make is especially important in the operation of a school system, for the administrative operation includes judicious management of many people in areas which obviously call for rules and regulations. Chapter 13, therefore, is devoted first of all to a discussion of the role of handbooks of rules and regulations; and then successively to suggestions for policies covering such diverse subjects as dismissal of students; preventing exploitation of pupils for commercial purposes; regulating extracurricular activities, social clubs, and musical organizations; homework; intraschool funds; and the evening use of school buildings.

HANDBOOK OF RULES AND REGULATIONS

As educational administration has rapidly become more complicated, the number and complexity of the decisions demanded of school administrators have grown proportionately. So, too, have the frequency, size, and scope of handbooks of rules and regulations governing the conduct of schools within a given school system.

238

The following ten rules were adopted to govern the schools of one township school district in 1864:

First—Each Sub School consist of all the Schollars within the limits of a District Established by The Board of Education and Shall be governed with the following rules.

Second—The hours of instruction Shall be from 8½ o'clock till 11½ o'clock in The forenoon and from one o'clock till four o'clock in The afternoon.

Third—Each pupil Shall have a Seat assigned him or her by the Teacher adapted to his or her Size and age.

Fourth—The Boys and girls are to be Seated Separate from each other and are expected to be of good conduct and at all times Readily obey the commands of Their Teacher.

Fifth—On entering The School room hats, bonnets, overcoats, and caps are to be hung up at The appointed place.

Sixth—No exchange of Seats is to take place between Schollars without the Teachers permission.

Seventh—It Shall be the chief duty of the Teacher to have every pupil well instructed in the Most useful and common branches of learning Such as Reading, Writing, and Arithmetic, and never to permit any to Spend Their Most precious time Studying higher branches when it Should necessarily be yet all devoted to that which is most useful for them to acquire.

Eighth—The Teacher should be undeviating in adherence to a mild but firm uniform and moderate System of School discipline and Shall pay most especial regard to moral habits and general behavior as well as the mental instruction of his Pupils.

Ninth—All quarling, fighting, Vulgar, profane or disrespectful language or conduct, Either in School, During intermission, or on the way to or from School shall not be tolerated; and any pupil guilty of Such conduct Shall be publicly admonished and if found to continue Such transgressions and disobey These regulations as well as the orders and admonitions of The Teachers; Such pupils may be reported to the directors that they May be admonished Suspended or Expelled.

Tenth—To preserve order, all punishments shall be Justly dealt in a measure Suitable to the offence, in a calm respectable and effective Manner. Corporal Punishment Shall only be inflicted in Extreme cases after all other reasonable methods have proved unavailing, and should be in a humane but impressive manner.

As late as 1940, one of the largest city school districts in the Middle West was still able to operate, albeit with some confusion, with a brief booklet of rules adopted and published in 1911, supplemented by board of education minutes interspersed with unrelated policies adopted over the intervening years. Today the general book of rules and regulations for the same system is over a hundred pages —codified, indexed, and augmented by detailed operational manuals covering such items as the evening use of school buildings, maintenance policies and responsibilities, and the handling of intraschool funds. Each item is keyed into the over-all numerical system of indexing.

DEVELOPING POLICIES FOR HANDBOOKS

While the governing board of an educational institution is basically responsible for adopting school policies, the chief executive is charged with developing and recommending such policy to the board for decision. The effectiveness of policies adopted depends in part on how they are developed. If those affected by the policy are represented in its formulation, the result will likely be both sound and respected.

In a handbook published to assist in the development of written school personnel policies, a committee of the Ohio Education Association makes these observations:[1]

> There may be temptation at this point to rush ahead without a sincere effort to get employee participation. Some boards and administrators, intentionally or unintentionally, have short-circuited staff member involvement in a vain effort to speed up the time required to complete the policy statement. This does save time but it also violates the basic principle which underlies the whole process.
>
> Staff participation is more important than any amount of time which might be saved. If those who must live by policies are to be expected to support them wholeheartedly, they must have a part in the development of those policies.
>
> Participation will be confined to representative teachers, principals, and non-teaching employees serving on policy study groups in most school systems. However, all school employees can take some part in the process in many systems.

[1] *School Personnel Policies,* Ohio Education Association, Commission on Teacher Education and Personnel Standards, Columbus, 1956.

The function of these work groups will be to study carefully board policy as it exists, to offer ideas and suggestions which they feel should be covered by policy, to review policies which have been adopted by other boards, and to help draft tentative policy statements. . . .

There are hazards to be encountered in trying to make policy statements too brief or too elaborate, too flexible or too inflexible. Broad participation by school personnel in the policy development project will help avoid these difficulties. Policy must be reasonably specific if it is to have value. On the other hand, a policy statement which attempts to govern rigidly in detail every action of every employee, represents an unrealistic effort to put a school system into a strait jacket. The chief shortcoming of such policy statements is that they become bogged down with too much administrative detail —the type of detailed regulations which would be based upon policy but published separately as regulations.

A middle ground must be reached somewhere between the extremes of meaningless generality and unyielding rigidity.

ORGANIZATION OF HANDBOOKS

A handbook of policies and general regulations must be organized with a flexible numbering system to permit additions at any point without disrupting the unity of the whole. Some schools and school systems find adequate a bound publication reissued every three to five years. Between printings, changes are duplicated and distributed as addenda. Other school systems, especially small systems that need relatively few copies, find desirable flexibility in loose-leaf folders in which each rule is entered on a separate page, with dividers separating one section from another.

In either case, a comprehensive numbering system is fundamental. A handbook could be organized in chapters following the general organization of Part 3 of this book. Each of the six major responsibilities of the administrator could be a chapter, with preceding chapters on the board of control and the general plan of organization. Administrators have found that assigning a thousand numbers to a section permits of adequate expansion of any one section without getting into complicated decimal designations for later insertions.

Thus a general pattern of numbers for a handbook could be:

The Board of Control	1000s
The Administrative Pattern	2000s
Instruction	3000s
Administrative Operation	4000s
Pupil Personnel Services	5000s
Business Management	6000s
Community Relations	7000s
Research	8000s

In turn, Business Management, arbitrarily assigned the 6000s, might have the following general numerology:

Finance	6000–6199
Housing	6200–6399
Supplies	6400–6599
Food Services	6600–6799

Or if regulations concerning teacher personnel were assigned a block of fifty numbers from 4100 to 4149, with item 4125 covering three-day absences without loss of salary for death in the family, tenths could be used for later definitions of who was considered "in the family." Thus 4125.1 might define any relative living in the household of the teacher as "in the family."

ILLUSTRATIVE POLICIES FOR HANDLING PUPILS

The following policies taken from the Handbook entitled *Rules and Regulations of the Cincinnati Public Schools 1955* are presented here for several reasons: they are illustrative of the numerology used in Chapter 10 of this handbook; they provoke thinking on a number of items on which administrative policy is necessary; and they are items which the author feels merit comment in any discussion of administrative operation.

Section 10.11—*Early Dismissal of School*
No school shall be dismissed before the regular hour nor the regularly established hours of the day be changed except with the knowledge and approval of the assistant superintendent in charge of the department of administration.

Comment. Since the school calendar is drawn up to provide the number of school days desired for children in a community, it follows that deviations from it must be approved by the official responsible for system-wide enforcement. Only an occasional grave emergency in which there is no time for consultation with such an official would justify an exception. Diocesan manuals seem to indicate that historically pastors and principals have awarded free days without regard to the official school calendar issued by the superintendent's office. This is reflected in such regulations as the following from the *Book of Policies,* Archdiocese of Chicago: "The School Calendar is sent from the office of the Archdiocesan Superintendent each year. Pastors and principals are expected to follow the Calendar strictly and should not grant any free days . . . with the exception of a patronal or traditionally observed feast. Each sister . . . is entitled to one free day each semester for the purpose of visiting other schools." These regulations usually refer to the minimum number of school days demanded by state school codes.

Section 10.12—*Dismissal of Individual Pupils*

No teacher or other employee shall permit or cause any pupil to leave school prior to the regular hour of dismissal except with the knowledge and approval of the principal or administrative assistants and with the knowledge of the parent or guardian.

No elementary school child shall be permitted to leave school prior to dismissal at the request of or in the company of anyone other than a school employee, a police officer, a court official, a public health official, or the parents or guardians of the child, unless the permission of the parent or guardian be first secured.

No pupil shall be permitted to leave school prior to dismissal except for reasons approved by the superintendent of schools, and such reasons shall give primary consideration to the welfare of the pupil.

Comment. A regulation such as this provides only the protection to which children, parents, teachers, and administrators are entitled. Clearly, children's lives are not to be risked by sending them from school at a time when they should be in attendance. Parents have a right to expect that when a child arrives in school he will remain in the relative safety of the school grounds during the school day. Teachers and principals who follow any other practices become liable for damages should injuries to a pupil result. Occasional well-publicized incidents of kidnapping underscore the necessity for vigilance in securing parental permission before releasing the child to anyone else, perhaps even a police officer, unless he is armed with a warrant.

Section 10.13—*Excursions*

Any teacher taking any group of pupils on a field trip or excursion off the school grounds must secure the approval of the principal in advance. In case the trip or excursion involves the transportation of a pupil in any vehicle, the written permission of the parent shall be secured in advance.

Comment. While the written permission of the parent is desirable so that he is kept informed about the whereabouts of his child, many teachers mistakenly believe that a note on file relieves them of responsibility in case of accident. If any accident occurs on such an excursion because of the negligence of the teacher, the note has no effect on the situation since one is always liable for his own negligence and since no one (not even a parent) can, in advance, sign away the rights of another to recover for damages owing to negligence. (For a discussion of negligence and legal liability of school personnel, see Chapter 14.)

Section 10.14—*Errands*

No pupil shall be sent from the school building during school hours to perform an errand or act as messenger, except with the knowledge and approval of the principal and then only for urgent and necessary school business and with the consent of the pupil's parent or guardian.

Comment. Left to themselves, some teachers will use pupils to run errands beyond school grounds. Even some principals have been known to use student messengers to take school money to the bank each day. The implications of risk to the student and to the financial solvency of the school official seem almost too obvious to mention.

Section 10.15—*Interviews*

No person other than an employee of the board of education or public health personnel assigned to the schools shall be allowed to interview a pupil at school except with the approval of the principal. The principal shall grant such approval only in case he is convinced that the interview is in the interest of the pupil or in the interest of justice. Such an interview shall be held in the presence of the principal or the administrative assistants.

Comment. Once again, the child must be protected, as must be the parents. With the number of broken homes today, the principal must exercise care that the parent legally responsible for the child is the one with whom he is dealing. Should any interview with a child be granted by a principal, the child's protection demands the presence of a school official at the interview.

Section 10.16—*Use of Records*

The records of the school concerning an individual pupil shall be used for the promotion of the welfare of the pupil, and shall not be made available to any outside person or agency unless it is reasonably clear that such person or agency will use the records to the advantage of the child or his family or in the interest of justice. No teacher shall ever give information from the child's record to anyone outside the school staff, except the child's parents, unless he shall first obtain the permission of the principal. Other school officials may give information from the records only to the child, his parents, the authorized representatives of the child and his parents, police officers or other public officials, prospective employers, representatives of recognized social agencies or other persons approved by the child's parents.

Comment. Appropriate safeguards must be taken in handling school records which are confidential and to be disclosed only to persons having a legitimate interest in them. Such persons include prospective employers, government officials, police departments, and of course, parents. An interesting related problem is whether the school should provide the insistent parent with information on the IQ or mental age of his child. Several basic considerations are involved. One is that this knowledge can be so used and abused that schools prefer not to divulge it except to professional persons. However, if the parent insists on knowing this information—since the parent is basically responsible for the education of the child—it is our opinion that the administrator ultimately should provide it. The number of obstacles he places in the way of the parent varies with the parent in question: the parent's background, the kind of interest he takes in the child, and his emotional stability.

Section 10.17—*Lists of Names*

Teachers shall not furnish lists of names and addresses of pupils to anyone other than school officials. No principal or other school official shall furnish any such list to any outside person or agency until he has made an investigation and satisfied himself that the list will not be used for any commercial gain and will not be used in any way to the embarrassment or annoyance of the school, the pupils, or the parents of the pupils, except that the superintendent may authorize the release of such lists of members of the senior class to local schools and colleges, which, in his opinion, offer educational opportunities of sufficient merit to interest high school graduates.

Nothing in this rule shall prohibit a parent-teacher association or parents' organization being given the names and addresses of the parents of pupils in the schools to be used in the promotion of activities approved by the superintendent of schools.

Comment. This regulation is based on the right of the child and his parent to be protected from commercial exploitation through the school. Obviously a salesman for a book firm will find his job facilitated if he can call on parents and leave the impression that he is working closely with the school in the educational development of their child. To gain this advantage some firms have been known to give themselves deceptive titles and to secure the cooperation of unwary principals in having children complete information blanks for "research surveys on educational problems." Armed with the name of the school, the pupil, his address, the subjects he is interested in, and the subjects he dislikes, engaging salesmen successfully assault the pocketbooks of the parents a short while later, apparently with the approval of the school principal, whose name is artfully bandied about in the sales line.

Section 10.18—*Eligibility for Participation*

Membership in all school organizations and participation in all pupil activities which are a part of the school's program and for which the schools accept responsibility shall be open to all pupils on the following terms of qualification:

a. The achievement and maintenance in each instance and for each activity of whatever level of scholarship may be required by the high school principals' council and approved by the superintendent of schools.

b. The maintenance of a level of school citizenship by pupil participants which is considered by the principal of the school to be satisfactory.

c. The possession by each pupil of sufficient physical well-being, stature, and strength to enable him to participate in a particular activity without endangering his health.

d. The possession by pupils of the modicum of talent and ability that the member or members of a faculty in charge of a particular activity may consider to be necessary.

School principals may at their discretion determine a maximum number of organizations and activities in which pupils of varying scholastic levels shall be permitted to participate.

Comment. This policy provides the essential controls on extracurricular activities which experience has proved necessary. It establishes a uniform standard of eligibility for athletic and nonathletic activities; it gives the principal adequate controls over who is permitted to participate in activities and to what extent; and it gives the faculty member in charge of an activity some control over who may participate in the activity for which he is responsible.

Section 10.19—*Social Clubs*

It is recognized that high school youths need an outlet for the social urge that is characteristic of adolescence. To insure insofar as possible that this urge finds expression in wholesome ways, the formation of social clubs of high school pupils and the making by high school principals of provisions for their supervision are authorized.

Comment. The tendency of high school youngsters to form secret fraternities and sororities has caused problems for school administrators for many years. Formerly, membership in such organizations was generally forbidden by school authorities, though the interdicts had little actual effect. The policy quoted above, as does the following one, envisions a newer approach to the problem: to eliminate undesirable features of secret social organizations through recognition, regulation, and supervision. While additional responsibilities fall on school personnel under these policies, some administrators have found results well worth the effort.

Section 10.20—*School Organizations in General*

In all organizations, including social organizations, in which membership is by invitation of the members, it shall be determined by majority vote of the members, or by some other equivalent democratic procedure approved by the principal of the school.

The constitution and by-laws, initiation procedures, activities and programs, size, grade levels of operation, times of holding meetings, and financial practices of all school organizations shall be subject to the supervision and approval of the school principal or faculty members designated by him for this purpose.

All pupils who desire to participate in any school activity and who meet eligibility requirements shall be permitted to do so and the schools shall establish a sufficient number of organizations or activities to make this possible.

It shall be the duty of the principal of each school to see that all activities in which pupils engage are properly supervised and that social activities are properly chaperoned by members of the school's staff or by committees of parents.

Under the direction of the superintendent of schools the high school principals' council may establish in the supervision of all student activities such operating procedures and regulations consistent with these regulations as it may deem necessary for the proper discharge of the responsibilities these regulations assign to the principals of the schools. . . .

The members of any organizations of high school pupils which are not under the supervision of other agencies approved by the superintendent of schools and which do not elect to accept the supervision and regulation of school authorities, shall not be permitted to engage in any extra-curriculum activity of the schools.

Comment. By providing for constitutions, membership invitations by democratic procedures, supervised activities and programs, larger numbers of organizations, eligibility requirements, and penalties for belonging to unrecognized organizations, the serious problems of secret fraternities and sororities are lessened. Yet the natural urge to join a social group at adolescence may still be satisfied, though directed and regulated.

Section 10.21—*Musical Organizations*

School bands and other musical organizations composed of pupils shall make public appearances only in the following instances:

a. At functions which are part of the school program, whether held in the school building or elsewhere.

b. At community functions organized in the interests of the schools.

c. At educational meetings or conventions.

d. On educational broadcasts designed to acquaint the public with the work of the schools.

e. On civic occasions when such participation does not encroach upon the opportunities of professional musicians for employment.

f. At benefit performances where professional musicians would likewise donate their services.

g. On other occasions only upon agreement between school authorities and official representatives of the organized professional musicians.

In case the appearance of any band or musical organization requires members to be absent from their homes overnight the approval of the superintendent shall be secured in advance.

Comment. The main purpose of this policy is to clarify relations with appropriate organizations of professional musicians, particularly musicians' unions.

HOMEWORK

Homework—should there be any, how much, and on what nights —has been a matter of considerable controversy between extremists for some years, with the pendulum currently swinging in the direction of more nightwork. While the answers to the problems of homework should flow out of instructional considerations, it is in another realm that the administrator's concern with this matter arises: parents who complain about too little or too much nightwork or parents who complain that too much comes from too many teachers on the same night; teachers who complain that other high school teachers monopolize all the students' time for home study. Problems like these make essential some school policies on the subject of nightwork.

INSTRUCTIONAL CONSIDERATIONS UNFAVORABLE TO HOMEWORK

Homework can be, and frequently has been, completely ineffective, a waste of time. This is amply demonstrated by many well-planned and well-conducted research studies, the results of which have generally indicated that whether homework was regularly assigned or was never assigned made absolutely no difference in the amount of subject matter learned by students. According to Otto,[2]

> Researches at the elementary-school level show: (*a*) there is a very small relationship between the amount of time spent in home study and pupil progress; (*b*) homework is not significantly related to achievement as measured by teachers' marks or standardized tests; (*c*) homework at the elementary-school level has a slight positive relationship to success in high school; (*d*) voluntary homework has about as many values as compulsory homework; (*e*) the benefits of assigned homework are too small to counterbalance the disadvantages, especially for pupils in poor homes; (*f*) compulsory homework does not result in sufficiently improved academic accomplishments to justify the retention of the "achievement argument" as the chief justification for home-study assignments.

Research at the high school level has generally been in accord with the above findings. One of the most careful studies involved American history in a large New York City high school. Students were matched by mental ability and divided into classes with the same teacher teaching both groups. The only difference between matched groups was that the usual substantial amount of homework was assigned to one group of classes and none to the second. Final achievement tests revealed no significant difference in the attainments of the two groups.

That homework should frequently be educationally ineffective is consistent with the general conclusion that what children learn academically is principally the result of what goes on between the teacher and pupils in the classroom. This is a generalization supported by research in areas other than that of homework. For example, in a controlled study of the influence of television on school achievement of sixth- and seventh-grade children, Walter J. Clarke reported in 1951 that no significant relationship existed between school achievement and televiewing habits of children.[3]

Not only has homework frequently been proved a waste of the students' time, but it is often accompanied by undesirable by-prod-

---

[2] *Encyclopedia of Educational Research,* Walter S. Monroe (ed.), rev. ed., The Macmillan Company, New York, 1950, pp. 380–381.

[3] Walter J. Clarke, *Of Children and Television,* report of research conducted by Xavier University, Cincinnati, 1951.

ucts such as permitting children to practice and fix errors when they have failed to learn adequately in class; rewarding students whose assignments are copied or are done by parents; fixing slovenly habits of study in children who are improperly supervised at home; interfering with family activities which are sometimes more educationally productive than many assignments; aggravating tensions in the slow-learning child who, after a hard day at school, may need physical exercise and recreation rather than harassment by overzealous parents to do in three hours what an average student may accomplish in an hour; and placing on parents tasks which demand emotional detachment and professional skills which they do not have. In view of probable by-products such as these, as well as the absence of adequate provisions for home study in many families, it is small wonder that research has discovered homework to be generally ineffective.

INSTRUCTIONAL CONSIDERATIONS FAVORABLE TO HOMEWORK

While it is generally true that children learn best in the classroom under the guidance of the teacher, children must gradually develop habits of independent study, since the ability to solve problems independently is an indispensable characteristic of an educated person. No matter how unfruitful nightwork has been in the past, one ought still to direct the pupil to independent study as he advances on the educational ladder.

To accomplish this, perhaps a different kind of home assignment should be given in a manner different from past practice. One educator describes homework thus:[4]

> The pupil whose homework is a monotonous continuum of stint after stint in a text-book followed by a classroom rehash is the child who complains, dawdles and accomplishes little. . . .
>
> A kind of activity, largely self-generated but organized through considerable planning in the classroom, now becomes his homework. It is no longer a stint of drudgery to satisfy a taskmaster; it is a means of fulfilling the child's normal desire to learn.
>
> Homework now takes on many aspects, some familiar in appear-

[4] Ablett H. Flury, "Putting Lifework in Homework," *New Jersey Education Association Review,* vol. 30, no. 7, March, 1957.

ance and others quite different. It may be taking a trip or writing a report. It may be the careful observation of the shapes of flowers and trees, or the planting of some seeds in a flower box to see them germinate and grow. It may be an excursion into art or music. It may be watching a particular television program, followed by a family discussion of its significance. . . . It may be memorizing poetry. It may be drill and practice for some learning in which a pupil recognizes that his automatic response is essential, such as in the use of number facts. . . .

Homework of this kind which grows out of a vitalized classroom is possible and desirable at all grade levels.

Besides developing habits of individual study, there is a second reason for an increasing amount of homework as the youngster advances up the educational ladder through secondary school. To achieve educational objectives in some fields, more time than is available in school is needed. For example, if youngsters going to school are to read novels, they must read them outside class hours since it would be impossible to cover several novels a year in class and accomplish anything else. The vocabulary of a foreign language or conjugations of irregular verbs must to some extent be mastered outside of class hours or again little progress will be made in a year. Longer compositions must be completed at home. Even in the elementary school, learning in subjects dependent on practice or drill will, for slower-learning students at least, demand more practice than can be given in school if the more capable students are not to be impeded. Fixing number facts, spelling, and memorization are examples of work requiring outside drill.

ELEMENTS OF A HOMEWORK POLICY

Three elements are suggested as desirable in a homework policy for schools.

1. In view of the real doubt which valid research studies have shed on the educational values of homework as commonly assigned, it is incumbent on teachers to justify each assignment. Does the assignment promote genuine self-study? Or does it represent a necessary extension of the time available in school? If the latter, is it necessary for all students or only for some? This approach clearly eliminates any policy requiring a specified length of time to be spent by the "average student" in homework every night.

2. If homework is to promote independent study, it obviously cannot be assigned in a routine manner. Painstaking motivation of the student, detailed advanced planning in class, and teacher originality are indispensable if the objective is to be realized.

3. If homework is assigned to supplement classroom learning by time taken from recreation, physical exercise, or family living, it should be assigned well in advance of the deadline for completing it. This provides opportunity for the high school youth to select his time for reading a novel, for example, and makes it less likely that too much work will be required by several teachers on a given night. Comprehensive instructional units with unit outlines will facilitate such budgeting of student time. Here again, teacher creativity in providing motivation will be the key to success.

At the elementary school level where nightwork will generally be of the time-extending type, usually with slower-learning children, directions to parents on long-term help to their children in specific tasks like the use of flash cards will make success more likely. If the work of the school is to be supplemented by unsupervised practice exercises at home, obviously the work should be started at school lest the wrong facts or approaches become fixed!

If the principles involved in the above three items are included in a statement of policy on homework adopted by a school or school system, it is probable that homework would be required in schools presently following a "no-homework" policy; less homework would be required in schools that currently evidence too much belief in it; and many of the unfortunate by-products of both extremes would be lessened.

ADMINISTRATION OF INTRASCHOOL FUNDS

One aspect of school finance is properly treated as a phase of administrative operation rather than of business management. (For the latter, see Chapter 17.) This is the administration of intraschool funds.

While there are some receipts which are difficult to classify sharply as belonging to the business function or to the function of administrative operation, most items of income are readily distinguishable. Income from taxes in public schools and income from tuitions or collections for the support of private schools are clearly to be classified as a part of the financial aspect of business management; so too are expenditures of such moneys. Just as evidently, however, income from dramatic productions, dues from clubs, or a gift to supply a scholarship or to purchase a projector for a given school are intraschool funds which fall logically into the area of administrative operation. The handling of such funds is properly the responsibility of the principal of a given school.

In general, the distinction between types of funds involved is this: Income secured to support the instructional program of the schools is part of school finance, a system-wide responsibility; in a public school such moneys are referred to as public funds. Income drawn from sources within the individual school which are properly extrainstructional are referred to as intraschool funds; in a public school system they may be called private funds. Actually this distinction is forced on some public schools by state laws which may forbid spending public funds for such purposes as the support of interscholastic athletics or the purchase of band uniforms.

While both the receipt and expenditure of intraschool funds are responsibilities of principals, who are directly charged with the administrative operation of the individual schools of a system, clearly no school system can safely leave the supervision of these matters completely to their discretion. In large city systems the total of intraschool funds may easily exceed a million dollars in one year. A typical public high school with an enrollment of around 3,000 students may receive and spend over $280,000 a year in intraschool funds.

The need for developing administrative policies for the effective handling of such substantial sums is obvious. Policies must include:

1. Clear definition of what kinds of income are public funds and what kinds are intraschool or private funds

2. Provision for orderly transfer of money collected within a school to a school treasurer, preferably in envelopes so printed as to become basic records

3. Provision for issuing formal receipts by the treasurer for all money received

4. Provision for bonding school treasurers

5. Requirements for regular bank deposits, usually daily, in a school account

6. Requirements for the orderly maintaining of accounting records

7. Insistence that all disbursements be by check signed by both the school treasurer and the principal

8. Provision for preventing the arbitrary transfer by the principal of substantial sums from one fund to a favorite project of his

9. Institution of at least an annual audit of all intraschool accounts

While many of the distinctions governing the handling of intraschool funds lose their force when individual schools are autonomous, or as in many Catholic schools autonomous for most practical purposes, maintaining the distinction does offer advantages; and some of the suggested policy provisions are important to the prudent administrative operation even of these schools.

EVENING USE OF SCHOOL BUILDINGS

An expanding area of school operation involves evening use of school buildings for purposes directly or indirectly concerned with adult education. Evening activity in schools is of two general kinds: evening educational programs operated by the schools and community use of school buildings.

An Office of Education analysis of adult education data covering 1956 revealed that about 9 million adults in the United States were estimated to have participated in adult education classes, exclusive of part-time attendance at college. Participants were younger than nonparticipants, with an average age of 37.6 to 43.9 years. About 7 out of 10 participants were employed, 75 per cent of women participating were married, and 71 per cent of those enrolled in classes of a recreational nature were women. Interestingly enough, participants had had over 2 years more formal education than nonparticipants (12.6 years of school completed compared to 10.4 years).[5]

[5] Marie D. Wann and others, *Participation in Adult Education*, U.S. Office of Education Circular 539, 1959.

EVENING SCHOOL PROGRAMS

Large city public school systems have traditionally offered evening programs for persons wishing to continue formal education at night and for immigrants who need to study English and American government to qualify for citizenship. These two functions of evening schools continue in large cities. In Cincinnati, for example, in 1955–1956, 503 adults were enrolled in elementary school work, 554 were graduated from vocational or academic high school programs, and 542 persons were enrolled in Americanization and citizenship classes.

In very recent years, however, the big developments in evening school work have come in two greatly expanding areas. The first is in helping workers up-grade themselves through improved vocational skills. Over 1,500 men and women in Cincinnati in 1951–1952 were enrolled in evening courses for technical training ranging from ground school in aeronautics to leadership training for department store supervisors. Included were courses in bricklaying, plumbing, pipe fitting, linoleum and carpet laying, tile setting, diesel engine repair, house wiring, refrigeration, television repair, presswork, linotype, lithography, and machine training on lathes, milling machines, shapers, and tool grinders. Special salesmanship courses, not always meeting in school buildings, have been organized for salesmen of paint, candy, and fruit and vegetables.

In the operation of these courses, some of them growing out of the requests of business, industrial, and other community agencies, problems do arise over how far the schools should go in cooperating with particular organizations in advancing their interests. A decision by the schools to provide or not to provide a specific course must ultimately be made in terms of basic educational policies. Does the content desired in a given course conform to the educational objectives of the school system?

In response to an even more swiftly growing community demand, schools are expanding their evening courses to meet avocational or leisure time interests of the public. In four years, enrollment in Cincinnati rose from 200 to 1,400 in such areas as painting pictures, restoring antiques, home decorating, dressmaking, slip-cover and drapery making, and food preparation. Not infrequently, husband and wife teams are to be found an evening or two a week in public school woodworking shops, building items of living-room or bedroom furniture under the guidance of a skilled cabinet maker. Classes in swimming, basketball, badminton, tennis, and golf, are offered regularly.

Reflecting an increasing interest in intellectual activities, community forums and discussion groups under skilled leaders on such topics as city planning, narcotics, economics, child behavior, and problems of foreign policy are increasingly being organized.

As evening classes of both the vocational and the leisure-time-activity type expand, of course, the chief administrative concern is with their financial support. For the kind of program described above, the Cincinnati public schools spend 1.1 per cent of their budget. A few years ago, 54 cities of over 100,000 population spent about $1 for adult education for every $50 spent on day school programs.

About 70 per cent of school systems providing adult education programs charge tuition to be applied toward the cost. Almost universally, the cost of materials for projects is charged to the students. Clearly, expenditures for adult education must not be allowed to cut into funds which are needed for the education of children. It is possible that the good will and public relations values of having the schools used profitably by large numbers of adults and business organizations could result in so much more enthusiastic financial support of schools that, rather than weakening the financial support of day school programs, funds available to it might actually be increased. This result will not come about without skilled administration, however.

CATHOLIC ADULT EDUCATION PROGRAMS

Traditionally, Catholic parishes have had activities of a generally educational nature, many of them carried on in school buildings in the evening. The number and kinds of these activities have varied considerably from parish to parish and diocese to diocese. In recent years, however, more formal and specifically educational programs for adults have been organized in some cities under diocesan auspices. Chicago, Cleveland, and Pittsburgh have programs of this kind. The Pittsburgh program is representative.

The Institute of Adult Education is an educational service of the Diocese of Pittsburgh. The director is appointed by the bishop. An Advisory Board assists him in planning the program which is designed to help adult Catholics, young and old, to play a more effective role in the reconstruction of modern society along Christian lines. Courses offered are open to anyone, regardless of creed, race, or previous educational background.

The faculty consists of priests and laymen drawn chiefly from educational institutions in the Pittsburgh area. They are paid a fee for their services according to the number of class hours they carry. Courses are offered in fall and spring semesters with fees ranging from $5 for one course to three courses for $10. Special rates for married or engaged couples are offered.

In one recent fall semester, thirty-eight courses were offered, including Book Review (a series of ten reviews), Introduction to Listening (Music), Shorthand II, How to Think, Labor Relations, and Your Moral I.Q. No academic credit is given for attendance at the Institute, and there are no entrance requirements. The program is comparable to the rapidly growing public school evening programs for adults—education for avocational and leisure-time pursuits.

Some individual parishes throughout the country have sponsored highly successful evening educational programs. Outstanding has been the program of St. John the Evangelist Parish in Philadelphia, where about 11,000 persons a year have enrolled in one or more of the 125 courses offered. Some other parishes have concerned themselves exclusively with educational programs for the aged.

COMMUNITY USE OF SCHOOL BUILDINGS

In addition to the evening use of school buildings for classes operated by school personnel, farsighted administrators, realizing that school buildings are an expensive community resource, are encouraging the wide use of buildings for other community activities when they are not needed for regular school purposes. This use, since it involves no direct contribution to the purposes of schools, is planned so that no cost to schools is involved, although detailed administrative planning is necessary and complicated problems do arise. The general reasons for encouraging the wide use of public school buildings are in great measure valid also for similar use of parochial school plants.

School facilities are being used for meetings of responsible civic organizations, labor unions, physical exercise groups, and community character-building groups such as the Boy and Girl Scouts. A schedule of fees covering the costs of custodial personnel, heat, and electricity must be established.

Policies must be set regarding use of facilities for commercial gain or for gambling and serving alcoholic beverages; regarding over-all hours for use, procedures for obtaining permits to use a facility, and checking availability of facilities at a given time; and regarding the very complicated question of use by controversial organizations. If the group requesting use of school facilities is so controversial that in the opinion of school authorities school property may be endangered by disorder, the request may be legitimately denied.

Large school systems will find it necessary to establish policies governing the evening use of school buildings by the school staff itself, since unlimited use becomes expensive. Costs of custodial employees, heat, and electricity may rise rapidly if limits to free evening use are not set. One large public school system limits the number of free permits per year for use of a school after 5 P.M. of school days to the following:

Principal's open house, parent meetings,
    commencement, alumni meetings,
    entertainments . . . . 5 per school
PTA or similar associations . . . . 6 per association
Meetings of school employees, approved
    by superintendent . . . . No limit
Approved employee organizations (for
    recreational or educational purposes
    only) . . . . 12 per organization

Questions for Discussion or Investigation

1. Discuss the temptation to circumvent staff member involvement in the formulation of policy molds.
2. What factors govern the decision to publish handbooks in bound or in loose-leaf form?

3. Formulate what you believe to be a defensible statement of policy on homework for the grade or subject with which you are most familiar.

4. List examples of public or school system funds which may be collected within individual schools. List as many examples as you can of truly intra-school funds.

5. What justification do you see for spending public school money for adult education of an avocational nature: bridge, woodworking, making slip covers, etc.?

6. What administrative considerations lead to a policy limiting the number of evenings a year on which a given school may be used free?

Readings and References

American Association of School Administrators and National School Boards Association: *Written Policies for School Boards,* American Association of School Administrators, Washington, 1955.

Bard, Harry: *Homework, a Guide for Secondary School Teachers,* Holt, Rinehart and Winston, Inc., New York, 1958.

Burns, Richard W.: "A Study of Directed Study in Selected High School Subjects," doctor's thesis, State University of Iowa, 1952.

Encyclopedia of Educational Research (See index: homogeneous grouping; homework), Chester W. Harris (ed.), 3d ed., The Macmillan Company, New York, 1960.

Essert, Paul L., and Coolie Verner: "Education for Active Adult Citizenship," *Columbia University Teachers College Record,* vol. 53, no. 1, pp. 16–31, October, 1951.

Flury, Ablett H.: "Putting Lifework in Homework," *New Jersey Education Association Review,* vol. 30, no. 7, March, 1957.

Holden, John B.: *Adult Education Services of State Departments of Education,* U.S. Office of Education Misc. 31, 1959.

How to Develop School Board Policies and Administrative Regulations, Arthur C. Croft Publications, New London, Conn.

Keeler, Sister Jerome: "Catholics Look at Adult Education," *America,* Oct. 4, 1958, pp. 14–16.

School Personnel Policies, Ohio Education Association, Commission on Teacher Education and Professional Standards, Columbus, 1956.

Sheats, Paul H., and others: *Adult Education, the Community Approach,* Holt, Rinehart and Winston, Inc., New York, 1953.

Staehle, John F.: *Characteristics of Administrative Handbooks for School Staff Personnel,* U.S. Office of Education Bulletin 1960, no. 13, 1960.

Strang, Ruth: *Guided Study and Homework,* National Education Association, What Research Says to the Teacher series, no. 8, Washington, 1955.

Walton, John: *Administration and Policy-making in Education,* Johns Hopkins Press, Baltimore, 1959.

Wann, Marie D.: *Participation in Adult Education,* U.S. Office of Education Circular 539, 1959.

White, Alpheus L.: *Characteristics of Local School Board Policy Manuals,* U.S. Office of Education Bulletin 1959, no. 14, 1959.

Woodward, Marthine V.: *Adult Education in Public Schools 1940–56,* U.S. Office of Education, OE-13000, 1960.

14. *Administrative Operation: Legal Liability*

Questions concerning the legal liability of school personnel have acquired increasing importance in recent years as school facilities expand and potentially dangerous situations become more common. Certainly it is true that with the equipment necessary for physical education, for various kinds of shops, and for other types of educational projects undertaken by modern schools, opportunities for injury to children have increased. Playground equipment on school property and bus transportation also make it possible that children will be injured while under school supervision.

A comprehensive discussion of the legal liability of school personnel is difficult, since it will depend ultimately on the provisions of statutory law and on precedents established under common law in the United States and, earlier, in Anglo-Saxon law. Since the interpretation of common law and the writing of statute law vary from state to state, general statements on this subject are somewhat dangerous. In general, however, valid statements can be made regarding the legal liability of public school districts and school board members and of other school personnel, public and private; and regarding some general precautions which the administrator should take in operating a school.

PUBLIC SCHOOL DISTRICTS AND BOARD
OF EDUCATION MEMBERS

Under English common law, which obtains in the absence of statutory provisions, school districts or school boards, acting as such, are not liable for injuries growing out of their negligence. The basis for this is threefold:

1. The old concept that the sovereign can do no wrong; the school board as an agency of the state is a part of the sovereign United States.

2. School boards are authorized to do certain things; since they are not authorized to do anything wrong, they can legally do no wrong.

3. School moneys can legally be dispensed only for maintaining schools, not for paying damage suits.

However, a few states, by specific statutes, have relinquished some of their immunity. The states of California, New York, and Washington have laws making school boards and their school districts liable for negligence. There has been considerable agitation on the part of school personnel throughout the country to increase the number of states making statutory provision for relinquishing immunity to successful suits. In one area in particular, states have moved in this direction. With the great increase in transportation of pupils by bus and the consequent increase in the possibilities of accidents, many states have made it possible for boards of education to pay the cost of liability insurance covering school bus transportation.

As to the personal liability of individual school board members, there are very few cases where board of education members have been held personally liable for negligence. When the negligence is alleged to have grown out of faulty judgment in establishing school policies, as long as the judgment was made in good faith, individual school board members are never held liable. If, however, the facts of the case indicate that school board members acted from malice or bad faith, they have on occasion been held liable for the results. One case of this kind occurred in North Carolina, where a suit was brought because of the death of a child in a bus accident. It was shown that the son of one board of education member had been chosen as the bus driver over the protests of parents that the young man was reckless and unfit. In this case, the court decided that the board members had not acted in good faith in hiring the particular young man.

OTHER SCHOOL PERSONNEL, PUBLIC AND PRIVATE

General principles regarding the liability of school personnel other than public school board of education members are equally applicable to public and Catholic school personnel—superintendents, principals, and teachers—with the exception that public school principals and teachers will not be held liable for negligence if they are merely enforcing school board policies, since the school board itself is an immune body and is completely responsible for the decision. In general, however, the fact that a public school teacher or pupil is an agent for an immune body does not make him immune to successful suits.

Since the public or private school administrator or teacher is liable for his own negligence, it is necessary to establish the concept of exactly what constitutes negligence. Legally speaking, negligence is the failure of anyone to act as a reasonably prudent and careful person would act under the circumstances involved. Consequently, negligence may involve doing something imprudent or failing to do something which would have been prudent. The decision on whether or not a teacher or principal acted as a reasonably prudent person under the circumstances is made by the jury.

When the jury is considering this question, two considerations regarding the circumstances are basic: that school personnel are generally held to be acting *in loco parentis;* that is, they have the same responsibilities regarding children as parents would have had under the same circumstances. The second very significant principle applied in the case of school personnel is that teachers and principals must protect children against themselves, against their own tendencies, and against self-injury as a result of "childish acts." In other words, teachers and principals are supposed to know that "children will be children." They therefore must act in terms of what children are likely to do: anticipating childish pranks or indiscretions and promptly reporting school hazards in which children are likely to find a source of injury. Exactly what a reasonably prudent teacher, protecting children against themselves and acting in the place of the parent, should anticipate is again a matter for a jury to decide.

Should a child be injured and suit be brought charging the school principal or teacher with negligence, certain defenses are possible. The suit can be defended by proof that the alleged negligence was not a proximate cause of the particular accident. Another defense is that the accident, rather than being caused by the school personnel, fell under the category of an "act of God." One court case along these lines involved a suit against a teacher whose glass transom to the schoolroom door was open when a sudden gust of wind slammed it shut, shattering the glass and cutting one of the students, causing facial disfiguration. The decision was that the sudden slamming of the glass transom was an act of God.

A third defense in certain circumstances is known as "assumption of risk." For example, when a young man, with the approval of his parents, undertakes to play football on an interscholastic team, he does assume some risk: the normal risk associated with playing football. If, however, the young man were to be injured in a football game, and because of his outstanding playing ability were to be sent back into the game, a development which resulted in aggravating the injury and perhaps doing permanent damage, the coach or other personnel involved could well be held liable, since sending the youngster back into the game was beyond the limits of assumption of normal risk involved in playing football.

Another defense involves the concept of contributory negligence. Even if the school person were negligent in a given situation, if it could be proved that the child was also negligent, then under the doctrine of contributory negligence, the school principal or teacher would not be held liable. The difficulty with this defense, however, is that because of the concept that "children will be children," contributory negligence by a child is difficult to prove except under extremely obvious circumstances.

LIABILITY CONDITIONS SPECIFIC TO CATHOLIC SCHOOL PERSONNEL

Under some circumstances priests and religious enjoy certain advantages as far as susceptibility to suits is concerned. First of all, their very religious status makes it less likely that the religious parent will bring suit, even though the teacher is responsible for injury to a child, legally speaking. Furthermore, certain provisions of canon law make it a serious religious offense to bring any priest into court as a defendant. Generally, while Catholic school personnel do not enjoy the immunity of public school personnel, neither do Catholic administrators have restrictions which prevent them from carrying adequate liability insurance. In all cases, insurance coverage should be obtained in Catholic schools, since sisters and priests as members of religious orders are generally held to be agents of that order; and the order itself may be successfully sued because of the negligence of one of its members. Today jury awards in liability suits not infrequently exceed $100,000. Consequently the importance of adequate liability insurance coverage cannot be overstressed.

SCHOOL SITUATIONS CONDUCIVE TO LIABILITY

In view of the general considerations governing liability of school personnel, public or private, teachers and principals should be aware of the situations around schools which are most dangerous to children and which, accordingly, call for special vigilance if the possibilities of successful suits for liability are to be minimized. A discussion of some of these danger spots and critical situations follows.

The operation of a school safety patrol is one situation which calls for caution. If a school has a right to run a school patrol, it clearly follows that those responsible for its operation have the duty to see that normal prudence characterizes their performance. The school's right to run a school patrol has generally been upheld by the courts. This follows from court decisions that the school may legitimately exercise jurisdiction over student actions beyond the actual boundaries of school property as long as the effectiveness of the school instructional program is involved. (Interestingly enough, public school teachers have been upheld for punishing children because of actions they have taken, even on the property of the child's parents.) In regard to the administration of safety patrols, therefore, school personnel are bound by the general principles of liability. The assignment of a child known to be particularly irresponsible and undependable to a critical post on a safety patrol could conceivably result in a successful suit against the school official involved in the decision.

If the school operates its own busses for pupil transportation, many opportunities for injuries to students exist, including the possibilities of injuries resulting from roughhousing in the bus when inadequate supervision has been provided. While court decisions vary from state to state, school bus drivers have been held negligent and liable for damages when, for instance, a driver permitted a young child to get off his bus some distance and on the opposite side of the street from his home and when a driver injured the arm of a boy by opening the bus door before the bus had stopped.

Gymnasiums, swimming pools, shops, laboratories, and playgrounds are key danger spots around modern school plants. The possibility of accidents and pupil injuries in each of these areas is ever present. Deteriorated equipment, inadequate supervision, overcrowding, the absence of safety equipment or the use of defective safety equipment, the lack of normal foresight by the teacher or principal—all may be held to have directly caused a given accident. A physical education teacher might be liable for injuries resulting from permitting two boys to box without previously warning them of the dangers involved or from allowing a pupil to overexert himself. A shop teacher may be responsible for damages if he permits a student to use equipment without adequate safety guards or if he permits a youth to operate power machinery with loosely fitting clothes which become entangled in the machinery with consequent injury to the student. The laboratory teacher who, because of the lack of normal supervision of his class, allows a dangerous experiment to be conducted by a student or who fails to warn of the dangers of handling certain chemicals may be found liable.

The actual violation of a school law or state code by a school official, if the violation results in injury to a child, puts the official in an indefensible position.

Sometimes the demands of modern extracurricular programs subject a principal to pressures which result in unwise decisions. Such pressures undoubtedly contributed to a multithousand-dollar verdict against one religious order. A member of the order, as principal of a high school, permitted some students to leave school grounds during school hours to collect furniture and other props for a school play. The students used a truck borrowed and driven by one student. An accident occurred and one student was killed.

Sending students off school grounds on errands during school hours, sending ill students home without adequate provisions for getting them there safely, or overzealous and imprudent application of first aid can all result in school personnel being held liable for resulting damages.

PRECAUTIONS AGAINST LIABILITY

Because the number of suits brought against school personnel is increasing, certain specific precautionary measures should be taken by superintendents, principals, and teachers to minimize the likelihood of successful suit against them. First, all accidents around school property should be recorded on forms which give the names of persons involved, the names of witnesses, and the approximate extent of injuries. Should suit be brought within the statute of limitations several years later, it is most embarrassing if none of the school personnel have any memory of the incident. The possibilities of refreshing one's memory through a written report on file in the school office and in the office of the superintendent of schools is of great assistance in such circumstances.

Second, school personnel should regularly inspect potential danger spots. For example, safety of equipment in gymnasiums or the condition of playground swings and their supports should be carefully determined. Wherever hazards are observed, the observer should immediately relieve himself of responsibility by making a formal report to his superior. Thus, the teacher who reports a situation to the principal has transferred responsibility to the principal; the principal who has done what he could and reported the situation to the business manager for immediate correction has discharged his responsibility, unless some other prudent action is also indicated.

For activities involving risk, such as interscholastic athletics, statements of permission from the parents of each child who participates should be on file in the proper administrative office. Generally speaking, schools do provide liability insurance covering such extracurricular activities, paying the premiums out of gate receipts where public funds may not be expended for this purpose.

Further, when teachers and other school personnel are not covered by school liability insurance policies, they should protect themselves by individually carrying personal liability insurance. The premium for such insurance is remarkably inexpensive. While accidents may not happen with great frequency, when one does occur and financial responsibility of school personnel is established, a major financial disaster can occur.

In recent years many school administrators have been sponsoring inexpensive liability insurance policies for each child in the school, encouraging parents to pay the annual premium on such policies. It should be clearly pointed out that the existence of such a policy in no way relieves the principal or teacher from financial responsibility for his own negligence. There is even some question whether the use of the school teacher and school facilities to promote individual liability policies for children, no matter how worthwhile the end, is a legitimate function of the school and whether or not the practice actually violates the general principle that schools are not to be used for the commercial profit of any organization or person.

The attorney general of one state, in an informal opinion in response to questions from the state superintendent of public instruction about the right of public school boards of education to select an insurance company to write group accident insurance policies and the right of public school teachers to serve as intermediaries between parents and the insurance company, said in part:[1]

> There can be no doubt of the right of the parents of such pupils to procure group coverage of this sort if they choose to do so, but the promotion of such a project by the board in a situation involving the encouragement by the board of a monopoly by one insurance company clearly appears to me to be well beyond the scope of the legitimate interests of the board. In a field in which the individual

[1] Informal Opinion No. 446, C. William O'Neill, Attorney General, State of Ohio, Apr. 29, 1955.

pupils and their parents are concerned, not as pupils but as individuals, it is difficult to perceive how the board could assert a proper interest; and when it is proposed in such field to foster, if not establish, a monopoly for the benefit of a private insurance company, it becomes necessary to conclude that the board's authority in such a project is *not* clearly and distinctly granted by law, and that such project is, therefore, not within its powers.

In view of the conclusion above reached that a project of this sort is not properly a school function, it necessarily follows that teachers as such, would be under no duty to distribute insurance literature or to aid in processing applications and collecting premiums. As to their legal right *as individuals* to do these things, there could be no question so far as the school code is concerned, but their right to engage in such activities under existing insurance laws involves questions of mixed law and fact which should properly be considered in the first instance by the state division of insurance.

Questions for Discussion or Investigation

1. Discuss whether or not states should pass statutes which make school districts liable for damages incurred through negligence.
2. Contrast the present status of most public school districts with that of private school corporations in regard to liability for negligence.
3. Compare the liability for negligence of a public school teacher with that of a member of a religious order with a vow of poverty.
4. Precisely what is the norm or standard used by a jury in determining negligence of school teachers or principals?
5. What effect would a permission note signed by the parent probably have on the success of a suit against teachers or principals in case of accidents?
6. What effect do so-called accident insurance policies, sold through schools, have on the liability of principals and teachers?
7. In your area, what is the annual cost of liability insurance policies covering school teachers and principals? Is there any difference in rate for teachers and principals? What are the limits of liability covered?
8. Does any part of the quotation from the informal opinion of the state attorney general concerning accident insurance policies for children have significance for administrators of private schools?

Readings and References

Drury, Robert L. (ed.): *Law and the School Superintendent,* W. H. Anderson Co., Cincinnati, 1958.

Edwards, Newton: *The Courts and the Public Schools,* rev., University of Chicago Press, Chicago, 1935.

Garber, Leo O., and others: *The Law and the Ohio Teacher,* The Interstate Printers and Publishers, Inc., Danville, Ill., 1956.

Hamilton, Robert R., and Paul R. Mort: *The Law and Public Education,* 2d ed., The Foundation Press, Chicago, 1959.

Keesecker, Ward W.: *Know Your School Law,* U.S. Office of Education Bulletin 1958, no. 8, 1958.

Kramer, Robert (ed.): "School Pupils and the Law," *Law and Contemporary Problems,* vol. 20, Winter, 1955.

The Legal Status of the Public-School Pupil, National Education Association, Research Bulletin 26, no. 1, Washington, February, 1948.

Punke, H. H.: *Law and Liability in Public Transportation,* University of Chicago Press, 1943.

Rosenfield, Harry N.: *Liability for School Accidents,* Harper & Brothers, New York, 1940.

Remmlein, Madeline Kinter: *School Law,* McGraw-Hill Book Company, Inc., New York, 1950.

————: *The Law of Public School Administration,* McGraw-Hill Book Company, Inc., New York, 1953.

———— and Martha L. Ware: *An Evaluation of Existing Forms of School Law,* W. H. Anderson Co., Cincinnati, 1957.

"School Law: Aid to the Administrator," *Educational Trend,* no. 652, Arthur C. Craft Publications, New London, Conn.

Trusler, H. R.: *Essentials of School Law,* The Bruce Publishing Company, Milwaukee, 1927.

Who Is Liable for Pupil Injuries? National Education Association, Research Division, Washington, 1950.

15. *Administrative Operation:*
Teacher Personnel

As times change, so does the relative emphasis which school administrators give to various aspects of their responsibilities. Nowhere is this more evident than in the relative emphasis given to the administration of teacher personnel today as compared to twenty-five years ago. The job of the director of teacher personnel in the larger school systems at that time was largely confined to screening the best from an avalanche of applicants for the few openings caused by deaths, retirement, and marriage. Serious mistakes were hard to make, and some directors of personnel even found time for a bit of slumber in an inner office.

Today to the active, personable recruiter who wanders far from his office goes the prize: a teacher hired. In fact, it can be said (with pardonable exaggeration) that if only *rigor mortis* has not yet set in on an applicant with certification requirements in mathematics or science, he'll be hired.

For the Catholic school administrator, teacher personnel problems are of two distinct kinds with little in common: those concerning religious teachers and those concerning lay teachers. The latter problems, new to the Catholic school administrator generally, are

272

almost identical with those faced in public schools, and their solutions will be much the same.

THE LAY TEACHER

As the child population continues to grow markedly while the supply of religious teachers comes from a less numerous generation, there is every likelihood that the role of the lay teacher in Catholic elementary and secondary education will be of increasing importance, both numerically and functionally.

The growth in number and percentage of lay teachers since 1950 in one Catholic school system is seen in Table 6, which includes only regular classroom teachers, not special teachers.

TABLE 6. GROWTH IN THE NUMBER OF LAY TEACHERS—
ONE CATHOLIC SCHOOL SYSTEM

Year	Elementary			High school			Per cent lay, elementary and high school
	Religious	Lay	Per cent lay	Religious	Lay	Per cent lay	
1950–1951	1,032	140	11.9	470	82	14.8	12.8
1951–1952	1,040	163	13.5	526	93	15.0	14.0
1952–1953	1,057	183	14.7	537	106	16.4	15.3
1953–1954	1,069	242	18.4	545	102	15.7	17.6
1954–1955	1,078	302	21.1	531	107	16.6	20.2
1955–1956	1,113	351	24.0	553	113	16.9	21.7
1956–1957	1,117	401	26.4	549	104	15.9	23.2
1957–1958	1,121	489	30.3	573	115	16.7	26.6
1958–1959	1,108	576	34.2	558	142	20.2	30.1
1959–1960	1,093	638	36.8	565	134	19.7	31.9

The relatively greater increase in the number of lay teachers in the elementary schools than in the high schools reflects the fact that up to 1955–1956 increased enrollment had been a far more acute problem in Catholic elementary schools than in high schools.

The relative increase in lay teachers is seen in another way. The school year 1953–1954 in the elementary schools saw an increase of 12 religious and 59 lay teachers; the year 1954–1955, an increase of 9 religious and 60 lay teachers; 1955–1956, an increase of 35 religious and 49 lay teachers; the next two years witnessed a decline of 28 religious teachers and an increase of 149 lay teachers. According to the Superintendent of Schools, the explanation is that some of the religious communities are giving their sisters more education before sending them into the schools. (See the discussion of the Sister Formation movement later in this chapter.)

At the national level between 1945 and 1956, there was an average yearly increase in sister-teachers of 1.75 per cent throughout the United States. At the same time lay teachers were increasing at an average rate of 11.22 per cent. By 1970, it has been estimated, lay teachers will outnumber sisters in the schools conducted by sisters.[1]

As the need for good lay teachers in Catholic elementary and secondary schools grows more accute, competition for their services with public schools will increase. In this competition, the experience and skill of a professional personnel administrator is as essential to the Catholic as to the public schools. This competitive activity must encompass the fields of teacher recruitment, retention, dismissal, and conditions of service. While the Catholic schools can draw with profit on the lessons being learned in Catholic colleges and universities which have earlier attacked similar problems, the professional equipment of the personnel administrator for these schools must include acquaintance with the techniques already developed by public school administrators. For conditions of life which the layman or laywoman must meet put severe limits on the sacrifices which the qualified teacher can make in the interests of a lay Catholic teaching apostolate, no matter how deep his religious motivation.

TEACHER RECRUITMENT

Teacher personnel problems begin with recruitment. This means getting out of the office and visiting the sources of teacher supply— teachers colleges and universities. It may also mean encouraging nearby colleges to assist in cooperative programs of emergency teacher training. In any case a school bureau of teacher personnel is more and more concerned with selling and advertising. Personal conferences with juniors and seniors in college, using all the tech-

---

[1] Sister Rose Matthew, "Sister Teachers in the United States: A Study of Their Status and Projected Role," in Sister Ritamary (ed.), *Planning for the Formation of Sisters,* Fordham University Press, New York, 1958, pp. 111–114.

niques of persuasion, are held. Attractive brochures describing the educational, recreational, and cultural advantages in a particular location read like advertisements for a good vacation spot. A Miami, Florida, teacher-recruitment folder which crossed the desk of this author on a winter day several years ago would have severely tempted the most confirmed Northerner, replete as it was with references to the closeness of the Gulf Stream with its gentle, warming winter breezes and cool summer breezes. The pictures included were luscious!

The volume of such mail coming to college teacher placement officers, the rapidly increasing number of requests to interview prospective teachers by searching administrators who are on trips of over a thousand miles, the number of long-distance telephone calls made to chairmen of college departments of education, and even the pitifully elaborate Christmas cards sent by the imaginative recruiter of teachers are all evidence of the emphasis given to this activity.

TEACHER RETENTION

Once the newly hired teacher arrives in town, another kind of staff activity begins. The teacher must be made happy; homesickness must not set in! The principal and staff of the school to which the young woman teacher is assigned must be enlisted to help her make satisfactory living arrangements. Invitations to dinner and entertainment must be forthcoming. The aid of professional teacher organizations is enlisted to provide group activities like bowling and square dancing. Above all, introductions to potential husbands must be provided. Nothing sends the young woman college graduate home, where she knows people, faster than the absence of dates. There is a delicate problem here, however, since too much success at providing social activities might easily have the same result as too little—the loss of the teacher. The calculated risk is considered well taken, however, since homesickness sets in faster than marriage is likely to occur.

TEACHER DISMISSAL

No matter how extraordinary the efforts which must be made toward teacher recruitment and retention, some teachers have to be dismissed if administrators are to discharge their basic responsibilities for providing children with a good instructional program. Out of fairness to the teacher as well as to the children, the weak teacher must be identified early, well before tenure is obtained. In a large system, a well-conceived teacher appraisal system with well-defined procedures for identifying the teacher who needs supervisory help must be set up. To this end, regular appraisal of new teachers by principals and supervisors each year for perhaps three years is essential. In one large school system, an operational timetable (see Table 7) is followed for all teachers in their first three years of service and for others classified as needing help.

While the principal and supervisor work cooperatively to bring the teacher up to a level satisfactory for continued employment, any granting of tenure status must, of course, be withheld. School systems, in addition to the supervisory techniques and procedures discussed in Chapter 8, frequently provide transfers for the teacher likely to be more effective in a different school situation. Generally speaking, by the end of the fifth year of employment decision must be finally reached as to whether or not a teacher is to be issued a continuing contract. State laws covering tenure of public school teachers usually make mandatory the issuance of a continuing contract granting permanent tenure to a teacher employed more than five years.

The decision is a critical one for the school system involved since tenure guarantees the right of the teacher to a job unless guilty of gross inefficiency or gross immorality. The right of public hearing and appeal to courts is given the teacher. The voluntary extension of similar tenure rights by contract to lay teachers in Catholic schools will be a necessary development if good teachers are to be secured on the competitive market. It has already become necessary on the college level.

If the decision to extend tenure privileges to a teacher has been made carefully, many much more severe problems will be avoided. However, even good teachers whose status was not questionable in their first three to five years of service may deteriorate in later years to the level where they must be removed from the classroom. Some teachers, particularly men frustrated in their administrative ambitions, cease to perform adequately, desiring only to collect their

TABLE 7. "NEEDS HELP" GROUP

By Oct. 15	Principal receives from Department of Personnel two copies of a list of his faculty with certain names checked as being automatically in "Needs Help" Group. Evaluation Forms are also received and distributed to teachers concerned.
By Nov. 15	Principal, in cooperation with supervisor, will check additional names on the list which should be placed in "Needs Help" group, giving a brief explanation for checking the name. It is necessary, of course, for the principal to discuss with the teacher the reasons for adding his name to the list. Principal then returns one copy of amended list to Department of Personnel.
Beginning Nov. 15	Principal, supervisor, and others work with "Needs Help" teachers, keeping a brief record of such contacts.
By Mar. 30	Principal and supervisor reach a cooperative decision as to future status of each "Needs Help" teacher. Those to be continued in "Needs Help" are to be appraised by principal using Column 2 of evaluation form. The teacher is to see the principal's appraisal, discuss it with him and sign the form as evidence of having conferred with the principal about it. Principal then submits the evaluation form along with a summary of his contacts with the teacher during the year (using the form provided) to the Department of Personnel. The supervisor will also submit to the Department of Personnel a summary of assistance given to the teacher with appropriate comments.
Mar. 30 to June	Continuation of assistance to teachers remaining in "Needs Help" Group.

salaries until retirement. Some teachers do lose their hearing, their sight, or other faculties essential to alert work in the classroom. Most tragic and difficult of all, however, are previously excellent teachers who, at an advanced stage of life, develop mental abnormalities obvious to their pupils but not to the teachers themselves.

Since no administrator wants to try to prove "gross inefficiency" at a public trial with skillful lawyers representing the teacher who may have performed so long and so well, persuading such a teacher to retire voluntarily and quietly is the only satisfactory solution. This calls for the utmost kindness, patience, tact, and persuasiveness. It is perhaps the most painful of all administrative tasks.

If cases of physical deterioration are to be discovered, regular physical examinations of all teachers must be required, perhaps every three to five years. Any smooth solution to this and the problem of mental deterioration depends upon the existence of an adequate retirement plan for school personnel.

Teacher retirement plans for public school teachers are usually covered by state retirement systems. They may or may not include Federal social security coverage. In Catholic schools, Federal social security coverage provides indispensable minimum retirement and survivor benefits. These provisions, as far as teachers are concerned, are only minimum and do not themselves constitute a program adequate to the needs of professional persons such as teachers. Supplementary retirement benefits purchased from private insurance companies are important if retirement provisions of Catholic schools are to be at all competitive with those of public school personnel. The expense of such plans is usually shared by employers and employees, most frequently on a matching basis. Generally, supplementary retirement plans involve a 5 per cent payroll deduction matched by 5 per cent contributed by the employer. State industrial insurance plans may cover injuries suffered by school personnel, public or Catholic, while on the job.

Group insurance covering major medical expenses and regular income payments if the teacher should become totally disabled are becoming more frequent in educational circles. The latter coverage is especially helpful when physical or mental disability forces premature retirement from teaching.

CONDITIONS OF SERVICE

Policies governing conditions of service for teachers employed by schools have frequently been the first area of rules and regulations developed for administrative handbooks. This is because teachers ordinarily want to know in advance of employment just what these policies are and because so frequently detailed questions arise concerning salaries, sick leave, other absences, outside employment, and standards of conduct expected from teachers in a system.

Salaries. The salaries of teachers are ordinarily provided for in a salary schedule which outlines minimum and maximum salaries for school personnel, detailing the amount of annual increases to be given for each year's satisfactory experience until a maximum is reached. While no salary differential is ordinarily provided for the different teaching levels of a school system, separate categories based upon level of academic preparation are usually outlined and separate salary schedules maintained for each category. Thus for salary purposes, teachers otherwise professionally qualified may be grouped into those not having the bachelor's degree, those having the bachelor's degree, those having the master's degree, and those with a specified amount of additional graduate work beyond the master's degree.

Extra compensation may be provided for nonclassroom responsibilities which are particularly time-consuming extracurricular activities, such as athletic coaching or supervising dramatics or musical organizations. School treasurers, particularly in large schools, may be teachers receiving extra pay. While it is generally accepted salary practice in public schools to pay men and women teachers of equal experience and training the same teaching salary, the assignment of extra responsibilities to men for extra pay is frequently deliberately used to provide a differential.

Since years of experience is usually an important determinant of salary, policies covering previous years of experience in other schools or credit for service in the armed forces must be specified.

Some idea of the strain placed on those who recruit lay teachers for the Catholic elementary schools in one Middle Western city can be gained by a comparison of the minimum salary schedule for teachers in the two systems in the same city (see Table 8). It should cause little surprise, under the circumstances, that about 40 per cent of the lay teachers employed in the Catholic elementary schools had completed less than two years of college.

Sick Leave. The usual practice of school systems is to determine maximum number of days per year for which the teacher will be paid while ill. Fifteen school days a year, or three teaching weeks, are commonly provided for a teacher who has taught for a full year. Unused sick leave may be accumulated up to a maximum number of days, frequently ninety, to provide insurance for the teacher against the financial blow of a major illness. The practice in some systems of paying extra for unused days of sick leave in a given year would seem to work against one major purpose of these provisions, that children be protected from the contagious illnesses of the teacher. Sick teachers are not to be encouraged to remain in the classroom.

TABLE 8. MINIMUM SALARY SCHEDULE FOR TEACHERS IN PUBLIC AND CATHOLIC ELEMENTARY SCHOOLS, A MIDDLE WESTERN CITY, 1960

Public schools:

Years experience	Class I Master's degree	Class II Bachelor-provisional certificate	Class III Unqualified for regular appointment
0	$4,650	$4,350	$4,050
1	4,850	4,550	4,200
2	5,050	4,750	4,350
3	5,350	5,050	4,500
4	5,550	5,250	4,650
5	5,750	5,450	4,800
6	5,950	5,650	4,950
7	6,150	5,850	5,100
8	6,350	6,050	
9	6,550	6,250	
10	6,750	6,450	
11	6,950	6,650	
12 (maximum)	7,150	6,850	

Catholic schools:

Years experience	Class A Provisional certificate	Class B Cadet certificate	Class C Temporary certificate
0	$3,400	$3,100	$2,800
1	3,450	3,150	2,850
2	3,500	3,200	2,900
3	3,550	3,250	2,950
4	3,600	3,300	3,000
5	3,650	3,350	3,050

Protracted illness should be certified by a doctor. After extended illness, perhaps one of three weeks, a physician's certificate of the fitness of the teacher to resume duties should be required. Absence because of illness or death in the immediate family of a teacher may legitimately be deducted from sick leave.

Other Absences. Typical of the details which must be spelled out in personnel policies are the following taken from the *Rules and Regulations* of the Board of Education of Cincinnati:

Death in Family

An employee shall be allowed 3 days of absence, and any additional days approved by the superintendent without loss of pay in event of the death of parent, child, spouse, sister, or brother, or in event of the death of any relative mentioned in the next paragraph who is a permanent resident in the employee's home.

An employee shall be allowed one day of absence, and any additional days approved by the superintendent without loss of pay to attend the funeral of an aunt, uncle, nephew, niece, grandparent or grandchild, father-in-law, mother-in-law, brother-in-law, sister-in-law, or the spouse of his child.

Family Events

An employee may, with the approval of the superintendent, be absent for not to exceed one day for a wedding, graduation, or similar event within the immediate family, and the salary deduction for such absence shall be only the amount necessary to pay the cost of any necessary substitution.

Appearance in Court

In case of absence from duty in response to a subpoena in a case in court or in an administrative hearing in which the employee is not a party, there shall be deducted from the salary of the employee the amount and only the amount of any witness fee or other compensation, exclusive of any reimbursement paid specifically for expenses incurred by reason of such subpoena. A certificate signed by the employee and stating the amount of such fee or other compensation, if any, must be submitted by the employee, or the full salary for the period of absence shall be deducted.

In case of absence from duty for any court proceeding or administrative hearing in which the employee is a party, no salary shall be paid to the employee for the period of absence.

In case of absence from duty in response to a jury summons, no salary shall be paid to the employee for the period of absence. Employees wishing exemption from jury duty should, immediately after receiving a summons, request instructions from the office of the clerk of the board of education.

Purposes for Which Leaves of Absence Are Granted

Upon proper application and approval thereof, any employee may be granted a leave of absence without pay for personal illness or illness on the part of the immediate family, and after three years of satisfactory service, for maternity, study, or exchange teaching in a school outside the Cincinnati Public School System when such teaching is clearly in the interests of the Cincinnati Public Schools or of the community. . . .

Duration of Leave

A leave of absence for maternity shall begin 5 months prior to the anticipated birth of the child and continue 19 months after the birth, if the child lives. If the child should not live, earlier return from leave may be authorized by the superintendent. . . .

Outside Employment. Teacher salaries, improving as they are, still fail to keep pace with increased costs of living and with increases in salary in other areas of employment. One large city public school system in 1956–1957 was paying teachers with master's degrees a maximum of $6,200 per year, while plumbers were receiving an annual salary of $6,800. The parochial school system in the same city was at the same time paying an average annual salary of $2,200 for lay elementary school teachers.

It is not surprising, therefore, that teachers, especially men with families, are increasingly looking to outside employment for supplementary income or that public school systems are sometimes assisting teachers to find outside employment, thus influencing the choice of employment so that the men are not tending bar or washing windshields in commercial establishments close to their schools. Some systems offer men teachers the opportunity, if such is the proper term, to work on plant painting and repair during summer months, a chance which is frequently seized.

Certain principles must be established regarding outside employment of teachers:

1. The work must not interfere with the success of their primary job of teaching.

2. The work should ordinarily not commence before 5 P.M., giving teachers the opportunity to discharge their obligations to attend faculty meetings or to participate in extracurricular activities.

3. The work should not exceed a maximum number of hours per school week (Monday through Friday), perhaps fifteen to twenty.

Standards of Conduct within and without the Classroom. By expressed policy, school personnel should be held to standards of personal and professional conduct in keeping with the standards set by the community involved. Such standards should be described in general terms in teacher contracts. Contracts for teachers in Catholic schools, in keeping with the purposes of these schools, should specifically provide for termination if the teacher knowingly and persistently teaches anything contrary to the doctrine of the Catholic Church, or if the teacher's personal conduct is a source of public scandal or grave embarrassment to the religious school to which the teacher is under contract.[2]

THE RELIGIOUS TEACHER

In addition to sharing in all the problems of public schools concerning teaching personnel, Catholic schools have distinctive problems in relation to religious teachers.

Religious teachers in Catholic schools have been both men and women: priests and brothers, and nuns. Close to 100,000 sisters are currently teaching in Catholic schools in this country. Parish schools especially have been made possible in the past only by the contributed services of the sisters whose lives have been dedicated to their work. New parish schools are staffed basically by contract between the pastor and the provincial superior of a religious community.[3] In the case of private religious schools, the religious community operating the school provides teachers. Diocesan high schools may be operated by a religious order under contract to the diocese or may be staffed by priests of the diocese, usually younger priests whose first years are spent teaching before assignment to full-time pastoral duties. Salaries of the religious teacher are nominal, frequently barely covering living expenses or, in the instance of members of religious communities whose members have vows of poverty, barely, or not actually, covering living and educational

[2] For suggested contract form for teachers in Catholic schools, see Appendix C.
[3] For a sample pastor-religious community contract, see Appendix C.

expenses, overhead of the mother house, or other community expenses.

Indispensable as religious teachers have been to the Catholic educational enterprise, and phenomenal as has been their contribution, their use has not been without problems. As American education has become more professional, more complicated, and more comprehensive in scope, so have some of these problems become more identifiable.

Two elements are necessary to the training of a good religious teacher: training as a good religious, one whose own spiritual development is promoted within the traditions of his or her religious order; and training as a professional teacher, one who is professionally equipped to do the important job of teaching school on the modern American scene. In the not-too-distant past, when the ability to read and write was about the only teaching requirement in all schools, it was not too inappropriate that major emphasis in the training of religious teachers was placed on the development of good religious. It was assumed for too long, however, that a good religious—priest, brother, or nun—would be able to do a good teaching job. Irrespective of how long this may have been true, the professional training for priestly duties or the spiritual development of a good member of a religious community can no longer be thought to guarantee automatically a professional teacher.

It is out of this setting that seminaries for training priests have been adding to their canonically prescribed programs experiences designed to develop the competent, dedicated priest-teacher; and it is out of this setting that there has recently developed in the United States the distinctively American Sister Formation movement, a movement which in less than ten years pioneered more significant advances in the education of sisters than had occurred for generations previous.

THE SISTER FORMATION MOVEMENT

In many ways the Sister Formation movement, only a few years old, is a distinctively American Catholic development. In the words of one expert observer,[4]

[4] Edward B. Rooney, "Incentives to Excellence," *Sister Formation Bulletin,* vol. 6, no. 1, p. 4, Autumn, 1959.

The strength of Sister Formation, perhaps its greatest strength, is that the inspiration for it operated from within the groups of Sisters themselves. It was a movement of religious, and especially of religious superiors. It was not imposed from without—not by states, nor by accrediting associations, nor by bishops or diocesan superintendents. It grew out of the fine, clear vision that the Sisters themselves had of the needs of Catholic education, and of its greatest need of well-trained, completely-trained Sisters.

True it is that the movement was an American response to Pope Pius XII's remarks at the First International Congress of Teaching Sisters in Rome in 1951:[5]

Many of your schools are being described and praised to us as being very good. But not all. It is our fervent wish that all endeavor to become excellent. This presupposes that your teaching sisters are masters of the subjects they expound. See to it, therefore, that they are well trained and that their academic education corresponds in quality and degrees to that demanded by the State. Be generous in giving them all they need, especially where books are concerned, so that they may continue their studies and thus offer young people a rich and solid harvest of knowledge. . . .

It is also true that the movement owes much to the National Catholic Educational Association which used the words of Pius XII as a basis for a panel discussion in the Teacher Education Section of the College and University Department at its annual convention at Kansas City in 1952; which helped organize exploratory regional conferences with an eye to establishing a national commission on sisters' educational and professional standards at its 1953 convention; which, in January, 1954, set up the Sister Formation Committee of the NCEA; and which organized the permanent Section on Sister Formation of the NCEA in 1957, with provision for an executive secretary at NCEA headquarters in Washington.

Furthermore, it is true that the first of a series of publications on Sister Formation was financed by a grant of $4,000 to Fordham University from the Michael Grace Trust, and that a $50,000 grant from the Fund for the Advancement of Education of the Ford Foundation made possible significant preliminary research and the devel-

[5] Quoted in Sister Ritamary (ed.), *The Mind of the Church in the Formation of Sisters,* Fordham University Press, New York, 1956, p. xv.

opment of a college curriculum for training sisters. Results achieved by the movement have been to some extent owing to the encouragement, help, and cooperative activity of members of the hierarchy, college administrators, and Catholic and non-Catholic expert educational advisors.

Yet all this only highlights the movement as a great American cooperative effort in which[6]

> "Nuns are planning together, teaching together, studying together in a way never known before. The variety in cuts and colors of the cornets, coifs, wimples, hoods and veils will remain the glory of the 377 women's teaching congregations and the exasperation of sometimes puzzled clerics. But of infinitely more moment than modifications in religious paraphernalia is the single-minded approach to the reorganization of sister education."

SOME ACCOMPLISHMENTS OF THE SISTER FORMATION MOVEMENT

In addition to the unprecedented cooperative efforts which have marked its brief history, the accomplishments of the movement are already impressive. They include the following:

1. The foundation of a voluntary national organization of sisters to study the problems of the professional training of sister-teachers (as well as sister–social workers and sister–hospital personnel).

2. The discovery of the facts concerning the status and problems of sister formation. Early in the movement the current status of teacher education for sisters and obstacles to adequate programs were uncovered through a national questionnaire addressed to 377 general superiors of all teaching communities in the United States. Several months later, in 1952, the financial problems of twenty-five selected communities were studied. A vocation survey of 14,000 students in high schools, colleges, and schools of nursing revealed significant facts about the attitudes of students toward sisters. Another research project reported responses of selected members of the clergy to a questionnaire on the spiritual and intellectual elements in the formation of sisters. Prior to the Everett Curriculum Workshop described below, and a part of that project supported by Ford

[6] Neil G. McCluskey, "The Education of Our Sisters," *America,* Apr. 23, 1960, p. 118.

Foundation money, two sisters traveled through 44 states visiting 125 different teaching communities to ascertain the curriculum needs of the communities, the impact of certification problems in the states, and the obstacles to pre-service training.

3. The production of a professional literature concerned with sister formation. *The Sister Formation Bulletin,* devoted exclusively to pre-service and in-service training of sisters, is published quarterly as a clearinghouse for accounts of meetings and regional conferences, reports of promising new practices in sister formation, and results of new research on the problems involved. A series of volumes on sister formation has been published through the Fordham University Press, beginning with the 1956 publication *The Mind of the Church in the Formation of Sisters* and continuing with *Spiritual and Intellectual Elements in the Formation of Sisters* (1957), *Planning for the Formation of Sisters* (1958), *The Juniorate in Sister Formation* (1960), and a forthcoming *In-service Sisters. A Directory of Catholic Women's Colleges Having Facilities for the Education of Sisters,* designed to assist the 118 small communities having no educational facilities of their own and no ready access to Catholic women's colleges, and the *Report of Everett Curriculum Workshop* are two additional publications of basic significance to the movement.

4. The development of a technique of regional conferences of major superiors of religious communities and those charged with the ascetical and professional training of teachers.

5. The delineation of desirable specific goals for the education of sister-teachers. Among these are:

a. A five-year college program. The movement has clearly established a five-year minimum college program as the goal for an integrated spiritual and professional education of sister-teachers. To the traditional year of postulancy and a two-year noviceship, including the year mainly devoted to religious formation in accordance with canon law, would be added a fourth and fifth year to complete a Bachelor of Arts degree program. This five-year program would be taught in a juniorate, a liberal arts college for "junior sisters." It would provide resistance to the short-term pressures to use teachers before they have received adequate formation and would envision ending the frustrating and unscholarly protraction of undergraduate studies through years of Saturday morning and summer courses. That such resistance to short-term pressures must increase is indicated by the observation that graduates of a five-year program can be expected to give individually an average of forty years of service to children in Catholic schools. Their training must be such as "to assure as well as humanly possible that each of those years shall have maximum value, before God and men." [7]

b. The Everett curriculum. A five-year curriculum for juniorates was constructed in a three-month workshop held from June 1 to August 30, 1956, at Providence School of Nursing, Everett, Washington. Participants were sister-experts (sisters with Ph.D. degrees in their fields) from seventeen Catholic women's colleges, each with a specialty in a different academic field; twelve part-time consultants, men and women, drawn from among college presidents, deans, and professional organizations, some non-Catholic; and a staff of sister-secretaries. The workshop group "attempted to analyze the sisters' roles and works in the light of what is predictable about the era ahead of us and to rethink the college curriculum in view of their conclusions. . . . Every effort was made, however, to see the college education of the Sister as designed for one who is a special kind of student with a special mission and dedication, and as taking place within the larger context of total and integrated spiritual and intellectual formation." [8]

c. Pilot juniorates. The movement has stimulated a diversified wealth of pilot approaches to the problem of providing juniorates for the college training of teachers, including those conducted by large religious congregations which may organize their juniorates in collaboration with one or more of their own colleges for women; cooperatively organized sister-training institutions for sisters of many orders (as in the new Marillac College near St. Louis, recently accredited by the North Central Association); or the new Providence Heights College for sisters which has been organized as one of the six major academic units of the Jesuit Seattle University.

d. Increase of vocations. The Sister Formation movement has

[7] Sister Ritamary, "Marillac—A Sister Formation College," *Sister Formation Bulletin,* vol. 6, no. 3, p. 3, Spring, 1960.

[8] *Report of Everett Curriculum Workshop,* Heiden's Mailing Bureau, Seattle, 1956, p. vii.

already given well-founded hope that with continued progress in the years ahead will come an increase in vocations to the sisterhoods, an increase of great importance to the future of Catholic education in the United States. This likelihood is implied in the 1954 vocation survey of 14,000 students of the sisters, a survey which found only 20 per cent of the students convinced that religious life is broadening, only 22 per cent rating sisters as professionals, and fewer than half considering sisters cultured.[9]

Questions for Discussion or Investigation

1. In your own school system, what approaches are being used to recruit new teachers (not religious teachers)? What additional measures have you to suggest?

2. What measures are taken in your school system to prevent inferior teachers from securing a formal tenure status? Discuss: There is a phenomenon which could be described as "informal tenure status" in systems which do not have policies covering tenure.

3. Are the conditions necessary for administrative handling of the problems of mental or physical deterioration of teachers present in your own school system? What are they?

4. Construct a statement of policy covering sick leave for teachers in a school system.

5. Critically review one of the publications listed below in *Readings and References* under the heading of Publications of the Sister Formation Conferences.

Readings and References

THE LAY TEACHER

Bicknell, John E.: *The Prediction of Effectiveness in Secondary School Teaching,* State Department of Education of New York, Summary Report of the Cooperative Study, Albany, June, 1959.

Chamberlain, Leo M., and Leslie W. Kindred: *The Teacher and School Organization,* Prentice-Hall, Inc., Englewood Cliffs, N.J., 1949.

Elsbree, Willard S.: *The American Teacher,* American Book Company, New York, 1939.

Huggett, Albert J., and Tim M. Stinnett: *Professional Problems of Teachers,* The Macmillan Company, New York, 1956.

Mason, Ward S., and Robert K. Bain: *Teacher Turnover in the Public Schools, 1957–58,* U.S. Office of Education, OE-23002, 1959.

[9] Sister Judith, "Report on the Sister Formation Conferences' Vocation Survey," *Sister Formation Bulletin,* vol. 3, no. 1, pp. 1–7, Autumn, 1956.

Moore, Harold E., and Newell B. Walters: *Personnel Administration in Education,* Harper & Brothers, New York, 1955.

The Postwar Struggle to Provide Teachers, National Education Association, Research Bulletin 35, no. 3, October, 1957.

Public-school Retirement at the Half-century, National Education Association, Research Bulletin 28, no. 4, December, 1950.

Reavis, W. C., and D. H. Cooper: *Evaluation of Merit in City School Systems,* University of Chicago Press, Chicago, 1945.

Ruml, Beardsley, and Sidney G. Tickton: *Teaching Salaries Then and Now,* Fund for the Advancement of Education, Bulletin 1, New York, 1955.

School Personnel Development Plans, Ohio Education Association, Commission on Teacher Education and Professional Standards, Columbus, 1958.

School Personnel Policies, Ohio Education Association, Commission on Teacher Education and Professional Standards, Columbus, 1956.

The Status of the American Public-school Teacher, National Education Association, Research Bulletin 35, no. 1, February, 1957.

Teachers for Tomorrow, Bulletin 2, Fund for the Advancement of Education, New York, 1955.

THE RELIGIOUS TEACHER

A. *Publications of the Sister Formation Conferences*

The Directory of Catholic Women's Colleges Having Facilities for the Education of Sisters, National Catholic Educational Association, Sister Formation Committee, College and University Department, Washington, 1955.

In-service Sisters in Sister Formation, scheduled for publication.

Report of Everett Curriculum Workshop, Heiden's Mailing Bureau, Seattle, Washington, 1956.

Sister Formation Bulletin, published quarterly since 1954, 4831-35th Avenue, S.W., Seattle 6, Washington.

Sister Ritamary (ed.): *The Juniorate in Sister Formation,* Fordham University Press, New York, 1960.

————: *The Mind of the Church in the Formation of Sisters,* Fordham University Press, New York, 1956.

————: *Planning for the Formation of Sisters,* Fordham University Press, New York, 1958.

————: *Spiritual and Intellectual Elements in the Formation of Sisters,* Fordham University Press, New York, 1957.

B. *Other Readings and References*

Bradley, Sister Ritamary: "Lavigerie and the Education of Sisters," *Thought,* vol. 34, no. 135, pp. 607–615, Winter, 1959–1960.

Emil, Sister Mary: "The Teaching Sister and the Vocation Crisis," *Catholic Mind,* vol. 54, pp. 190–196, April, 1956.

————: "The Survey Report on Teacher Preparation," *National Catholic Educational Association Bulletin,* vol. 50, no. 2, pp. 224–226, August, 1953.

Farrell, Benjamin: *Rights and Duties of Ordinary Regarding Women Religious,* The Catholic University of America Press, Washington, 1941.

"The In-service Sister and the Problem of Time," a symposium, *Sister Formation Bulletin,* vol. 5, no. 2, pp. 10–19, Winter, 1959.

Lynch, Timothy: *Contracts between Bishops and Religious Congregations,* The Catholic University of America Press, Washington, 1946.

McCarthy, T. P.: *Guide to the Catholic Sisterhoods in the United States,* 4th ed., The Catholic University of America Press, Washington, 1958.

McCluskey, Neil G.: "The Education of Our Sisters," *America,* pp. 118–127, Apr. 23, 1960.

McGrath, Robert E.: *The Local Superior in Non-exempt Clerical Congregations,* The Catholic University of America Press, Washington, 1954.

Meyer, Sister Bertrande: *The Education of Sisters,* B. Herder Book Company, St. Louis, 1941.

Religious Sisters, English version of *Directoire des supérieures* and *Les Adaptations de la vie religieuse,* The Newman Press, Westminster, Md., 1950.

Ryan, Leo V.: "Central Catholic High-school Employee Benefit Programs," *Catholic Educational Review,* vol. 58, no. 2, February, 1960.

16. Pupil
Personnel Services

Responsibility for pupil personnel services in a large school system is frequently assigned to a major assistant superintendent; duties include enforcing compulsory attendance; providing school health services for the children; supervising psychological services for the unusual student who has been referred by school personnel for intensive individual diagnosis; and transporting children who live beyond fixed distances from school. Special education is sometimes also included as a pupil personnel service, since the unity gained by such classification may facilitate participation in state or Federal money available to public school systems. Generally speaking, however, special education is more properly thought of as part of the regular instructional program of schools rather than as a pupil personnel service.

To the extent that there is a logical unity underlying the category of pupil personnel services, it is found in the concept of services not actually a part of the educational offerings of the school proper, but rather auxiliary to the educational program, as are child accounting, bus transportation of children to school, and health services. Special facilities extended to exceptional children, for example, psychological diagnosis of individual children or case-study techniques used in dealing with chronic truants, also may be included here. It is somewhat because of this concept of services auxiliary to education rather than a part of educational offerings themselves that the Supreme Court of the United States has found nothing unconstitutional in extending such services to children attending parochial schools when local communities see fit to do so. Consequently, the extent to which pupil personnel services are made available to children of all schools depends on state and local initiative and legislation.

In the usual Catholic school system, the whole area of pupil personnel services occupies a rather small part of the total responsibilities of school administrators. The reasons for the relative lack of emphasis are several. The parochial school responsibility for attendance has been mainly to comply with regulations set up by public school authorities; for health services, mainly to fit in with, or promote services from, public health authorities; for psychological services and special education, mainly to cooperate with other diocesan agencies to whom these functions are delegated: typically with Catholic Charities for psychological services and with special educational institutions for the blind, deaf, or predelinquents.

While public schools can themselves frequently centralize these functions, many of them very expensive, with the assistance of public funds available to them, Catholic schools have found an approach to financing them with the assistance of the Community Chest or United Appeal. Centralization under school authorities generally makes possible a more coordinated use of special services for the educational welfare of the child; in the Catholic diocese, where Community Chest funds make some of them possible, these services must be classified as primarily welfare rather than educational concerns if such funds are to be obtained.

It is within this general framework that many pupil personnel services in Catholic schools must be compared to those in public school systems.

ENFORCEMENT OF COMPULSORY ATTENDANCE LAWS

Since Catholic schools must be an integral part of the machinery for enforcing compulsory attendance laws, some understanding of developments in this field is important to the administrator of Catholic schools. Included are the school census, the attendance department, exclusion from school, work permits, and relations with juvenile court.

SCHOOL CENSUS

If compulsory attendance is to be enforced adequately, local school officials must know as accurately as possible who should be in school. Traditionally, two sources of information were relied on to supply this information: an in-school census, taken early each school year, through which each child enrolled in school was asked to complete a card giving vital information about himself and all brothers and sisters; and an out-of-school census taken up annually by paid census-takers who went from house to house listing vital information about all child residents of a school district.

Since some parents became adept at avoiding listing children who were not in school, but should have been, both in the in-school and out-of-school censuses, many large cities in the past thirty years have shifted to a continuous census which begins with the birth records, five or six years prior to the date of expected first entrance to school. This basic file is then modified in the light of in-school and outside enumerations, the reports of school teachers and principals, and the reports of attendance officers on the comings and goings within a particular attendance district. Thus by hard and painstaking work, a reasonably accurate list of children of school age is kept by an alert public school office of the school census.

ATTENDANCE DEPARTMENT

Once school authorities know who ought to be in school, they must see to it that these children actually get to school and continue to attend until they move beyond the limits of a given system or are beyond the age limits for compulsory attendance. The key to this phase of child accounting is the attendance officer, whose function has broadened as his title has been changed in many parts of the country over the past thirty years. Formerly known as the truant officer, his job was pretty much one of catching truants and physically depositing them in the school principal's office. Not infrequently was he aptly described as strong of body but weak in mind. Today he may be known by the pleasanter title of home visitor or visiting teacher; but more than the title has changed.

The job now involves more than catching the truant and delivering him to school. It includes finding the answer for his frequent absence, helping the teacher and principal understand reasons for unauthorized absence and dealing with parents on these matters, acting rapidly when a chronic case is reported as absent by an alert principal's phone call, knowing the place where the repeater is likely to be found, recommending special diagnostic procedures where they seem needed, preparing reports for case workers, cooperating with other community agencies in instances where the truant's problems interrelate with the concerns of those agencies, and preparing recommendations and a case for presentation to juvenile court when legal action against the offender or his parents is warranted. With duties like these, the newer type of attendance officer is increasingly found to be a trained and certificated professional person with requirements and salary at least equal to those of a teacher, though his training may have also included some of the techniques of the social worker. Both men and women have proved highly successful in the work. Experienced young professional attendance officers, after a few years in this kind of work, have been found to make excellent teachers, especially in schools having a high concentration of problem students. After some teaching experience, they have proved a valuable source of supply for filling openings as counselors, assistant principals, and principals.

Enforcing the Exceptions to Compulsory Attendance

Intimately related to enforcing compulsory attendance laws is the enforcement of state child-labor regulations. To secure coordination in the operation of both sets of laws, school officials may be charged with issuing work permits. Compulsory attendance laws, while specifying the age limits of compulsory school attendance, also may provide for exceptions, such as children of a specified minimum age for whom work certificates may be issued while they are employed. A particularly prudent approach is to provide for the permit to be issued to the employer with the provision that the permit be returned to the issuing office if the child's services cease for any reason.

In such an eventuality the attendance department is alerted to seeing that he reenters school promptly.

A second exception to compulsory education provisions of state laws is the small group of youngsters officially declared to be incapable of profiting from further schooling. With the scope of special educational opportunities available today to all kinds of children—the bedside cases, the very slow learners, the physically handicapped, and the behavior problems—very few children in a large city qualify for official action of this kind.

RELATIONS WITH JUVENILE COURT

Since most school relationships with juvenile courts grow out of truancy, or are in some way related to attendance problems, it is usual that in a large city system a specialist in handling all court cases will be a member of the staff of the division concerned with enforcing compulsory attendance. His responsibilities will ordinarily include:

1. Formally summoning parents or guardians to conferences on serious attendance problems.

2. If such measures fail to secure adequate corrective action, initiating legal action against the parents or legal guardians. Punitive action or even court commitment to a corrective institution may be involved.

Relations of a Catholic school with juvenile courts will ordinarily be coordinated through a division of Catholic Charities.

CATHOLIC SCHOOL RESPONSIBILITIES

In adopting compulsory school-attendance regulations, the state is clearly acting within its responsibility for the welfare of the children of the state. In following necessary procedures and in supplying the necessary reports, Catholic schools fulfill their legal responsibility to comply with the legitimate demands of civil society as it is organized in the United States.

Obviously, unless Catholic schools participate thoroughly in the in-school census procedures, in the regular weekly or monthly attendance reporting, in using attendance officers to assist with chronic truancy problems, and in keeping the attendance department informed as to transfers in, out, or within school district lines, enforcement procedures may break down and the common welfare is endangered.

Some Catholic school teachers, in their natural dislike for completing forms and reports, will occasionally refer to these reports as devices by which local public school authorities collect state money for children they do not have to educate. This is not often as true as it is rumored; whether or not it is the case can easily be checked. If state reimbursement to local school districts is based on children of educable age, the claim is partly true; however, such funds, in by far the greater number of states, are based on children in ADM (average daily membership) or ADA (average daily attendance) only in the public schools receiving the funds.

HEALTH SERVICES

Since how much children learn in school can on occasion be determined by the health of the child, alert school administration is interested in uncovering physical defects which may influence the child's school performance. It is also interested in providing a healthy environment for learning and in controlling as much as possible the spread of communicable disease throughout a school. These two responsibilities—uncovering physical impediments to learning and helping prevent the spread of communicable diseases in school—provide the basic reasons for organized health services, generally under the supervision of a physician who may be known as the director of health services. Necessary physical examinations of children by school doctors, dentists, and nurses; daily health inspection by teachers, especially at the primary level; school nursing services; policies and advice on administering first aid in schools; exclusion of children suspected of having communicable diseases; and informing parents of physical conditions needing treatment by family physicians and dentists or at public clinics are all part of well-organized school health programs.

In some school districts, where municipal or county health departments are strongly organized and well financed, the division of school health services may consist only of a director whose chief function is to coordinate the use of board of health physicians and public health nurses who are assigned to schools. In other school districts, the school authorities have their own staff of physicians, dentists, and nurses.

Obviously, where public health authorities provide staff for health work, public and parochial school children have an equal claim on their services, as in Pennsylvania where state laws provide for health services for all children. Where local school authorities completely staff their own services, parochial school health services are less likely, or they must be developed on a volunteer basis. When a division of health services is organized in a public school system, desirable functions other than those for which it was specifically organized soon accrue to it. The division may administer a compulsory health examination required for *initial* or *continued* employment in the school system, both in teaching positions or in such nonprofessional jobs as are found in school lunchrooms. Advising and counseling with the department of instruction concerning the curriculum in health, with the department of administrative operation (e.g., on whether or not a school should be closed because of heavy incidence of flu), and with the department of business (e.g., health and sanitary requirements of school buildings) also are frequently added to the primary functions of this area of pupil personnel services.

Provisions for adequate school health services should include:

1. Physical examinations and immunizations of children at preschool roundups.

2. Periodic examinations to uncover physical conditions needing treatment or corrective action if children are to profit from school activities, for example, sight, hearing, and dental examinations. It should be noted here that treatment of physical defects is not an elementary or secondary school service. This service is generally limited to advising parents of the need for private treatment or, if requested, referring them to clinics maintained in the community for free medical or dental treatment.

3. Assistance in control of communicable diseases by recommending exclusion from school for children suspected of having one of these diseases or for children who fail to present evidence of immunizations required by law.

4. Assisting teachers, especially primary teachers, with help in

discovering children whose symptoms warrant examination by the school physician or nurse.

5. Administering first aid, when health staff members are in the building, or advising principals and teachers on emergency first-aid treatment needed when health staff members are not in the building.

6. Advising administrators on policies to follow in the event of emergency health situations—serious injury in an accident or sudden illness. It should be pointed out that the school administrator frequently finds himself in a dilemma in these situations. He can do too little and be guilty of negligence; or he can do too much and be guilty of negligence, as well as personally liable for medical or hospital bills for treatment he has authorized. The prudent principle for administrators to follow in these situations is to do as little as is necessary pending authorization from a parent. The child should be safely placed in the hands of the parents even if it means driving him home. Advance arrangements may often be made with the local police authorities to have emergency cases driven home by them; if hospitalization is called for before parents can be reached, again the police may secure entrance to a hospital as an emergency measure, avoiding personal liability by school personnel.

PSYCHOLOGICAL SERVICES

A substantial number of children in any school need intensive diagnostic examination if the causes of their unusual behavior are to be discovered and their responses to educational opportunities are to be improved. Unfortunately, even diagnostic procedures are time-consuming and expensive. Individual mental testing, individual aptitude testing, detailed case-study techniques, liaison with community social agencies, psychological and psychiatric diagnosis —all these may be indicated. Thus, in order to study at all adequately the complicated problems of the severely atypical child, expensive staffs of psychometrists, case workers, school psychologists, and medically trained psychologists and psychiatrists are needed. It is safe to say that no school system is able to provide a staff which has more than begun on the serious problems of severely disturbed children, the number of whom is considerably larger than generally suspected.

The magnitude of the problems involved, however, is hardly an excuse for failure to do everything possible along these lines. The bare minimum which should be provided is as highly trained a staff member as possible to serve as the schools' clearing agency with other community psychological and psychiatric services, private or public. Such a person would serve as an expert advisor to schools and parents on the need for, and availability of, such technical services. In turn, this staff member would channel back to the principal and teacher the results of detailed diagnosis with suggestions on how best to conform to the treatment which may be in process. In Catholic schools such a staff member would generally coordinate school efforts and the appropriate Catholic Charities agency.

Almost as essential to a minimum program of psychological services, are as many skilled psychometrists for individual mental testing, and as many trained case workers for developing social histories as any school organization is likely to afford. In Catholic school situations, generally speaking, this will have to be left to Catholic social agencies receiving Community Chest or governmental support. If the schools and the social agencies are to work together successfully, however, liaison cannot be left to chance or the initiative of an outside agency.

TRANSPORTATION OF PUPILS

Transporting children to school has been a greatly expanding service of public school systems. More recently it has become increasingly a responsibility of Catholic school administrators. While all school administrators are still in the process of learning the best answers to problems connected with this service, research studies and experience have isolated many of these problems and are indicating some desirable answers.

TRANSPORTING PUBLIC SCHOOL PUPILS

State laws which provide for compulsory school attendance and those which encourage consolidation of school districts into larger units make it necessary that children be transported safely to school if they lived beyond a certain distance from their assigned building. According to the National Council on Schoolhouse Construction, such limits are generally three-quarters of a mile each way for elementary school, one and a half miles for junior high school, and two miles for senior high school pupils.[1] Table 9 presents a picture of the increasing scope of pupil transportation in the United States.

TABLE 9. NUMBER AND PER CENT OF PUBLIC SCHOOL PUPILS TRANSPORTED AT PUBLIC EXPENSE, AND EXPENDITURES FOR TRANSPORTATION: CONTINENTAL UNITED STATES, 1929–1930 TO 1955–1956

Year	Enrollment		Per cent of enrolled pupils transported	Expenditures of public funds for transportation excluding capital outlay, thousands of dollars
	Total	Pupils transported at public expense		
1	2	3	4	5
1929–1930	25,678,015	1,902,826	7.4	$ 54,823
1931–1932	26,275,441	2,419,173	9.2	58,078
1933–1934	26,434,193	2,794,724	10.6	53,908
1935–1936	26,367,098	3,250,658	12.3	62,653
1937–1938	25,975,108	3,769,242	14.5	75,637
1939–1940	25,433,542	4,144,161	16.3	83,283
1941–1942	24,562,473	4,503,081	18.3	92,922
1943–1944	23,266,616	4,512,412	19.4	107,754
1945–1946	23,299,941	5,056,966	21.7	129,756
1947–1948	23,944,532	5,854,041	24.4	176,265
1949–1950	25,111,427	6,947,384	27.7	214,504
1951–1952	26,562,664	7,697,130	29.0	268,827
1953–1954	*25,643,871	*8,411,719	*32.8	307,437
1955–1956	*27,740,149	*9,695,819	*35.0	353,972

* Number of pupils in average daily attendance.
SOURCE: *Biennial Survey of Education in the United States, 1954–1956*, U.S. Office of Education, chap. 1.

By 1960 over 12 million children were being transported to school in the fifty states of the union at a public expense of close to 500 million dollars per year. Well over one-third of all public school pupils are transported to school at public expense.

Frequently suburban and rural public school districts go beyond

[1] *Guide for Planning School Plants,* National Council on Schoolhouse Construction, George Peabody College for Teachers, Nashville, Tenn., 1949, p. 18.

the requirements of state laws and in many school districts today, virtually every child is transported in a school bus, chiefly as a safety measure.

The expanding nature of this service is indicated by Reeder as follows: "Since its beginning in Quincy, Massachusetts, in 1874, the transportation of pupils at public expense has had a phenomenal growth. . . . The percentage of the school budget going for pupil transportation has been gradually increasing in most states and approximately 4.5 per cent of the budget goes for transportation." [2]

Most, but not all, transportation of school children is in school busses. In large city school systems, peculiarities of school district lines sometimes make a school board contract with a taxicab company the most feasible approach. Where the system requires attendance at special classes at a distance from the child's home, the child's fare on public transportation is defrayed by issuing pupil bus tickets. Sometimes when the child is severely handicapped—for example, students with gravely impaired vision—local districts, helped by state reimbursement, may even provide a student guide, paying an extra bus fare and even a stipend.

TRANSPORTING CATHOLIC SCHOOL PUPILS

Few issues have engendered more emotional bitterness in recent years than that concerning the transportation of parochial school children in public school busses at public expense. The Catholic parent who must drive his youngster to school—perhaps even to a building located next door to the public school—is daily irritated by the inconvenience as he views other children on his street riding a bus for which he, as a taxpayer, is paying. On the other hand, his neighbors are frequently ready to take all possible steps to keep the parochial school youngster off the school bus lest the "wall of separation between Church and State" be dented or breached.

As we have seen when discussing the New Jersey Bus case in Chapter 4, the Supreme Court majority sees nothing contrary to the Constitution of the United States should a state provide transportation service to parochial school children under circumstances which

[2] Ward G. Reeder, *The Fundamentals of Public School Administration,* The Macmillan Company, New York, 1958, p. 332.

are not deemed by state supreme courts in violation of state constitutions. Within the state, therefore, the question generally comes down to the attitude of the local board on extending the service or the results of any legal action that may be taken by a taxpayer in protest of a board's action favorable to the parochial school child.

Local boards, particularly where the support of Catholic parents is essential to passing school bond or special tax-levy proposals, frequently have extended this service without any taxpayer opposition. When a suit results, however, the phraseology of the state law and the wording of state constitutional provisions preventing public aid to religiously controlled schools become issues.

In Kentucky, for example, a state law specifically phrased to permit transportation of pupils to school as a public safety, not educational, measure was ruled constitutional. The law could be applied to children irrespective of the school attended on the grounds that the state was equally interested in the safety of all children. Where state laws are not so specifically worded, the status of public transportation of parochial school children depends upon the court's interpretation as to whether transportation is essentially an educational measure, and so violates a state constitutional provision preventing state educational funds from religious control; or whether it is essentially a service to children and, as such, is extendable to all children. State courts have decided this question differently in different states. However, by 1960 nineteen states had some statutory provision for transporting children attending nonpublic schools.

The net result of the varying status of public transportation of Catholic school children is that in most localities in the country where transportation is provided, it is done so by Catholic school authorities at the expense of the parents of the children using the busses. As more and more parish schools are located in more sparsely settled suburban or rural areas, Catholic pastors and principals find themselves involved in solving the many problems with which the literature of public education has for some years been concerned.

PROBLEMS OF TRANSPORTING PUPILS

The basic question facing school authorities launching a transportation service for children is whether it is better for the schools to own and run their own busses or to contract with a private firm or public utility to provide the service. The answer to this question depends partly on costs, a subject equally important to the public school administrator or to the Catholic school administrator who is interested in keeping the expenses of attending his school as low as possible for the parents who must pay them.

Generally speaking, as would be expected, almost all studies have indicated the desirability of school ownership of busses. According to a summary by Clayton D. Hutchins in the *Encyclopedia of Educational Research,* school ownership has the advantages of lower costs, better control, greater flexibility, safer transportation, better drivers, improved maintenance, and more adequate service. School-owned equipment results in cost 30 to 40 per cent less than contract plans; since, of course, contractors must make a profit, they must provide for possible nonrenewal of contracts, and they must pay high charges for financing purchases of busses; also, they may have to pay some taxes which even parochial school authorities may not have to pay.[3]

With school ownership, Hutchins further points out, there is more complete control, changes in route can be made more easily as need arises, variations in bus schedules can be arranged on a given day, and the selection of drivers and standards of safety can be better controlled. Furthermore, school busses are available for other educational activities growing out of the school curriculum, such as transporting the faculty to educational institutes.

Of course these advantages, in some circumstances, can be nullified if the numbers to be transported are small, or if a school district serves widely scattered homes in sparsely settled areas. Joint ownership and operation of a school bus by two or three parishes may be indicated to offset the too-few children in one parish. Actually the staggering of school hours between parishes involved in a joint operation may be more easily arranged than in a larger public school where staggered school hours lead only to confusion and administrative complications.

Assistance in administrative planning for pupil transportation is widely available in the literature of education: manuals published by

[3] *Encyclopedia of Educational Research,* 2d ed., Walter S. Monroe (ed.), The Macmillan Company, New York, 1950, pp. 1490–1491.

state departments of education, articles by experienced administrators, and United States Office of Education bulletins. Problems generally covered in this literature include mapping transportation routes, circular or loop versus shoestring routes, spacing of bus stops, standards for busses, liability and property-damage insurance, selection of drivers, and use of teachers as drivers, a device which increases their salaries, but limits their after-hour services as teachers.

Questions for Discussion or Investigation

1. Does your own community use the continuous census technique, or does it rely on one or more spot censuses?

2. What qualifications are set for attendance officers in your schools?

3. What provisions cover the issuance of work permits in your community?

4. Who controls the use of school physicians or nurses in your community? Are they equally available to public and private schools?

5. What psychological services are available to students in public schools upon referral by teachers and principals of your locality? In parochial schools? How are the latter financed?

6. What public school pupils may be transported at public expense in your state? In your local community? Precisely what is the situation of Catholic school pupils in your community as regards transportation to school at public expense? Could they be transported legally with public funds if they are not?

Readings and References

Ankenbrandt, Richard: "Health Services in the Catholic Secondary Schools," unpublished master's thesis, The Catholic University of America, Washington, 1957.

Belknap, Burton H.: *The School Bus,* Educational Publishers, Minneapolis, 1951.

Cutts, Norma E. (ed.): *School Psychologists at Mid-century,* American Psychological Association, Washington, 1955.

Featherston, E. Glen, and John B. Murray: *Requirements and Training Programs for School Bus Drivers,* U.S. Office of Education Circular 465, rev., 1960.

————, and ————: *State Provisions for Transporting Pupils,* U.S. Office of Education Circular 453, rev., 1960.

————, and Robert F. Will: *Pupil Transportation Responsibilities and Services of State Departments of Education,* U.S. Office of Education Misc. 27, 1956.

Grieder, Calvin, and William Everett Rosenstengel: *Public School Administration,* The Ronald Press Company, New York, 1954.

Jones, Arthur J.: *Principles of Guidance and Pupil Personnel Work,* McGraw-Hill Book Company, Inc., New York, 1951.

National Commission on Safety Education: *Standards and Training Programs for School Bus Drivers,* National Education Association, Washington, 1949.

National Society for the Study of Education: *Personnel Services in Education,* Fifty-eighth Yearbook, Part II, University of Chicago Press, Chicago, 1959.

Pupil Transportation, Yearbook 1953, National Education Association, Department of Rural Education, Washington, 1953.

Reeder, Ward G.: *The Fundamentals of Public School Administration,* The Macmillan Company, New York, 1958.

Roesch, Winston L.: *Statutory Basis for Administrative and Specialized Service Staffing in Local School Districts,* U.S. Office of Education Bulletin 1960, no. 1, 1960.

Suggested School Health Problems, 3d ed., National Education Association, Joint Committee on Health Problems in Education, Washington, 1956.

Turner, Clair E.: *School Health and Health Education,* The C.V. Mosby Company, St. Louis, 1952.

Umbeck, Nelda: *State Legislation on School Attendance and Related Matters,* U.S. Office of Education Circular 615, 1960.

Wall, William D. (ed.): *Psychological Services for Schools,* New York University Press, New York, 1957.

Wilson, Charles C. (ed.): *School Health Services,* National Education Association, Joint Committee on Health Problems in Education, Washington, 1954.

Yeager, William A.: *Administration and the Pupil,* Harper & Brothers, New York, 1949.

17. *Business Management: School Finance*

Business management is one of the sixfold responsibilities of school administration. The efficiency with which the function of business management is discharged within a school system will determine to a considerable extent the effectiveness of the instructional program which it supports. School business management includes financial management, housing the instructional program, furnishing school supplies, and operating school lunchrooms. The first of these, school finance, is treated in the present chapter. Chapter 18 is devoted to housing; Chapter 19, to supplies and food services.

School finance, whether in public or Catholic schools, includes responsibility for receiving all income and spending all school moneys other than those properly classified as intra-school funds, which are the responsibility of the principal of the school which raised them from such sources as admissions, dues, entertainments, and socials.

A clear distinction in school finance is made between current expenditures and current income, on the one hand, and capital outlay and income for capital expenses, on the other. As the name implies, current expenditures include all the on-going expenses of running schools, and current income consists of all the funds available in a fiscal year for defraying these expenses. Capital outlay includes all funds spent for plant expansion—new schoolhouses or additions to school plants. Income for capital outlay is money specifically secured for financing new schools or additions to school plants. In public schools the cost of capital outlay is ordinarily secured from specifically approved bond issues which are retired over a period of years through special real estate taxes authorized for this purpose prior to issuance of the bonds. In Catholic schools, whatever the sources used for defraying capital costs, separate accounting is necessary if the on-going picture of current expenditures and income is not to become too confused for efficient administration.

In financial matters state law may provide a basis for a conflict between sound theories of administration and legal provisions outlining the responsibilities of the clerk of the board of education of a public school district. As observed earlier, sound administrative theory provides for a unitary delegation of administrative responsibility to a chief executive who, in turn, delegates part of his responsibilities to a business manager who, in his turn, may have an assistant known as director of finance. Yet, state law may reserve the actual receiving of income and signing of checks to another servant of the board of education, the clerk. In a private corporation a similar situation may be found when certain financial responsibilities are allocated to a treasurer who is responsible directly to the board of trustees.

To reconcile this conflict and to avoid nullifying the advantages of the unitary concept of administrative delegation, the duties of the clerk of the board should be restricted to the minimum financial duties specifically directed by law; likewise, in a private corporation the responsibilities of a corporation treasurer should be limited to the minimum necessary for adequate control, chiefly those of signing checks. Otherwise, the clerk or treasurer may develop in fact into a business manager, or financial manager, operating outside of the professional administrator's area of responsibility and increasing the likelihood of conflict between financial policies and other administrative functions.

The concept of school finance as responsible for handling income and expenditures necessarily includes responsibilities for adequate accounting for all funds available, studies of costs and trends, and providing the chief administrator with information on income and expenditures so necessary for effective school management.

THE BUDGET, A KEY TO SOUND FINANCIAL PRACTICES

The school budget is selected for detailed discussion, since as the administrator moves toward effective budgetary procedures, other financial responsibilities must automatically be discharged better. Thus, the school budget can well be the key to improved accounting, improved financial planning, and improved procedures for controlling expenditures, and can bring about an increased awareness of the necessity for cost accounting. These are not the only good results of effective budget procedures, however, for actually the budget may well be called the greatest single tool which the school administrator has available to him: its by-product is over-all administrative efficiency.

By state law, public school districts must have a school budget submitted on proper forms for approval by state school authorities; by growing custom, most Catholic schools have budgets. Having a budget in itself, though, is no guarantee that valuable by-products will be realized. The potential over-all administrative results of a budget will be completely missed by any institution, Catholic or public, if it has a budget just because some law makes it mandatory; or because everyone is doing it; or because an accrediting agency will demand one; or because sometimes businessmen members of advisory councils want to know about expected deficits, surpluses, or allocation of expenditures before supporting fund drives. In fact, *pro forma* budgets may well contribute some new sources of financial waste: padding of budget requests, spending allotments recklessly before they are forever lost as the fiscal year closes, and fostering an attitude that the less one spends in a given year, the less he will receive to spend in the following one.

To bring about the general administrative efficiency which justifies labeling the budget as the greatest single tool of the effective administrator, it must be properly prepared, properly justified, and properly controlled. These three steps in budgetary procedures make possible, and even almost inevitable, a detailed awareness of financial facts, informed policy-making decisions, good staff communications, controlled executive activity, and piercing evaluation of the many features of a school program.

BUDGET PREPARATION

Basically good budget preparation is a mechanical procedure. Precisely from this fact flow advantages to the good administrator and disadvantages to the weak one. From following sound mechanics of budget preparation, there can come to the alert only a large number of questions "why?" As the why's are effectively answered, efficient administration is promoted. But because budget preparation can be so largely mechanical, chief administrators frequently go through the mechanics oblivious to the why's demanding answer; or they prejudge that nothing illuminating to the artistic administrator could emerge from so prosaic a tool; or they fail to see that in involving all staff members concerned in answering the why's, vital staff communication can be obtained. All three failures are disastrous to schools and school systems fighting for survival among today's problems of school finance.

A budget is a statement of expected income for a fiscal year balanced against a statement of expected expenditures for the same year. The fiscal year for the private school best coincides with the school year—September 1 through August 31. Why July 1 through June 30 should be used in a private school seems difficult to explain since, if there are summer operations, the beginning of the new fiscal year is in the middle of them; and if there are no summer operations, any salary payments made during the summer are at the rates of the previous school year and complicate budget planning. Public schools may by law have to use the calendar year as the fiscal year because the school board's term is on a January through December basis, and tax rates and distributions are so based. Such a fiscal year, however, adds unnecessary computational intricacies for the private school.

Since the statement of expected income for a fiscal year is less detailed and more easily anticipated, it is to the expenditures aspect of the budget that more detailed attention is given here.

1. The approach begins with a form which in horizontal columns provides for recording actual expenditures for at least three and perhaps five years past, and one column for entering anticipated

expenditure figures for the same item in the fiscal year ahead. This obviously presupposes an accounting system which is designed to provide this information accurately and easily.

2. Expenditure items are arranged vertically and grouped logically under general headings or categories. Budget categories, if logically planned, ought to coincide with the categories basic to the accounting system employed and, if maximum administrative efficiency is to be gained, both should follow a pattern being used in comparable school systems or institutions (cf. "Budget Justification," below). The categories adopted will bear a recognizable relationship to the functions of school administration—instruction, administrative operation, pupil personnel services, business management, community relations, and research.

3. One staff member—the director of finance if there is one, the business manager himself if he has no assistant charged with the job, or in a small system, perhaps the chief executive himself—must be charged with initiating and coordinating budget development. He is the budget officer.

4. The entry for each category of expected expenditures will be initiated by the staff member responsible for administering the funds. This is the person most able to anticipate program modification—whether expanding or contracting—and estimate financial ramifications of such changes. His budget estimate should be the result of conferences with the budget officer, a process giving essential insights to both. The administrator of a department or bureau discovers general financial developments which set over-all limitations on expansion likely to be approved. The budget officer becomes aware of extraordinary developments influencing a departmental request. Conferences held between division heads and the budget officer and between the division heads and their staffs provide a two-way route for the intra-organizational communication so needed in institutions of complex structure.

5. The chief executive, be he superintendent or institutional president, with his budget officer and major administrative assistants, reviews budget estimates and justification. While always maintaining proper communications with those initiating requests, they isolate the policy decisions needed to bring the total budget in balance. The chief administrator recommends to the board of education or

institutional board of control a balanced budget with the alternative policy decisions needed to achieve it. The board makes the final decisions and adopts an official budget for the next fiscal year.

BUDGET JUSTIFICATION

Budget justification consists in answering the why's which arise in the months immediately preceding the adoption of the budget as it is in preparation. The questions may come from a variety of activities. As they are reasonably and effectively answered, wise administrative decisions are facilitated by budgetary procedures. If the questions do not even come up, an educational venture will develop Topsy-like.

The first source of the question "why?" is the mechanical form itself. Suppose, for example the budget summary for a large school operation contains, in part, the following items:

	Expenditures			Budget
	1958–1959	1959–1960	1960–1961	1961–1962
Administration, general:				
Office of Superintendent				
salaries	28,000	29,500	31,000	40,000
Supervision and instruction:				
Teachers' salaries	9,000,000	9,500,000	10,000,000	11,500,000
Maintenance of buildings:				
Salaries	262,500	287,500	312,500	412,500
All other	157,500	172,500	187,500	222,500
Total	420,000	460,000	500,000	635,000

As the administrator examines the budget item by item, under the first excerpt the question arises: why, after a normal yearly rise of $1,500, does next year's budget call for a rise of $9,000 in salaries? The normal $1,500 for salary increases is included, but a new position of administrative assistant to the superintendent is proposed at $7,500. Reasons for creating the position are specified.

The "Teachers' Salaries" item shows a past progression of $500,-000 per year covering salary increments and additional teachers to meet the tidal wave of students. Next year's budget proposes a 1½-million-dollar increase—why? Justification includes a similar $500,-000 to cover the same factors as past years with an additional $200,-

000 to cover costs of hiring fifty additional teachers at an average salary of $4,000. These new teachers are necessary because an extraordinary 1,500 enrollment over that of the past three years is expected. The provision for meeting the costs of a new teacher salary schedule is $800,000.

The third excerpt indicates a rise of $135,000 for total building maintenance. Why? Explanation: school painting maintenance under the pressure of other financial demands has been neglected somewhat over the past three years. An emergency need now exists. To meet it will cost $75,000 in salaries over the usual $25,000 cost for increments to maintenance personnel and $20,000 for supplies over the usual $15,000 per year increased cost of all maintenance supplies.

As budget justification reaches its final stages, the superintendent and his staff, and ultimately the board which must determine policy, have choices to make if anticipated expenditures are larger (as is usual) then anticipated income.

Is this the year to spend $7,500 for an administrative assistant to the superintendent?

Since the new teacher salary schedule has already been adopted, shall class size be increased beyond past practice to save all or part of the $200,000 planned for additional teaching?

Shall the painting program be authorized? or half of it? or none of it?

If the proposed expenditures are all indispensable, is the justification sound enough to request additional income from the people who support the school?

A second source of why's coming from good budget procedures arises from comparing a school system or institution with comparable systems or institutions, providing standard accounting categories and procedures are used. Such comparisons raise such questions as these:

Why is our system spending only 65 per cent of its income on supervision and instruction if comparable systems spend an average of 72 per cent on this function?

Why are we spending 14 cents of every current-expense dollar on operation of plant when national figures may indicate 10 cents is about average?

Why are our per-pupil costs higher or lower than the average of comparable institutions?

The answers to these and similar questions may fully justify our practices. For example, in the first instance, a low salary schedule may be indicated; in the second, an antiquated plant may necessitate extraordinary janitorial or fuel expenditures; or in answer to the last, data on cost of living or relative wealth available may indicate the practice justified. The point, however, is that proper budget justification procedures make for alert administration as the why's arise and are answered.

Catholic and private schools may have initial difficulty in securing comparable figures on expenditures in comparable systems on two counts: the factor of contributed services in parochial school finance may seem to make comparisons difficult or impossible; and few figures have been gathered on Catholic school per-pupil costs or on the percentage of the school dollar that is spent on each function.

The solution of the first solves the second since, if contributed or nominal salaries of religious are handled properly, comparisons can be made with either public or parochial schools. Techniques developed by Catholic colleges and universities for handling contributed services may be applied to elementary and secondary schools. Salaries of religious staff are constructed on the same bases used for determining salaries paid laymen of similar experience and training. These constructed salaries are entered in the accounting records as expenses in the same way that lay salaries are. On the income side is entered as return from a living endowment the difference between constructed salaries and actual cost of the religious community to the school, or nominal salaries plus living, according to the facts. The total difference for all religious is capitalized at prevailing interest rates on gilt-edged securities, and the resulting figure constitutes the dollar value of the "living endowment."

If Catholic school books are kept in this manner, the figures are then perfectly comparable to public school figures, providing the accounting categories are identical. Detailed guides to proper school accounting and the meaning of standard categories are available, including two publications of the U.S. Office of Education: Bulletin 1957, no. 4, *Financial Accounting for Local and State School Sys-*

tems, and Bulletin 1959, no. 21, *Financial Accounting for School Activities.*

With standardization of budget categories, national figures, such as those issued by the U.S. Office of Education on percentage of expenditures by function or annual per-pupil costs, may then be used by Catholic schools in budget justification. Following are summary figures on both of these items for school systems in cities and counties with 100,000 population or more for 1957–1958:[1]

Per Cent of Expenditures by Function

Administration	2.4
Instruction	74.8
Attendance and Health Services	1.6
Pupil Transportation Services	.5
Operation	10.6
Maintenance	4.7
Fixed Charges	3.7

Annual Current Expenditure per Pupil in Average Daily Attendance

Average	$344

It is significant that a comparison with comparable figures four years earlier reveals a higher percentage of expenditures now going to instruction (in which teacher salary is the largest item) with lesser percentages being devoted to administration and auxiliary services as a whole. The percentage devoted to maintenance has remained relatively constant. Chief costs under fixed charges are pension and retirement, the costs of which are rising.

BUDGET CONTROL

Once a budget has been adopted for a school organization, if the adoption is to make any sense, expenditures must be controlled within the allocations of money provided for each item. The staff member assigned financial responsibility must be made controller to see that before expenditures are made, funds are available in the budget.

The necessity for clearing expenditures in advance with the controller leads inevitably to a system of requisitions. Expenditures must be requisitioned by the heads of departments. The controller

[1] Gerald Kahn, *Current Expenditures per Pupil in Public School Systems: Urban School Systems, 1957–58,* U.S. Office of Education Circular 595, 1959, p. 8.

must indicate the availability of budgeted funds. Where funds are not available, procedures for transfer from other funds administered by the same executive may be made. If this source is not productive, on recommendation of the chief executive, transfers may be authorized from a contingency fund which always is part of a good budget.

Since the controller and the administrative staff must know whether or not funds are available, accounting procedures must be accurate and speedy. Budget reports must be issued promptly, preferably monthly, but at least quarterly. Periodically during the school year, budget review must be instituted so that urgent unanticipated financial developments may find their way promptly into the total budget picture. Again, the necessary staff conferences have the important by-products of stimulating policy decisions and providing for two-way staff communications.

FINANCING DIOCESAN SCHOOLS

With the ever-accelerating growth of Catholic schools in the United States has come an ever-increasing problem of financing these schools. All the developments along the route to an inevitably more complex administration of modern schools take more money. The most significant increase in expenditure for Catholic schools, now and in the years ahead, must be for salaries for lay teachers. As the trend is now established, by 1970 the number of lay teachers in parish schools throughout the United States should exceed the number of sisters; and the cost of one lay teacher at a maximum salary in a public school (the standard of competition) frequently exceeds the cost of an equally qualified sister in a comparable diocese by a ratio of 9 to 1. Even at minimum salaries substantially inferior to those paid in public schools, five sisters (if available) could be supported for the cost of one lay teacher.

As has been pointed out repeatedly in previous chapters, Catholic school administration has been traditionally decentralized. In the financing of the parish school, each parish has been, for all practical purposes, a "district unit." The pastor has been responsible for financing the parish school; he generally has depended upon monthly or weekly collections for school support, supplemented by other workable means for raising money including income from parish socials, festivals, and paper drives. In some dioceses, a modest tuition has been collected from the parents who could afford to pay it.

With the growth of centralized diocesan high schools in this century, the costs of conducting these schools have generally been shared by the feeder parishes themselves and by the parents through tuitions. Specifically, in one diocese in 1959–1960, tuition of $90 per year for each pupil was charged; $45 was contributed by the parish to which the youth belonged and $45 by the parents of the youth. At the same time the cost per pupil for one youngster in the neighboring public high schools was about $400 per year.

The diocesan office of the superintendent of schools has, typically, not been involved with problems of school finance. It has been sufficiently occupied with the problem of securing adequate finances to conduct its own educational services at a minimum level. The superintendent of one diocesan school system in a large metropolitan area, when he was assigned to his position some years ago, was allotted a sum of $500 on which to perform his functions for a year. Currently the beginnings of a diocesan-wide school financing program are to be seen in those dioceses assessing parish schools 25 or 50 cents per pupil for the support of the office of the superintendent.

As diocesan school systems are forced by the complexity of today's problems to greater centralization of school administration, and as the costs of running diocesan schools continue to soar, the unequal distribution of financial resources among parishes will make itself even more apparent. Just as in public school districts the problem of financing adequate education in relatively impoverished districts forced a solution in the form of state-foundation programs, so the problem of financing adequate Catholic education in relatively impoverished parishes is increasingly demanding a solution.

AN APPROACH TO THE PROBLEM

As the more insistent problems in financing centralized diocesan high schools are studied and resolved, it is our opinion that the way will be paved for a more comprehensive approach to diocesan-wide financing of Catholic school systems, for the financing of a centralized high school supported jointly by a group of parishes constitutes definite inroads on the relative financial autonomy of the individual pastor; it has highlighted in some dioceses the inability of some parishes to pay an equal share of the total costs of the school; it has occasioned some research into techniques for evaluating the ability of parishes to pay for education and some specific plans for effecting diocesan school foundation programs. A particularly comprehensive research study leading to specific proposals is the doctoral study of Robusto.[2]

As a result of his research, Robusto presents three general plans for the proposed financing of the central Catholic high schools of the Diocese of Trenton as illustrations of the adaptability of public school finance techniques applied to Catholic schools. The three plans involve total diocesan support, a partnership plan of support, and total regional support, respectively.

Plan for Total Diocesan Support. The total diocesan support plan would establish a foundation program of education for the entire diocese, defined in terms of the total unit-cost index of $110.47 per pupil in average daily attendance. This unit-cost index is a measure of needed services and facilities including a plant charge. The diocesan foundation program would be flexible and permit maximum adaptability by the individual schools. To increase local initiative and promote diocesan-wide interest, each school would be permitted to use all high school revenue receipts, except tuition, to enrich the educational offerings beyond the minimum program. The cost of the diocesan foundation program would be borne entirely by all the parishes of the diocese by a tax or assessment based upon the parish index of relative financial ability, regardless of the number of children that the parish sends to the central Catholic high school. The diocese could assure that the required school funds would be available for the educational program through the establishment of a central high school finance office, the chief function of which would be the collection of the parish tax or assessment, and the apportionment and distribution of the funds to the central Catholic high schools. The apportionment and distribution of the high school funds would be made on the basis of average daily attendance.

The Partnership Plan. The partnership plan of support would establish a foundation program which is identical to that of the

[2] Carmine C. Robusto, "The Financial Support of Catholic Diocesan Secondary Schools," unpublished doctoral dissertation, Fordham University, New York, 1954.

total diocesan support plan except in its method of support. This program would be supported through the joint participation of the parishes of the diocese, the central Catholic high schools, and the Diocese of Trenton. This program would also be flexible and permit maximum adaptability by the individual schools. Each high school would be encouraged to enrich its educational offerings beyond the foundation program by permitting the use of those high school revenue receipts which exceed a certain per cent of the total annual high school expenditures. On the basis that the parishes contributed approximately 50 per cent of the total high school expenditures for the year 1950–1951, parishes would support 50 per cent of the total cost of the foundation program. Thus, this share of the total cost of the foundation program would be borne by all parishes of the diocese by a tax or assessment based upon the parish index of relative financial ability. On the basis that the total high school expenditures of each central high school reflected the relative financial ability of the area in which it was located, it was determined that each central high school would contribute 5 per cent of the total high school expenditures for 1950–1951 for the support of the foundation program. On the basis of current practice in financing central Catholic high schools throughout the United States, it was considered desirable to include a tuition charge, to be borne directly by the student, as part of this plan. The average tuition charge of the central high schools of the United States was used as the basis for setting this tuition charge at $35 per year. The contribution by the Diocese of Trenton, as a grant-in-aid, would be the difference between the total cost of the foundation program and the total of parish assessments, tuition, and central high school contributions. The diocese could assure that the required school funds would be available for the educational program through the establishment of a central finance office, the chief responsibility of which would be the collection of the school funds and the apportionment and distribution of these funds to the central Catholic high schools. As in the total diocesan support plan, the apportionment and distribution of high school funds would be made on the basis of average daily attendance.

The Regional Support Plan. The total regional support plan would establish a foundation program for each region of the diocese. Since the Diocese of Trenton is divided into seven regions, the foundation program of each region is defined in terms of the total-unit-cost index (per-pupil cost in average daily attendance) as a measure of needed services and facilities. The total-unit-cost index includes a plant charge. The regional foundation program would be flexible and permit maximum adaptability by the individual regions. To increase local initiative and promote diocesan-wide interest, each region would be permitted to use all high school revenue receipts, except tuition, to enrich the regional educational offerings beyond the minimum program. The cost of the regional foundation program would be borne entirely by all the parishes of the region by a tax or assessment based upon the parish index of relative financial ability determined on a regional basis. As in the previous plans, the diocese could assure that the funds would be available for the regional foundation programs through the establishment of a central high school finance office. The apportionment and distribution of the high school funds would be made on the basis of average daily attendance of the regions.

DIOCESAN FOUNDATION PROGRAMS

The research of Robusto suggesting the detailed plans included above, while specifically addressed to the financing of diocesan centralized high schools, would seem to contain the essential elements of a comprehensive diocesan foundation for financing all diocesan schools. These elements are:

1. Establishing a minimum financial level of expenditure to be guaranteed by the diocese.

2. Establishing an index of ability to pay, applicable to the individual parishes after research.

3. Establishing an adequate source of financial income with which to defray the cost of the diocesan guarantee—either parish assessments or a diocesan tax based on the parish index of ability to pay.

4. Leaving other traditional sources of income to the local parish for enrichment of its parish school program beyond the minimum guaranteed.

5. Establishing a division of school finance in the office of superintendent to conduct the necessary studies to maintain a per-pupil

cost index, to maintain a current index of ability to pay, and to distribute diocesan funds to diocesan schools in proportion to their number of pupils. One modification of Robusto's plans might be profitably adopted: distribution according to average daily membership rather than average daily attendance. The former is a more stable figure, is more easily handled, and reflects the fact that school expenditures are incurred in terms of membership rather than in terms of how many students actually attend.

Questions for Discussion or Investigation

1. In what ways can you justify the thesis that the budget can be a key to sound financial practices? To sound administrative practices other than financial?

2. How is the important question "why?" answered by adequate budget justification?

3. In Robusto's three plans for financing diocesan central high schools, what similarities to state foundation programs do you find? What differences?

4. In figures presented in this chapter on percentages expended by major function, 0.5 per cent is given for transportation of pupils. Can you reconcile this figure with the fact that Chapter 15 shows well over a third of all public school pupils transported at public expense?

5. After consulting a publication on school accounting procedures and standardized budget categories, under what major category do you find the costs of the business manager's office? Those of a public relations bureau? The salaries of principals? The salaries of supervisors? The salaries of supervisors of custodians?

Readings and References

Breheny, John P.: "Diocesan Administration of Catholic Secondary Education in the United States: Its Status—With a Design for the Future," unpublished doctoral thesis, Harvard University, 1954.

Burke, Arvid J.: *Financing Public Schools in the United States,* Harper & Brothers, New York, 1951.

Fiscal Authority of City Schoolboards, National Education Association, Research Bulletin 28, no. 2, Washington, April, 1950.

Flynn, Sister Elizabeth Ann: "Cost Differentials and Sources of Revenue in the Expansion of Parochial Schools," *Research Newsletter,* Immaculate Heart College, Los Angeles, February, 1957.

Freeman, Roger A.: *School Needs in the Decade Ahead,* The Institute for Social Science Research, Washington, 1958.

Hutchins, Clayton D., and Elmer C. Deering: *Financing Public School Facilities,* U.S. Office of Education Misc. 32, 1959.

————, and others: *Trends in Significant Facts on School Finance, 1929–30 —1953–54,* U.S. Office of Education Circular 498, Washington, 1957.

Johns, R. L., and E. L. Morphet: *Problems and Issues in Public School Finance,* Bureau of Publications, Teachers College, Columbia University, New York, 1952.

Kahn, Gerald: *Current Expenditures per Pupil in Public School Systems: Urban School Systems, 1957–58,* U.S. Office of Education Circular 595, 1959.

Knezevich, Stephen J., and John Guy Fowlkes: *Business Management of Local School Systems,* Harper & Brothers, New York, 1960.

Linn, Henry H. (ed.): *School Business Administration,* The Ronald Press Company, New York, 1956.

Mort, Paul R., and others: *Public School Finance,* 3d ed., McGraw-Hill Book Company, Inc., New York, 1960.

Munse, Albert R., and Eugene P. McLoone: *Public School Finance Programs of the United States, 1957–58,* U.S. Office of Education Bulletin 1959, no. 21, 1959.

————, and Edna D. Booher: *Selected References on School Finance,* U.S. Office of Education Circular 462, 1956.

Ovsiew, Leon, and William B. Castetter: *Budgeting for Better Schools,* Prentice-Hall, Inc., Englewood Cliffs, N.J., 1960.

Reason, Paul L., and Alpheus L. White: *Financial Accounting for Local and State School Systems,* Bulletin 1957, no. 4, 1957.

————, and George G. Tankard, Jr.: *Property Accounting for Local and State Systems,* U.S. Office of Education Bulletin 1959, no. 22, 1959.

Robusto, Carmine C.: "The Financial Support of Catholic Diocesan Secondary Schools," unpublished doctoral dissertation, Fordham University, New York, 1954.

Ryan, Leo V.: "The Business Management of Central Catholic High Schools," *National Catholic Educational Association Bulletin,* vol. 54, pp. 33–38, November, 1957.

Samuelson, Everett V., and others: *Financial Accounting for School Activities,* U.S. Office of Education Bulletin 1959, no. 21, 1959.

18. *Business Management:*
School Housing

In its business department, a school system will have to provide for the adequate discharge of the function of housing—providing buildings, operating them, and maintaining them. This means that today when school construction is as widespread an activity of administrators as it has been in recent decades, there has to be adequate planning of school buildings; and there has to be effective management of building operation and maintenance. Certainly when 10 to 15 per cent of total school costs is going into new buildings and when an additional 13 per cent is devoted to operation of school plants, any inefficiency or waste represents serious misuse of badly needed school income.

THE CONSTRUCTION OF NEW SCHOOLS

The whole area of school housing, but especially the matter of building new buildings, involves such detailed and complex knowledge and skills that any single chapter on this subject must limit itself to basic considerations and the general principles which must be part of the total professional equipment of the school administrator. It is possible only to hint at the detailed knowledge of con-

323

struction techniques, the relative usefulness of various building materials, the cost of the several materials, the values of modular construction, the advantages of "bearing" or "curtain" walls, the standards for adequate lighting, and the hundreds of other concerns on which the school administrator must make decisions when schools are being built. These are decisions which must be made with considerable reliance on expert assistance.

In the large public school system, the school administrator's expert assistance will come from his staff official who has specialized in school construction and from his architect. In the smaller public school system, he will have to get his advice from school building experts on the staff of the state department of education and from the architect employed by the school district on a particular project.

In the typical Catholic school situation, reliance generally has been heavily on the architect, since expert assistance has generally not been provided on the staff of Catholic school administrators. In fact in most diocesan school systems, the function of building new buildings is almost completely separated from the professional educator's responsibilities. New buildings are usually constructed by the pastor, whose plans must be approved by a diocesan building commission which represents the bishop. In the past, diocesan school superintendents have usually neither claimed, nor had the opportunity to develop, any expertness in this field, although sometimes they are also members of the diocesan building commission. Far from typical, but rather representative of a more highly developed diocesan school system, is the following excerpt from a diocesan handbook. It indicates the very minimum relationship of the superintendent to school construction.[1]

> *School Planning*—The Superintendent of Schools conducts surveys and projects studies to determine where new school facilities may be required or where existing buildings may need expansion. He advises pastors on the development of their school plant. He meets with members of the Archdiocesan Building Commission, architects, and contractors to make certain that school buildings will meet the requirements of the educational program of the Archdiocese.

[1] *Administrative Manual for the Elementary Schools,* Archdiocese of New York, 1956, p. 4.

Religious orders conducting a number of schools throughout the United States, probably through a number of autonomous regional provinces, are increasingly faced with the complex problems of construction of college, high school, and elementary school buildings, usually with a most uneven availability of expert staff assistance. It would seem to this author that such orders might profitably develop a cooperative system whereby at least one genuine school building expert would be available for detailed and extensive consultation with individual school administrators of the order throughout the country, since probably no one province has an on-going need for the full-time services of such a skilled person. While the educational expert on school buildings in no way replaces the need for an experienced school architect, he does bring to planning conferences the professional educator's knowledge of school needs combined with a knowledge of building techniques and costs gained from both training and ever-increasing experience.

The Relationship of School Program to School Plant

The necessity for an expert educator–building specialist grows from the fundamental principle that school plants are constructed to house school programs. Accordingly, the school building is a facility which is to serve the instructional program; it is neither an end in itself (as it may become if the building is built and then turned over to professional school administrators to use), nor is it of coordinate importance with the instructional program (as it may become if a building authority or commission has responsibilities equal to those of instructional officials for decisions which actually determine how teaching will be conducted when the building is completed).

The basic instructional policies of schools influence the kind of plant needed. An extreme subject-matter centered school needs many fewer square feet of classroom space per pupil than an extreme child-centered school with an activity curriculum. A school which accepts as its unique purpose the development of the intellect needs fewer square feet of classroom space per pupil than one which considers the social development of the youngster of equal importance. Obviously, if a class in homemaking for boys and girls can with validity on Fridays become a class in social dancing, space is needed.

If the school conceives of its purpose as meeting the needs of its students to learn to swim, then square footage per pupil is needed for the pool, showers, lockers, plumbing, fixtures, filter, etc. The instructional role of physical education in the school will determine, in part, the size of the gymnasium and in part, whether the gymnasium will be a single-purpose facility or will serve also as an auditorium or lunchroom. If the classroom-library concept is a part of the instructional program of a school, the size and shape of classrooms will be modified. If movable classroom furniture is essential to the instructional program of the school, the classrooms will be larger.

The Cost of School Buildings

All the above illustrations of how instructional programs must influence school plants, and many others, directly influence school costs. The basic unit for comparing school costs is cost per square foot per pupil.

Many factors will influence the cost per square foot per pupil, or resulting cost per classroom of one school building as compared to another. For example, cost of labor varies in different localities throughout the country; less expensive, but equally durable, materials may be used in one building as compared to another; costs for the same materials may vary somewhat from one locality to another; relative climatic conditions determine the feasibility of some construction economies; luxury of facilities provided influences price; and construction costs vary from year to year, and sometimes from month to month.

The chief single factor of cost of school buildings, however, is the number of square feet per pupil, and this arises from the nature of the educational program of the school. As summarized by Freeman in *School Needs in the Decade Ahead,* "It seems that the cost of building schools, on a dollar per square foot basis, has gone up less than the general construction indices over the past 20 or 30 years. This is partly due to the fact that classroom ceilings have come down from 12 feet to 10 feet or 9½ feet. . . . The often-quoted decorative waste may sometimes be conspicuous to the eye, but in the aggregate does not amount to very much." [2]

[2] Roger A. Freeman, *School Needs in the Decade Ahead,* The Institute for Social Science Research, Washington, 1958, p. 223.

What has gone up is the number of square feet per pupil provided in many new schools! It is this factor which chiefly accounts for the wide variations in total costs in schools built to accommodate the same number of pupils. In 1930 the elementary and junior high schools in New York City averaged 39.5 square feet per pupil and high schools 53.6 square feet. Today New York standards provide 80 to 117 square feet per pupil in elementary schools and 97 to 115 square feet per pupil in high schools for 1,000 to 1,500 pupils, respectively.

The essential impact of square feet per pupil in total school costs is also indicated by Freeman,[3] who analyzed the difference in costs between a public high school in Los Angeles and a Catholic high school in Philadelphia. Each was built for about 3,000 students. The first cost $3.8 million; the second, $1.3 million. The first provided 83 square feet per pupil; the second, 45 square feet. The first cost $15.64 per square foot; the second, $10.04. While the Catholic school was built three years later when construction costs were 11 per cent lower, nevertheless, after adjusting figures for this difference and discovering the Catholic school had been built for 28 per cent less per square foot, Freeman finds the major difference in total costs was the difference in square feet provided per pupil. Whether 45 square feet or 83 square feet or 115 square feet or some other number of square feet per pupil is required by educational policies must be decided by administrators in terms of why schools exist; but three facts are indisputable: upon this answer school costs mainly depend; to the answer school plants must be fitted; and many millions of dollars are at stake.

Comparative costs of school buildings are most frequently cited in terms of cost per pupil or cost per classroom (average number of pupils per classroom multiplied by the cost per pupil). These figures are insufficient by themselves as bases for comparison because they give no inkling of the square footage provided per pupil, the critical factor in indicating how much has been secured for the price of the classroom. The classroom-unit figures, furthermore, reveal nothing of the capacities of the classrooms in terms of students per room. Really useful statements of comparative costs should be along these lines: School A was built at a per-pupil cost of $_____, providing __ square feet per pupil. Or School A was built at a per-

[3] *Ibid.,* p. 220.

classroom cost of $_____ with the capacity of each room aver-aging _____ pupils and with an over-all building average of __ square feet provided per pupil. Otherwise, cost comparisons on a per pupil or per classroom basis are of little significance.

Catholic school buildings have generally been constructed at lower total costs and lower per-classroom and per-pupil costs than public schools planned for a comparable enrollment. From the fore-going it is clear that these facts do not prove efficiency or inefficiency; of themselves, they merit neither approval nor disapproval, profes-sionally. Significant conclusions as to efficiency or inefficiency of construction come only from the answers to a lot of questions, the most important of which are these two: is the square footage per pupil suitable to a well-conceived educational program? Is the cost per square foot more or less than the cost per square foot in schools of comparable size, other factors also being equal?

EDUCATIONAL PLANNING FOR BUILDINGS

Schools are generally built to last at least fifty years, though some stay in use much longer than that. It follows, then, that serious mis-takes resulting from inadequate planning in advance of construction will be haunting some school administrator or limiting the effective-ness of a school's instructional program for generations. The ad-ministrator who fully realizes this runs some risk of freezing up under the serious responsibility involved. His is the obligation of discovering the middle ground between inaction, because of the irrevocable nature of decisions concerning a new school plant, and snap judgments, which have a fifty-fifty chance of being wrong.

All the techniques of adequate planning must be marshaled so that his recommendations, which usually will strongly influence the board of control ultimately making the decision, will be the best recommendations possible at the time. For, no one can know how schools should be built for educational programs fifty years or more hence.

Here, as in so many of his jobs, the administrator must involve peo-ple in decision making: the people who must pay for the building; the teachers who must teach in it and who in many cases will have ideas as to what kinds of rooms they can work best in; the administrative staff, health staff, guidance officers, and maintenance officials; professional consultants; and of course the architect himself, whose function is described at greater length below. All these people may have roles to play before the chief executive of the school makes the final recommendations for the design of the building.

Research and investigation will also be necessary to provide basic facts about population trends, projected enrollments, probable centers of population, best methods of construction financing, and the financial implications regarding the operation and maintenance of the facilities planned. There is no substitute for visiting newly completed schools and discussing the results with those actually using the new facilities. Probably no one who has been responsible for building a new school has failed to discover some things he would have done differently if he had another chance. Even the selection of the best architect will require research of a sort!

SELECTING A SITE

Much of the research and investigation preliminary to building a new school building will be directed to the selection of an adequate site. Accessibility, centralized location, availability of an adequate parcel of land, and size of the plot will all figure strongly in the final decision, but in varying proportions according to whether a high school or an elementary school is being planned, according to finances available, and according to the nature of the educational program to be conducted.

The following criteria for selecting a school site are based on suggestions of Taylor in an Office of Education publication devoted to sites.[4]

1. The inherent health and safety factors of any piece of land are to be considered in its selection.

2. School sites, in addition to providing a foundation for building, furnish play areas and facilities for the school's recreation and physical education program.

3. School sites should be selected with long-range economy in mind. Factors such as natural drainage, natural landscaping, availability of utilities, and closeness to a municipal park (actual or pro-

[4] James L. Taylor, *School Sites: Selection, Development, and Utilization,* U.S. Office of Education Special Publication 7, 1958.

jected) or to recreational facilities may cause a site initially more expensive to be cheaper in the long-run.

4. A school site should be attractive since it becomes an environmental influence on the student.

5. A school site should be large enough for the purpose. The National Council on Schoolhouse Construction suggests a minimum of 5 acres for an elementary school, 20 acres for a junior high, and 30 for a senior high.[5] The increasing necessity for adequate student parking at the high school level must not be overlooked.

In coming to a decision recommending a site for a new school, the administrator responsible usually finds an advisory committee particularly valuable. He needs engineering or architectural reaction, and he needs the reactions of responsible citizens who will be paying for the new building. Realtors, principals, and teachers can all supplement his own experiences as to desirable features of the site.

THE ROLE OF THE ARCHITECT

It is hard to overestimate the importance of the architect in the construction of a new building. The school will need its own expert to participate in planning and perhaps to serve as "clerk of the works"—that is, to spend much of his time on the job to ensure that all the terms and conditions of the contract have been met. It is the architect, however, who will translate the plans which grow out of the instructional program into a building which is functional, beautiful, and structurally sound.

The specific responsibilities of the architect include designing the building and preparing preliminary sketches, models, specifications, and cost estimates; recommending materials and equipment; preparing drawings and specifications for bidding and eventual construction; evaluating qualifications of contractors and coordinating their work; and issuing certificates for periodic payments to contractors. He employs and deals with any specialized engineering services required.

It follows that the selection of an architect must be made carefully. It would seem desirable that he be a good school architect, one who is experienced in building schools and in the features peculiar to

[5] *Guide for Planning School Plant,* National Council on Schoolhouse Construction, George Peabody College for Teachers, Nashville, Tenn., 1958, p. 23.

schools, one who has demonstrated the personal capability, imagination, and administrative skill necessary to good design and proper construction.

Architects are generally paid a uniform percentage of the total cost of the construction plus reimbursement for necessary drawings and engineering services. A standard contractual form is available from the American Institute of Architects. Since reputable architects, in terms of their code of ethics, may not compete with each other on the basis of cutting the standard percentage or by using donations as a device for securing a contract, shopping for a reputable architect on the basis of a lower fee will prove futile or, even if successful, will prove risky. The only determinant in selecting an architect should be his qualifications.

Awarding the Contracts

The conditions and procedures for selecting a general contractor for building public schools—or several contractors if the project requires separate contracts—are generally specified by state or local statutes. These provide for competitive, sealed bids based on architectural drawings and specifications,[6] public opening of all bids submitted, and submission of a certified check or a bond to be forfeited if the contractor fails to accept the contract.

While no such legal provisions cover the awarding of contracts on privately owned schools, the general procedures outlined are equally suitable to Catholic schools. The primary goal is the same: realization of specifications at the lowest possible cost. Incidental factors—the temptation to select a particular contractor because he is a heavy contributor to church projects or some particular subcontractors because they are active alumni or friends of active alumni—generally lead school authorities into making difficult decisions amidst conflicting pressures. According to general experience, the results frequently are greater expense (even with contributions deducted) and loss of those "friends" whose firms were not awarded the contract—as well as loss of their gifts. In general, objective procedures giving everyone an equal opportunity to secure the contract will prove the most satisfactory to all concerned.

[6] For illustrative proposal form for contractor's bids, see Appendix E.

SOME GENERAL FEATURES OF DESIGN

As has been restated throughout this treatment of general problems of school building, superintendents of schools or other chief school executives must depend on their staff experts or on their architect for technical features of design. There are, however, several developments in schoolhouse design with which they should have some general familiarity. Among them are prefabricated schools and modular construction.

Prefabricated Schools. The techniques of prefabrication which have been increasingly accepted in the construction of private homes have been tried in relatively few new schools in this country, though considerably employed in some other countries. Prefabrication techniques, which promise considerable economies in construction, generally have met community resistance from persons committed to more traditional building methods: architects, skilled building tradesmen and their unions, local contractors, and local suppliers. Furthermore, sometimes outmoded local building code regulations make expensive modifications to prefabricated schools necessary, with the result that potential savings disappear. Obviously, prefabrication can effect savings only as it involves mass production. Should the concept of prefabrication of school buildings find wider public acceptance, it would seem to offer considerable simplification and not an inconsiderable saving to those charged with schoolhouse construction. In the meantime, firms interested in the prefabrication approach have generally shifted to a more limited concept known as modular or unit construction.

Modular Construction. Modular construction emphasizes prefabricated building components in contrast to prefabrication of the whole building. Under the original initiative of the American Standards Association, the concept of standardizing dimensions in buildings in terms of a basic unit or module was developed. A 4-inch module was recommended as standard. With over-all dimensions for school buildings developed as multiples of the 4-inch module, it is possible to develop building components as multiples of this size so that they can be fitted into individually designed buildings without trimming, cutting, or wasting space.

Obviously, as bricks, cement blocks, girders, window sash, wall panels, chalkboards, partitions, cabinets, and other components of the school building are constructed in relationship to a basic module, more and more prefabricated items can be worked into a new building. Also, carried to its ultimate development, the result would approach the prefabricated or packaged school. One large firm, which has done much of the development of modular construction, cites as major advantages speed of construction and easier and more accurate cost estimates, as well as economy.

Other Design Features. The alert school administrator involved in a school building program will want to get a general insight into other newer developments in school planning and design, including the relative suitability of bearing walls versus skeletonal construction with curtain walls, the possible use of hexagon-shaped classrooms arranged in clusters of four to six to save corridor and other wasted interior space, newer trends in the design of elementary or secondary school functional classrooms, flexibility through movable partitions, and the campus-type versus the multistoried school building—all treated in the professional literature of schoolhouse construction.

MAINTENANCE AND OPERATION OF PLANT

Once the building is a reality it must be maintained with adequate janitorial services. A large school may have a chief custodian with various assistants responsible to him. Many decisions must be made. What are the duties of the chief custodian? How many times per year are the windows to be washed? How often should the floors be washed or waxed? Is he to cut the grass? If so, how frequently? Standards must be developed in these and many other aspects of good janitorial performance. If the plant is large enough, skilled engineers will be needed to control the heating. Plant maintenance means painters, plumbers, electricians, carpenters, and glaziers. All these employees must be hired, supervised, and paid at current rates. Job descriptions and operational policies have to be developed in manuals available to all concerned. Some idea of the complexity of the maintenance job in school systems is seen from the fact that when a teacher in the Cincinnati public schools with a master's degree was being paid a maximum of $6,200 per year, a plumber was receiving $6,800; or is seen from the fact that the cost for replacing broken windows in school buildings in the city of Chicago is over $35,000 annually.

In the typical parochial school, janitorial services and maintenance are handled on a much more informal basis than in public schools. Frequently, teachers handle a good portion of the janitorial services, and one janitor takes care of an entire building. He is not only chief janitor, but chief painter, chief engineer, chief glazier, and chief everything. In the past, parochial schools in general have not had to consider unions and union demands. The result, whether efficient or not, is that janitorial and maintenance services in parochial schools tend to be less expensive than they are in the public schools, where every member of the maintenance staff is a member of a union, and where the janitor may not drive a nail because that is a function of the carpenter. Nor may he do anything resembling plumbing, since that is a function of the plumber. What the janitor actually does, of course, frequently depends on how well the principal and teachers get along with him. It is doubtful, therefore, that there would be any great economy involved in the adoption by parochial school systems of custodial standards similar to those used in public schools. However, as teacher loads become heavier and more lay teachers are employed in Catholic schools, economical use of teacher time will make more formal organization of maintenance services desirable. There is one other factor in the operation and maintenance of Catholic schools to be considered: there is a developing movement by labor unions toward organizing nonprofessional employees in nonprofit institutions. It has reached hospitals and some colleges and universities. The complete decentralization of parochial elementary school operation and maintenance under individual pastors, as long as it continues, will make the Catholic school janitor or maintenance man an unlikely recruit for unionization.

Questions for Discussion or Investigation

1. In the opening paragraph of this chapter, the figure of 13 per cent was used to describe operation and maintenance funds; Chapter 17 gives some percentages for operation and maintenance for 1957–1958. Can you discover why the figures are not identical?

2. Contrast the role in schoolhouse construction of the educational expert

in housing, who is a member of the professional staff of the larger school systems, with the role of the architect employed on a given project. To what extent should the school's chief executive be a part of the total picture?

3. Cite specific ways, other than those suggested in this chapter, in which features of a school instructional program should influence the construction of a new school.

4. Why is cost per square foot, by itself, an inadequate measure of relative school costs? per-pupil cost? per-classroom cost? Small differences in cost per square foot may not indicate anything significant about efficiency of construction if the schools compared are in different locations. Why?

5. Discuss the desirability of involving a committee in site selection. Whom would you involve in your school situation? Why?

6. Why might modular construction lead ultimately to the packaged or completely prefabricated school?

7. Through outside readings prepare a brief report on newer design features of elementary or secondary school classrooms.

Readings and References

American School Buildings, Twenty-seventh Yearbook of the American Association of School Administrators, Washington, 1949.

Campbell, Paul E., and others: *Schoolhouse Planning and Construction,* Joseph F. Wagner, Inc., New York, 1950.

Economy Handbook, New York State Commission on School Buildings, Albany, 1953.

Engelhardt, Nickolaus L., and others: *School Planning and Building Handbook,* F. W. Dodge Corp., New York, 1956.

Guide for Planning School Plants, National Council on Schoolhouse Construction, George Peabody College for Teachers, Nashville, Tenn., 1958.

Herrick, John H., and others: *From School Program to School Plant,* Holt, Rinehart and Winston, Inc., New York, 1956.

How Much Should a Good School Cost? a portfolio of 14 reprints, American Association of School Administrators, Washington.

Linn, Henry H., and others: *The School Custodian's Housekeeping Handbook,* Bureau of Publications, Teachers College, Columbia University, New York, 1948.

————, and Schyler C. Joyner: *Insurance Practices in School Administration,* The Ronald Press Company, New York, 1952.

MacConnell, James D.: *Planning for School Buildings,* Prentice-Hall, Inc., Englewood Cliffs, N.J., 1957.

More Schools for Your Money! New York State Commission on School Buildings, Albany, 1954.

Peters, Jon S. (ed.): *Planning Tomorrow's Secondary Schools,* School Planning Laboratory, Stanford University, Stanford, Calif., 1954.

Planning America's School Buildings, American Association of School Administrators, Washington, 1960.

School Plant Maintenance, American Association of School Administrators, Washington, 1951.

Sumption, Merle R., and Jack L. Landes: *Planning Functional School Buildings,* Harper & Brothers, New York, 1957.

Taylor, James L.: *Administrative Facilities in School Buildings,* U.S. Office of Education Special Publication 6, 1957.

————: *School Sites: Selection, Development, and Utilization,* U.S. Office of Education Special Publication 7, 1958.

————, and others: *Designing Elementary Classrooms,* U.S. Office of Education Special Publication 1, 1953.

Viles, Nelson E.: *Improving School Custodial Service,* U.S. Office of Education Bulletin 1949, no. 13, 1949.

————: *School Buildings: Remodeling, Rehabilitation, Modernization, Repair,* U.S. Office of Education Bulletin 1950, no. 17, 1950.

19. *Business Management:*
Supplies and Food Services

SUPPLIES

Providing the supplies and equipment needed to operate schools is a major function of business management. Extensive savings in the cost of these items are possible to those schools which are part of a system which follows well-conceived procedures; this is in sharp contrast to schools which handle their own supply needs individually, more or less haphazardly, and at excessive costs.

Effective procedures for providing supplies for a school system will usually include the centralized purchasing, warehousing, and delivery of the equipment and materials needed in each of the major areas of school administration—instruction, administrative operation, pupil personnel services, business management, community relations, and research.

SELECTION OF SUPPLIES

The selection of supplies and equipment originates within the department needing them, though generally speaking, decisions regarding specific quality and brand are made in cooperation with a skilled purchasing agent, whose duties are described below. The

337

chief exceptions to this are certain instructional supplies and equipment—textbooks and such teaching aids as supplementary books,
maps, magazines, films, recordings, charts, models, or tools. The
decision of instructional officials governs the selection of such instructional materials, for the experience and knowledge of the teachers, principals, and supervisors must be fully utilized in the process.
Consequently, the school system will ordinarily make these selections
through committees of instructional officers. For example, in selecting supplementary textbooks, one system uses a committee of 100
teachers who reexamine existing books and review recent publications with a view to making recommendations for a supplementary
book list. A catalogue of 150 pages containing about 3,000 elementary supplementary books approved for purchase is prepared by
this committee. Within the financial allotments assigned to each
school, teachers may then requisition supplementary books from this
catalogue. In the same school system a separate catalogue of some
2,800 visual and auditory aids was prepared after the items to be
included were selected by committees involving 75 teachers. In the
same way, the type of seating to be used in local classrooms may be
chosen by committees of teachers, principals, and supervisors who
examine manufacturers' catalogues and samples, consult with seating experts, and even visit other school systems. Where no manufactured furniture meets the requirements of a given committee, it
may on occasion be necessary to order special furniture constructed
according to exact specifications which the committee has in mind.

A particularly sensitive area, and one demanding specific procedures and safeguards, is that of textbook selection. It has been true
in the past that, because of inadequate textbook selection procedures,
temptations for financial gain have been difficult to resist for some
individuals charged with responsibility in this field. As a protection
to the administrator from any suspicion along these lines, the following type of policy is wise:

1. When a textbook in a given field is to be chosen, all publishers
are asked to submit books which they have available in the field
under consideration.

2. A committee is appointed by the superintendent of schools to
recommend a textbook for adoption.

3. Publishers are advised of the names of those on the textbook

committee and of the ground-rules they must follow in presenting the advantages of their particular book to the committee.

Procedures may further specify that in addition to a general presentation before the committee, an interested textbook publisher may have a representative call on each teacher for a specified length of time on school premises. There is to be no outside contact between committee members and publishers' agents. The formal decision of a committee on a book is to be submitted to the assistant superintendent in charge of instruction for his recommendation, then to the superintendent of schools for his recommendation, and then to the board of education for adoption. Should the selection not be recommended by one of the higher authorities involved, procedure should consist in returning the recommendation to the committee with reasons for nonapproval, indicating perhaps that some other book be selected. However, initial selection of a particular book should come from the committee itself.

In one city school system it is estimated that it takes about 400 hours of deliberation on the part of members of a textbook selection committee to arrive at a selection. With 286 textbooks used in the school system in question, and each of them systematically reviewed every five years for readoption or change, considerable committee action is involved.

The selection of other types of supplies, such as the soap, brooms, or ash cans needed by the business department, involves less selective procedures on the part of the department originating the request, since materials of this kind ordinarily will have been purchased in accordance with standard specifications and will be stored in a warehouse from which they may be requisitioned.

PURCHASING

Basic to economy in providing schools with the supplies needed for their operation is mass purchasing carried on by a specialist known as a purchasing agent. This staff member becomes expert in the economies to be obtained through purchase of large lots, through testing given products to get maximum efficiency in relation to unit cost, through advertising adequately for bids on all large-scale purchases, and through determining which items should be stocked in a school warehouse.

It is sometimes desirable that the schools combine with other agencies in their purchasing. Public school systems may sometimes purchase certain items in cooperation with other governmental units —the city and the county. The advantage of mass purchasing of items is well illustrated by the experience of the Cincinnati Public Schools in effecting economies in the purchase of coal. Approximately six trains of sixty cars each would be needed to haul the coal supply for the Cincinnati Public Schools for one year. Purchasing involves setting specifications, including the British thermal unit (Btu) specification of the amount of heat which must be put out from the coal purchased. The joint purchasing of coal by the city, county, and school district, in the first year it was put into effect, saved the taxpayers over $100,000 in the price of the coal bought. When the savings to the school board of their share of the $100,000 is added to the savings effected in the purchasing of the 48,000 pounds of soap cleaner, the 640 brooms and floor brushes, the 2,300 light bulbs, the nearly 11,000,000 paper towels, and the 2,100 gallons of liquid soap, the mimeograph, the ditto, stationery and other paper supplies, and the countless other materials used in a single year, it can be seen how the entire cost of skilled purchasing, warehousing, and delivery of supplies can be defrayed, and other substantial savings be made through adequate procedures and staff.

The effect of quantity buying of white mimeograph paper, a substantial item in most schools, is illustrative of the savings available to schools through purchasing in large lots. Prices of mimeograph paper decrease according to quantity purchased; price changes occur among smaller lots when 2,000, 15,000, and 60,000 sheets are ordered at once. Because the paper itself may be either 16- or 20-pound weight and either letter or legal size, the most appropriate choices must be made.

Table 10, based on 1959 prices for good-quality mimeograph paper, indicates, for example, that 60,000 sheets of 16-pound letter-size paper could be bought exactly $163 cheaper in the larger lot than 20-pound paper in the smaller lots; yet for many school purposes 16-pound paper is perfectly adequate and may lead to additional savings in postage and filing or storage space. In larger lots, of course, even greater savings are possible than are indicated in Table 10. For example, bought in 600,000-sheet lots, 20-pound paper becomes about as cheap as 16-pound bought at the 60,000-sheet rate, or over $100 cheaper than 16-pound paper bought at the 2,000-sheet rate.

TABLE 10. COST OF 60,000 SHEETS OF MIMEOGRAPH PAPER OF DIFFERENT SIZE AND QUALITY, PURCHASED IN DIFFERENT QUANTITY LOTS

Size and weight	Lot	Cost	Lot	Cost	Lot	Cost
Letter, 16 lb	2,000	$237.00	15,000	$145.80	60,000	$129.60
Letter, 20 lb	2,000	$282.60	15,000	$177.00	60,000	$156.60
Legal, 16 lb	2,000	$299.40	15,000	$185.40	60,000	$164.40
Legal, 20 lb	2,000	$355.80	15,000	$225.00	60,000	$199.20

As an individual department, school, or school teacher needs supplies, one of two kinds of requisitions is used, a requisition for outside purchase of the supply or a warehouse requisition.

When a "purchase" requisition is used, an extra procedural step is required. On receipt of the goods or services by the requisitioner, he must immediately forward to the finance office an "Advice of Goods Received" form so that the bill can be paid. Only if this advice is received can a bill be safely paid and advantage taken of any allowable discounts for prompt payment.

Adequate requisitioning of supplies or services, therefore, must include the following general steps:

1. A requisition, either warehouse or purchase, must be completed.

2. The requisition must be forwarded to the head of the major administrative department involved for approval and signature.

3. The requisition must be forwarded to the finance officer who serves as controller of the budget so that he can indicate the availability of budgeted funds.

4. The requisition must be forwarded to the purchasing officer for ordering the delivery of the supplies or services.

5. On outside purchases, the advice of receipt must be forwarded promptly to the finance officer who pays the bill.

To secure the flexibility necessary for handling emergency purchases by responsible officials, institutional purchasing procedures usually permit purchases not to exceed a specific sum of money through a telephoned request for a purchase order number and direct placing of the order. They may even permit an occasional requisition for reimbursement of an official for small emergency purchases.

WAREHOUSING

While it is not always necessary to accept delivery of an entire lot at one time in order to secure favorable prices, mass purchasing ordinarily leads to the maintenance of some type of storage or warehousing facility. The supplies generally used in the system will normally be warehoused. A catalogue of the types of supplies, with specific items numbered, is basic to requisitioning on a warehouse requisition. Obviously, in addition to the expense of warehousing, there will be some expense for personnel—perhaps a chief stock clerk and several assistants. In conjunction with warehouse operation some school systems have found it economical to maintain a bookbinding department for the repair of books in use in the schools.

DELIVERY

The maintenance of a warehouse, itself dictated by mass-purchasing procedures, in turn necessitates the maintenance of a delivery system. A large school system may find it desirable to schedule a fleet of trucks traveling from school to school daily on a more or less fixed schedule. Thus, fast service is maintained between the requisitioning of supplies from the warehouse and their delivery. Such a delivery system can also carry intra-system mail, saving postage and express fees. The maintenance of a fleet of trucks also makes possible the efficient operation of an audio-visual aids bureau, with regular truck delivery schedules. For example, the teacher who has requisitioned a film or filmstrip for a given day can receive the teaching aid on the delivery trip scheduled the day before the film is to be presented. The film can then be had for the day of presentation and can be returned by truck the following day to the audio-visual aids bureau, where it can be rewound or repaired in time to be of use to someone else on the following day.

APPLICATION TO CATHOLIC SCHOOLS

Clearly, if public school systems are able to maintain skilled purchasing, warehousing, and delivery services and still effect substantial economies, the same would be possible to parochial schools. In addition to the economies which result from efficient operations of this kind, the parochial schools would receive the advantage of some important by-products. Not the least of these is making possible an efficient audio-visual aids bureau. If the use of audio-visual teaching aids is as effective as all research tends to indicate that it can be, then any approach to making their use easier for teachers will serve to improve the instructional program. As it is, the maximum use of these teaching aids is frequently severely impeded by the inconvenience caused the teacher who uses them. Going to the public library, locating the material, charging it out, taking it out, taking it to the school, showing it, and then returning it to the library —all involve complexities for the average parochial school teachers which will make the use of audio-visual aids unlikely. In the same way, audio-visual aids gathered from out-of-town sources with the uncertainties of mail delivery dates, the necessity for repacking and preparing for return shipment, and the necessity for insuring the package—all make their use so inconvenient as to become unlikely.

The organization of institutional purchasing offices has been a first step instituted in some dioceses to take advantage of economies available through mass purchases, although the by-products to be realized through warehousing and delivery are not generally found in Catholic schools. Ordinarily, such centralized services have been confined to publishing a catalogue of items available at discounts from a few specific firms, with the purchasing being done either through a central office or directly by the participating school with those firms. Delivery is made directly to the institution itself by the seller. Institutions of higher education are eligible to join an educational and institutional cooperative to secure mass-purchasing opportunities.

In his 1954 research on diocesan secondary schools, Breheny found that of eight dioceses reporting a system of central purchasing used by high schools, there were six in which purchasing was a function of the diocesan office of education and two in which schools reported using the services of a diocesan purchasing office.[1]

---

[1] John P. Breheny, "Diocesan Administration of Catholic Secondary Education in the United States—With a Design for the Future," unpublished doctoral thesis, Harvard University, 1954, p. 286.

In view of the widespread purchasing of materials and supplies in Catholic institutions, ordinarily by persons not specifically trained for performing this function, the following remarks of William A. Regan, Legal Consultant to the Catholic Hospital Association of the United States and Canada, are presented for their pertinence to Catholic institutional purchasing, whether in hospital or in school:[2]

We have been surprised to find from time to time that certain religious institutions carry on their business transactions with manufacturers and distributors on a "telephone-matter-of-fact" basis with no written provisions regarding the nature of the commitment between the institution and business house with which it has contracted. We submit that this is poor administration and does not serve to edify the business houses that are engaged in rendering services to our colleges or hospitals. For this reason again we suggest that arrangements between our religious institutions and commercial business houses should be reduced to writing and conducted on a formal business basis. Such business acumen on the part of the hospital will serve to put business houses on notice that the hospital is interested in protecting its legal position with reference to its contractual obligations.

There are three basic elements that must be found in every contract if it is to prove effective and satisfactory for the purpose of establishing a valid business relationship between the parties. Every contract must contain an *Offer* in the form of the goods, supplies or services which will be delivered. It must contain *Acceptance* in the form of a signature of the contracting parties. The contract must contain some evidence of *Consideration* being the price or fee that the institution will pay for the good, supplies or services rendered by the other party to the contract. It is usually not too difficult to make out these elements of *Offer, Acceptance* and *Consideration* in even the most simple form of invoice manifesting the contractual relationship between the parties.

There is a concept in the law of contracts known as the *Meeting of the Minds*. A mutual understanding of the provisions contained in a contract must exist before a valid contract comes into existence. We have often wondered how a meeting of the minds can exist in many of the oral agreements which we have come upon between

[2] William A. Regan, "Civil Law and Religious Institutions," a paper presented to the Fifth Conference on Business Problems, Xavier University, July 21, 1957, pp. 9–10.

religious institutions and vendors and purveyors of supplies and equipment. By way of contrast, a written contract generally lends itself to a clear meeting of the minds as the terms and provisions of the agreement such as the quantity and quality of goods, supplies or services contracted for, are clearly established.

It is sometimes possible to negotiate for certain special considerations to be included as part of an agreement between contracting parties. These special guaranties are designated in the law as "expressed warranties." Frequently it is advisable to have such expressed warranties spelled out in the contract. We suggest that when a religious institution is making a commitment involving any great expenditure of money a conference should be held with legal counsel regarding the desirability of having certain expressed warranties incorporated by reference into such a contract.

In addition to expressed warranties there are certain implied warranties which are contained in every contract. The warranty that the seller has good title to the goods or supplies and the authority to contract is usually implied in every contract. Likewise, in contracts for the sale of consumable goods, there is implied the guaranty that such goods are fit for human consumption.

FOOD SERVICES

The management of school lunchrooms is a major business operation in large city systems today, whether in public or parochial schools. In fact, few restaurant chains in a given city can approach the number of meals served per year in the public and private schools of that city.

IMPROVING PRACTICES

As school systems have perfected techniques for serving excellent meals at lowest-possible costs over the past twenty to thirty years, practices of school systems doing the best jobs include:

1. Centralized management of cafeterias in one head, a supervisor of school food services, experienced in both dietary and business aspects of lunchroom management

2. Centralized planning of school menus to use large quantities of seasonal foods at low prices, while preserving balanced dietary requirements

3. Centralized purchasing of foods with the savings involved in mass purchasing

4. Standardization of servings to avoid fluctuations of cost because of overly large, wasteful servings

5. Catered hot meals from a central location to smaller schools to save on labor and equipment costs

6. In-service training programs for school cooks in order to develop maximum integration with a system-wide approach

7. Extensive use of voluntary help for all but the skilled jobs of management and cooking in school lunchrooms, thus cutting labor costs substantially

8. Last, but far from least, participation in the Federal School Lunch Program, not only because its contribution is substantial financially, but also because, from the standpoint of efficient management of the school lunchroom, the standards required for participation in the program are such as to force the school system to real improvements in most cases

All eight of these practices contribute to effective management of school lunchrooms to the end that quality meals are served at lowest possible costs. Special attention to the importance of participation in the Federal Lunch Program is given in the following sections of this chapter. Since costs of school lunches are basically determined by cost of foods, cost of labor, and cost of equipment in that order, special notice should be taken of the importance of the widest-possible use of voluntary lunchroom assistance drawn from PTA or other organizational groups.

Parochial schools, as a rule, excel in their success at using such voluntary help in school lunchrooms. Not infrequently, the cost of lunch in public schools will be found to exceed that in Catholic schools where both participate in the Federal School Lunch Program, despite the fact that the public schools may be stronger in some or all of the other six desirable practices. The advantages thus gained are completely offset, however, by the wider use of voluntary help in the Catholic school lunchroom. Maximum efficiency in both systems would seem to lie, however, in using all of the practices which would help bring about the goal of good lunches at the cheapest prices without financial loss.

THE FEDERAL SCHOOL LUNCH PROGRAM

The Federal School Lunch Program was initiated in 1946 with two major purposes: to promote the health of school children by helping schools provide a balanced nutritional meal at noon through subsidizing a portion of the cost of hot meals which meet specific standards, and to distribute surplus commodities bought by the Federal government in its program of maintaining agricultural price supports. Both public and private school lunchrooms are eligible.

Since in most states constitutional provisions prevent the distribution of state funds to religious schools, provisions have been made for channeling Federal funds directly to Catholic schools from regional Federal offices. A precise picture of how the Federal Lunch Program aids school lunchrooms is gained from the following report on the school lunch program of one diocesan school system made after ten years of participation in this program.[3]

School Lunch Program

1955–56

June 4, 1956, marks an important date in the history of the National School Lunch Program of the Archdiocese of Cincinnati. On that date ten years ago, the National Lunch Program was enacted into law and the Archdiocese of Cincinnati became a member of this vital program.

As measured against the first years of the National School Lunch Program, we can report definite visible signs of the progress in the past ten years. Lunches served are increasingly better designed to meet the nutritional requirements of the child. The standard type hot meal or "Type A" as set up by the Government has become synonymous with a well balanced nutritional meal and its components.

Nutritional Meal Pattern

½ pt. milk—3.5 or over butterfat
2 oz. of protein   2 slices of bread
½ cup of vegetable   2 tsp. of butter
½ cup of fruit

[3] From *Annual Report of the Superintendent of Schools, 1955–56*, Archdiocese of Cincinnati.

This meal pattern is becoming widely known and understood, not only by school lunch personnel, but also by children, parent-teacher groups, business concerns and professional people in the field of food and nutrition and Public Health.

Schools in Program

There were 103 schools in the Archdiocese holding Federal School Lunch contracts for the Type A program. Type A provides for ⅓ of the child dietary requirements for the day. Of these 103 Type A schools, 65 held a Special Milk Program contract. There were 18 schools which held Special Milk contracts only. These 18 schools did not have the physical facilities to serve hot lunches. A breakdown of the schools in the Archdiocese holding Federal contracts were as follows:

Cincinnati (Elementary Schools)	31
Hamilton County (excluding Cinti.)	21
Outside Hamilton County	20
Dayton	17
High Schools	8
Institutions	6
Total	103

Six schools were approved the past year for Federal aid: Immaculate Heart of Mary, Cincinnati, Ohio; Resurrection, Dayton, Ohio; St. Patrick, Bellefontaine, Ohio; St. Mary's, Russell's Point, Ohio; St. Mary, Springfield, Ohio; Holy Angels High School, Sidney, Ohio.

Food Reimbursement

After each program was reviewed by the Chicago Regional Office and our Archdiocesan Office as to the specific needs of each school, and in conjunction with the allotted funds appropriated by Congress, a variable rate was established for each school. In our Archdiocese, the rates for Type A meals were set at .07; .06; .05; .04; .03 per meal. There were 3,761,787 Type A lunches served to our children during the 1955–56 school year; in addition 1,400,744 extra bottles of milk were served to children bringing a cold packed lunch from home.

The total amount of cash reimbursement from the Treasurer of the United States for Type A hot meal paid to schools holding contracts the past year was $176,551,43; for the Special Milk

Program, $51,016.93, making a total of $227,568.36 paid to our program by the U.S. Government.

Meal Cost

The cost of preparing and serving a hot lunch that meets Federal standards has increased considerably. The Schools continue to have as their major purpose a well balanced nutritional meal, served to the children at a reasonable price. The three determining factors of course are with us always—(1)—continued high cost of food; (2)—labor; (3)—equipment.

Meal Charge to Children

Seven	Schools	Charged	No charge
Five	"	"	$.12
Two	"	"	.15
One	"	"	.18
Fourteen	"	"	.20
Two	"	"	.22
Sixty-nine	"	"	.25
Three High	"	"	.28
Three High	"	"	.30

——
106 schools

A majority of the schools have a family rate. Some offer reduced rates to children if they pay by the week, others give rates to families having three or more children. All children who are in need are served a meal free. The Pastor, Principal, and Manager determine the need of free meals and the cost according to conditions that exist in each school area. There were 432,696 free meals served to needy children last year.

Food Costs

The total amount of food purchased by the 103 schools amounted to $873,661.89. Of this amount, including Special Milk Program, $355,675.87 was spent for milk alone. Below is a breakdown of total expenditures for all of the schools during the past year.

Food costs	$ 873,661.89
Labor	272,061.15
All other costs including all non-food items—equipment	110,592.88
Total costs	$1,256,315.92

These figures may seem staggering, but School Lunch is big business and our labor costs particularly are low throughout the diocese due to large amounts of donated labor.

Our schools are encouraged to buy "Special Monthly Foods." These "Specials" are usually seasonal and reasonably priced so that each program benefits by the savings and helps to carry out one of the prime requisites of the program, namely "to help the farmers market their products."

Direct Distribution of Surplus Commodities

The Office of Commodity Distribution of the State of Ohio at Columbus allocates surplus commodities to this area through the offices of the Archdiocese of Cincinnati, to the Dayton area through Rev. Edward Connaughton, Assistant Superintendent of Parochial Schools, and in the northern area of the Archdiocese through the County Superintendents of Public Welfare in their respective communities. The following surplus commodities [tabulated on the following page] were distributed to our schools and institutions in the three areas under Section 6; 32; and institutions.

The cost of these commodities if our schools and institutions had purchased them at the market price of April 26th, 1956 would have been in the Cincinnati area, $230,884.48; in the Dayton area, $73,548.79; and in the Northern area, $31,218.16 making a grand total of $335,651.43.

Our schools realize the savings to the program and are very grateful for the surplus commodities made possible by the Ohio State Department of Welfare and the National School Lunch Program.

Special Milk Program

The Special Milk Program, now in the second year of operation, was designed to help relieve the over-supply of the dairy industry, and to increase consumption of milk by school children, both in the schools which have feeding facilities and in schools where space limitations or other factors prevent the establishment of food preparation and service facilities.

Congress appropriated all told, $60,000,000 to this program the past year. Schools participating in the National School Lunch (Type A—hot lunch) who took advantage of this Special Milk Program were able to offer ½ pint of milk to a child for .03. The Government reimbursed the school .04 for each bottle of milk sold

Types of Food	Cincinnati	Dayton	Northern Area	Total
Shortening	739 cases	218 cases	33 cases	990
Salad oil	193 "	61 "	9 "	266
Rice	348 (50# bags)	90 bags	8 bags	446
Dry milk	506 cases	244 cases	36 cases	786
Cherries	478 "	122 "	55 "	655
Grapefruit sections	782 "	311 "	120 "	1213
Peas	1209 "	388 "	140 "	1737
Butter	3176 "	1085 "	290 "	4551
Cheddar cheese	219 (65 lb)	55	13	287
Process "	1690 cases	534 cases	180 cases	2404
Lima beans	165 (100# bag)	63 bags	18 bags	246
French prunes	286 baskets	171 baskets	32 baskets	489
Peanut butter	243 cases	96 cases	48 cases	387
Tomatoes	697 "	178 "	92 "	967
Dry apricots	329 "	105 "	72 "	506
Sweet potatoes	227 crates	7 crates	—	234
Orange juice	230 cases	78 cases	47 cases	355
Cnd. pork & gravy	1011 "	338 "	210 "	1559
Pork luncheon meat	625 "	173 "	155 "	953
Cnd. hams	385 "	90 "	45 "	520
Frozen hamburger	283 "	119 "	74 "	476
Pork loins	73 "	—	—	73
Cube butter	80 (65#)	11	—	91
Frozen smoked hams	—	31	—	31
Kidney beans	—	1 (100# bag)	4 bags	5

351

to children. Sixty-five of our schools holding Type A Government contracts took advantage of the program.

Eighteen schools held contracts for Special Milk Program only. These schools charged .04 per ½ pint and the Government paid .03 per ½ pint for all milk sold to children. The number of ½ pint bottles of milk sold on the Special Milk Program only was 1,304,304 and the amount of reimbursement from the U.S. Government was $27,269.07.

Donated Labor

We are quite proud of the important role the women of our parishes are playing in donating their time and energy to the Lunch Program. It is because of their services that we are able to continue to serve the children with wholesome, nutritious meals at minimum cost. Figured at just .50 per hour (below minimum wage standards) we find that the P. T. A. and other organizational groups donated 231,555 hours of work, making a direct contribution of $115,797.46 to the program.

Training Program

Each year we plan training programs and workshops to stimulate thought and discussion of common problems and new ideas in order to sustain the high level of effort and performance among our supervisors, managers and cooks. This past year during the last week in August we had our usual one day workshops in Cincinnati and Dayton. Then we had two baking institute demonstrations put on by the Pillsbury Company for all managers. Our schools in each area cooperated and attended sanitation conferences by each local Board of Health in order to improve and to be ever vigilant in this most important segment of administration of the lunch program. The Cincinnati Office also provides technical guidance in all phases of the program development.

The school lunch personnel of the Archdiocese is genuinely interested in the betterment of each program and is always seeking ways and means to improve and to interest children in accepting nutritional meals.

The success of our School Lunch Program can be attributed greatly to the cooperation of the pastors and teachers and their ever-ready assistance in improving each year the physical aspects of the cafeterias. Their interest in seeing that the children are served nutritious meals in attractive surroundings is a dominant factor in our total program.

Questions for Discussion or Investigation

1. In your school system, how are supplies or equipment procured? Evaluate the procedures in effect against the standards proposed in this chapter.

2. For what reason is it said that mass purchasing ordinarily leads to warehousing, at least in large systems? In a small system or in one large autonomous school, to what does mass purchasing lead?

3. List as many as you can of the instructional advantages to a school system which accrue from organization for efficient purchasing.

4. Can you think of any likely emergency situations in which school personnel need to make purchases in other than the standard procedure?

5. Discuss the essential elements of a good contract.

6. Why can it be said that Catholic school participation in the Federal Lunch Program moved diocesan systems along the road to more centralized administration?

7. Under what circumstances would centralized catering of lunches to a number of schools seem advantageous within a school system?

8. From the detailed report of the operation of one diocesan school system, find the total financial savings to the children coming from governmental contributions. What benefits to the school system in question do you find reflected in the report?

Readings and References

1. SUPPLIES

Daum, George F.: "Supply Management," in Henry H. Linn (ed.), *School Business Administration*, The Ronald Press Company, New York, 1956.

George, Norvil L.: "Selection of Supplies and Equipment," *School Executive*, vol. 67, pp. 36–37, July, 1948.

Lawson, Douglas E.: *School Administration*, The Odyssey Press, Inc., New York, 1953.

Melton, Monroe: "Buying School Supplies Out of Season," *American School Board Journal*, vol. 128, pp. 53–54, May, 1954.

Mort, Paul R., and Donald H. Ross: *Principles of School Administration*, McGraw-Hill Book Company, Inc., New York, 1957.

University of the State of New York: *Purchases and Stores*, School Business Management Handbook, no. 5, New York State Education Department, Albany, 1955.

Reeder, Ward G.: *The Fundamentals of Public School Administration*, The Macmillan Company, New York, 1958.

Sholz, G. I.: "Better Local School Purchasing," *American School Board Journal*, vol. 128, pp. 43, 90, March, 1954.

Smith, George F.: "Purchasing," in Henry H. Linn (ed.), *School Business Administration*, The Ronald Press Company, New York, 1956.

2. FOOD SERVICES

Bryan, Mary deGarmo, and Neva Henrietta Radell: "Food Service in Schools," in Henry H. Linn (ed.), *School Business Administration,* The Ronald Press Company, New York, 1956.

Colton, M. L., and B. Hurley: "Training Program for Lunch Employees," *American School Board Journal,* vol. 138, p. 45, June, 1959.

Eckel, Howard: "School Lunch Management Practices," *School Executive,* vol. 71, pp. 105–106, December, 1951; vol. 71, pp. 151–152, January, 1952; vol. 71, pp. 129–130, February, 1952.

Farley, T. J.: "Good School Lunch Programs Cost Less than Poor Ones," *Catholic School Journal,* vol. 59, pp. 79–82, June, 1959.

McClees, Estelle: "Central Purchasing Saves Money," *Nation's Schools,* vol. 54, no. 1, pp. 72–74, July, 1954.

Planning and Equipping School Lunchrooms, U.S. Office of Education Bulletin 1946, no. 19, 1946.

Reeves, Robert E.: "A Study of Administrative Controls with Emphasis on Financial Controls of School Food Service Programs in Selected Cities of the United States," doctoral thesis, University of Southern California, Berkeley, Calif., 1955.

Russell, M. A.: "Planning Food Services for the Large High School," *American School Board Journal,* vol. 135, pp. 45–47, July, 1957.

20. Community Relations

The essential importance of each of the major functions of school administration is no more easily demonstrated than for community or public relations. Schools, school systems, and school personnel, public and Catholic, need the support of their public, a support which invariably includes financial aid for public schools in the form of tax money or bond issues, and for private or religious schools, in the form of tuition or voluntary contributions. The amount of such financial support will inevitably depend on what the school's public thinks of it. It is, therefore, the attitude of those served by the school which will substantially determine the success of a school administrator and of the instructional program for which he is responsible.

It is axiomatic that all school activities of necessity are involved with public relations. The public relations of any school are either good or bad, since the attitude of any individual toward the school always reflects the impression, good or bad, which he has received from his contacts with it. It is the responsibility of all school personnel to attempt constantly and consciously to leave a favorable impression of the school or system with the many individuals com-

355

prising a school's public; that is, to carry on a successful program of external relations.

While the school administrator uses all possible avenues to develop strongly favorable attitudes toward the school, it must be remembered that to develop understanding alone is not enough. Understanding must be touched by pleasant feelings; that is, favorable emotional reactions must be the goal of public relations, for people generally react in any situation according to pre-set emotionalized attitudes.

As a long-term program of prejudicing the public in a school's favor has been successful, the reaction of the individuals comprising the public will withstand the strains put upon it. Just such a strain comes when the public is asked to spend money for schools, either by voting to levy extra tax money or by contributing substantial sums to a school. Public support for schools, however, is inevitably tested in other ways.

Perhaps three or four students of one high school are arrested for joy-riding in a stolen car. Since the name of the school may be the only specific given in newspaper articles involving juvenile offenders, two reactions are possible: "Isn't it strange that that could happen in such a good school?" or, "What else could you expect from such a place?"

Teachers may be charged with being "too progressive" or "leftist." A pressure group may allege that a textbook contains Communist propaganda. A charge that Johnny can't read may be circulated. Whether an individual reacts favorably or unfavorably when such things happen will depend on the emotionalized attitude which he has previously formed toward the school; and that attitude will have depended upon how effectively school personnel have sought to make it favorable.

Since it is the responsibility of school administration to develop a favorable attitude through all the means by which impressions are made on the public, it follows that thorough consideration be given to just what some of these means are. The staff must be public relations-conscious; techniques for involving the public in school problems must be used; full advantage of all the media for good community relations should be taken; and the skills and information comprising the new concept of *development* should be part of the total community relations program.

PUBLIC RELATIONS THROUGH THE SCHOOL'S STUDENTS

The indispensable element of the school public relations program is the student. The student's attitude toward his school, its program, its teachers, and its principal, whether favorable or unfavorable, directly reaches the two publics on which the school most immediately relies for support—the parents and their close friends. Not only are the attitudes of the students themselves caught by those closely associated with them, but there is no escaping the judgment of the school by the quality of its products. In surprisingly few years, furthermore, it is these same students who are the taxpayers or community leaders or financial contributors on whom the school will be depending for its support.

In a most real sense, then, good public relations depends on a good school; and good public relations begins with the students. No amount of techniques for developing favorable attitudes toward a school among the general public can take effect if the students themselves have no enthusiasm for the school or if they do not exemplify the characteristics which their parents and associates expect the school to have developed.

PUBLIC RELATIONS THROUGH THE SCHOOL STAFF

Each contact the school staff has with the public helps to strengthen the general attitude that "this is a fine school" or helps to weaken that general attitude. When the teacher or principal deals with a parent, when the teacher or principal participates in community activities, projects, or organizations, either good or bad community relations result. It is for this reason that no longer is a school principal appointed merely because he is a good scholar in a particular field. A well-rounded personality is essential. What is sought is a principal who is in no sense of the word peculiar. There was a time when it was claimed that a male school teacher or principal could be recognized anywhere because of some characteristic trait, such as producing a change purse when paying fare on a streetcar. Too frequently, with reason, principal or teacher could be caricatured, as happened when Stephen Leacock described his classics professor as a man who always carried an umbrella and wore rubbers no matter what the weather; and who claimed that all he was or all he ever hoped to be he owed to the study of classics—a serious charge, if true, observed Leacock. By contrast, today's school administrator is expected to be the sort of person who mixes in community affairs, who can make a good speech without boring people, and who is thought of, superficially at least, as much the same species as his nonteaching associates in service or civic clubs.

One aspect of the parochial school administrator's responsibilities should be emphasized: If personal public relations is important to the public school administrator, it is even more important to the Catholic school administrator, because when people react unfavorably to the Catholic school administrator, who wears clerical garments or the habit of a religious order, the emotional reaction is likely to be just as pronounced against the Church itself as against the school. On the public relations consciousness of a Catholic school teacher or principal, therefore, may rest the salvation of an immortal soul.

PUBLIC PARTICIPATION IN SCHOOL ADMINISTRATION

A good public relations program involves the concept of public participation in school administration. In so far as the advice and help of representatives of the public is secured in the operation of a school or system, an increase in the public understanding of the problems faced by the school results. More than that, there is a relationship between one's emotionalized attitudes and the degree to which he becomes personally involved in related activity. If one wants to gain the support of someone, it is best to involve him actively. Getting people of different beliefs or persons with varying ideas to work together generally causes changed attitudes. Sympathetic emotional responses occur as people develop an understanding of one another's problems through joint participation in their solution. Thus the lay advisory board, the citizens' committee, and the approach of the White House Conference on Education are vehicles for involving people in school administration so that a better understanding of mutual problems may result and, even more important, so that sympathetic emotional responses are likely.

Citizen participation in the schools need not and does not have any specific pattern. Different approaches in different communities have been equally successful. Citizen participation in school improvement is described by Dreiman through detailed reports of such activities on behalf of the public schools of five communities—Corning, New York; Minneapolis, Minnesota; New Canaan, Connecticut; Houston, Texas; and Bellevue, Washington. In referring to the work of the National Citizens Commission for the Public Schools, Dreiman writes:[1]

> Since then the Commission has had confirmed repeatedly its original conviction that school problems are faced and solved (or *not* solved) every week of the year in thousands of communities throughout the nation—but only to the degree that the citizens themselves contribute their thought and energy.
>
> So long as Americans retain local responsibility for their local schools, these problems will be local problems. In essence the problems reduce to what goes on—or what should go on—in each individual classroom of each individual school.
>
> In the tens of thousands of variegated communities that make up the United States—rural, small town, suburban, and metropolitan—these problems can be approached realistically, and moved ultimately toward solution, by local action.
>
> But neither money nor oratory nor good intentions can accomplish much without the essential fuel—the will to assert for community good the massive muscle that citizens in concert possess.
>
> No town ever has a better school system than its people want and are willing to work for. No school system can be better than the community at large.

An outstanding example of the possibilities of community participation in school problems occurred in Arlington County, Virginia, when the citizens, dissatisfied with the school situation, proceeded to do something about it. Major public school improvements were brought about through the work of three community-

[1] David B. Dreiman, *How to Get Better Schools,* Harper & Brothers, New York, 1956, p. 5.

wide organizations: The first, the Citizen Committee for School Improvement, with a membership of 2,500, organized a School Board Nominating Convention representative of all civic organizations in the community. The convention nominated six representative, devoted persons for membership on the board of education. The second, the County Council of Parent-Teacher Associations, representing individual schools, discusses school problems and policies and expresses its views at monthly meetings of the board of education. The third group, the Civic Federation, a composite of all the county civic organizations, is concerned with the general welfare of the community. Its interest covers a wide range of problems, including those of schools.

Not the least of the results of such widespread participation by the public in school problems was to vote substantially larger school budgets for Arlington County in successive years. Some of the story of the success of citizen participation in the Arlington County schools is the subject of a March of Time Forum film entitled *The Fight for Better Schools.*

PARENT-TEACHER ORGANIZATONS

Closely related to the techniques used to secure effective citizen participation in school problems are those used in securing a good parent-teacher organization. A parent and teacher organization, which basically has tremendous possibilities for helping an individual school do an excellent job, can easily, however, become a vehicle for exceptionally poor public relations. Experience has demonstrated that a PTA which wanders off on its own unguided course often causes such a disturbance in the community that the school rapidly finds itself with a new principal. For this reason, too frequently principals are afraid of a PTA, delay in helping to organize one, or are content to have a dull organization weighted down with uninteresting meetings devoted to poorly read, lengthy, boring committee reports. Subconsciously, many principals are happy if the PTA remains innocuous, though worthless.

The challenge which the PTA presents to the principal is how to help it function as an interesting and important organization without becoming a mouthpiece for a clique or an irresponsible minority of parents.

In meeting this challenge the principal has one great asset, if he and his staff are competent to use it. Parents are usually intensely interested in their children and the education they are receiving. Thus, programs of frank discussion of important educational problems will prove a basis for a live organization. What is the value of homework? How is spelling taught in the school? How is reading taught? What about Flesch's book *Why Johnny Can't Read*? [2] Parents are interested in such problems as these, as contrasted to PTA programs devoted to hearing a speaker who was dragged in because he happened to spend five years many years ago in the mission fields of Africa.

In Catholic school systems the parent-school group may be known by various names. Sometimes called the PTA, sometimes the Parent-Teachers Guild, and increasingly the Home and School Association, there are about 1,800 such organizations connected with the Catholic schools of this country. In 1960 a new national service office was inaugurated for Catholic parent-teacher oriented groups throughout the country. Known as the National Catholic Home and School Association, it is operated by the National Council of Catholic Women and by the National Council of Catholic Men. It utilizes the consultative services of the Department of Education, National Catholic Welfare Conference, and the National Catholic Educational Association.

The services of the National Catholic Home and School Association, for which affiliates are charged dues between $15 and $30, depending on the enrollment of each school affiliated, include the following:

1. Representation of home-school interests at national and regional meetings
2. Clearing house for information on home-school associations
3. Special bulletin ten times a year
4. Program planning: yearly theme with implementation of subject
5. Correspondence, including assistance with individual programming

[2] Harper & Brothers, New York, 1955.

6. Speakers' bureau set up on a regional basis

7. Organization aids, including a *Manual for Home and School Associations,* containing a suggested constitution and bylaws, installation ceremony, home-school committees, agenda for meetings

8. Workshops, institutes and training, especially in conjunction with conventions or other meetings of the National Council of Catholic Women, the National Council of Catholic Men, and the National Catholic Educational Association

As illustrative of effective parent-teacher organizations, two examples are cited, one from a parochial school and one from a public school. The object and sole purpose of the PTA of Holy Angels School, Dayton, Ohio, is to promote a closer relationship between the home and the school, to create a better understanding between parents and teachers, and likewise to foster proper cooperation between parents, priests, and teachers for the best interests of the child in the school.

Of this PTA, the pastor in charge of the school writes:[3]

> It has been found advantageous to have panel discussions concerning topics of educational value at many of the meetings. No school activity such as orchestra, scout work, or the like is given at any of these meetings. The time is devoted solely to the purpose of enlightening all the members concerning things beneficial both for the present and the future welfare of the children. Members from the faculty of the University of Dayton, members of the Dayton public school systems, and other individuals of prominence, whom we have felt could give the parents something worthwhile, have spoken at our meetings. The best attendance is always at the panel discussions when the parents are free to ask the panel members questions concerning the welfare of their children. . . .
>
> From personal observation during the six years as pastor of the Church of the Holy Angels, I feel the Parent-Teacher Association, properly organized and directed, is beneficial to teachers, students and parents. . . .

The following excerpts from an article in *Time* describes the public relations activities of a New Orleans public school principal

[3] Joseph D. McFarland, "The Parent-Teacher Association at Holy Angels School," *Catholic Educator,* pp. 424–425, March, 1956.

with his PTA. While the description is necessarily brief, effective results are apparent.[4]

New Orleans Eye Opener

From the outside, the Beauregard grammar school on busy Canal Street seems as antiquated and drab as any. Inside, its floors gleam with wax polish; its walls are freshly washed. Built for 500 pupils, it expects to house 650 this fall; last year it had to turn down 300 applicants from other parts of the city. The man responsible for Beauregard's high regard is 33-year-old Principal Joseph Salvador Schwertz.

When Schwertz took over in 1942, Beauregard was a dirty, dilapidated place. His predecessor had kept the toilets locked to prevent pupils from writing on the walls. Enrollments had dropped to 384, and many parents had sent their children to the parochial school across the street.

Parents' Clubs. Soft-spoken Principal Schwertz, a product of New Orleans schools himself (before going to Loyola University of the South), soon began to change things. He wanted a playground and went direct to Beauregard parents for the money. Before long, he had enough to cover the muddy schoolyard with all-weather asphalt. Then he set up tennis, badminton and volleyball courts. For the youngest kids, he put in a basketball court with baskets five feet off the ground.

There were a lot of other things Schwertz wanted. Instead of waiting for the school board to dribble him the funds, he kept going to the parents. Members of the Beauregard Mothers' Club flocked to meetings just to keep up with his new schemes. The fathers formed a Dads' Club.

One paper drive, organized by the mothers, raised enough money to buy Beauregard the first telebinocular (for eye tests) and Audiograph (for hearing tests) in any New Orleans public school. Among the first 65 children tested, Schwertz found 38 who needed glasses or other eye treatment, and several who were being handicapped by deafness. . . .

Children's Chance. Last week, though school was closed for the summer, Principal Schwertz was still busy in his office, working on his latest scheme. He wanted Beauregard to be the first U.S. grammar school to have its own radio station, to give the children a

[4] "Education: New Orleans Eye Opener," *Time,* July 28, 1949.

chance to broadcast their own historical dramas, music, and student forums.

After watching wide-eyed for five years, the New Orleans school board had decided to chip in $2,000 toward a broadcasting studio. The dads had promised the rest: a 10-watt transmitter, a tape recorder, two turntables and a record library. They figured $3,000 was not much to raise for the man they call "the best damn principal in town."

USE OF MEDIA

A third approach to good community relations is to use all available media of mass communication to bring about a harmony of understanding between any group and the public it serves and upon whose goodwill it depends.

THE PRESS

If the school administrator or teacher has something of a nose for news, he will see the possibilities of developing newspaper stories about students, their activities, and their school life. Newer educational trends, school dramatic productions, foreign students, or faculty professional activities are among the possible sources of school news stories. So also are special educational opportunities such as education of the handicapped, enrollment trends, building programs, and financial news.

Certain mechanical arrangements have been found useful by school administrators as they strive to keep an adequate flow of news to the papers. Among those suggested in the Twenty-eighth Yearbook of the American Association of School Administrators are the following: that the superintendent in every district should maintain his own news notebook, perhaps in the form of a desk calendar on which pertinent news items and news deadlines can be noted; that forms convenient for filling in details of forthcoming news stories be placed in the hands of all teachers to facilitate the flow of news to the school's news bureau; and that superintendents should plan some form of regular contact with the press, perhaps informal visits to the newspaper in small systems and scheduled press conferences in larger ones.[5]

[5] *Public Relations for America's Schools,* Twenty-eighth Yearbook of the American Association of School Administrators, Washington, 1950, pp. 277–279.

Since the success of this phase of a public relations program depends upon the story actually being published, it must be realized that its chances are enhanced if it has been submitted in a form that the city desk finds easy to use. If rewriting at the city desk is needed, the possibilities of a story disappearing into a wastebasket are great.

The mechanics of preparing news stories with a professional flavor are relatively simple—the lead, the supporting details in short paragraphs arranged in order of decreasing importance, room for headlines, triple spacing, etc. In general, when a story is so written that it is easy for an editor to use as it is, it probably will appear in print, unchanged. The school publicist has one natural advantage in seeking newspaper space: newsmen realize the appeal of children's names, especially to relatives!

The school's own publications—the student newspaper, the annual, the literary magazines—have significant public relations impact. While these are primarily student learning activities, the administrator will find it necessary to develop in the students and their teacher-advisers an awareness of responsibility to reflect school policies and school objectives fairly. Particularly in regard to student newspapers, skill and tact are needed if extremes of sensationalism are to be avoided without stifling the interest of the student staff. Unfortunate public relations result if local merchants are subjected to pressure to purchase advertising space or if advertising which is considered offensive by some parents is accepted.

RADIO AND TELEVISION

These are two media for good public relations from which schools frequently secure only a small part of their potential. Generally speaking, school personnel wait for some member of the staffs of radio or television stations to approach them to participate in a program. This happens about as often as reporters come to schools to locate news stories.

But like newspapermen, radio and television program officials ordinarily welcome the schoolman who comes to them with ideas and materials for a good program. The future of radio and television as instruments of school public relations is excellent if educators join with community groups in furthering the use of these media for educational purposes. Programs in which schools share responsibility with a local council on world affairs, safety council, or other community organization with educational purposes may have better public relations effects than programs arranged directly by the schools themselves.

In general, schools will find it desirable to avoid becoming involved in any sustaining programs that go on the air week in and week out; the strain on school staffs becomes too great. But when the school has a good spot program to present, airing the program cannot help but cause a few more parents to believe that the participating school is an alert institution. This is especially true for the parents of the youngsters involved.

ANNUAL REPORTS

The annual report of the superintendent of schools, well planned and strategically distributed, plays an important public role in community relations.

Present-day reports are far removed from the painfully monotonous presentation of statistics so typical of earlier reports. Comprehensive statistical tables, important as they are, are generally relegated to a separate statistical supplement, or to the appendix. The report itself follows one of two general approaches: the highlights of the year's work are presented attractively with appropriate pictures, charts, and sketches so as to inform the public of the year's significant developments; or one important and timely aspect of the school program is selected for intensive treatment as one of a series of yearly reports, each devoted to a separate phase. Attractively covered and imaginatively titled, the report is sent to influential members of the community, especially those whose support is essential if adequate support is to be secured.

Some idea of what can be attempted, and probably accomplished, can be gained from the themes of some of the annual reports which have come across this writer's desk in the last twenty years: "Your Schools in Wartime," "Education for the Production of Goods and Services in the Vocational High Schools," "Schools and the Means of Education," "That All May Learn," "Opportunities for the Handicapped," "The Able Learner," "Foundation Values of American Life," "We Hold These Truths . . . ," "Writing: The Second R," "Responsibility: The Fourth R," and from another public school system another fourth R—"The Four R's: Reading, 'Riting, 'Rithmetic, Reverence." This last is particularly interesting as an apparent attempt to offset an impression of "the Godless public schools." With a cover suggesting a church, a striking illustration of two members of a choral group in choir garb, and old Gothic type used for the title, it is effective. All sections of the report are introduced with appropriate Biblical quotations italicized in red ink. For example, following a picture of a kindergarten class saying grace before their midsession milk and cookies, comes the quotation from *Psalms*: "It is a good thing to give thanks unto the Lord." Included in the script is this statement: "We hope by the process of having the latter ask the grace of Almighty God at such times to make such an imprint on his personality as to lend him throughout his life the capacities for standing humbly before all that is good."

Apparently for the same purpose, another public school system in an annual report of the superintendent, lists as its eighth instructional objective "to develop in young people a strong and vital religious spirit." This objective is also introduced with a picture of a school choir in garb and is followed by this expansion on the objective:

> We seek to encourage the development of those qualities of unselfishness and love of fellowmen which, coupled with recognition of a higher Being, represent that spirit.
>
> We seek to encourage in youth an appreciation of the role that this spirit has played in the development of civilization and the personal value to the individual in regulating his life in accordance with such a plan.

COMMUNICATIONS TO THE PARENTS

Whenever it is necessary to send communications home, the administrator with a keen public relations sense will take advantage of the opportunity to strengthen favorable attitudes toward the school. One device successfully used in the Cincinnati public schools is to send home with report cards an attractive, brief leaflet explaining one aspect of the child's educational program. For example, one leaflet called "Your Child Learns to Spell" contained a discussion of questions parents will ask concerning the what, where, when, how, and why of the teaching program in spelling in the schools. The general impression that the schools have a well-conceived program in this skill is widely disseminated. The same result, at other report periods, has been secured through such other titles in the series as "Your Child Learns to Read," "How Children Learn Words," "Your Child Learns to Write," and "What about Homework?"

Another effective communication with parents is illustrated by an attractive booklet presented at the preschool roundup to parents of the Goodman Primary School in North College Hill, Ohio. An intro-

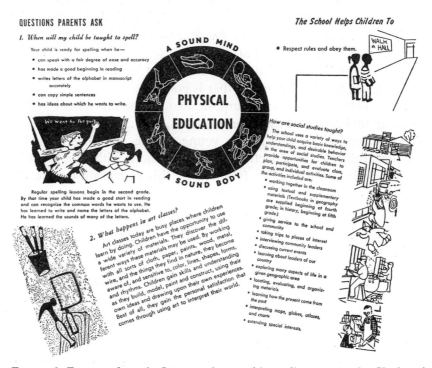

FIGURE 6. Excerpts from leaflets sent home with pupil report cards. Cincinnati public schools.

ductory letter from the principal begins: "HELLO! And now we are FIVE! How very important that number is in every child's life because we are all ready to ride the 'School Train' just as far as it is possible to go."

Included is a reminder to the parents to bring the child's birth certificate on the day of registration as proof of age. The booklet, charmingly illustrated with simple sketches, goes on to outline the four major social events of the kindergarten year at Halloween,

Christmas, Valentine's Day, and Easter—events all sponsored by the PTA. According to the bulletin, birthday parties are celebrated on the last Friday of each month unless changed because of conflicting dates. Further, the bulletin outlines the ways in which children develop in the school, it describes report procedures, and it concludes with suggested literature for parents of small children and for the children themselves. This approach to the problems of public relations gives evidence of foresight, planning, cleverness, thoroughness, sound administration, and excellent public relations techniques. Favorable attitudes to the school are built at the first contact the parents have with it.

Conversely, of course, only an adverse reaction can result from sending home a communication which is sloppily prepared, poorly spelled, and poorly thought out.

PARENT-TEACHER CONFERENCES

While the quarterly or semiannual conference of teacher and parent, regularly scheduled for a discussion of the child's performance in school, is primarily a technique for helping the child progress better in school, it has also frequently proved to have such public relations advantages that it should well be thought of as being, incidental to its major purpose, an important part of the external relations program of a school.

The conference provides opportunities for realizing some key public relations objectives: better communication between school and home, resulting in less likelihood of continued misunderstanding; genuine involvement of the parent in the child's schooling, resulting generally in improved parental attitude toward the school; greater parental understanding of school policy which, if the policy is sound, should lead to greater acceptance; and a chance to know, like, and respect the child's teacher. Here, as in so many public relations activities, the success or failure will depend, of course, upon the individual teacher—his essential fitness for the job and his public relations sense.

SCHOOL DEVELOPMENT PROGRAMS

In recent years, first in private colleges and universities and more recently in many private secondary schools, those external relations

activities specifically directed toward fund raising have been centralized under a director of development. Clearly, the function of fund
raising and the function of community or public relations are inter-
related. How to translate the interrelationship of the two functions
in an administrative chart has proved a vexing problem in many
private institutions. Should development be an aspect of public relations? Should public relations be an aspect or subdivision of development? Or should the two be separate functions, separately
administered, and each headed by coordinate officials responsible
to the chief executive of the institution?

It would seem clear that the two cannot be thought of as discrete,
coordinate functions. Fund raising, for its success, depends too
intimately on a total public relations program for the two not to be
coordinated under one person, not the chief executive who has to
give proportionate emphasis to his whole sixfold responsibility. Furthermore, he ought not to multiply the number of subordinates
reporting directly to him. The public relations function would seem
to be the broader; fund raising is but one aspect of external relations.
It depends on the success of all other facets of a comprehensive
community relations program. Looked at in another way, fund raising itself must be carried on within the framework of a sound public
relations program. To consider development, therefore, as the major
function, with public relations subordinate to fund-raising considerations, would seem to be permitting the tail to wag the dog, or the
result to become the cause. Increasingly important as development
or fund raising has become to the private school administrator,
especially at the college level, it is the overemphasis of development
in the organizational structure of an institution that can give some
substance to the charge by a former college administrator that "the
colleges and universities of this country have, in their desire for
popularity and money, gladly responded to every pressure and demand . . . reflecting the whims, no matter how frivolous or temporary, of those whose support they hope to gain." [6]

Placed in the proper framework as a part of, and a result of, a
sound program of school external relations, the newly developing
experts in institutional fund raising, or directors of development,
have specific skills, techniques, and knowledge to bring to bear upon

[6] From "The Administrator Reconsidered," remarks by Robert M. Hutchins to
the American College of Hospital Administrators, Atlantic City, Sept. 19, 1955.

their job. Precampaign analysis, planning, and setting of attainable goals; involving "corporate citizens"; pace-setting gifts, special gift solicitation, the training of solicitors, and the kick-off; the report meetings; the victory dinner—all unobtrusively managed by a director of development on salary or by a professional fund-raising counsel on a fee basis—have become increasingly a part of private institutional management and the fruition of long-term public relations programs. The results have frequently been spectacular, though not always. Where campaigns have been conducted professionally with a zeal which has burst through a basic framework of sound public relations policies, years of solid progress have sometimes been nullified. For this reason, the long-term director of development who is a regular member of the professional staff of the institution's public relations department is preferable to the short-term services of fund-raising organizations employed for a specific campaign. A desirable combination of the two is found in the staff director of development who is supplemented by a firm of professional consultants that is paid for regular evaluation of the development program and for suggestions for further refinements in both the long-term public relations and the development plans of the institution.

PUBLIC RELATIONS IN CATHOLIC SCHOOLS

Some additional observations should be made regarding public relations and Catholic education:

1. Limitations of staff in diocesan school offices have severely restricted diocesan superintendents in the discharge of their public relations responsibilities. This undoubtedly accounts for research findings that diocesan superintendents frequently equate public relations with making public appearances or with soliciting the cooperation of pastors, principals, and parents.[7]

2. Catholic schools have frequently not capitalized on the potential usefulness specific to lay teachers in strengthening community relations. For example, lay teachers can bridge a gap between life in the community at large and what goes on in the school, since they

[7] Sister M. Ruth Albert Ward, *Patterns of Administration in Diocesan School Systems,* The Catholic University of America Press, Washington, 1957, pp. 134–135.

have a better chance than religious of knowing what is going on in the neighborhood after school.

3. Catholic schools have frequently been slow to accept the advantages of involving the laity in administrative decision making.

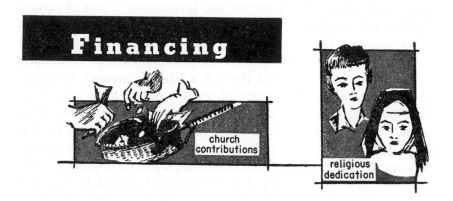

Catholics save the taxpayers of Ohio more than $100,000,000.00 each year by operating their own school system. This figure is based on a report issued in June 1959 by the Bureau of Educational Research of The Ohio State University. The report stated that the average cost to educate one pupil in the state during 1957-58 was $301.32. There are more than 338,000 pupils in the Ohio Catholic school system.

In addition, Catholics of Ohio have capital investments for school buildings and equipment representing other hundreds of millions of dollars.

This is accomplished by the heavy financial sacrifices of Catholic parents and the sacrifice of dedicated lives of both religious and lay teachers.

The primary source of funds is the Sunday collection in each parish church. This is supplemented by money-raising events, fund drives, book rentals and fees.

Each Parish church constructs and maintains its own elementary school. Some also finance their own high schools. Parishes sometimes join together to support a central or interparochial high school.

Religious communities of men and women also conduct high schools, schools of nursing, colleges and universities.

Teacher Salaries account for more than half of the money spent for current expenses in public schools. The remuneration for sisters, brothers and priests teaching in the Catholic schools is much less than public school teachers since they are unmarried and live a community life. This magnificent contribution makes our Catholic school system possible.

FIGURE 7. These panels are reproduced from a public relations folder on the Catholic school system in Ohio. Notice the presentation of specific information, the attractive layout.

This is the import of the article written by an experienced school superintendent, who says in part:[8]

Trusteeism is no longer a problem for the Church in this country. It has left us a legacy which has been hard to dispel—the fear of entrusting to the laity their share in the work of the Church. This article will attempt to show that the time is ripe to give the laity a

Curriculum

Elementary and secondary state standards outline the curriculum to be followed in all schools in Ohio. The Catholic schools carry out this curriculum in a religious atmosphere. Religion is taught formally in the classroom but finds its most fruitful expression as it penetrates the teaching of every subject during the school day.

The Catholic school system also meets state requirements for the number of school days and class hours in an academic year.

Shown here is a typical Catholic elementary school curriculum and daily time schedule.

A TYPICAL DAILY TIME SCHEDULE FOR CATHOLIC ELEMENTARY SCHOOLS
MINUTES PER DAY

SUBJECT	Grade 1	Grade 2	Grade 3	Grade 4	Grade 5	Grade 6	Grade 7	Grade 8
Religion	25	25	30	35	35	35	45	45
Arithmetic	25	25	30	45	45	45	45	45
Phonics	75	60	50	—	—	—	—	—
Reading	90	90	90	60	50	50	45	45
Handwriting	20	20	20	20	15	15	—	—
Spelling	—	20	15	15	15	15	15	15
English	25	25	25	35	35	35	40	40
Social Studies (History, Geography, Civics)	—	—	—	35	50	50	55	55
Science—Health Safety	5	5	10	25	30	30	30	30
Music	20	20	20	20	15	15	15	15
Art	15	15	15	15	15	15	15	15
Physical Ed.	15	10	10	10	10	10	10	10
Recess	15	15	15	15	15	15	15	15
Total Minutes per day	330	330	330	330	330	330	330	330

[8] Carl J. Ryan, "Ghosts of Trusteeism," *Homiletic and Pastoral Review*, p. 705, May, 1957.

greater measure of responsibility in Catholic education on the elementary and secondary levels.

4. While the philosophical and theological bases for Catholic schools have been widely communicated, particularly through statements of the hierarchy reported in the public press, only recently have Catholic administrators given adequate emphasis to presenting specific information on Catholic schools. Some of the facts are readily "sellable" and are potentially influential in forming favorable attitudes toward Catholic education. Among such specifics are enrollment figures, savings to taxpayers as compared to educating the same number of children at the per-pupil costs of public education, the actual annual cost of the religious teacher to the school, and the sources of financing Catholic schools.

5. Public relations programs for Catholic education must seek to emphasize and reemphasize that the United States is a pluralistic society; therefore education must be pluralistic. The responsibility for formal education is a shared responsibility—shared by schools controlled by the public, by the Catholic Church, by certain Protestant and Jewish educators, and by private corporations of a nonreligious nature. But at the elementary and secondary levels, the responsibility for America's schools falls largely on those administering her public and Catholic schools.

Questions for Discussion or Investigation

1. On the basis of material in this chapter, what definitions of school public relations could you formulate? Can you locate several definitions through outside investigation? Which definition do you prefer? Why?

2. Public relations activities, like many other activities of school administrators, are concerned with establishing or changing attitudes. Discuss indispensable elements of any program which would change attitudes. How are these elements included as a part of a total program of community relations?

3. Specialists in public relations frequently refer to a school's publics rather than public. In what ways would this seem to be a helpful concept in the discharge of public relations responsibilities?

4. Early in this chapter, public relations is described as a "long-term program of prejudicing the public in a school's favor." To what extent do you find this a valid description? Do you think specialists in public relations would use this description as a definition of the field? If not, why not?

5. Can you conceive of public relations being overemphasized by any school administrators? If your answer is in the affirmative, under what specific circumstances could this happen, in your opinion?

6. Have you attended PTA or Home and School Association meetings on several occasions? Evaluate your experience in the light of public relations values to the particular school.

7. Under what circumstances could you envision a director of development too influential on the staff of the chief executive of a school or school system?

Readings and References

A B C's of School Public Relations, a Check List, American Association of School Administrators, Washington, 1959.

Brownell, Clifford Lee, and others: *Public Relations in Education,* McGraw-Hill Book Company, Inc., New York, 1955.

Campbell, Roald F., and John A. Ramseyer: *The Dynamics of School-Community Relationships,* Allyn and Bacon, Inc., Englewood Cliffs, N.J., 1955.

Cooper, Dan H., and Louis A. Bergdolt: "Selected References on Public School Administration: Public Relations," *Elementary School Journal,* vol. 57, pp. 285–286, February, 1957.

Dreiman, David B.: *How to Get Better Schools,* Harper & Brothers, New York, 1956.

Education and Industry Cooperate, Hill and Knowlton, Inc., Public Relations Counsel, New York, 1951.

Fine, Benjamin: *Educational Publicity,* Harper & Brothers, New York, 1951.

Gerber, J. Jay: "Good Public Relations—An Aid to Education," *National Catholic Educational Association Bulletin,* vol. 51, no. 2, pp. 7–10, November, 1954.

Kindred, Leslie W.: *School Public Relations,* Prentice-Hall, Inc., Englewood Cliffs, N.J., 1957.

Moehlman, Arthur B., and James A. Van Zwoll: *School Public Relations,* Appleton-Century-Crofts, New York, 1957.

"Parochial Schools Rest on Good Will," *The Catholic Educator,* vol. 26, pp. 493–494, April, 1956.

Person to Person, The Classroom Teacher's Public Relations, National Education Association, National School Public Relations Association, Washington, 1956.

Phillips, Gerard: *The Role of the Laity in the Church,* translated by John R. Gilbert and James W. Moudry, Fides Publishers Association, Chicago, 1956.

Public Relations for America's Schools, Twenty-eighth Yearbook of the American Association of School Administrators, Washington, 1950.

Public Relations for Rural and Village Teachers, Office of Education Bulletin 1946, no. 17, 1946.

Richardine, Sister Mary: "Home-School Association: Action Ahead," *National Catholic Educational Association Bulletin,* vol. 56, no. 1, p. 276, August, 1959.

Ryan, Carl J.: "Ghosts of Trusteeism," *Homiletic and Pastoral Review,* pp. 705–714, May, 1957.

Stearns, Harry L.: *Community Relations and the Public Schools,* Prentice-Hall, Inc., Englewood Cliffs, N.J., 1955.

Ten Criticisms of Public Education, National Education Association, Research Bulletin 35, no. 4, Washington, December, 1957.

21. Research

Just as staff members of a school system, no matter what their particular titles or assignments, have some responsibility for carrying on activities in each of the five major areas of administration previously treated, so too, they must become involved with the sixth, research. The classroom teacher, the principal, the director of a division, the supervisor, or the assistant superintendent of schools must all carry on those research activities necessary to discovering the best answers to the questions which might arise in day-to-day activity. These problems must be solved if job performance is to be adequate.

In addition to research which is carried on at all levels of administration, however, there is that which enables the highest levels of administration to bring about the effective operation of the educational venture as a whole. The school administrator at this level is also responsible for cooperation with research being carried on by others so that national or regional efforts will add to the whole body of knowledge about educational administration. To these two responsibilities of the school administrator for research—carrying on studies to help in solving the problems which continually arise in the operation of schools and participating in the research studies carried on by research agencies outside the schools—should be added a third: regularly keeping adequate statistics.

377

A business executive's view of the need for research in administering America's schools was presented by Ralph Lazarus in an address to the National School Boards Association in 1960. In urging members of boards of education to allocate more money for research, Mr. Lazarus, who had served as chairman of the Committee on Economic Development study "Paying for Better Public Schools," said:[1]

> Modern enterprise lives by the axiom you either go into research to improve your business or you go out of business.
>
> Today, many industrial corporations set aside 5–10% of their annual budgets for research. In our overall educational budget, the total amount spent for educational research and development probably comes to about one-tenth of one percent.
>
> This year the federal government is spending $119 million for research in agriculture, which is plagued by surpluses. The money available to the Office of Education for research in education, which is plagued by shortages, is only $6.2 million. When educational research can claim only one-twentieth of what we are spending for farm research, isn't there a lesson for us in the contrast.

RESEARCH FOR ADMINISTRATIVE EFFICIENCY

Actually it is with annoying frequency in the conduct of schools that questions demanding wise answers arise; and the larger the enterprise, the more numerous, the more challenging, and the more varied are the problems demanding such solutions.

For example, a question may arise about the adequacy of the vocational education program of a school system. The board of education itself may raise the question. The answer may lead to other complicated problems. What should a vocational education program adequate to our times be like? The answer to this may require a thorough study of available professional literature in order to arrive at a statement of principles or criteria for such a program, all thoroughly documented and supported by factual data of trends; perhaps a questionnaire survey of how outstanding school systems are organizing their programs; or a report of visits to selected schools enjoying reputations for excellent programs. It is easy to envision

---

[1] As reported in *The Post & Times-Star,* Cincinnati, Apr. 27, 1960.

such an answer covering several hundred pages while merely presenting reasoned conclusions as to what a good program ought to be. But
this can be only the beginning!

As the board considers the blueprint suggested, other questions
soon follow. How would current expenses be affected—upwards or
downwards? Would per-pupil costs be greater or smaller? For which
vocational areas in a given community should instruction be provided? What is the reaction of industrial management or labor likely
to be? Will additional high school buildings be needed anyway? How
would building costs be affected by the new program?

Other problems of similar magnitude might involve a study of
costs as found in basic changes in teacher salary schedules; a ten-
year projection of prospective enrollment figures grade by grade;
a detailed study of school building needs; or the effect of proposed
changes in state foundation programs.

Not all of the questions which come up, however, are as comprehensive as these. Others are more simple, though some are perhaps more delicate. Should high school students be exempted from
final examinations if they have a specified average? To what extent
can the flag-salute requirement be enforced? How effective are half-
day sessions? What effect is increasing class size likely to have on
the learning of children? In a UN Day program, how should the
United Nations flag be displayed relative to the flag of the United
States? The best answer to these and similar questions must be
found swiftly and skillfully, and frequently under pressure from a
community organization which may have a vested interest in a particular answer to the problem posed.

Research on such problems, whether large or small, can hardly
be left as leisure-time activity for the superintendent of a large city
school system. Rather are they generally delegated to another
administrative arm: a division, department, or bureau of school research headed by a skilled director who is assisted by an adequate
staff of clerks, stenographers, and professional assistants. In the
small school system, once again they become part of a big one-man
job. In the small system, however, specialized assistance on specific
research problems is available through expert consultants or school
survey teams of experts frequently drawn from university departments of education. Through them, for a cost that the smaller school

systems can bear, some of the advantages of full-time research bureaus can be realized.

Securing the data upon which school policy decisions can be made may occasionally depend on the more complex types of research such as controlled experimentation or detailed case studies. More frequently they may involve normative survey techniques to get guidance about present practice. Most frequently, however, they involve a study of the results of educational research completed outside the school system.

For the harried and hurried school administrator, the following technique for a rapid overview of research results on school problems is suggested:

1. Start with the *Encyclopedia of Educational Research*. The third revision, published in 1960, contains in its center pages a good index to its contents. On any subject treated, a summary of principal research findings is followed by a bibliography selected by an expert. The summary itself makes specific enough reference to bibliographic listings that the alert reader has a valid idea as to whether or not a given entry will probably be pertinent to his problem.

2. For studies completed from about 1958 to within three years of the date of the search, consult appropriate issues of the *Review of Educational Research*. This periodical is published by the American Educational Research Association five times a year. Each issue is devoted to summarizing research on one of fifteen areas into which school problems are divided. Each area is treated every three years in cycle; the manner of treatment of summaries and bibliography is similar to that of the *Encyclopedia of Educational Research*.

3. From the date of the last coverage in the cycle of issues of the *Review of Educational Research* to the present consult the *Education Index*. While this publication lacks the summary and annotation features of the *Encyclopedia* and the *Review*, all professional publications are thoroughly indexed by topics.

The administrator of Catholic schools will want to supplement this technique for expeditiously canvassing the general field of education for information on his problems by consulting several sources for locating literature on specifically Catholic educational problems. The *Guide to Catholic Literature,* now published by the Catholic Library Association, and the *Catholic Periodical Index,* published by The Catholic University of America, are two bibliographic sources of considerable assistance to him.

PARTICIPATION IN OUTSIDE RESEARCH

As progress is made regionally and nationally on solving the great problems of education, researchers around the country must secure the basic facts on which decisions can be made. This sometimes means calling on school administrators to participate in experiments; it sometimes means permitting investigations to be held within school situations; and school administrators need no reminder that it sometimes means an awesome quantity of questionnaires to answer.

The U.S. Office of Education sponsors much of the fact finding on which alert administrators depend for help. While research and publications of research findings receive heavy emphasis in all the divisions of the Office of Education, that conducted by the Division of State and Local School Systems is particularly helpful to elementary and secondary school administrators. According to the 1960 *Handbook* of the Office, pages 15 and 16, the School Administration Branch of this Division carries on research studies in the following fields:

1. *State School Administration:* The organization and administration of the State and State Agencies for education and State administration of educational programs.

2. *Local School Administration:* The organization of local school districts; administrative staffing patterns and services in local school systems; organization and working procedures of local school boards; and practices in instructional personnel administration, including merit-rating of teachers.

3. *School Finance and School Business Administration:* State provisions for financing education, local tax revenues for capital outlay and current operation, Federal funds for schools; and the business administration of all funds available to local school authorities for the construction and operation of schools.

4. *School Housing:* The planning of immediate and long-range school construction programs; functional planning of school facilities to meet modern educational requirements; the sizing and designing of school furniture and equipment; school-plant management, including operation, maintenance and insurance; school-plant ad-

ministration, including financing and contractual procedures in the design, construction, equipping, and acceptance of school facilities, liaison between school officials and technological research agencies.

Other branches and divisions of the U.S. Office of Education conduct research in:

1. *Elementary Education:* School organization and curriculum development in the early elementary years—nursery, kindergarten, primary—and in the intermediate and upper grades; current instructional practices; and supervision in the elementary schools.

2. *Secondary Education:* Status, trends and emerging problems; analyses of research; and descriptions of current practices in instruction, organization, and supervision.

3. *Adult Education:* Education for the aging; fundamental and literacy education; citizenship education; intergroup education; leisure-time and worker education; and general adult education.

4. *Radio-Television Education:* Planning and developing instructional, evaluative, remedial, guidance, and administrative uses of radio and television and related content materials, methods, and technical facilities.

5. *Visual Education:* Analytical studies of audio-visual education; service as a source of information on all U.S. Government films; and nonbook instructional materials.

6. *Guidance and Student Personnel:* The development and guidance of student personnel services and the preparation of educational personnel workers at all levels.

7. *Exceptional Children and Youth:* Education of children whose needs are unusual because of mental retardation, mental giftedness, serious social or emotional maladjustment, or marked physical limitations.

Research materials of the Office of Education are made available in two forms: sales publications, which are printed and sold by the Superintendent of Documents, Government Printing Office; and free publications, which are multilithed, mimeographed, or dittoed and distributed without cost by the Office. A limited supply of sales publications may be obtained free from the Office of Education as long as the supply lasts.

National and regional professional organizations such as the National Education Association, the National Catholic Educational

Association, and accrediting associations, carry on basic research and publish their findings in their own periodicals and in yearbooks and bulletins, as do most state departments of education. Individual university professors, university research bureaus, and university graduate students preparing dissertations are additional sources of research inquiries and published findings.

Since school administrators clearly stand to benefit by all the knowledge which research workers can obtain regarding any part of the field of education, it is only reasonable to expect that they co-operate with outside research, providing that it is being conducted under responsible auspices, providing that any questionnaire received evidences careful forethought, and providing that responding does not demand an unreasonable amount of effort or time.

Where responsibility for administrative efficiency is centralized in a staff member or a bureau, this person or office will ordinarily be assigned the responsibility of overseeing participation in outside research projects, including receiving questionnaires—many of them needing information from several divisions of a system; of forwarding sections of the inquiry to the appropriate divisions concerned; and of coordinating, assembling, and forwarding the responses gathered.

SCHOOL STATISTICS

A third function of formally organized bureaus of school research accrues from the first two: research for administrative efficiency and participation in outside research. This involves responsibility for co-ordinating the keeping of statistics on a regular basis by all departments, and ordinarily includes planning with department heads the nature of the statistics which should regularly be available in their departments. The most essential information for administrative planning and for answering the questions most frequently received from outside serve as criteria. The bureau will ordinarily be in the best position to advise on the most generally useful classifications of statistical data, since, unless comparable categories are used, significant comparisons are impossible. Prudent advance planning of which statistics are to be kept regularly prevents frequent interruption of the on-going work of a department by frenzied efforts to discover facts which are urgently needed to satisfy demands from within or without the school organization itself.

Questions for Discussion or Investigation

1. Industry frequently uses the terms *operations research* and *product research*. Since the terms are somewhat self-explanatory, who in a school system carries on operations research? Who would carry on something akin to product research?

2. Of the professional studies referred to in this volume, cite at least one which was the result of survey techniques; of case-study technique; of historical technique. Which might be called creative research?

3. What sources of research findings, other than the U.S. Office of Education, did the author of this volume draw upon in previous chapters?

4. Discuss: All questionnaires on school problems should be answered by the conscientious school administrator.

Readings and References

Alexander, Carter, and Arvid J. Burke: *How to Locate Educational Information,* 3d ed., Bureau of Publications, Teachers College, Columbia University, New York, 1950.

Best, John W.: *Research in Education,* Prentice-Hall, Inc., Englewood Cliffs, N.J., 1959.

Encyclopedia of Educational Research, 3d ed., Chester W. Harris (ed.), The Macmillan Company, New York, 1960.

Garrett, Henry E.: *Statistics in Psychology and Education,* 5th ed., Longmans, Green & Co., Inc., New York, 1958.

Good, Carter V.: *Introduction to Educational Research,* Appleton-Century-Crofts, Inc., New York, 1959.

Parke, Beryl, and others: *Publications of the Office of Education,* U.S. Office of Education Bulletin 1959, no. 25, 1959.

Remmers, H. H., and H. L. Gage: *Educational Measurement and Evaluation,* rev. ed., Harper & Brothers, New York, 1955.

Wahlquist, John T., and others: *The Administration of Public Education,* The Ronald Press Company, New York, 1952.

What Research Says to the Teacher series, National Education Association, Washington, 1955.

Whitney, Frederick L.: *The Elements of Research,* Prentice-Hall, Inc., Englewood Cliffs, N.J., 1942.

Appendix A

KEY DECISIONS OF THE SUPREME COURT OF THE UNITED STATES INFLUENCING THE ADMINISTRATION OF SCHOOLS [1]

The Right of Independent Schools to Exist

THE OREGON SCHOOL CASE
Pierce v. Society of Sisters, 268 U.S. 510.

These appeals are from decrees, based upon undenied allegations, which granted preliminary orders restraining appellants from threatening or attempting to enforce the Compulsory Education Act[2] adopted November 1, 1922,

---

[1] The decisions as presented are complete except for legal bibliographic references, unless introduced with the phrase "in part."

[2] *Be it Enacted by the People of the State of Oregon:*

Section 1. That Section 5259, Oregon Laws, be and the same is hereby amended so as to read as follows:

Sec. 5259. *Children Between the Ages of Eight and Sixteen Years*—Any parent, guardian or other person in the State of Oregon having control or charge or custody of a child under the age of sixteen years and of the age of eight years or over at the commencement of a term of public school of the district in which said child resides, who shall fail or neglect or refuse to send such child to a public school for the period of time a public school shall be held during the current year in said district, shall be guilty of a misdemeanor and each day's failure to send such child to a public school shall constitute a separate offense; provided, that in the following cases, children shall not be required to attend public schools.

(a) *Children Physically Unable*—Any child who is abnormal, subnormal or physically unable to attend school.

(b) *Children Who Have Completed the Eighth Grade*—Any child who has

385

under the initiative provision of her Constitution by the voters of Oregon. . . . They present the same points of law; there are no controverted questions of fact. Rights said to be guaranteed by the federal Constitution were specially set up, and appropriate prayers asked for their protection.

The challenged Act, effective September 1, 1926, requires every parent, guardian or other person having control or charge or custody of a child between eight and sixteen years to send him "to a public school for the period of time a public school shall be held during the current year" in the district where the child resides; and failure so to do is declared a misdemeanor. There are exemptions—not specially important here—for children who are not normal, or who have completed the eighth grade, or who reside at considerable distances from any public school, or whose parents or guardians hold special permits from the County Superintendent. The manifest purpose is to compel general attendance at public schools by normal children, between eight and sixteen, who have not completed the eighth grade. And without doubt enforcement of the statute would seriously impair, perhaps destroy, the profitable features of appellees' business and greatly diminish the value of their property.

Appellee, the Society of Sisters, is an Oregon corporation, organized in

---

completed the eighth grade, in accordance with the provisions of the state course of study.

(c) *Distance from School*—Children between the ages of eight and ten years, inclusive, whose place of residence is more than one and one-half miles, and children over ten years of age whose place of residence is more than three miles, by the nearest traveled road, from a public school; provided, however, that if transportation to and from school is furnished by the school district, this exemption shall not apply.

(d) *Private Instruction*—Any child who is being taught for a like period of time by the parent or private teacher such subjects as are usually taught in the first eight years in the public school; but before such child can be taught by a parent or a private teacher, such parent or private teacher must receive written permission from the county superintendent, and such permission shall not extend longer than the end of the current school year. Such child must report to the county school superintendent or some person designated by him at least once every three months and take an examination in the work covered. If, after such examination, the county superintendent shall determine that such child is not being properly taught, then the county superintendent shall order the parent, guardian or other person, to send such child to the public school the remainder of the school year.

If any parent, guardian or other person having control or charge or custody of any child between the ages of eight and sixteen years, shall fail to comply with any provision of this section, he shall be guilty of a misdemeanor, and shall, on conviction thereof, be subject to a fine of not less than $5, nor more than $100, or to imprisonment in the county jail not less than two nor more than thirty days, or by both such fine and imprisonment in the discretion of the court.

This Act shall take effect and be and remain in force from and after the first day of September, 1926.

1880, with power to care for orphans, educate and instruct the youth, establish and maintain academies or schools, and acquire necessary real and personal property. It has long devoted its property and effort to the secular and religious education and care of children, and has acquired the valuable good will of many parents and guardians. It conducts interdependent primary and high schools and junior colleges, and maintains orphanages for the custody and control of children between eight and sixteen. In its primary schools many children between those ages are taught the subjects usually pursued in Oregon public schools during the first eight years. Systematic religious instruction and moral training according to the tenets of the Roman Catholic Church are also regularly provided. All courses of study, both temporal and religious, contemplate continuity of training under appellee's charge; the primary schools are essential to the system and the most profitable. It owns valuable buildings, especially constructed and equipped for school purposes. The business is remunerative—the annual income from primary schools exceeds thirty thousand dollars—and the successful conduct of this requires long time contracts with teachers and parents. The Compulsory Education Act of 1922 has already caused the withdrawal from its schools of children who would otherwise continue, and their income has steadily declined. The appellants, public officers, have proclaimed their purpose strictly to enforce the statute.

After setting out the above facts the Society's bill alleges that the enactment conflicts with the right of parents to choose schools where their children will receive appropriate mental and religious training, the right of the child to influence the parents' choice of a school, the right of schools and teachers therein to engage in a useful business or profession, and is accordingly repugnant to the Constitution and void. And, further, that unless enforcement of the measure is enjoined the corporation's business and property will suffer irreparable injury.

Appellee, Hill Military Academy, is a private corporation organized in 1908 under the laws of Oregon, engaged in owning, operating and conducting for profit an elementary, college preparatory and military training school for boys between the ages of five and twenty-one years. The average attendance is one hundred, and the annual fees received for each student amount to some eight hundred dollars. The elementary department is divided into eight grades, as in the public schools; the college preparatory department has four grades, similar to those of the public high schools; the courses of study conform to the requirements of the State Board of Education. Military instruction and training are also given, under the supervision of an Army officer. It owns considerable real and personal property, some useful only for school purposes. The business and incident good will are very valuable. In order to conduct its affairs long time contracts must be made for supplies, equipment, teachers and pupils. Appellants, law officers of the State and County, have publicly announced that the Act of November 7, 1922, is valid and have declared their intention to enforce it. By reason of the statute and threat of enforcement appellee's business is being destroyed and its property depreciated; parents and guardians are refusing to make contracts for the future instruction of their sons, and some are being withdrawn.

The Academy's bill states the foregoing facts and then alleges that the challenged Act contravenes the corporation's rights guaranteed by the Fourteenth Amendment and that unless appellants are restrained from proclaiming its validity and threatening to enforce it irreparable injury will result. The prayer is for an appropriate injunction.

No answer was interposed in either cause, and after proper notices they were heard by three judges . . . on motions for preliminary injunctions upon the specifically alleged facts. The court ruled that the Fourteenth Amendment guaranteed appellees against the deprivation of their property without due process of law consequent upon the unlawful interference by appellants with the free choice of patrons, present and prospective. It declared the right to conduct schools was property and that parents and guardians, as a part of their liberty, might direct the education of children by selecting reputable teachers and places. Also, that these schools were not unfit or harmful to the public, and that enforcement of the challenged statute would unlawfully deprive them of patronage and thereby destroy their owners' business and property. Finally, that the threats to enforce the Act would continue to cause irreparable injury; and the suits were not premature.

No question is raised concerning the power of the State reasonably to regulate all schools, to inspect, supervise and examine them, their teachers and pupils; to require that all children of proper age attend some school, that teachers shall be of good moral character and patriotic disposition, that certain studies plainly essential to good citizenship must be taught, and that nothing be taught which is manifestly inimical to the public welfare.

The inevitable practical result of enforcing the Act under consideration would be destruction of appellees' primary schools, and perhaps all other private primary schools for normal children within the State of Oregon. These parties are engaged in a kind of undertaking not inherently harmful, but long regarded as useful and meritorious. Certainly there is nothing in the present records to indicate that they have failed to discharge their obligations to patrons, students or the State. And there are no peculiar circumstances or present emergencies which demand extraordinary measures relative to primary education.

Under the doctrine of *Meyer* v. *Nebraska,* 262 U.S. 390, we think it entirely plain that the Act of 1922 unreasonably interferes with the liberty of parents and guardians to direct the upbringing and education of children under their control. As often heretofore pointed out, rights guaranteed by the Constitution may not be abridged by legislation which has no reasonable relation to some purpose within the competency of the State. The fundamental theory of liberty upon which all governments in this Union repose excludes any general power of the State to standardize its children by forcing them to accept instruction from public teachers only. The child is not the mere creature of the State; those who nurture him and direct his destiny have the right, coupled with the high duty, to recognize and prepare him for additional obligations.

Appellees are corporations and therefore, it is said, they cannot claim for themselves the liberty which the Fourteenth Amendment guarantees. Accepted in the proper sense, this is true. . . . But they have business and property for which they claim protection. These are threatened with destruction through the unwarranted compulsion which appellants are exercising over present and prospective patrons of their schools. And this court has gone very far to protect against loss threatened by such action. . . .

The courts of the State have not construed the Act, and we must determine its meaning for ourselves. Evidently it was expected to have general application and cannot be construed as though merely intended to amend the charters of certain private corporations, as in *Berea College* v. *Kentucky,* 211 U.S. 45. No argument in favor of such view has been advanced.

Generally it is entirely true, as urged by counsel, that no person in any business has such an interest in possible customers as to enable him to restrain exercise of proper power of the State upon the ground that he will be deprived of patronage. But the injunctions here sought are not against the exercise of any *proper* power. Plaintiffs asked protection against arbitrary, unreasonable and unlawful interference with their patrons and the consequent destruction of their business and property. Their interest is clear and immediate, within the rule approved in *Truax* v. *Raich, Truax* v. *Corrigan* and *Terrace* v. *Thompson,* . . . and many other cases where injunctions have issued to protect business enterprises against interference with the freedom of patrons or customers. . . .

The suits were not premature. The injury to appellees was present and very real, not a mere possibility in the remote future. If no relief had been possible prior to the effective date of the Act, the injury would have become irreparable. Prevention of impending injury by unlawful action is a well recognized function of courts of equity.

The decrees below are

Affirmed

THE DARTMOUTH COLLEGE CASE

Trustees of Dartmouth College v. Woodward, 4 Wheat. 518 U.S. 1819.

This case grew out of New Hampshire legislation which placed Dartmouth College, a chartered Congregational college, under state control despite its original charter as a private institution. The New Hampshire Court of Appeals held the state legislation modifying the charter to be valid. The Supreme Court of the United States reversed the New Hampshire court, stating in part:

From the review of this charter which has been taken it appears that the whole power of governing the college, of appointing and removing tutors, of fixing their salaries, of directing the course of study to be pursued by the students, and of filling up vacancies created in their own body, was vested in the trustees. On the part of the Crown it was expressly stipulated that this corporation, thus constituted, should continue forever; and that the number of trustees should forever consist of twelve, and no more. By this contract the Crown was bound, and could have made no violent alteration in its essential terms without impairing its obligation.

By the revolution the duties as well as the powers of government devolved on the people of New Hampshire. It is admitted that among the latter was comprehended the transcendent power of parliament, as well as that of the executive department. It is too clear to require the support of argument that all contracts and rights respecting property remained unchanged by the Revolution. The obligations, then, which were created by the charter to Dartmouth College were the same in the new that they had been in the old government. The power of the government was also the same. A repeal of this charter at any time prior to the adoption of the present Constitution of the United States would have been an extraordinary and unprecedented act of power, but one which could have been contested only by the restrictions upon the legislature to be found in the constitution of the state. But the Constitution of the United States has imposed this additional limitation, that the legislature of a state shall pass no act "impairing the obligation of contracts."

It has been already stated that the act "to amend the charter and enlarge and improve the corporation of Dartmouth College" increased the number of trustees to twenty-one, gives the appointment of the additional members to the executive of the state, and creates a board of overseers, to consist of twenty-five persons, of whom twenty-one are also appointed by the executive of New Hampshire, who have power to inspect and control the most important acts of the trustees.

On the effect of this law two opinions cannot be entertained. Between acting directly and acting through the agency of trustees and overseers no essential difference is perceived. The whole power of governing the college is transformed from trustees appointed according to the will of the founder, expressed in the charter, to the executive of New Hampshire. The management and application of the funds of this eleemosynary institution, which are placed by the donors in the hands of trustees named in the charter, and empowered to perpetuate themselves, are placed by this act under the control of the government of the state. The will of the state is substituted for the will of the donors in every essential operation of the college. This is not an immaterial change. The founders of the college contracted, not merely for the perpetual application of funds which they gave to the objects for which those funds were given; they contracted also to secure that application by the constitution of the corporation. They contracted for a system which, as far as human foresight can provide, retain forever the government of the literary institution they had formed, in the hands of persons approved by themselves. This system is totally changed. The charter of 1769 exists no longer. It is reorganized; and reorganized in such a manner as to convert a literary institution, molded according to the will of its founders and placed under the control of private literary men, into a machine entirely subservient to the will of government. This may be for the advantage of this college in particular, and may be for the advantage of literature in general; but it is not according to the will of the donors, and is subversive of that contract on the faith of which their property was given.

In the view which has been taken of this interesting case, the Court has confined itself to the rights possessed by the trustees, as the assignees and representatives of the donors and founders, for the benefit of religion and literature. Yet it is not clear that the trustees ought to be considered as destitute of such beneficial interest in themselves as the law may respect. In addition to their being the legal owners of the property, and to their having a freehold right in the powers confided to them, the charter itself countenances the idea that trustees may also be tutors with salaries. The first president was one of the original trustees; and the charter provides, that in case of vacancy in that office, "the senior professor or tutor, being one of the trustees shall make choice of, and appoint a president." According to the tenor of the charter, then, the trustees might, without impropriety, appoint a president and other professors from their own body. This is a power not entirely unconnected with an interest. Even if the proposition of the counsel for the defendant were sustained; if it were admitted that those contracts only are protected by the Constitution, a beneficial interest in which is vested in the party who appears in court to assert that interest; yet it is by no means clear that the trustees of Dartmouth College have no beneficial interest in themselves.

But the Court has deemed it unnecessary to investigate this particular point, being of opinion, on general principles that in these private eleemosynary institutions, the body corporate, as possessing the whole legal and equitable interest, and completely representing the donors, for the purpose of executing the trust, has rights which are protected by the Constitution.

It results from this opinion, that the acts of the legislature of New Hampshire, which are stated in the special verdict found in this cause, are repugnant to the Constitution of the United States; and that the judgment on this special verdict ought to have been for the plaintiffs. The judgment of the state court must therefore be reversed.

Reversed

THE NEBRASKA CASE
Meyer v. State of Nebraska, 262 U.S. 390.

Plaintiff in error was tried and convicted in the District Court for Hamilton County, Nebraska, under an information which charged that on May 25, 1920, while an instructor in Zion Parochial School, he unlawfully taught the subject of reading in the German language to Raymond Parpart, a child of ten years, who had not attained and successfully passed the eighth grade.

The information is based upon "An act relating to the teaching of foreign languages in the State of Nebraska," approved April 9, 1919, which follows:

"Section 1. No person, individually or as a teacher, shall, in any private, denominational, parochial or public school, teach any subject to any person in any language other than the English language.

"Sec. 2. Languages, other than the English language, may be taught as languages only after a pupil shall have attained and successfully passed the eighth grade as evidenced by a certificate of graduation issued by the county superintendent of the county in which the child resides.

"Sec. 3. Any person who violates any of the provisions of this act shall be deemed guilty of a misdemeanor and upon conviction, shall be subject to a fine of not less than twenty-five dollars ($25), nor more than one hundred dollars ($100) or be confined in the county jail for any period not exceeding thirty days for each offense.

"Sec. 4. Whereas, an emergency exists, this act shall be in force from and after its passage and approval."

The Supreme Court of the State affirmed the judgment of conviction. . . . It declared the offense charged and established was "the direct and intentional teaching of the German language as a distinct subject to a child who had not passed the eighth grade," in the parochial school maintained by Zion Evangelical Lutheran Congregation, a collection of Biblical stories being used therefore. And it held that the statute forbidding this did not conflict with the Fourteenth Amendment, but was a valid exercise of the police power. The following excerpts from the opinion sufficiently indicate the reasons advanced to support the conclusion.

"The salutary purpose of the statute is clear. The legislature had seen the baneful effects of permitting foreigners, who had taken residence in this country, to rear and educate their children in the language of their native land. The result of that condition was found to be inimical to our own safety. To allow the children of foreigners, who had emigrated here, to be taught from early childhood the language of the country of their parents was to rear them with that language as their mother tongue. It was to educate them so that they must always think in that language, and, as a consequence, naturally inculcate in them the ideas and sentiments foreign to the best interests of this country. The statute, therefore, was intended not only to require that the education of all children be conducted in the English language, but that, until they had grown into that language and until it had become a part of them, they should not in the schools be taught any other language. The obvious purpose of this statute was that the English language should be and become the mother tongue of all children reared in this state. The enactment of such a statute comes reasonably within the police power of the state. . . .

"It is suggested that the law is an unwarranted restriction, in that it applies to all citizens of the state and arbitrarily interferes with the rights of citizens who are not of foreign ancestry, and prevents them, without reason, from having their children taught foreign languages in school. That argument is not well taken, for it assumes that every citizen finds himself restrained by the statute. The hours which a child is able to devote to study in the confinement of school are limited. It must have ample time for exercise or play. Its daily capacity for learning is comparatively small. A selection of subjects for its education, therefore, from among the many that might be taught, is obviously necessary. The legislature no doubt had in mind the practical operation of the law. The law affects few citizens, except those of foregin lineage. Other citizens, in their selection of studies, except perhaps in rare instances, have never deemed it of importance to teach their children foreign languages before such children have reached the eighth grade. In the legislative mind, the salutary effect of the statute no doubt outweighed the restriction upon the citizens generally, which, it appears, was a restriction of no real consequence."

The problem for our determination is whether the statute as construed and applied unreasonably infringes the liberty guaranteed to the plaintiff in error by the Fourteenth Amendment. "No State shall . . . deprive any person of life, liberty, or property, without due process of law."

While this Court has not attempted to define with exactness the liberty thus guaranteed, the term has received much consideration and some of the included things have been definitely stated. Without doubt, it denotes not merely freedom from bodily restraint but also the right of the individual to contract, to engage in any of the common occupations of life, to acquire useful knowledge, to marry, establish a home and bring up children, to worship God according to the dictates of his own conscience, and generally to enjoy those privileges long recognized at common law as essential to the orderly pursuit of happiness by free men. . . . The established doctrine is that this liberty may not be interfered with, under the guise of protecting the public interest, by legislative action which is arbitrary or without reasonable relation to some purpose within the competency of the State to effect. Determination by the legislature of what constitutes proper exercise of police power is not final or conclusive but is subject to supervision by the courts. . . .

The American people have always regarded education and acquisition of knowledge as matters of supreme importance which should be diligently promoted. The Ordinance of 1787 declares, "Religion, morality, and knowledge being necessary to good government and the happiness of mankind, schools and the means of education shall forever be encouraged." Corresponding to the right of control, it is the natural duty of the parent to give his children education suitable to their station in life; and nearly all the States, including Nebraska, enforce this obligation by compulsory laws.

Practically, education of the young is only possible in schools conducted by especially qualified persons who devote themselves thereto. The calling always has been regarded as useful and honorable, essential, indeed, to the public welfare. Mere knowledge of the German language cannot reasonably be regarded as harmful. Heretofore it has been commonly looked upon as helpful and desirable. Plaintiff in error taught this language in school as part of his occupation. His right thus to teach and the right of parents to engage him so to instruct their children, we think, are within the liberty of the Amendment.

The challenged statute forbids the teaching in school of any subject except in English; also the teaching of any other language until the pupil has attained and successfully passed the eighth grade, which is not usually accomplished before the age of twelve. The Supreme Court of the State has held that "the so-called ancient or dead languages" are not "within the spirit or the purpose of the act." . . . Latin, Greek, Hebrew are not proscribed; but German, French, Spanish, Italian and every other alien speech are within the ban. Evidently the legislature has attempted materially to interfere with the calling of modern language teachers, with the opportunities of pupils to acquire knowledge, and with the power of parents to control the education of their own.

It is said the purpose of the legislation was to promote civic development by inhibiting training and education of the immature in foreign tongues and ideals before they could learn English and acquire American ideals; and "that the English language should be and become the mother tongue of all children reared in this State." It is also affirmed that the foreign born population is very large, that certain communities commonly use foreign words, follow foreign leaders, move in a foreign atmosphere, and that the children are thereby hindered from becoming citizens of the most useful type and the public safety is imperiled.

That the State may do much, go very far, indeed, in order to improve the quality of its citizens, physically, mentally and morally, is clear; but the individual has certain fundamental rights which must be respected. The protection of the Constitution extends to all, to those who speak other languages as well as to those born with English on the tongue. Perhaps it would be highly advantageous if all had ready understanding of our ordinary speech, but this cannot be coerced by methods which conflict with the Constitution— a desirable end cannot be promoted by prohibited means.

For the welfare of his Ideal Commonwealth, Plato suggested a law which should provide: "That the wives of our guardians are to be common, and their children are to be common, and no parent is to know his own child, nor any child his parent. . . . The proper officers will take the offspring of the good parents to the pen or fold, and there they will deposit them with certain nurses who dwell in a separate quarter; but the offspring of the inferior, or of the better when they chance to be deformed, will be put away in some mysterious, unknown place, as they should be." In order to submerge the individual and develop ideal citizens, Sparta assembled the males at seven into barracks and intrusted their subsequent education and training to official guardians. Although such measures have been deliberately approved by men of great genius, their ideas touching the relation between individual and State were wholly different from those upon which our institutions rest; and it hardly will be affirmed that any legislature could impose such restrictions upon the people of a State without doing violence to both letter and spirit of the Constitution.

The desire of the legislature to foster a homogeneous people with American ideals prepared readily to understand current discussions of civic matters is easy to appreciate. Unfortunate experiences during the late war and aversion toward every characteristic of truculent adversaries were certainly enough to quicken that aspiration. But the means adopted, we think, exceed the limitations upon the power of the State and conflict with rights assured to plaintiff in error. The interference is plain enough and no adequate reason therefor in time of peace and domestic tranquility has been shown.

The power of the State to compel attendance at some school and to make reasonable regulations for all schools, including a requirement that they shall give instructions in English, is not questioned. Nor has challenge been made of the State's power to prescribe a curriculum for institutions which it supports. Those matters are not within the present controversy. Our concern is with the prohibition approved by the Supreme Court. *Adams* v. *Tanner* . . . pointed out that mere abuse incident to an occupation ordinarily useful is not enough to justify its abolition, although regulation may be entirely proper. No emergency has arisen which renders knowledge by a child of some language other than English so clearly harmful as to justify its inhibition with the consequent infringement of rights long freely enjoyed. We are constrained to conclude that the statute as applied is arbitrary and without reasonable relation to any end within the competency of the State.

As the statute undertakes to interfere only with teaching which involves a modern language, leaving complete freedom as to other matters, there seems no adequate foundation for the suggestion that the purpose was to protect the child's health by limiting his mental activities. It is well known that proficiency in a foreign language seldom comes to one not instructed at an early age, and experience shows that this is not injurious to the health, morals or understanding of the ordinary child.

The judgment of the court below must be reversed and the cause remanded for further proceedings not inconsistent with this opinion.

Reversed

The "Wall of Separation"

The Indian Affairs case, the Louisiana Textbook case, the New Jersey School Bus case, the Illinois Released Time case, and the New York Released Time case.

THE INDIAN AFFAIRS CASE
Quick Bear v. Leupp, 210 U.S. 50.

This case grew out of the efforts of members of the Sioux Indian Tribe to stop payment of tribal funds by the executives of the United States government for the support of sectarian schools, particularly Catholic schools on their reservation. The government had since 1819 been regularly contracting with sectarian agencies for the education of Indians and had been paying for this by appropriating public moneys. The Court in its decision said in part:

As has been shown, in 1868 the United States made a treaty with the Sioux Indians, under which the Indians made large cessions of land and other rights. In consideration of this the United States agreed that for every thirty children a house should be provided and a teacher competent to teach the elementary branches of our English education should be furnished for twenty years. In 1877, in consideration of further land cessions, the United States agreed to furnish all necessary aid to assist the Indians in the work of civilization, and furnish them schools and instruction in mechanical and agricultural arts, as provided by the treaty of 1868. In 1899, Congress extended the obligation of the treaty for twenty years, subject to such modifications as Congress should deem most effective, to secure the Indians equivalent benefits of such education. Thereafter in every annual Indian appropriation act, there was an appropriation to carry out the terms of this treaty, under the heading, "Fulfilling Treaty Stipulation with, and Support of, Indian tribes."

These appropriations rested on different grounds from the gratuitous appropriations of public moneys under the heading, "Support of Schools." The two subjects were separately treated in each act, and naturally they are essentially different in character. One is the gratuitous appropriation of public money in this sense. It is the Indians' money, or, at least, is dealt with by the government as if it belonged to them, as morally it does. It differs from the "trust fund" in this: The trust fund has been set aside for the Indians, and the income expended for their benefit, which expenditure required no annual appropriation. The whole amount due the Indians for certain land cessions was appropriated in one lump sum by the act of 1889. . . . This "trust fund" is held for the Indians, and not distributed in accordance with the discretion of the Secretary of the Interior, but really belongs to the Indians. The President declared it to be the moral right of the Indians to have this "trust fund" applied to the education of the Indians in schools of their choice, and the same view was entertained by the Supreme Court of the District of Columbia and the Court of Appeals of the District. But the treaty fund has exactly the same characteristics. They are moneys belonging really to the Indians. They are the price of land ceded by the Indians to the government. The only difference is that, in the "treaty fund," the debt to the Indians created and secured by the treaty is paid by annual appropriations of public moneys, but the payment, as we repeat, of a treaty debt in installments. We perceive no justification for applying the proviso or declaration of policy to the payment of treaty obligations, the two things being distinct and different in nature, and having no relation to each other, except that both are technically appropriations.

Some reference is made by the Constitution, in respect to this contract with the Bureau of Catholic Indian Missions. It is not contended that it is unconstitutional, and it could not be. . . . But it is contended that the spirit of the Constitution requires that the declaration of policy that the government "shall make no appropriation whatever for education in any sectarian schools" should be treated as applicable, on the ground that the actions of the United States were to always be undenominational, and that, therefore, the government can never act in a sectarian capacity, either in the use of its own funds or in that of the funds of others, in respect of which it is a trustee; hence, that even the Sioux trust fund cannot be applied for education in Catholic schools, even though the owners of the fund so desires it. But we cannot concede the proposition that Indians cannot be allowed to use their own money to educate their own children in the schools of their own choice because the government is necessarily undenominational, as it cannot make any law respecting an establishment of religion or prohibiting the free exercise thereof. The court of appeals well said:

"The 'treaty' and 'trust' moneys are the only moneys which the Indians can lay claim to as a matter of right; the only sums on which they are entitled to rely as theirs for education; and while these moneys are not delivered to them in hand, yet the money must not only be provided, but be expended, for their benefit, and in part for their education; it seems inconceivable that Congress shall have intended to prohibit them from receiving religious education at their own cost if they desire it; such an intent would be one to prohibit the free exercise of religion amongst the Indians, and such would be the effect of the construction for which the complainants contend."

The *cestius que trust* cannot be deprived of their rights by the trustee in the exercise of power implied.

Affirmed

THE LOUISIANA TEXTBOOK CASE
Cochran v. Louisiana State Board of Education, 281 U.S. 370.

The appellants, as citizens and taxpayers of the State of Louisiana, brought this suit to restrain the state board of education and other state officials from expending any part of the severance tax fund in purchasing school books and in supplying them free of cost to the school children of the state, under Acts No. 100 and No. 143 of 1928, upon the ground that the legislation violated specific provisions of the constitution of the state and also Section 4 of Article IV and the Fourteenth Amendment of the Federal Constitution. The supreme court of the state affirmed the judgment of the trial court, which refused to issue an injunction. 168 La. 1030.

Act No. 100 of 1928 provided that the severance tax fund of the state, after allowing funds and appropriations as required by the state constitution, should be devoted "first, to supplying school books to the school children of the state." The board of education was directed to provide school books for school children free of cost to such children." Act No. 143 of 1928 made appropriations in accordance with the above provisions.

The supreme court of the state, following its decision in *Borden v. Louisiana State Board of Education*, 168 La. 1005, held that these acts were not repugnant to either the state or the Federal Constitution. . . .

The contention of the appellant under the Fourteenth Amendment is that taxation for the purchase of school books constituted a taking of public property for a private purpose. . . . The purpose is said to be to aid private, religious, sectarian, and other schools not embraced in the public educational system of the state by furnishing textbooks free to the children attending such private schools. The operation and effect of the legislation in question were described by the supreme court of the state as follows. . . .

"One may scan the acts in vain to ascertain where any money is appropriated for the purchase of school books for the use of any church, private, sectarian, or even public school. The appropriations were made for the specific purpose of purchasing school books for the use of the school children of the state free of cost to them. It was for their benefit and the resulting benefit to the state that the appropriations were made. True, these children attend some school; public or private, the latter, sectarian or nonsectarian, and that the books are to be furnished them for their use, free of cost, whichever they attend. The schools, however, are not the beneficiaries of these appropriations. They obtain nothing from them, nor are they relieved of a single obligation because of them. The school children and the state alone are the beneficiaries. It is also true that the sectarian schools, which some of the children attend, instruct their pupils in religion, and books are used for that purpose, but one may search diligently the acts, though without result, in an effort to find anything to the effect that it is the purpose of the state to furnish religious books for the use of such children. . . . What the statutes contemplate is that the same books that are furnished children attending public schools shall be furnished children attending private schools. This is the only practical way of interpreting and executing the statutes, and this is what the state board of education is doing. Among these books, naturally, none is to be expected, adapted to religious instruction." The court also stated, although the point is not of importance in relation to the federal question, that it was "only the use of the books that is granted to the children or, in other words, the books are lent to them."

Viewing the statute as having the effect thus attributed to it, we cannot doubt that the taxing power of the state is exerted for a public purpose. The legislation does not segregate private schools, or their pupils, as its beneficiaries or attempt to interfere with any matters of exclusively private concern. Its interest is education, broadly; its method, comprehensive. Individual interests are aided only as the common interest is safeguarded.

Affirmed

THE NEW JERSEY SCHOOL BUS CASE
Everson v. *Board of Education,* 330 U.S. 1.

A New Jersey statute authorizes its local school districts to make rules and contracts for the transportation of children to and from schools.[1] The ap-

---

[1] "Whenever in any district there are children living remote from any schoolhouse, the board of education of the district may make rules and contracts for the transportation of such children to and from school, including the transportation of

pellee, a township board of education, acting pursuant to this statute, authorized reimbursement to parents of money expended by them for the bus transportation of their children on regular busses operated by the public transportation system. Part of this money was for the payment of transportation of some children in the community to Catholic parochial schools. These church schools give their students, in addition to secular education, regular religious instruction conforming to the religious tenets and modes of worship of the Catholic Faith. The superintendent of these schools is a Catholic priest.

The appellant, in his capacity as a district taxpayer, filed suit in a state court challenging the right of the Board to reimburse parents of parochial school students. He contended that the statute and the resolution passed pursuant to it violated both the State and the Federal Constitutions. That court held that the legislature was without power to authorize such payment under the state constitution. . . . The New Jersey Court of Errors and Appeals reversed, holding that neither the statute nor the resolution passed pursuant to it was in conflict with the State constitution or the provisions of the Federal Constitution in issue. . . .

Since there has been no attack on the statute on the ground that a part of its language excludes children attending private schools operated for profit from enjoying State payment for their transportation, we need not consider this exclusionary language; it has no relevancy to any constitutional question here presented. Furthermore, if the exclusion clause had been properly challenged, we do not know whether New Jersey's highest court would construe its statutes as precluding payment of the school transportation of any group of pupils, even those of a private school run for profit. Consequently, we put to one side the question as to the validity of the statute against the claim that it does not authorize payment for the transportation generally of school children in New Jersey.

The only contention here is that the state statute and the resolution, insofar as they authorized reimbursement to parents of children attending parochial schools, violate the Federal Constitution in these two respects, which to some extent overlap. *First.* They authorize the State to take by taxation the private property of some and bestow it upon others, to be used for their own private purposes. This, it is alleged, violates the due process clause of the Fourteenth Amendment. *Second.* The statute and the resolution forced inhabitants to pay taxes to help support and maintain schools which are dedicated to, and which regularly teach, the Catholic Faith. This is alleged to be a use of state power to support church schools contrary to the prohibition of

---

school children to and from school other than a public school, except such school as is operated for profit in whole or in part.

"When any school district provides any transportation for public school children to and from school, transportation from any point in such established school route to any other point in such established school route shall be supplied to school children residing in such school district in going to and from school other than a public school, except such school as is operated for profit in whole or in part." . . .

the First Amendment which the Fourteenth Amendment made applicable to the states.

First. The due process argument that the state law taxes some people to help others carry out their private purposes is framed in two phases. The first phase is that a state cannot tax A to reimburse B for the cost of transporting his children to church schools. This is said to violate the due process clause because the children are sent to these church schools to satisfy the personal desires of their parents, rather than the public's interest in the general education of all children. This argument, if valid, would apply equally to prohibit state payment for the transportation of children to any non-public school, whether operated by a church or any other non-government individual or group. But, the New Jersey legislature has decided that a public purpose will be served by using tax-raised funds to pay the bus fares of all school children, including those who attend parochial schools. The New Jersey Court of Errors and Appeals has reached the same conclusion. The fact that a state law, passed to satisfy a public need, coincides with the personal desires of the individuals most directly affected is certainly an inadequate reason for us to say that a legislature has erroneously appraised the public need.

It is true that this Court has, in rare instances, struck down state statutes on the ground that the purpose for which tax-raised funds were to be expended was not a public one. . . . But the Court has also pointed out that this far-reaching authority must be exercised with the most extreme caution. . . . Otherwise, a state's power to legislate for the public welfare might be seriously curtailed, a power which is a primary reason for the existence of states. Changing local conditions create new local problems which may lead a state's people and its local authorities to believe that laws authorizing new types of public services are necessary to promote the general well-being of the people. The Fourteenth Amendment did not strip the states of their power to meet problems previously left for individual solution. . . .

It is much too late to argue that legislation intended to facilitate the opportunity of children to get a secular education serves no public purpose. . . . The same thing is no less true of legislation to reimburse needy parents, or all parents, for payment of the fares of their children so that they can ride in public busses to and from schools rather than run the risk of traffic and other hazards incident to walking or "hitchhiking." . . . Nor does it follow that a law has a private rather than a public purpose because it provides that tax-raised funds will be paid to reimburse individuals on account of money spent by them in a way which furthers a public program. . . . Subsidies and loans to individuals such as farmers and home-owners, and to privately owned transportation systems, as well as many other kinds of businesses, have been commonplace practices in our state and national history.

Insofar as the second phase of the due process argument may differ from the first, it is by suggesting that taxation for transportation of children to church schools constitutes support of a religion by the State. But if the law is invalid for this reason, it is because it violates the First Amendment's prohibition against the establishment of religion by law. This is the exact question raised by appellant's second contention, to consideration of which we now turn.

Second. The New Jersey statute is challenged as a "law respecting an establishment of religion." The First Amendment, as made applicable to the states by the Fourteenth, *Murdock* v. *Pennsylvania,* 319 U.S. 105, commands that a state "shall make no law respecting an establishment of religion, or prohibiting the free exercise thereof. . . ." These words of the First Amendment reflected in the minds of early Americans a vivid mental picture of conditions and practices which they fervently wished to stamp out in order to preserve liberty for themselves and for their posterity. Doubtless their goal has not been entirely reached; but so far has the Nation moved toward it that the expression "law respecting an establishment of religion," probably does not so vividly remind present-day Americans of the evils, fears, and political problems that caused that expression to be written into our Bill of Rights. Whether this New Jersey law is one respecting an "establishment of religion" requires an understanding of the meaning of that language, particularly with respect to the imposition of taxes. Once again, therefore, it is not inappropriate briefly to review the background and environment of the period in which that constitutional language was fashioned and adopted.

A large proportion of the early settlers of this country came here from Europe to escape the bondage of laws which compelled them to support and attend government-favored churches. The centuries immediately before and contemporaneous with the colonization of America had been filled with turmoil, civil strife, and persecutions, generated in large part by established sects determined to maintain their absolute political and religious supremacy. With the power of government supporting them, at various times and places, Catholics had persecuted Protestants, Protestants had persecuted Catholics, Protestant sects had persecuted other Protestant sects, Catholics of one shade of belief had persecuted Catholics of another shade of belief, and all of these had from time to time persecuted Jews. In efforts to force loyalty to whatever religious group happened to be on top and in league with the government of a particular time and place, men and women had been fined, cast in jail, cruelly tortured, and killed. Among the offenses for which these punishments had been inflicted were such things as speaking disrespectfully of the views of ministers of government-established churches, non-attendance at those churches, expressions of non-belief in their doctrines, and failure to pay taxes and tithes to support them.

These practices of the old world were transplanted to and began to thrive in the soil of the new America. The very charters granted by the English Crown to the individuals and companies designated to make the laws which would control the destinies of the colonials authorized these individuals and companies to erect religious establishments which all, whether believers or non-believers, would be required to support and attend. An exercise of this authority was accompanied by a repetition of many of the old-world practices and persecutions. Catholics found themselves hounded and proscribed because of their faith; Quakers who followed their conscience went to jail; Baptists were peculiarly obnoxious to certain dominant Protestant sects; men and women of varied faiths who happened to be in a minority in a particular locality were persecuted because they steadfastly persisted in worshipping God only as their own consciences dictated. And all of these dissenters were compelled to pay tithes and taxes to support government-sponsored churches whose ministers preached inflammatory sermons designed to strengthen and consolidate the established faith by generating a burning hatred against dissenters.

These practices became so commonplace as to shock the freedom-loving colonials into a feeling of abhorrence. The imposition of taxes to pay ministers' salaries and to build and maintain churches and church property aroused their indignation. It was these feelings which found expression in the First Amendment. No one locality and no one group throughout the Colonies can rightly be given entire credit for having aroused the sentiment that culminated in adoption of the Bill of Rights' provisions embracing religious liberty. But Virginia, where the established church had achieved a dominant influence in political affairs and where many excesses attracted wide public attention, provided a great stimulus and able leadership for the movement. The people there, as elsewhere, reached the conviction that individual religious liberty could be achieved best under a government which was stripped of all power to tax, to support, or otherwise to assist any or all religions, or to interfere with the beliefs of any religious individual or group.

The movement toward this end reached its dramatic climax in Virginia in 1785–86 when the Virginia legislative body was about to renew Virginia's tax levy for the support of the established church. Thomas Jefferson and James Madison led the fight against this tax. Madison wrote his great Memorial and Remonstrance against the law. In it, he eloquently argued that a true religion did not need the support of law; that no person, either believer or non-believer, should be taxed to support a religious institution of any kind; that the best interest of a society required that the minds of men always be wholly free; and that cruel persecutions were the inevitable result of government-established religions. Madison's Remonstrance received strong support throughout Virginia, and the Assembly postponed consideration of the proposed tax measure until its next session. When the proposal came up for consideration at that session, it not only died in committee, but the Assembly enacted the famous "Virginia Bill for Religious Liberty" originally written by Thomas Jefferson. The preamble to that Bill stated among other things that "Almighty God hath created the mind free; that all attempts to influence it by temporal punishments or burthens, or by civil incapacitations, tend only to beget habits of hypocrisy and meanness, and are a departure from the plan of the Holy author of our religion, who being Lord both of body and mind, yet chose not to propagate it by coercions on either . . . ; that to compel a man to furnish contributions of money for the propagation of opinions which he disbelieves, is sinful and tyrannical; that even the forcing him to support this or that teacher of his own religious persuasion, is depriving him of the comfortable liberty of giving his contributions to the particular pastor, whose morals he would make his pattern. . . ." And the statute itself enacted "That no man shall be compelled to frequent or support any religious worship, place, or ministry whatsoever, nor shall be enforced, restrained, molested, or burthened in his body or goods, nor shall otherwise suffer on account of his religious opinions or belief. . . ."

This Court has previously recognized that the provisions of the First Amendment, in the drafting and adoption of which Madison and Jefferson played such leading roles, had the same objective and were intended to provide the same protection against governmental intrusion on religious liberty as the Virginia statute. . . . Prior to the adoption of the Fourteenth Amendment, the First Amendment did not apply as a restraint against the states. Most of them did soon provide similar constitutional protections for religious liberty. But some states persisted for about half a century in imposing restraints upon the free exercise of religion and in discriminating against particular religious groups. In recent years, so far as the provision against the establishment of a religion is concerned, the question has most frequently arisen in connection with proposed state aid to church schools and efforts to carry on religious teachings in the public schools in accordance with the tenets of a particular sect. Some churches have either sought or accepted state financial support for their schools. Here again the efforts to obtain state aid or acceptance of it have not been limited to any one particular faith. The state courts, in the main, have remained faithful to the language of their own constitutional provisions designed to protect religious freedom and to separate religions and governments. Their decisions, however, show the difficulty in drawing the line between tax legislation which provides funds for the welfare of the general public and that which is designed to support institutions which teach religion.

The meaning and scope of the First Amendment, preventing establishment of religion or prohibiting the free exercise thereof, in the light of its history and the evils it was designed forever to suppress, have been several times elaborated by the decisions of this Court prior to the application of the First Amendment to the states by the Fourteenth. The broad meaning given the Amendment by these earlier cases has been accepted by this Court in its decisions concerning an individual's religious freedom rendered since the Fourteenth Amendment was interpreted to make the prohibitions of the First applicable to state action abridging religious freedom. There is every reason to give the same application and broad interpretation to the "establishment of religion" clause. The interrelation of these complementary clauses was well summarized in a statement of the Court of Appeals of South Carolina, quoted with approval by this Court in *Watson* v. *Jones,* 13 Wall. 679, 730: "The structure of our government has, for the preservation of civil liberty, rescued the temporal institutions from religious interference. On the other hand, it has secured religious liberty from the invasion of the civil authority."

The "establishment of religion" clause of the First Amendment means at least this: Neither a state nor the Federal Government can set up a church. Neither can pass laws which aid one religion, aid all religions, or prefer one religion over another. Neither can force nor influence a person to go to or to remain away from church against his will or force him to profess a belief or disbelief in any religion. No person can be punished for entertaining or professing religous beliefs or disbeliefs, for church, attendance or non-attendance. No tax in any amount, large or small, can be levied to support any religious activities or institutions, whatever they may be called, or whatever form they may adopt to teach or practice religion. Neither a state nor the Federal Government can, openly or secretly, participate in the affairs of any religious organizations or groups and *vice versa*. In the words of Jefferson, the clause against establishment of religion by law was intended to erect "a wall of separation between church and State.". . .

We must consider the New Jersey statute in accordance with the foregoing limitations imposed by the First Amendment. But we must not strike that state statute down if it is within the State's consitutional power even though it approaches the verge of that power. . . . New Jersey cannot consistently with the "establishment of religion" clause of the First Amendment contribute tax-raised funds to the support of an institution which teaches the tenets and faith of any church. On the other hand, other language of the amendment commands that New Jersey cannot hamper its citizens in the free exercise of their own religion. Consequently, it cannot exclude individual Catholics, Lutherans, Mohammedans, Baptists, Jews, Methodists, Nonbelievers, Presbyterians, or the members of any other faith, *because of their faith, or lack of it,* from receiving the benefits of public welfare legislation. While we do not mean to intimate that a state could not provide transportation only to children attending public schools, we must be careful, in protecting the citizens of New Jersey against state-established churches, to be sure that we do not inadvertently prohibit New Jersey from extending its general state law benefits to all its citizens without regard to their religious belief.

Measured by these standards, we cannot say that the First Amendment prohibits New Jersey from spending tax-raised funds to pay the bus fares of parochial school pupils as a part of a general program under which it pays the fares of pupils attending public and other schools. It is undoubtedly true that children are helped to get to church schools. There is even a possibility that some of the children might not be sent to the church schools if the parents were compelled to pay their children's bus fares out of their own pockets when transportation to a public school would have been paid for by the State. The same possibility exists where the state requires a local transit company to provide reduced fares to school children including those attending parochial schools, or where a municipally owned transportation system undertakes to carry all school children free of charge. Moreover, state-paid policemen, detailed to protect children going to and from church schools from the very real hazards of traffic, would serve much the same purpose and accomplish much the same result as state provisions intended to guarantee free transportation of a kind which the state deems to be best for the school children's welfare. And parents might refuse to risk their children to the serious danger of traffic accidents going to and from parochial schools, the approaches to which were not protected by policemen. Similarly, parents might be reluctant to permit their children to attend schools which the state had cut off from such general government services as ordinary police and fire protection, connections for sewage disposal, public highways and sidewalks. Of course, cutting off church schools from these services, so separate and so indisputably marked off from the religious function, would make it far more difficult for the schools to operate. But such is obviously not the purpose of the First Amendment. That Amendment requires the state to be a neutral in its relations with groups of religious believers and non-believers; it does not require the state to be their adversary. State power is no more to be used so as to handicap religions than it is to favor them.

This Court has said that parents may, in the discharge of their duty under state compulsory education laws, send their children to a religious rather than a public school if the school meets the secular educational requirements which the state has power to impose. . . . It appears that these parochial schools meet New Jersey's requirements. The State contributes no money to the schools. It does not support them. Its legislation, as applied, does no more than provide a general program to help parents get their children, regardless of their religion, safely and expeditiously to and from accredited schools.

The First Amendment has erected a wall between church and state. That wall must be kept high and impregnable. We could not approve the slightest breach. New Jersey has not breached it here.

Affirmed

THE ILLINOIS RELEASED TIME CASE
McCollum v. Board of Education, 333 U.S. 203.

This case relates to the power of a state to utilize its tax-supported public school system in aid of religious instruction insofar as that power may be restricted by the First and Fourteenth Amendments to the Federal Constitution.

The appellant, Vashti McCollum, began this action for mandamus against the Champaign Board of Education in the Circuit Court of Champaign County, Illinois. Her asserted interest was that of a resident and taxpayer of Champaign and of a parent whose child was then enrolled in the Champaign public schools. Illinois has a compulsory education law which, with exceptions, requires parents to send their children, aged seven to sixteen, to its tax-supported public schools where the children are to remain in attendance during the hours when the schools are regularly in session. Parents who violate this law commit a misdemeanor punishable by fine unless the children attend private or parochial schools which meet educational standards fixed by the State. District boards of education are given general supervisory powers over the use of the public school buildings within the school districts. . . .

Appellant's petition for mandamus alleged that religious teachers, employed by private religious groups, were permitted to come weekly into the school buildings during the regular hours set apart for secular teaching, and then and there for a period of thirty minutes substitute their religious teaching for the secular education provided under the compulsory education law. The petitioner charged that this joint public-school religious-group program violated the First and Fourteenth Amendments to the United States Constitution. The prayer of her petition was that the Board of Education be ordered to "adopt and enforce rules and regulations prohibiting all instruction in and teaching of religious education in all public schools in Champaign School District Number 71, . . . and in all public school houses and buildings in said district when occupied by public schools."

The board first moved to dismiss the petition on the ground that under Illinois law appellant had no standing to maintain the action. This motion was denied. An answer was then filed, which admitted that regular weekly religious instruction was given during school hours to those pupils whose parents consented and that those pupils were released temporarily from their regular secular classes for the limited purpose of attending the religious classes. The answer denied that this coordinated program of religious instruction violated the State or Federal Constitution. Much evidence was heard, findings of fact were made, after which the petition for mandamus was denied on the ground that the school's religious instruction program violated neither the federal nor state constitutional provisions invoked by the appellant. On appeal the State Supreme Court affirmed. . . .

The appellees press a motion to dismiss the appeal on several grounds, the first of which is that the judgment of the State Supreme Court does not draw in question the "validity of a statute of any State" as required by 28 U.S.C. § 344 (a). This contention rests on the admitted fact that the challenged program of religious instruction was not expressly authorized by statute. But the State Supreme Court has sustained the validity of the program on the ground that the Illinois statutes granted the board authority to establish such a program. This holding is sufficient to show that the validity of an Illinois statute was drawn in question within the meaning of 28 U.S.C. § 344 (a). . . . A second ground for the motion to dismiss is that the appellant lacks standing to maintain the action, a ground which is also without merit. . . . A third ground for the motion is that the appellant failed properly to present in the State Supreme Court her challenge that the state program violated the Federal Constitution. But in view of the express rulings of both state courts on this question, the argument cannot be successfully maintained. The motion to dismiss the appeal is denied.

Although there are disputes between the parties as to various inferences that may or may not properly be drawn from the evidence concerning the religious program, the following facts are shown by the record without dispute. In 1940 interested members of the Jewish, Roman Catholic, and a few of the Protestant faiths formed a voluntary association called the Champaign Council on Religious Education. They obtained permission from the Board of Education to offer classes in religious instruction to public school pupils in grades four to nine inclusive. Classes were made up of pupils whose parents signed printed cards requesting that their children be permitted to attend; they were held weekly, thirty minutes for the lower grades, forty-five minutes for the higher. The council employed the religious teachers at no expense to the school authorities, but the instructors were subject to the approval and supervision of the superintendent of schools. The classes were taught in three separate religious groups by Protestant teachers, Catholic priests, and a Jewish rabbi, although for the past several years there have apparently been no classes instructed in the Jewish religion. Classes were conducted in the regular classrooms of the school building. Students who did not choose to take the religious instruction were not released from public school duties; they were required to leave their classrooms and go to some other place in the school building for pursuit of their secular studies. On the other hand, students who were released from secular study for the religious instructions were required to be present at the religious classes. Reports of their presence or absence were to be made to their secular teachers.

The foregoing facts, without reference to others that appear in the record, show the use of tax-supported property for religious instruction and the close cooperation between the school authorities and the religious council in promoting religious education. The operation of the State's compulsory education system thus assists and is integrated with the program of religious instruction carried on by separate religious sects. Pupils compelled by law to go to school for secular education are released in part from their legal duty upon the condition that they attend the religious classes. This is beyond all question a utilization of the tax-established and tax-supported public school system to aid religious groups to spread their faith. And it falls squarely under the ban of the First Amendment (made applicable to the States by the Fourteenth) as we interpreted it in *Everson* v. *Board of Education,* 330 U.S. 1. There we said: "Neither a state nor the Federal Government can set up a church. Neither can pass laws which aid one religion, aid all religions, or prefer one religion over another. Neither can force or influence a person to go to or to remain away from church against his will or force him to profess a belief or disbelief in any religion. No person can be punished for entertaining or professing religious beliefs or disbeliefs, for church attendance or non-attendance. No tax in any amount, large or small, can be levied to support any religious activities or institutions, whatever they may be called, or whatever form they may adopt to teach or practice religion. Neither a state nor the Federal Government can, openly or secretly, participate in the affairs of any religious organizations or groups and *vice versa*. In the words of Jefferson, the clause against establishment of religion by law was intended to erect 'a wall of separation between church and State.' " . . . The majority in the *Everson* case, and the minority . . . agreed that the First Amendment's language, properly interpreted, had erected a wall of separation between Church and State. They disagreed as to the facts shown by the record and as to the proper application of the First Amendment's language to those facts.

Recognizing that the Illinois program is barred by the First and Fourteenth Amendments if we adhere to the views expressed both by the majority and the minority in the *Everson* case, counsel for the respondents challenge those views as dicta and urge that we reconsider and repudiate them. They argue that historically the First Amendment was intended to forbid only government preference of one religion over another, not an impartial governmental assistance of all religions. In addition they ask that we distinguish or overrule our holding in the *Everson* case that the Fourteenth Amendment made the "establishment of religion" clause of the First Amendment applicable as a prohibition against the States. After giving full consideration to the arguments presented we are unable to accept either of these contentions.

To hold that a state cannot consistently with the First and Fourteenth Amendments utilize its public school system to aid any or all religious faiths or sects in the dissemination of their doctrines and ideals does not, as counsel urge, manifest a governmental hostility to religion or religious teachings. A manifestation of such hostility would be at war with our national tradition as embodied in the First Amendment's guaranty of the free exercise of religion. For the First Amendment rests upon the premise that both religion and government can best work to achieve their lofty aims if each is left free from the other within its respective sphere. Or, as we said in the *Everson* case, the First Amendment has erected a wall between Church and State which must be kept high and impregnable.

Here not only are the State's tax-supported public school buildings used for the dissemination of religious doctrines. The State also affords sectarian groups an invaluable aid in that it helps to provide pupils for their religious classes through use of the State's compulsory public school machinery. This is not separation of Church and State.

The cause is reversed and remanded to the State Supreme Court for proceedings not inconsistent with this opinion.

Reversed and remanded

THE NEW YORK RELEASED TIME CASE
Zorach v. Clauson, 343 U.S. 306.

New York City has a program which permits its public schools to release students during the school day so that they may leave the school building and school grounds and go to religious centers for religious instruction or devotional exercises. A student is released on written request of his parents. Those not released stay in the classrooms. The churches make weekly reports to the schools, sending a list of children who have been released from public school but who have not reported for religious instruction.

This "released time" program involves neither religious instruction in public school classrooms nor the expenditure of public funds. All costs, including the application blanks, are paid by the religious organizations. The case is therefore unlike *McCollum* v. *Board of Education,* 333 U.S. 203, which involved a "released time" program from Illinois. In that case the classrooms were turned over to religious instructors. We accordingly held that the program violated the First Amendment which (by reason of the Fourteenth Amendment) prohibits the states from establishing religion or prohibiting its free exercise.

Appellants, who are taxpayers and residents of New York City and whose children attend its public schools, challenge the present law, contending it is in essence not different from the one involved in the *McCollum* case. Their argument, stated elaborately in various ways, reduces itself to this: the weight and influence of the school is put behind a program for religious instruction; public school teachers police it, keeping tab on students who are released; the classroom activities come to a halt while the students who are released for religious instruction are on leave; the school is a crutch on which the churches are leaning for support in their religious training; without the cooperation of the schools this "released time" program, like the one in the *McCollum* case, would be futile and ineffective. The New York Court of Appeals sustained the law against this claim of unconstitutionality. . . .

The briefs and arguments are replete with data bearing on the merits of this type of "released time" program. Views *pro* and *con* are expressed, based on practical experience with these programs and with their implications. We do not stop to summarize these materials nor to burden the opinion with an analysis of them. For they involve considerations not germane to the narrow constitutional issue presented. They largely concern the wisdom of the system, its efficiency from an educational point of view, and the political considerations which have motivated its adoption or rejection in some communities. Those matters are of no concern here, since our problem reduces itself to whether New York by this system has either prohibited the "free exercise" of religion or has made a law "respecting an establishment of religion" within the meaning of the First Amendment.

It takes obtuse reasoning to inject any issue of the "free exercise" of religion into the present case. No one is forced to go to the religious classroom and no religious exercise or instruction is brought to the classrooms of the public schools. A student need not take religious instruction. He is left to his own desires as to the manner or time of his religious devotions, if any.

There is a suggestion that the system involves the use of coercion to get public school students into religious classrooms. There is no evidence in the record before us that supports that conclusion. The present record indeed tells us that the school authorities are neutral in this regard and do no more than release students whose parents so request. If in fact coercion were used if it were established that any one or more teachers were using their office to persuade or force students to take the religious instruction, a wholly different case would be presented. Hence we put aside that claim of coercion both as respects the "free exercise" of religion and "an establishment of religion" within the meaning of the First Amendment.

Moreover, apart from that claim of coercion, we do not see how New York by this type of "released time" program has made a law respecting an establishment of religion within the meaning of the First Amendment. There is much talk of the separation of Church and State in the history of the Bill of Rights and in the decisions clustering around the First Amendment. . . . There cannot be the slightest doubt that the First Amendment reflects the philosophy that Church and State should be separated. And so far as interference with the "free exercise" of religion and an "establishment" of religion are concerned, the separation must be complete and unequivocal. The First Amendment within the scope of its coverage permits no exception; the prohibition is absolute. The First Amendment, however, does not say that in every and all respects there shall be a separation of Church and State. Rather, it studiously defines the manner, the specific ways, in which there shall be no concert or union or dependency one on the other. That is the common sense of the matter. Otherwise the state and religion would be aliens to each other—hostile, suspicious, and even unfriendly. Churches could not be required to pay even property taxes. Municipalities would not be permitted to render police or fire protection to religious groups. Policemen who helped parishioners into their places of worship would violate the Constitution. Prayers in our legislative halls; the appeals to the Almighty in the messages of the Chief Executive; the proclamations making Thanksgiving Day a holiday; "so help me God" in our courtroom oaths—these and all other references to the Almighty that run through our laws, our public rituals, our ceremonies would be flouting the First Amendment. A fastidious atheist or agnostic could even object to the supplication with which the Court opens each session: "God save the United States and this Honorable Court."

We would have to press the concept of separation of Church and State to these extremes to condemn the present law on constitutional grounds. The nullification of this law would have wide and profound effects. A Catholic student applies to his teacher for permission to leave the school during hours on a Holy Day of Obligation to attend a mass. A Jewish student asks his teacher for permission to be excused for Yom Kippur. A Protestant wants the afternoon off for a family baptismal ceremony. In each case the teacher requires parental consent in writing. In each case the teacher, in order to make sure the student is not a truant, goes further and requires a report from the priest, the rabbi, or the minister. The teacher in other words cooperates in a religious program to the extent of making it possible for her students to participate in it. Whether she does it occasionally for a few students, regularly for one, or pursuant to a systematized program designed to further the religious needs of all the students does not alter the character of the act.

We are a religious people whose institutions presuppose a Supreme Being. We guarantee the freedom to worship as one chooses. We make room for as wide a variety of beliefs and creeds as the spiritual needs of man deem necessary. We sponsor an attitude on the part of government that shows no partiality to any one group and that lets each flourish according to the zeal of its adherents and the appeal of its dogma. When the state encourages religious instruction or cooperates with religious authorities by adjusting the schedule of public events to sectarian needs, it follows the best of our traditions. For it then respects the religious nature of our people and accommodates the public service to their spiritual needs. To hold that it may not would be to find in the Constitution a requirement that the government show a callous indifference to religious groups. That would be preferring those who believe in no religion over those who do believe. Government may not finance religious groups nor undertake religious instruction nor blend secular and sectarian education nor use secular institutions to force one or some religion on any person. But we find no constitutional requirement which makes it necessary for government to be hostile to religion and to throw its weight against efforts to widen the effective scope of religious influence. The government must be neutral when it comes to competition between sects. It may not thrust any sect on any person. It may not make a religious observance compulsory. It may not coerce anyone to attend church, to observe a religious holiday, or to take religious instruction. But it can close its doors or suspend its operations as to those who want to repair to their religious sanctuary for worship or instruction. No more than that is undertaken here.

This program may be unwise and improvident from an educational or a community viewpoint. That appeal is made to us on a theory, previously advanced, that each case must be decided on the basis of "our own prepossessions." . . . Our individual preferences, however, are not the constitutional standard. The constitutional standard is the separation of Church and State. The problem, like many problems in constitutional law, is one of degree. . . .

In the *McCollum* case the classrooms were used for religious instruction and the force of the public school was used to promote that instruction. Here, as we have said, the public schools do no more than accommodate their schedules to a program of outside religious instruction. We follow the *McCollum* case. But we cannot expand it to cover the present released time program unless separation of Church and State means that public institutions can make no adjustments of their schedules to accommodate the religious needs of the people. We cannot read into the Bill of Rights such a philosophy of hostility to religion.

Affirmed

Racial Segregation in Schools

The Missouri case, the Sweatt case, the McLaurin case, and the Integration cases.

THE MISSOURI CASE

Missouri ex rel. Gaines v. Canada, 305 U.S. 337.

This case is one of a series in which the Court narrowed its concept of separate but equal facilities until in 1954, in the integration cases, the concept was eliminated as applicable to education. The decision in the Missouri Case reads in part:

Petitioner Lloyd Gaines, a negro, was refused admission to the School of Law at the State University of Missouri. Asserting that this refusal constituted a denial by the State of the equal protection of the laws in violation of the Fourteenth Amendment of the Federal Constitution, petitioner brought this action for mandamus to compel the curators of the University to admit him. . . .

Petitioner is a citizen of Missouri. In August, 1935, he was graduated with the degree of Bachelor of Arts at the Lincoln University, an institution maintained by the State of Missouri for the higher education of negroes. That University has no law school. Upon the filing of his application for admission to the law school of the University of Missouri, the registrar advised him to communicate with the president of Lincoln University and the latter directed petitioner's attention to § 9622 of the Revised Statutes of Missouri (1929), providing as follows:

"Sec. 9622. *May arrange for attendance at university of any adjacent state —Tuition fees.*—Pending the full development of the Lincoln University, the board of curators shall have the authority to arrange for the attendance of negro residents of the state of Missouri at the university of any adjacent state to take any course or to study any subjects provided for at the state university of Missouri and which are not taught at the Lincoln University and to pay the reasonable tuition fees for such attendance; provided that whenever the board of curators shall deem it advisable they shall have the power to open any necessary school or department."

We must regard the question whether the provision for the legal education in other states of negroes resident in Missouri is sufficient to satisfy the constitutional requirement of equal protection, as the pivot upon which this case turns.

The state court stresses the advantages that are afforded by the law schools of the adjacent states, Kansas, Nebraska, Iowa and Illinois, which admit non-resident negroes. . . .

We think that these matters are beside the point. The basic consideration is not as to what sort of opportunities other states provide, or whether they are as good as those in Missouri, but as to what opportunities Missouri itself furnishes to white students and denies to negroes solely upon the ground of color. The admissibility of laws separating the races in the enjoyment of privileges afforded by the state rests wholly upon the quality of the privileges which the laws give to the separated groups within the state. The question here is not of a duty of the state to supply legal training, or of the quality of the training which it does supply, but of its duty when it provides such training to furnish it to the residents of the state upon the basis of an equality of right. By the operation of the laws of Missouri a privilege has been created for white law students which is denied to negroes by reason of their race. The white resident is afforded legal education within the state; the negro resident having the same qualifications is refused it there and must go outside the state to obtain it. That is a denial of the equality of legal right to the enjoyment of the privilege which the state has set up, and the provision for the payment of tuition fees in another state does not remove the discrimination.

The equal protection of the laws is "a pledge of the protection of equal laws" . . . Manifestly, the obligation of the state to give the protection of equal laws can be performed only where its laws operate, that is, within its own jurisdiction. It is there that the equality of legal right must be maintained. . . . We find it impossible to conclude that what otherwise would be an unconstitutional discrimination, with respect to the legal right to the enjoyment of opportunities within the state, can be justified by requiring resort to opportunities elsewhere. That resort may mitigate the inconvenience of the discrimination but cannot serve to validate it.

Nor can we regard the fact that there is but a limited demand in Missouri for the legal education of negroes as excusing the discrimination in favor of whites. . . .

Here, petitioner's right was a personal one. It was as an individual that he was entitled to the equal protection of the laws, and the state was bound to furnish him within its borders facilities for legal education substantially equal to those which the state there afforded for persons of the white race, whether or not other negroes sought the same opportunity.

It is urged, however, that the provision for tuition outside the state is a temporary one,—that it is intended to operate merely pending the establishment of a law department for negroes at Lincoln University. While in that sense the discrimination may be termed temporary, it may neverthless continue for an indefinite period by reason of the discretion given to the curators of Lincoln University and the alternative of arranging for tuition in other states, as permitted by the state law as construed by the state court, so long as the curators find it unnecessary and impracticable to provide facilities for the legal instruction of negroes within the state. In that view, we cannot regard the discrimination as excused by what is called its temporary character. . . .

We are of the opinion that . . . petitioner was entitled to be admitted to the law school of the state university in the absence of other and proper provision for his legal training within the state. . . .

Reversed

THE SWEATT CASE
Sweatt v. Painter, 339 U.S. 629.

The decision of the Court reads in part:

This case and *McLaurin v. Oklahoma State Regents* . . . present different aspects of this general question: To what extent does the Equal Protection Clause of the Fourteenth Amendment limit the power of a state to distinguish between students of different races in professional and graduate education in a state university? Broader issues have been urged for our consideration but we adhere to the principle of deciding constitutional questions only in the context of the particular case before the Court. . . .

In the instant case, petitioner filed an application for admission to the University of Texas Law School for the February, 1946, term. His application was rejected solely because he is a Negro. Petitioner thereupon brought this suit for mandamus against the appropriate school officials, respondents here, to compel his admission. At that time, there was no law school in Texas which admitted Negroes.

The State trial court recognized that the action of the State in denying petitioner the opportunity to gain a legal education while granting it to others deprived him of the equal protection of the laws guaranteed by the Fourteenth Amendment. The Court did not grant the relief requested, however, but continued the case for six months to allow the State to supply substantially equal facilities. At the expiration of the six months, in December, 1946, the court denied the writ on the showing that the authorized university officials had adopted an order calling for the opening of a law school for Negroes the following February. While petitioner's appeal was pending, such a school was made available, but petitioner refused to register therein. The Texas Court of Civil Appeals set aside the trial court's judgment and ordered the cause "remanded generally to the trial court for further proceedings without prejudice to the right of any party to this suit." . . .

The University of Texas Law School, from which petitioner was excluded, was staffed by a faculty of sixteen full-time and three part-time professors, some of whom are nationally recognized authorities in their field. Its student body numbered 850. The library contained over 65,000 volumes. Among the other facilities available to the students were a law review, moot court facilities, scholarship funds, and Order of the Coif affiliation. The school's alumni occupy the most distinguished positions in the private practice of the law and in the public life of the State. It may properly be considered one of the nation's ranking law schools.

The law school for Negroes which was to have opened in February, 1947, would have had no independent faculty or library. The teaching was to be carried on by four members of the University of Texas Law School faculty, who were to maintain their offices at the University of Texas while teaching at both institutions. Few of the 10,000 volumes ordered for the library had arrived; nor was there any full-time librarian. The school lacked accreditation.

Since the trial of this case, respondents report the opening of a law school at the Texas State University for Negroes. It is apparently on the road to full accreditation. It has a faculty of five full-time professors; a student body of 23; a library of some 16,500 volumes serviced by a full-time staff; a practice court and legal aid association; and one alumnus who has become a member of the Texas Bar.

Whether the University of Texas Law School is compared with the original or the new law school for Negroes, we cannot find substantial equality in the educational opportunities offered white and Negro law students by the State. In terms of number of the faculty, variety of courses and opportunity for specialization, size of the student body, scope of the library, availability of law review and similar activities, the University of Texas Law School is superior. What is more important, the University of Texas Law School possesses to a far greater degree those qualities which are incapable of objective measurements but which made for greatness in a law school. Such qualities, to name but a few, include reputation of the faculty, experience of the administration, position and influence of the alumni, standing in the community, traditions and prestige. It is difficult to believe that one who had a free choice between these law schools would consider the question close.

Moreover, although the law is a highly learned profession, we are well aware that it is an intensely practical one. The law school, the proving ground for legal learning and practice, cannot be effective in isolation from the individuals and institutions with which the law interacts. Few students and no one who has practiced law would choose to study in an academic vacuum, removed from the interplay of ideas and the exchange of views with which the law is concerned. The law school to which Texas is willing to admit petitioner excludes from its student body members of the racial groups which number 85% of the population of the State and include most of the lawyers, witnesses, jurors, judges and other officials with whom petitioner will inevitably be dealing when he becomes a member of the Texas Bar. With such a substantial and significant segment of society excluded, we cannot conclude that the education offered petitioner is substantially equal to that which he would receive if admitted to the University of Texas Law School.

It may be argued that excluding petitioner from that school is no different from excluding white students from the new law school. This contention overlooks realities. . . .

In accordance with these cases, petitioner may claim his full constitutional right: legal education equivalent to that offered by the State to students of other races. Such education is not available to him in a separate law school as offered by the State. We cannot, therefore, agree with respondents that the doctrine of *Plessy v. Ferguson,* 163 U.S. 537 (1896), requires affirmance of the judgment below. Nor need we reach petitioner's contention that *Plessy v. Ferguson* should be reexamined in the light of contemporary knowledge respecting the purposes of the Fourteenth Amendment and the effects of racial segregation. . . .

We hold that the Equal Protection Clause of the Fourteenth Amendment requires that petitioner be admitted to the University of Texas Law School. The judgment is reversed and the cause is remanded for proceedings not inconsistent with this opinion.

THE McLAURIN CASE
McLaurin v. Oklahoma State Regents, 339 U.S. 637.

The decision of the Court reads in part:

In this case, we are faced with the question whether a state may, after admitting a student to graduate instruction in its state university, afford him different treatment from other students solely because of his race. . . .

In the interval between the decision of the court below and the hearing in this Court, the treatment afforded appellant was altered. For some time, the section of the classroom in which appellant sat was surrounded by a rail on which there was a sign stating, "Reserved For Colored", but these have been removed. He is now assigned to a seat in the classroom in a row specified for colored students; he is assigned to a table in the library on the main floor; and he is permitted to eat at the same time in the cafeteria as other students although here again he is assigned to a special table.

It is said that the separation imposed by the State in his case is in form merely nominal. McLaurin uses the same classroom, library and cafeteria as students of other races; there is no indication that the seats to which he is assigned in these rooms have any disadvantage of location. He may wait in line in the cafeteria and there stand and talk with his fellow students, but while he eats he must remain apart.

These restrictions were obviously imposed in order to comply, as nearly as could be, with the statutory requirements of Oklahoma. But they signify that the State, in administering the facilities it affords for professional and graduate study, sets McLaurin apart from the other students. The result is that appellant is handicapped in his pursuit of effective graduate instruction. Such restrictions impair and inhibit his ability to study, to engage in discussions and exchange views with other students, and, in general, to learn his profession.

Our society grows increasingly complex, and our need for trained leaders increases correspondingly. Appellant's case represents, perhaps, the epitome of that need, for he is attempting to obtain an advanced degree in education, to become, by definition, a leader and trainer of others. Those who will come under his guidance and influence must be directly affected by the education he receives. Their own education and development will necessarily suffer to the extent that his training is unequal to that of his classmates. State-imposed restrictions which produce such inequalities cannot be sustained.

It may be argued that appellant will be in no better position when these restrictions are removed, for he may still be set apart by his fellow students. This we think irrelevant. There is a vast difference—a Constitutional difference—between restrictions imposed by the state which prohibit the intellectual commingling of students, and the refusal of individuals to commingle where the state presents no such bar. . . .

The removal of the state restrictions will not necessarily abate individual and group predilections, prejudices and choices. But at the very least, the state will not be depriving appellant of the opportunity to secure acceptance by his fellow students on his own merits.

We conclude that the conditions under which this appellant is required to receive his education deprive him of his personal and present right to the equal protection of the laws. See *Sweatt* v. *Painter,* 339 U.S. We hold that under these circumstances the Fourteenth Amendment precludes differences in treatment by the state based upon race. Appellant, having been admitted to a state-supported graduate school, must receive the same treatment at the hands of the state as students of other races. . . .

Reversed

THE INTEGRATION CASES

Brown v. Board of Education of Topeka, 347 U.S. 483.

These cases come to us from the States of Kansas, South Carolina, Virginia, and Delaware. They are premised on different facts and different local conditions, but a common legal question justifies their consideration together in this consolidated opinion.

In each of these cases, minors of the Negro race, through their legal representatives, seek the aid of the courts in obtaining admission to the public schools of their community on a nonsegregated basis. In each instance, they had been denied admission to schools attended by white children under laws requiring or permitting segregation according to race. This segregation was alleged to deprive the plaintiffs of the equal protection of the laws under the Fourteenth Amendment. In each of the cases other than the Delaware case, a three-judged federal district court denied relief to the plaintiffs on the so-called "separate but equal" doctrine announced by this Court in *Plessy* v. *Ferguson,* 163 U.S. 537. Under that doctrine, equality of treatment is accorded when the races are provided substantially equal facilities, even though these facilities be separate. In the Delaware case, the Supreme Court of Delaware adhered to that doctrine, but ordered that the plaintiffs be admitted to the white schools because of their superiority to the Negro schools.

The plaintiffs contend that segregated public schools are not "equal" and cannot be made "equal," and that hence they are deprived of the equal protection of the laws. Because of the obvious importance of the question presented, the Court took jurisdiction. Argument was heard in the 1952 Term, and reargument was heard this Term on certain questions propounded by the Court.

Reargument was largely devoted to the circumstances surrounding the adoption of the Fourteenth Amendment in 1868. It covered exhaustively consideration of the Amendment in Congress, ratification by the states, then existing practices in racial segregation, and the views of proponents and opponents of the Amendment. This discussion and our own investigation convince us that, although these sources cast some light, it is not enough to resolve the problem with which we are faced. At best, they are inconclusive. The most avid proponents of the post-War Amendments undoubtedly intended them to remove all legal distinctions among "all persons born or naturalized in the United States." Their opponents, just as certainly, were antagonistic to both the letter and the spirit of the Amendments and wished them to have the most limited effect. What others in Congress and the state legislature had in mind cannot be determined with any degree of certainty.

An additional reason for the inconclusive nature of the Amendment's history, with respect to segregated schools, is the status of public education at that time. In the South, the movement toward free common schools, supported by general taxation, had not yet taken hold. Education of white children was largely in the hands of private groups. Education of Negroes was almost nonexistent, and practically all of the race were illiterate. In fact, any education of Negroes was forbidden by law in some states. Today, in contrast, many Negroes have achieved outstanding success in the arts and sciences as well as in the business and professional world. It is true that public school education at the time of the Amendment had advanced further in the North, but the effect of the Amendment on Northern States was generally ignored in the congressional debates. Even in the North, the conditions of public education did not approximate those existing today. The curriculum was usually rudimentary; ungraded schools were common in rural areas; the school term was but three months a year in many states; and compulsory school attendance was virtually unknown. As a consequence, it is not surprising that there should be so little in the history of the Fourteenth Amendment relating to its intended effect on public education.

In the first cases in this Court construing the Fourteenth Amendment, decided shortly after its adoption, the Court interpreted it as proscribing all state-imposed discriminations against the Negro race. The doctrine of "separate but equal" did not make its appearance in this Court until 1896 in the case of *Plessy* v. *Ferguson*, . . . involving not education but transportation. American courts have since labored with the doctrine for over half a century. In this court, there have been six cases involving the "separate but equal" doctrine in the field of public education. In *Cumming* v. *County Board of Education*, 175 U.S. 528, and *Gong Lum* v. *Rice*, 275 U.S. 78, the validity of the doctrine itself was not challenged. In more recent cases, all on the graduate school level, inequality was found in that specific benefits enjoyed by white students were denied to Negro students of the same educational qualifications. . . . In none of these cases was it necessary to reexamine the doctrine to grant relief to the Negro plaintiff. And in *Sweatt* v.

Painter, . . . the Court expressly reserved decision on the question whether *Plessy* v. *Ferguson* should be held inapplicable to public education.

In the instant cases, that question is directly presented. Here, unlike *Sweatt* v. *Painter,* there are findings below that the Negro and white schools involved have been equalized, or are being equalized, with respect to buildings, curricula, qualifications and salaries of teachers, and other "tangible" factors. Our decision, therefore, cannot turn on merely a comparison of these tangible factors in the Negro and white schools involved in each of the cases. We must look instead to the effect of segregation itself on public education.

In approaching this problem, we cannot turn the clock back to 1868 when the Amendment was adopted, or even to 1896 when *Plessy* v. *Ferguson* was written. We must consider public education in the light of its full development and its present place in American life throughout the Nation. Only in this way can it be determined if segregation in public schools deprives these plaintiffs of the equal protection of the laws.

Today, education is perhaps the most important function of state and local governments. Compulsory school attendance laws and the great expenditures for education both demonstrate our recognition of the importance of education to our democratic society. It is required in the performance of our most basic public responsibilities, even service in the armed forces. It is the very foundation of good citizenship. Today it is a principal instrument in awakening the child to cultural values, in preparing him for later professional training, and in helping him to adjust normally to his environment. In these days, it is doubtful that any child may reasonably be expected to succeed in life if he is denied the opportunity of an education. Such an opportunity, where the state has undertaken to provide it, is a right which must be made available to all on equal terms.

We come then to the question presented: Does segregation of children in public schools solely on the basis of race, even though the physical facilities and other "tangible" factors may be equal, deprive the children of the minority group of equal educational opportunities? We believe that it does.

In *Sweatt* v. *Painter,* . . . in finding that a segregated law school for Negroes could not provide them equal educational opportunities, this Court relied in large part on "those qualities which are incapable of objective measurement but which make for greatness in a law school." In *McLaurin* v. *Oklahoma State Regents,* . . . the Court, in requiring that a Negro admitted to a white graduate school be treated like all other students, again resorted to intangible considerations: ". . . his ability to study, to engage in discussions and exchange views with other students, and, in general, to learn his profession." Such considerations apply with added force to children in grade and high schools. To separate them from others of similar age and qualifications solely because of their race generates a feeling of inferiority as to their status in the community that may affect their hearts and minds in a way unlikely ever to be undone. The effect of this separation on their educational opportunities was well stated by a finding in the Kansas case by a court which nevertheless felt compelled to rule against the Negro plaintiffs: "Segregation of white and colored children in public schools has a detrimental effect upon the colored children. The impact is greater when it has the sanction of the law; for the policy of separating the races is usually interpreted as denoting the inferiority of the negro group. A sense of inferiority affects the motivation of a child to learn. Segregation with the sanction of law, therefore, has a tendency to [retard] the educational and mental development of negro children and to deprive them of some of the benefits they would receive in a racial[ly] integrated school system." Whatever may have been the extent of psychological knowledge at the time of *Plessy* v. *Ferguson,* this finding is amply supported by modern authority. Any language in *Plessy* v. *Ferguson* contrary to this finding is rejected.

We conclude that in the field of public education the doctrine of "separate but equal" has no place. Separate educational facilities are inherently unequal. Therefore, we hold the plaintiffs and others similarly situated for whom the actions have been brought are, by reason of the segregation complained of, deprived of the equal protection of the laws guaranteed by the Fourteenth Amendment. This disposition makes unnecessary any discussion whether such segregation also violates the Due Process Clause of the Fourteenth Amendment.

Because these are class actions, because of the wide applicability of this decision, and because of the great variety of local conditions, the formulation of decrees in these cases presents problems of considerable complexity. On reargument, the consideration of appropriate relief was necessarily subordinated to the primary question—the constitutionality of segregation in public education. We have now announced that such segregation is a denial of the equal protection of the laws. In order that we may have the full assistance of the parties in formulating decrees, the cases will be restored to the docket, and the parties are requested to present further argument on Questions 4 and 5 previously propounded by the Court for the reargument this Term. The Attorney General of the United States is again invited to participate. The Attorneys General of the states requiring or permitting segregation in public education will also be permitted to appear as *amici curiae* upon request to do so by September 15, 1954, and submission of briefs by October 1, 1954.

It is so ordered.

Appendix B

NATIONAL DEFENSE EDUCATION ACT OF 1958
Public Law 85–864
85th Congress, H.R. 13247
September 2, 1958

AN ACT

To strengthen the national defense and to encourage and assist in the expansion and improvement of educational programs to meet critical national needs; and for other purposes.

Be it enacted by the Senate and House of Representatives of the United States of America in Congress assembled, That this Act, divided into titles and sections according to the following table of contents, may be cited as the "National Defense Education Act of 1958."

TABLE OF CONTENTS

TITLE I—GENERAL PROVISIONS

FINDINGS AND DECLARATION OF POLICY

SEC. 101. The Congress hereby finds and declares that the security of the Nation requires the fullest development of the mental resources and technical skills of its young men and women. The present emergency demands that additional and more adequate educational opportunities be made available. The defense of this Nation depends upon the mastery of modern techniques developed from complex scientific principles. It depends as well upon the discovery and development of new principles, new techniques, and new knowledge.

We must increase our efforts to identify and educate more of the talent of our Nation. This requires programs that will give assurance that no student of ability will be denied an opportunity for higher education because of financial need; will correct as rapidly as possible the existing imbalances in our educational programs which have led to an insufficient proportion of our population educated in science, mathematics, and modern foreign languages and trained in technology.

The Congress reaffirms the principle and declares that the States and local communities have and must retain control over and primary responsibility for public education. The national interest requires, however, that the Federal Government give assistance to education for programs which are important to our defense.

To meet the present educational emergency requires additional effort at all levels of government. It is therefore the purpose of this Act to provide substantial assistance in various forms to individuals, and to States and their subdivisions, in order to insure trained manpower of sufficient quality and quantity to meet the national defense needs of the United States.

FEDERAL CONTROL OF EDUCATION PROHIBITED

SEC. 102. Nothing contained in this Act shall be construed to authorize any department, agency, officer, or employee of the United States to exercise any direction, supervision, or control over the curriculum, program of instruction, administration, or personnel of any educational institution or school system.

DEFINITIONS

SEC. 103. As used in this Act—

(a) The term "State" means a State, Alaska, Hawaii, Puerto Rico, the District of Columbia, the Canal Zone, Guam, or the Virgin Islands, except that as used in sections 302 and 502, such term does not include Alaska, Hawaii, Puerto Rico, the Canal Zone, Guam, or the Virgin Islands.

(b) The term "institution of higher education" means an educational institution in any State which (1) admits as regular students only persons having a certificate of graduation from a school providing secondary education, or the recognized equivalent of such a certificate, (2) is legally authorized within such State to provide a program of education beyond secondary education, (3) provides an educational program for which it awards a bachelor's degree or provides not less than a two-year program which is acceptable for full credit toward such a degree, (4) is a public or other nonprofit institution, and (5) is accredited by a nationally recognized accrediting agency or association or, if not so accredited, is an institution whose credits are accepted, on transfer, by not less than three institutions which are so accredited, for credit on the same basis as if transferred from an institution so accredited. For purposes of title II, such term includes any private business school or technical institution which meets the provisions of clauses (1), (2), (3), (4), and (5). For purposes of this subsection, the Commissioner shall publish a list of nationally recognized accrediting agencies or associations which he determines to be reliable authority as to the quality of training offered.

(c) The term "Commissioner" means the Commissioner of Education.

(d) The term "Secretary" means the Secretary of Health, Education, and Welfare.

(e) The term "State educational agency" means the State board of education or other agency or officer primarily responsible for the State supervision of public elementary and secondary schools, or, if there is no such officer or agency, an officer or agency designated by the governor or by State law.

(f) The term "school-age population" means that part of the population which is between the ages of five and seventeen, both inclusive, and such school-age population for the several States shall be determined by the Commissioner on the basis of the population between such ages for the most recent year for which satisfactory data are available from the Department of Commerce.

(g) The term "elementary school" means a school which provides elementary education, as determined under State law.

(h) The term "secondary school" means a school which provides secondary education, as determined under State law, except that it does not include any education provided beyond grade 12. For the purposes of sections 301 through 304, the term "secondary school" may include a public junior college, as determined under State law.

(i) The term "public" as applied to any school or institution does not include a school or institution of any agency of the United States.

(j) The term "nonprofit", as applied to a school or institution, means a school or institution owned and operated by one or more nonprofit corporations or associations no part of the net earnings of which inures, or may lawfully inure, to the benefit of any private shareholder or individual, and, for purposes of part A of title V, includes a school of any agency of the United States.

(k) The term "local educational agency" means a board of education or other legally constituted local school authority having administrative control and direction of public elementary or secondary schools in a city, county, township, school district, or political subdivision in a State.

TITLE II—LOANS TO STUDENTS IN INSTITUTIONS OF HIGHER EDUCATION

APPROPRIATIONS AUTHORIZED

SEC. 201. For the purpose of enabling the Commissioner to stimulate and assist in the establishment at institutions of higher education of funds for the making of low-interest loans to students in need thereof to pursue their courses of study in such institutions, there are hereby authorized to be appropriated $47,500,000 for the fiscal year ending June 30, 1959, $75,000,-000 for the fiscal year ending June 30, 1960, $82,500,000 for the fiscal year ending June 30, 1961, $90,000,000 for the fiscal year ending June 30, 1962, and such sums for the fiscal year ending June 30, 1963, and each of the three succeeding fiscal years as may be necessary to enable students who have received a loan for any school year ending prior to July 1, 1962, to continue or complete their education. Sums appropriated under this section for any fiscal year shall be available, in accordance with agreements between the Commissioner and institutions of higher education, for payment of Federal capital contributions which, together with contributions from the institutions, shall be used for establishment and maintenance of student loan funds.

ALLOTMENTS TO STATES

SEC. 202. (a) From the sums appropriated pursuant to section 201 for any fiscal year ending prior to July 1, 1962, the Commissioner shall allot to each State an amount which bears the same ratio to the amount so appropriated as the number of persons enrolled on a full-time basis in institutions of higher education in such State bears to the total number of persons enrolled on a full-time basis in institutions of higher education in all of the States. The number of persons enrolled on a full-time basis in institutions of higher education for purposes of this section shall be determined by the Commissioner for the most recent year for which satisfactory data are available to him.

(b) Sums appropriated pursuant to section 201 for any fiscal year ending after June 30, 1962, shall be allotted among the States in such manner as the Commissioner determines to be necessary to carry out the purpose for which such amounts are appropriated.

PAYMENT OF FEDERAL CAPITAL CONTRIBUTIONS

SEC. 203. (a) The Commissioner shall from time to time set dates by which institutions of higher education in a State must file applications for Federal capital contributions from the allotment of such State. In the event the total requested in such applications, which are made by institutions with which he has agreements under this title and which meet the requirements established in regulations of the Commissioner, exceeds the amount of the allotment of such State available for such purpose, the Federal capital contribution from such allotment to each such institution shall bear the same ratio to the amount requested in its application as the amount of such allotment available for such purpose bears to the total requested in all such applications. In the event the total requested in such applications which are made by institutions in a State is less than the amount of the allotment of such State available for such purpose, the Commissioner may reallot the remaining amount from time to time, on such date or dates as the Commissioner may fix, to other States in proportion to the original allotments to such States under section 202 for such year. The Federal capital contribution to an institution shall be paid to it from time to time in such installments as the Commissioner determines will not result in unnecessary accumulations in the student loan fund established under its agreement under this title.

(b) In no case may the total of such Federal capital contributions to any institution of higher education for any fiscal year exceed $250,000.

CONDITIONS OF AGREEMENTS

SEC. 204. An agreement with any institution of higher education for Federal capital contributions by the Commissioner under this title shall—

(1) provide for establishment of a student loan fund by such institution;

(2) provide for deposit in such fund of (A) the Federal capital contributions, (B) an amount, equal to not less than one-ninth of such Federal contributions, contributed by such institutions, (C) collections of principal and interest on student loans made from such fund, and (D) any other earnings of the fund;

(3) provide that such student loan fund shall be used only for loans to students in accordance with such agreement, for capital distributions as provided in this title, and for costs of litigation arising in connection with the collection of any loan from the fund or interest on such loan;

(4) provide that in the selection of students to receive loans from such student loan fund special consideration shall be given to (A) students with a superior academic background who express a desire to teach in elementary or secondary schools, and (B) students whose academic background indicates a superior capacity or preparation in science, mathematics, engineering, or a modern foreign language; and

(5) include such other provisions as may be necessary to protect the financial interest of the United States and promote the purposes of this title and as are agreed to by the Commissioner and the institution.

TERMS OF LOANS

SEC. 205. (a) The total of the loans for any fiscal year to any student made by institutions of higher education from loan funds established pursuant to agreements under this title may not exceed $1,000, and the total for all years to any student from such funds may not exceed $5,000.

(b) Loans from any such loan fund to any student by any institution of higher education shall be made on such terms and conditions as the institution may determine; subject, however, to such conditions, limitations, and requirements as the Commissioner may prescribe (by regulation or in the agreement with the institution) with a view to preventing impairment of the capital of the student loan fund to the maximum extent practicable in the light of the objective of enabling the student to complete his course of study; and except that—

(1) such a loan shall be made only to a student who (A) is in need of the amount of the loan to pursue a course of the study at such institution, and (B) is capable, in the opinion of the institution, of maintaining good standing in such course of study, and (C) has been accepted for enrollment as a full-time student at such institution or, in the case of a student already attending such institution, is in good standing and in full-time attendance there either as an undergraduate or graduate student;

(2) such a loan shall be evidenced by a note or other written agreement which provides for repayment of the principal amount, together with interest thereon, in equal annual installments, or, if the borrower so requests, in graduated periodic installments (determined in accordance with such schedules as may be approved by the Commissioner), over a period beginning one year after the date on which the borrower ceases to pursue a full-time course of study at an institution of higher education and ending eleven years after such date, except that (A) interest shall not accrue on any such loan, and periodic installments need not be paid, during any period (i) during which the borrower is pursuing a full-time course of study at an institution of higher education, or (ii) not in excess of three years during which the borrower is a member of the Armed Forces of the United States, (B) any such period shall not be included in determining the ten-year period during which the repayment must be completed, (C) such ten-year period may also be extended for good cause determined in accordance with regulations of the Commissioner, and (D) the borrower may at his option accelerate repayment of the whole or any part of such loan;

(3) not to exceed 50 per centum of any such loan (plus interest) shall be canceled for service as a full-time teacher in a public elementary or secondary school in a State, at the rate of 10 per centum of the amount of such loan plus interest thereon, which was unpaid on the first day of such service, for each complete academic year of such service;

(4) such a loan shall bear interest, on the unpaid balance of the loan, at the rate of 3 per centum per annum except that no interest shall accrue before the date on which repayment of the loan is to begin;

(5) such a loan shall be made without security and without endorsement except that, if the borrower is a minor and the note or other evidence of obligation executed by him would not, under the applicable

law, create a binding obligation, either security or endorsement may be required;

(6) the liability to repay any such loan shall be canceled upon the death of the borrower, or if he becomes permanently and totally disabled as determined in accordance with regulations of the Commissioner;

(7) such a loan by an institution for any year shall be made in such installments as may be provided in regulations of the Commissioner or the agreement with the institution under this title and, upon notice to the Commissioner by the institution that any recipient of a loan is failing to maintain satisfactory standing, any or all further installments of his loan shall be withheld, as may be appropriate; and

(8) no note or other evidence of such a loan may be transferred or assigned by the institution of higher education making the loan except, upon the transfer of the borrower to another institution of higher education participating in the program under this title (or, if not participating, is eligible to do so and is approved by the Commissioner for such purpose), to such institution.

(c) An agreement under this title for payment of Federal capital contributions shall include provisions designed to make loans from the student loan fund established pursuant to such agreement reasonably available (to the extent of the available funds in such fund) to all eligible students in such institution in need thereof.

DISTRIBUTIONS OF ASSETS FROM STUDENT LOAN FUNDS

SEC. 206. (a) After June 30, 1966, and not later than September 30, 1966, there shall be a capital distribution of the balance of the student loan fund established under this title by each institution of higher education as follows

(1) The Commissioner shall first be paid an amount which bears the same ratio to the balance in such fund at the close of June 30, 1966, as the total amount of the Federal capital contributions to such fund by the Commissioner under this title bears to the sum of such Federal capital contributions and the institution's capital contributions to such fund.

(2) The remainder of such balance shall be paid to the institution.

(b) After September 30, 1966, each institution with which the Commissioner has made an agreement under this title shall pay to the Commissioner, not less often than quarterly, the same proportionate share of amounts received by the institution after June 30, 1966, in payment of principal or interest on student loans made from the student loan fund established pursuant to such agreement (which amount shall be determined after deduction of any costs of litigation incurred in collection of the principal or interest on loans from the fund and not already reimbursed from the student loan fund or such payments of principal or interest) as was determined for the Commissioner under subsection (a).

(c) Upon a finding by the institution or the Commissioner prior to July 1, 1966, that the liquid assets of a student loan fund established pursuant to an agreement under this title exceed the amount required for loans or otherwise in the foreseeable future, and upon notice to such institution or to the Commissioner, as the case may be, there shall be, subject to such limitations as may be included in regulations of the Commissioner or in such agreement, a capital distribution from such fund. Such capital distribution shall be made as follows:

(1) The Commissioner shall first be paid an amount which bears the same ratio to the total to be distributed as the Federal capital contributions by the Commissioner to the student loan fund prior to such distribution bear to the sum of such Federal capital contribution and the capital contributions to the fund made by the institution.

(2) The remainder of the capital distribution shall be paid to the institution.

LOANS TO INSTITUTIONS

SEC. 207. (a) Upon application by any institution of higher education with which he has made an agreement under this title, the Commissioner may make a loan to such institution for the purpose of helping to finance the institution's capital contributions to a student loan fund established pursuant to such agreement. Any such loan may be made only if such institution shows it is unable to secure such funds from non-Federal sources upon terms and conditions which the Commissioner determines to be reasonable and consistent with the purposes of this title. Loans made to institutions under this section shall bear interest at a rate which the Commissioner determines to be adequate to cover (1) the cost of the funds to the Treasury as determined by the Secretary of the Treasury, taking into consideration the current average yields of outstanding marketable obligations of the United States having maturities comparable to the maturities of loans made by the Commissioner under this section, (2) the cost of administering this section, and (3) probable losses.

(b) There are hereby authorized to be appropriated such sums as may be necessary to carry out the purposes of this section, but not to exceed a total of $25,000,000.

(c) Loans made by the Commissioner under this section shall mature within such period as may be determined by the Commissioner to be appropriate in each case, but not exceeding fifteen years.

PAYMENTS TO COVER REDUCTIONS IN AMOUNTS OF LOANS

SEC. 208. In addition to the payments otherwise authorized to be made pursuant to this title, the Commissioner shall pay to the appropriate institution, at such time or times as he determines, an amount which bears the same ratio to the interest which has been prevented from accruing and the portion of the principal which has been canceled on student loans pursuant to paragraph (3) of section 205 (b) (and not previously paid pursuant to this subsection) as the total amount of the institution's capital contributions to such fund under this title bears to the sum of such institution's capital contributions and the Federal capital contributions to such fund.

ADMINISTRATIVE PROVISIONS

SEC. 209. (a) The Commissioner, in addition to the other powers conferred upon him by this title, shall have power to agree to modifications of agreements or loans made under this title and to compromise, waive, or release any right, title, claim, or demand, however arising or acquired under this title.

(b) Financial transactions of the Commissioner pursuant to this title, and vouchers approved by him in connection with such financial transactions, shall be final and conclusive upon all officers of the Government; except that all such transactions shall be subject to audit by the General Accounting Office at such times and in such manner as the Comptroller General may by regulation prescribe.

TITLE III—FINANCIAL ASSISTANCE FOR STRENGTHENING SCIENCE, MATHEMATICS, AND MODERN FOREIGN LANGUAGE INSTRUCTION

APPROPRIATIONS AUTHORIZED

SEC. 301. There are hereby authorized to be appropriated $70,000,000 for the fiscal year ending June 30, 1959, and for each of the three succeeding fiscal years, for (1) making payments to State educational agencies under this title for the acquisition of equipment (suitable for use in providing education in science, mathematics, or modern foreign language) and for minor remodeling described in paragraph (1) of section 303 (a), and (2) making loans authorized in section 305. There are also authorized to be appropriated $5,000,000 for the fiscal year ending June 30, 1959, and for each of the three succeeding fiscal years, for making payments to State educational agencies under this title to carry out the programs described in paragraph (5) of section 303 (a).

ALLOTMENTS TO STATES

SEC. 302. (a) (1) From the sums appropriated pursuant to the first sentence of section 301 for any fiscal year the Commissioner shall reserve such amount, but not in excess of 2 per centum thereof, as he may determine for allotment as provided in section 1008, and shall reserve 12 per centum for loans authorized in section 305. From the remainder of such sums the Commissioner shall allot to each State an amount which bears the same ratio to the amount of such remainder as the product of—

(A) the school-age population of the State, and

(B) the State's allotment ratio (as determined under paragraph (2)), bears to the sum of the corresponding products for all the States.

(2) The "allotment ratio" for any State shall be 100 per centum less the product of (A) 50 per centum and (B) the quotient obtained by dividing the income per child of school age for the State by the income per child of school age for the continental United States except that the allotment ratio shall in no case be less than 33⅓ per centum or more than 66⅔ per centum. The allotment ratios shall be promulgated by the Commissioner as soon as possible after enactment of this Act, and again between July 1 and August 31 of the year 1959, on the basis of the average of the incomes per child of school age for the States and for the continental United States for the three most recent consecutive years for which satisfactory data are available from the Department of Commerce. The first such promulgation shall be conclusive for each of the two fiscal years in the period beginning July 1, 1958, and ending June 30, 1960, and the second shall be conclusive for each of the two fiscal years in the period beginning July 1, 1960, and ending June 30, 1962.

(3) For the purposes of this title—

(A) The term "child of school age" means a member of the population between the ages of five and seventeen, both inclusive.

(B) The term "continental United States" does not include Alaska.

(C) The term "income per child of school age" for any State or for the continental United States means the total personal income for the State and the continental United States, respectively, divided by the number of children of school age in such State and in the continental United States, respectively.

(4) A State's allotment under this subsection shall remain available for payment pursuant to section 304 (a) for projects in such State until the end of the fiscal year following the year for which the allotment is made.

(b) From the sums appropriated pursuant to the second sentence of section 301 for any fiscal year the Commissioner shall reserve such amount, but not in excess of 2 per centum thereof, as he may determine for allotment as provided in section 1008. From the remainder of such sums the Commissioner shall allot to each State an amount which bears the same ratio to the amount of such remainder as the school-age population of such State bears to the total of the school-age populations of all of the States. The amount allotted to any State under the preceding sentence for any fiscal year which is less than $20,000 shall be increased to $20,000, the total thereby required being derived by proportionately reducing the amount allotted to each of the remaining States under the preceding sentence, but with such adjustments as may be necessary to prevent the allotment of any of such remaining States from being thereby reduced to less than $20,000.

STATE PLANS

Sec. 303. (a) Any State which desires to receive payments under this title shall submit to the Commissioner, through its State educational agency, a State plan which meets the requirements of section 1004 (a) and—

(1) sets forth a program under which funds paid to the State from its allotment under section 302 (a) will be expended solely for projects approved by the State educational agency for (A) acquisition of laboratory and other special equipment, including audio-visual materials and equipment and printed materials (other than textbooks), suitable for use in providing education in science, mathematics, or modern foreign language, in public elementary or secondary schools, or both, and (B) minor remodeling of laboratory or other space used for such materials or equipment;

(2) sets forth principles for determining the priority of such projects in the State for assistance under this title and provides for undertaking such projects, insofar as financial resources available therefor make possible, in the order determined by the application of such principles;

(3) Provides an opportunity for a hearing before the State educational agency to any applicant for a project under this title;

(4) provides for the establishment of standards on a State level for laboratory and other special equipment acquired with assistance furnished under this title;

(5) sets forth a program under which funds paid to the State from its allotment under section 302 (b) will be expended solely for (A) expansion or improvement of supervisory or related services in public elementary and secondary schools in the fields of science, mathematics, and modern foreign languages, and (B) administration of the State plan.

(b) The Commissioner shall approve any State plan and any modification thereof which complies with the provisions of subsection (a).

PAYMENTS TO STATES

SEC. 304. (a) From a State's allotment for a fiscal year under section 302 (a), the Commissioner shall from time to time during the period such allotment is available for payment as provided in paragraph (4) of section 302 (a), pay to such State an amount equal to one-half of the expenditures for projects for acquisition of equipment and minor remodeling referred to in paragraph (1) of section 303 (a) which are carried out under its State plan approved under section 303 (b); except that no State shall receive payments under this subsection for any period in excess of its allotments for such period under section 302 (a).

(b) From a State's allotment under section 302 (b) for the fiscal year ending June 30, 1959, the Commissioner shall from time to time pay to such State an amount equal to the amount expended by such State for such year to carry out the program referred to in paragraph (5) of section 303 (a) under its State plan approved under section 303 (b). From a State's allotment under section 302 (b) for the fiscal year ending June 30, 1960, and for each of the two succeeding fiscal years, such payments shall equal one-half of the amount so expended under its State plan approved under section 303 (b); except that no State shall receive payments under the subsection for any fiscal year in excess of its allotment under section 302 (b) for that fiscal year.

LOANS TO NONPROFIT PRIVATE SCHOOLS

SEC. 305. (a) The Commissioner shall allot, out of funds reserved for each fiscal year for the purposes of this section under the provisions of section 302 (a), to each State for loans under the provisions of this section an amount which bears the same ratio to such funds as the number of persons in such State enrolled in private nonprofit elementary and secondary schools bears to the total of such numbers for all States.

(b) From the sums allotted to each State under the provisions of this section the Commissioner is authorized to make loans to private nonprofit elementary and secondary schools in such State for the purposes for which payments to State educational agencies are authorized under the first sentence of section 301. Any such loan—

(1) shall be made upon application containing such information as may be deemed necessary by the Commissioner;

(2) shall be subject to such conditions as may be necessary to protect the financial interest of the United States;

(3) shall bear interest at the rate arrived at by adding one-quarter of 1 per centum per annum to the rate which the Secretary of the Treasury determines to be equal to the current average yield on all outstanding marketable obligations of the United States as of the last day of the month preceding the date the application for the loan is approved and by adjusting the result so obtained to the nearest one-eighth of 1 per centum; and

(4) shall mature and be repayable on such date as may be agreed to by the Commissioner and the borrower, but such date shall not be more than ten years after the date on which such loan was made.

TITLE IV—NATIONAL DEFENSE FELLOWSHIPS

APPROPRIATIONS AUTHORIZED

SEC. 401. There are hereby authorized to be appropriated such sums as may be necessary to carry out the provisions of this title.

NUMBER OF FELLOWSHIPS

SEC. 402. During the fiscal year ending June 30, 1959, the Commissioner is authorized to award one thousand fellowships under the provisions of this title, and during each of the three succeeding fiscal years he is authorized to award one thousand five hundred such fellowships. Such fellowships shall be for periods of study not in excess of three academic years.

AWARD OF FELLOWSHIPS AND APPROVAL OF INSTITUTIONS

SEC. 403. (a) The Commissioner shall award fellowships under this title to individuals accepted for study in graduate programs approved by him under this section. The Commissioner shall approve a graduate program of an institution of higher education only upon application by the institution and only upon his finding:

(1) that such program is a new program or an existing program which has been expanded.

(2) that such new program or expansion of an existing program will substantially further the objective of increasing the facilities available in the Nation for the graduate training of college or university level teachers and of promoting a wider geographical distribution of such facilities throughout the Nation, and

(3) that in the acceptance of persons for study in such programs preference will be given to persons interested in teaching in institutions of higher education.

(b) The total of the fellowships awarded under this title for pursuing a course of study in a graduate program at any institution of higher education may not exceed a limit established by the Commissioner in the light of the objective referred to in subsection (a) (2).

FELLOWSHIP STIPENDS

SEC. 404. (a) Each person awarded a fellowship under the provisions of this title shall receive a stipend of $2,000 for the first academic year of this study after the baccalaureate degree, $2,200 for the second such year, and $2,400 for the third such year, plus an additional amount of $400 for each such year on account of each of his dependents.

(b) In addition to the amounts paid to persons pursuant to subsection (a) there shall be paid to the institution of higher education at which each such person is pursuing his course of study such amount, not more than $2,500 per academic year, as is determined by the Commissioner to constitute that portion of the cost of the new graduate program or of the expansion in an existing graduate program in which such person is pursuing his course of study, which is reasonably attributable to him.

FELLOWSHIP CONDITIONS

SEC. 405. A person awarded a fellowship under the provisions of this title shall continue to receive the payments provided in section 404 only during such periods as the Commissioner finds that he is maintaining satisfactory proficiency in, and devoting essentially full time to, study or research in the field in which such fellowship was awarded, in an institution of higher education, and is not engaging in gainful employment other than part-time employment by such institution in teaching, research, or similar activities, approved by the Commissioner.

TITLE V—GUIDANCE, COUNSELING, AND TESTING; IDENTIFICATION AND ENCOURAGEMENT OF ABLE STUDENTS

PART A—STATE PROGRAMS

APPROPRIATIONS AUTHORIZED

SEC. 501. There are hereby authorized to be appropriated $15,000,000 for the fiscal year ending June 30, 1959, and for each of the three succeeding fiscal years, for making grants to State educational agencies under this part to assist them to establish and maintain programs of testing and guidance and counseling.

ALLOTMENTS TO STATES

SEC. 502. From the sums appropriated pursuant to section 501 for any fiscal year the Commissioner shall reserve such amount, but not in excess of 2 per centum thereof, as he may determine for allotment as provided in section 1008. From the remainder of such sums the Commissioner shall allot to each State an amount which bears the same ratio to the amount of such remainder as the school-age population of such State bears to the total of the school-age populations of all of the States. The amount allotted to any State under the preceding sentence for any fiscal year which is less than $20,000 shall be increased to $20,000, the total of increases thereby required being derived by proportionately reducing the amount allotted to each of the remaining States under the preceding sentence, but with such adjustments as may be necessary to prevent the allotment of any such remaining States from being thereby reduced to less than $20,000.

STATE PLANS

SEC. 503. (a) Any State which desires to receive payments under this part shall submit to the Commissioner, through its State educational agency, a State plan which meets the requirements of section 1004 (a) and sets forth—

(1) a program for testing students in the public secondary schools, and if authorized by law in other secondary schools, of such State to identify students with outstanding aptitudes and ability, and the means of testing which will be utilized in carrying out such program; and

(2) a program of guidance and counseling in the public secondary schools of such State (A) to advise students of courses of study best suited to their ability, aptitudes, and skills, and (B) to encourage students with outstanding aptitudes and ability to complete their secondary school education, take the necessary courses for admission to institutions of higher education, and enter such institutions.

(b) The Commissioner shall approve any State plan and any modification thereof which complies with the provisions of subsection (a).

PAYMENTS TO STATES

SEC. 504. (a) Payment under this part shall be made to those State educational agencies which administer plans approved under section 503. For the fiscal year ending June 30, 1959, such payments shall equal the amount expended by the State in carrying out its State plan, and for the fiscal year ending June 30, 1960, and for each of the two succeeding fiscal years, such payments shall equal one-half of the amount so expended; except that no State educational agency shall receive payment under this part for any fiscal year in excess of that State's allotment for that fiscal year as determined under section 502.

(b) In any State which has a State plan approved under section 503 and in which the State educational agency is not authorized by law to make payments to cover the cost of testing students in any one or more secondary schools in such State to determine student abilities and aptitudes, the Commissioner shall arrange for the testing of such students and shall pay the cost thereof for the fiscal year ending June 30, 1959, and one-half of the cost thereof for any of the three succeeding fiscal years out of such State's allotment. Testing of students pursuant to this subsection shall, so far as practicable, be comparable to, and be done at the same grade levels and under the same conditions as in the case of, testing of students in public schools under the State plan.

PART B—COUNSELING AND GUIDANCE TRAINING INSTITUTES

AUTHORIZATION

SEC. 511. There are hereby authorized to be appropriated $6,250,000 for the fiscal year ending June 30, 1959, and $7,250,000 for each of the three succeeding fiscal years, to enable the Commissioner to arrange, by contracts with institutions of higher education, for the operation by them of short-term or regular session institutes for the provision of training to improve the qualifications of personnel engaged in counseling and guidance of students in secondary schools, or teachers in such schools preparing to engage in such counseling and guidance. Each individual, engaged, or preparing to engage, in counseling and guidance in a public secondary school, who attends an institute operated under the provisions of this part shall be eligible (after application therefor) to receive a stipend at the rate of $75 per week for the period of his attendance at such institute, and each such individual with one or more dependents shall receive an additional stipend at the rate of $15 per week for each such dependent for the period of such attendance.

TITLE VI—LANGUAGE DEVELOPMENT

PART A—CENTERS AND RESEARCH STUDIES

LANGUAGE AND AREA CENTERS

SEC. 601. (a) The Commissioner is authorized to arrange through contracts with institutions of higher education for the establishment and operation by them, during the period beginning July 1, 1958, and ending with the close of June 30, 1962, of centers for the teaching of any modern foreign language with respect to which the Commissioner determines (1) that individuals trained in such language are needed by the Federal Government or by business, industry, or education in the United States, and (2) that adequate instruction in such language is not readily available in the United States. Any such contract may provide for instruction not only in such modern foreign language but also in other fields needed to provide a full understanding of the areas, regions, or countries in which such language is commonly used, to the extent adequate instruction in such fields is not readily available, including fields such as history, political science, linguistics, economics, sociology, geography, and anthropology. Any such contract may cover not more than 50 per centum of the cost of the establishment and operation of the center with respect to which it is made, including the cost of grants to the staff for travel in the foreign areas, regions, or countries with which the subject matter of the field or fields in which they are or will be working is concerned and the cost of travel of foreign scholars to such centers to teach or assist in teaching therein and the cost of their return, and shall be made on such conditions as the Commissioner finds necessary to carry out the purposes of this section.

(b) The Commissioner is also authorized, during the period beginning July 1, 1958, and ending with the close of June 30, 1962, to pay stipends to individuals undergoing advanced training in any modern foreign language (with respect to which he makes the determination under clause (1) of subsection (a)), and other fields needed for a full understanding of the area, region, or country in which such language is commonly used, at any short-term or regular session of any institution of higher education, including allowances for dependents and for travel to and from their places of residence, but only upon reasonable assurance that the recipients of such stipends will, on completion of their training, be available for teaching a modern foreign language in an institution of higher education or for such other service of a public nature as may be permitted in regulations of the Commissioner.

RESEARCH AND STUDIES

SEC. 602. The Commissioner is authorized, directly or by contract, to make studies and surveys to determine the need for increased or improved instruction in modern foreign languages and other fields needed to provide a full understanding of the areas, regions, or countries in which such languages are commonly used, to conduct research on more effective methods of teaching such languages and in such other fields, and to develop specialized materials for use in such training, or in training teachers of such languages or in such fields.

APPROPRIATIONS AUTHORIZED

SEC. 603. There are hereby authorized to be appropriated such sums as may be necessary to carry out the provisions of this part, not to exceed $8,000,000 in any one fiscal year.

PART B—LANGUAGE INSTITUTES

AUTHORIZATION

SEC. 611. There are hereby authorized to be appropriated $7,250,000 for the fiscal year ending June 30, 1959, and each of the three succeeding fiscal years, to enable the Commissioner to arrange, through contracts with institutions of higher education, for the operation by them of short-term or regular session institutes for advance training, particularly in the use of new teaching methods and instructional materials, for individuals who are engaged in or preparing to engage in the teaching, or supervising or training teachers, of any modern foreign language in elementary or secondary schools. Each individual (engaged, or preparing to engage, in the teaching, or supervising or training teachers, of any modern foreign language in a public elementary or secondary school) who attends an institute operated under the provisions of this part shall be eligible (after application therefor) to receive a stipend at the rate of $75 per week for the period of his attendance at such institute, and each such individual with one or more dependents shall receive an additional stipend at the rate of $15 per week for each such dependent for the period of such attendance.

TITLE VII—RESEARCH AND EXPERIMENTATION IN MORE EFFECTIVE UTILIZATION OF TELEVISION, RADIO, MOTION PICTURES, AND RELATED MEDIA FOR EDUCATIONAL PURPOSES

PART A—RESEARCH AND EXPERIMENTATION

FUNCTIONS OF THE COMMISSIONER

SEC. 701. In carrying out the provisions of this part the Commissioner, in cooperation with the Advisory Committee on New Educational Media (established by section 761), shall (through grants or contracts) conduct, assist, and foster research and experimentation in the development and evaluation of projects involving television, radio, motion pictures, and related media of communciation which may prove of value to State or local educational agencies in the operation of their public elementary or secondary schools, and to institutions of higher education, including the development of new and more effective techniques and methods—

(1) for utilizing and adapting motion pictures, video tapes and other audio-visual aids, film strips, slides and other visual aids, recordings (including magnetic tapes) and other auditory aids, and radio or television program scripts for such purposes;

(2) for training teachers to utilize such media with maximum effectiveness; and

(3) for presenting academic subject matter through such media.

GRANTS-IN-AID; CONTRACTS

SEC. 702. In carrying out the provisions of section 701, the Commissioner—

(1) may make grants-in-aid, approved by the Advisory Committee on New Educational Media, to public or nonprofit private agencies, organizations, and individuals for projects of research or experimentation referred to in section 701;

(2) may enter into contracts, approved by the Advisory Committee on New Educational Media, with public or private agencies, organizations, groups, and individuals for projects of research or experimentation referred to in section 701; and

(3) shall promote the coordination of programs conducted or financed by him under this title with similar programs conducted by other agencies, institutions, foundations, organizations, or individuals.

PART B—DISSEMINATION OF INFORMATION ON NEW EDUCATIONAL MEDIA

FUNCTIONS OF THE COMMISSIONER

SEC. 731. In order to disseminate information concerning new educational media (including the results of research and experimentation conducted under part A of this title) to State or local educational agencies, for use in their public elementary or secondary schools, and to institutions of higher education, the Commissioner—

(1) shall make studies and surveys to determine the need for increased or improved utilization of television, radio, motion pictures, and related media of communication by State or local educational agencies and institutions of higher education for educational purposes;

(2) shall prepare and publish catalogs, reviews, bibliographies, abstracts, analyses of research and experimentation, and such other materials as are generally useful in the encouragement and more effective use of television, radio, motion pictures, and related media of communication for educational purposes;

(3) may, upon request, provide advice, counsel, technical assistance, and demonstrations to State or local educational agencies and institu-

tions of higher education undertaking to utilize such media of communication to increase the quality or depth or broaden the scope of their educational programs;

(4) shall prepare and publish an annual report setting forth (A) projects carried out under this title and the cost of each such project, and (B) developments in the utilization and adaptation of media of communication for educational purposes; and

(5) may enter into contracts with public or private agencies, organizations, groups, or individuals to carry out the provisions of this part.

PART C—GENERAL PROVISIONS

ESTABLISHMENT OF THE ADVISORY COMMITTEE

SEC. 761. (a) There is hereby established in the Office of Education an Advisory Committee on New Educational Media (hereafter in this title referred to as the "Advisory Committee"). The Advisory Committee shall consist of the Commissioner, who shall be chairman, a representative of the National Science Foundation and twelve persons appointed, without regard to the civil-service laws, by the Commissioner with the approval of the Secretary. Three of such appointed members shall be individuals identified with the sciences, liberal arts, or modern foreign languages in institutions of higher education; three shall be individuals actually engaged in teaching or in the supervision of teaching in elementary or secondary schools; three shall be individuals of demonstrated ability in the utilization or adaptation of television, radio, motion pictures, and related media of communication for educational purposes, and three shall be individuals representative of the lay public who have demonstrated an interest in the problems of communication media.

(b) The Advisory Committee shall—

(1) advise, consult with, and make recommendations to the Commissioner on matters relating to the utilization or adaptation of television, radio, motion pictures, or related media of communication for educational purposes, and on matters of basic policy arising in the administration of this title;

(2) review all applications for grants-in-aid under part A of this title for projects of research or experimentation and certify approval to the Commissioner of any such projects which it believes are appropriate for carrying out the provisions of this title; and

(3) review all proposals by the Commissioner to enter into contracts under this title and certify approval to the Commissioner of any such contracts which it believes are appropriate to carry out the provisions of this title.

(c) The Commissioner may utilize the services of any member or members of the Advisory Committee in connection with matters relating to the provisions of this title, for such periods, in addition to conference periods, as he may determine.

(d) Members of the Advisory Committee shall, while serving on business of the Advisory Committee or at the request of the Commissioner under subsection (c) of this section, receive compensation at rates fixed by the Secretary, not to exceed $50 per day, and shall also be entitled to receive an allowance for actual and necessary travel and subsistence expenses while so serving away from their places of residence.

SPECIAL PERSONNEL

SEC. 762. The Commissioner may secure from time to time and for such periods as he deems advisable, without regard to the civil-service laws, the assistance and advice of persons in the United States and from abroad who are experts in the utilization and adaptation of television, radio, motion pictures, and other related media of communication for educational purposes.

APPROPRIATIONS AUTHORIZED

SEC. 763. There are hereby authorized to be appropriated the sum of $3,000,000 for the fiscal year ending June 30, 1959, and the sum of $5,-000,000 for each of the three succeeding fiscal years for carrying out the provisions of this title.

TITLE VIII—AREA VOCATIONAL EDUCATION PROGRAMS

STATEMENT OF FINDINGS AND PURPOSE

SEC. 801. The Congress hereby finds that the excellent programs of vocational education, which States have established and are carrying on with the assistance provided by the Federal Government under the Smith-Hughes Vocational Education Act and the Vocational Education Act of 1946 (the George-Barden Act), need extension to provide vocational education to residents of areas inadequately served and also to meet national defense requirements for personnel equipped to render skilled assistance in fields particularly affected by scientific and technological developments. It is therefore the purpose of this title to provide assistance to the States so that they may improve their vocational education programs through area vocational education programs approved by State boards of vocational education as providing vocational and related technical training and retaining for youths, adults, and older persons, including related instruction for apprentices, designed to fit them for useful employment as technicians or skilled workers in scientific or technical fields.

AMENDMENT TO VOCATIONAL EDUCATION ACT OF 1946

SEC. 802. The Vocational Education Act of 1946 (20 U. S. C. 15i–15m, 15o–15q, 15aa–15jj) is amended by adding after title II the following new title:

"TITLE III—AREA VOCATIONAL EDUCATION PROGRAMS

"AUTHORIZATION OF APPROPRIATIONS

"SEC. 301. There is authorized to be appropriated for the fiscal year ending June 30, 1959, and for each of the three succeeding fiscal years the sum of $15,000,000 for area vocational education programs, to be apportioned for expenditure in the States as provided in section 302.

"ALLOTMENTS TO STATES

"SEC. 302. (a) From the sums appropriated for any fiscal year pursuant to section 301, each State shall be entitled to an allotment of an amount bearing the same ratio to such sums as the total of the amounts apportioned under title I of this Act, the Act of March 18, 1950 (20 U. S. C. 31–33), and section 9 of the Act of August 1, 1956 (20 U. S. C. 34), to such State for such year bears to the total of the amounts so apportioned to all the States for such year.

"(b) The amount of any allotment to a State under subsection (a) for any fiscal year which the State certifies to the Commissioner will not be required for carrying out area vocational education programs (under the part of the State plan meeting the requirements of section 305) shall be available for re-allotment from time to time, on such dates as the Commissioner may fix, to other States in proportion to the original allotments to such States under subsection (a) for such year. Any amount so reallotted to a State shall be deemed part of its allotment under subsection (a).

"PAYMENTS TO STATES

"SEC. 303. (a) Any amount paid to a State from its allotment under section 302 for any fiscal year shall be paid on condition:

"(1) that there shall be spent for such year an equal amount in State or local funds, or both, for area vocational education programs operated under the provisions of this title;

"(2) that funds appropriated under this title will not be used to reduce the amount of State or local funds, or both, being spent for vocational education programs operated under provisions of the Smith-Hughes Vocational Educaton Act and titles I and II of this Act and reported to the Commissioner, but such State or local funds, or both, in excess of the amount necessary for dollar for dollar matching of funds allotted to a State under provisions of the Smith-Hughes Vocational Education Act and titles I and II of this Act may be used to match funds appropriated under this title;

"(3) that funds appropriated under section 301 of this title shall be used exclusively for the training of individuals designed to fit them for useful employment as highly skilled technicians in recognized occupations requiring scientific knowledge, as determined by the State board for such State, in fields necessary for the national defense.

"(b) The Commissioner shall, prior to the beginning of each calendar quarter or other period prescribed by him, estimate the amount to be paid to each State for area vocational education programs under this title for such period; and shall pay to the State, from the allotment available therefor, the amount so estimated by him for such period, reduced or increased, as the case may be, by any sum (not previously adjusted under this subsection) by which he finds that his estimate of the amount to be paid to the State for any prior period for such purpose under this title was greater or less than the amount which should have been paid to the State for such prior period under this title for such purpose. Such payments shall be made in such installments as the Commissioner may determine.

"USE OF FUNDS

"SEC. 304. (a) Funds paid to a State under this title for area vocational education programs may be used, in carrying out such programs (under the part of the State plan meeting the requirements of section 305), for—

"(1) maintenance of adequate programs of administration, supervision, and teacher-training;

"(2) salaries and necessary travel expenses of State or local school personnel, including teachers, coordinators, supervisors, vocational guidance counselors, teacher-trainers, directors, administrators, and others;

"(3) travel expenses of members of advisory committees or State boards;

"(4) purchase, rental, or other acquisition, and maintenance and repair, of instructional equipment;

"(5) purchase of instructional supplies and teaching aids;

"(6) necessary costs of transportation of students;

"(7) securing necessary educational information and data as a basis for the proper development of area vocational education programs and programs of vocational guidance;

"(8) training and work-experience training programs for out-of-school youths;

"(9) related instruction for apprentices; and

"(10) determining the need for, and planning and developing, area vocational education programs.

"(b) Any equipment and teaching aids purchased with funds appropriated to carry out the provisions of this title shall become the property of the State.

"ADDITIONAL STATE PLAN REQUIREMENTS

"SEC. 305. (a) To be eligible to participate in this title the State plan must be amended to include a new part which—

"(1) designates the State board as the sole agency for administration of such part of the plan (or for the supervision of the administration thereof by State or local educational agencies);

"(2) provides minimum qualifications for teachers, teacher-trainers, supervisors, directors and others having responsibilities under the plan;

"(3) shows the plans, policies, and methods to be followed in carrying out such part of the State plan;

"(4) provides such accounting, budgeting, and other fiscal methods and procedures as are necessary for the proper and efficient administration of such part of the State plan; and

"(5) provides that the State board will make such reports to the Commissioner, in such form and containing such information, as are reasonably necessary to enable the Commissioner to perform his functions under this title.

"(b) The Commissioner shall approve a part of any plan for purposes of this title if he finds that it fulfills the conditions specified in subsection (a) of this section.

"(c) Whenever the Commissioner after reasonable notice and opportunity for hearing to the State board finds that—

"(1) the part of the State plan approved under subsection (b) has been so changed that it no longer complies with any provision required by subsection (a) of his section to be included in such part; or

"(2) in the administration of such part of the plan there is a failure to comply substantially with any such provision;

the Commissioner shall notify such State board that no further payments will be made to the State from its allotments under section 302 (or, in his discretion, that further payments will not be made to the State for projects under or portions of such part of the State plan affected by such failure) until he is satisfied that there is no longer any such failure. Until he is so satisfied the Commissioner shall make no further payments to such State from its allotments under section 302 (or shall limit payments to projects under or portions of such part of the State plan in which there is no such failure).

"(d) (1) If any State is dissatisfied with the Commissioner's action under subsection (c) of this section, such State may appeal to the United States court of appeals for the circuit in which such State is located. The summons and notice of appeal may be served at any place in the United States. The Commissioner shall forthwith certify and file in the court the transcript of the proceedings and the record on which he based his action.

"(2) The findings of fact by the Commissioner, unless substantially contrary to the weight of the evidence, shall be conclusive; but the court, for good cause shown, may remand the case to the Commissioner to take further evidence, and the Commissioner may thereupon make new or modified findings of fact and may modify his previous action, and shall certify to the court the transcript and record of the further proceedings. Such new or modified findings of fact shall likewise be conclusive unless substantially contrary to the weight of the evidence.

"(3) The court shall have jurisdiction to affirm the action of the Commissioner or to set it aside, in whole or in part. The judgment of the court shall be subject to review by the Supreme Court of the United States upon certiorari or certification as provided in title 28, United States Code, section 1254.

"APPROPRIATIONS FOR ADMINISTRATION

"SEC. 306. There are hereby authorized to be included for each fiscal year in the appropriations for the Department of Health, Education, and Welfare such sums as are necessary to administer the provisions of this title.

"DEFINITIONS

"SEC. 307. For purposes of this title—

"(a) The term 'State' includes Alaska, Hawaii, the Virgin Islands, Puerto Rico, the District of Columbia, and Guam.

"(b) The term 'Commissioner' means the Commissioner of Education.

"(c) The terms 'State plan' and 'State board' shall have the meaning which said terms have in the Act approved February 23, 1917 (39 Stat. 929, ch. 114).

"(d) The term 'area vocational education program' means a program consisting of one or more less-than-college-grade courses conducted under public supervision and control and on an organized, systematic class basis, which is designed to fit individuals for useful employment as technicians or skilled workers in recognized occupations requiring scientific or technical knowledge, and which is made available to residents of the State or an area thereof designed and approved by the State board, who either have completed junior high school or, regardless of their school credits, are at least sixteen years of age and can reasonably be expected to profit by the instruction offered."

TITLE IX—SCIENCE INFORMATION SERVICE

FUNCTIONS OF THE SERVICE

SEC. 901. The National Science Foundation shall establish a Science Information Service. The Foundation, through such Service, shall (1) provide, or arrange for the provision of, indexing, abstracting, translating, and other services leading to a more effective dissemination of scientific information, and (2) undertake programs to develop new or improved methods, including mechanized systems, for making scientific information available.

SCIENCE INFORMATION COUNCIL

SEC. 902. (a) The National Science Foundation shall establish, in the Foundation, a Science Information Council (hereafter in this title referred to as the "Council") consisting of the Librarian of Congress, the director of the National Library of Medicine, the director of the Department of Agriculture library, and the head of the Science Information Service, each of whom shall be ex officio members, and fifteen members appointed by the Director of the National Science Foundation. The Council shall annually elect one of the appointed members to serve as chairman until the next election. Six of the appointed members shall be leaders in the fields of fundamental science, six shall be leaders in the fields of librarianship and scientific documentation, and three shall be outstanding representatives of the lay public who have demonstrated interest in the problems of communication. Each appointed member of such Council shall hold office for a term of four years, except that (1) any member appointed to fill a vacancy occurring prior to the expiration of the term for which his predecessor was appointed shall be appointed only for the remainder of such term, and (2) that of the members first appointed, four shall hold office for a term of three years, four shall hold office for a term of two years, and three shall hold office for a term of one year, as designated by the Director of the National Science Foundation at the time of appointment. No appointed member of the Council shall be eligible for reappointment until a year has elapsed since the end of his preceding term.

(b) It shall be the duty of the Council to advise, to consult with, and to make recommendations to, the head of the Science Information Service. The Council shall meet at least twice each year, and at such other times as the majority thereof deems appropriate.

(c) Persons appointed to the Council shall, while serving on business of the Council, receive compensation at rates fixed by the National Science Foundation, but not to exceed $50 per day, and shall also be entitled to receive an allowance for actual and necessary travel and subsistence expenses while so serving away from their places of residence.

AUTHORITY FOR CERTAIN GRANTS AND CONTRACTS

SEC. 903. In carrying out its functions under this title, the National Science Foundation shall have the same power and authority it has under the National Science Foundation Act of 1950 to carry out its functions under that Act.

APPROPRIATIONS AUTHORIZED

SEC. 904. There are hereby authorized to be appropriated for the fiscal year ending June 30, 1959, and for each succeeding fiscal year, such sums as may be necessary to carry out the provisions of this title.

TITLE X—MISCELLANEOUS PROVISIONS

ADMINISTRATION

SEC. 1001. (a) The Commissioner is authorized to delegate any of his functions under this Act, except the making of regulations, to any officer or employee of the Office of Education.

(b) In administering the titles of this Act for which he is responsible, the Commissioner is authorized to utilize the services and facilities of any agency of the Federal Government and, without regard to section 3709 of the Revised Statutes of the United States (41 U. S. C., sec. 5), of any other public or nonprofit agency or institution, in accordance with agreements between the Secretary and the head thereof.

(c) The Commissioner shall include in his annual report to the Congress a full report of the activities of the Office of Education under this Act, including recommendations for needed revisions in the provisions thereof.

(d) The Secretary shall advise and consult with the heads of departments and agencies of the Federal Government responsible for the administration of scholarship, fellowship, or other educational programs with a view to securing full information concerning all specialized scholarship, fellowship, or other educational programs administered by or under any such department or agency and to developing policies and procedures which will strengthen the educational programs and objectives of the institutions of higher education utilized for such purposes by any such department or agency.

(e) Any agency of the Federal Government shall exercise its functions under any other law in such manner as will assist in carrying out the objectives of this Act. Nothing in this Act shall be construed as superseding or limiting the authority of any such agency under any other law.

(f) No part of any funds appropriated or otherwise made available for expenditure under authority of this Act shall be used to make payments or loans to any individual unless such individual (1) has executed and filed with the Commissioner an affidavit that he does not believe in, and is not a member of and does not support any organization that believes in or teaches, the overthrow of the United States Government by force or violence or by any illegal or unconstitutional methods, and (2) has taken and subscribed to an oath or affirmation in the following form: 'I do solemnly swear (or affirm) that I will bear true faith and allegiance to the United States of America and will support and defend the Constitution and laws of the United States against all its enemies, foreign and domestic." The provisions of section 1001 of title 18, United States Code, shall be applicable with respect to such affidavits.

ADVISORY COMMITTEES

SEC. 1002. (a) The Commissioner, with the approval of the Secretary, may appoint an advisory committee, or advisory committees, to advise and consult with him with respect to the administration of the provisions of this Act for which he is responsible. Any such committee shall have twelve members as follows:

(1) Four members who are recognized scholars in any of the following fields: engineering, mathematics, or science;

(2) Four members who are recognized scholars in any of the fields of the humanities; and

(3) Four members from such fields of endeavor as the Commissioner deems appropriate.

Members of an advisory committee appointed under this section, while attending conferences or meetings of the committee, shall be entitled to receive compensation at a rate to be fixed by the Secretary, but not exceeding $50 per diem, and while away from their homes or regular places of business they may be allowed travel expenses, including per diem in lieu of subsistence, as authorized by law for persons in the Government service employed intermittently.

EXEMPTION FROM CONFLICT-OF-INTEREST LAWS OF MEMBERS OF ADVISORY COMMITTEES OR INFORMATION COUNCIL

SEC. 1003. (a) Any member of an advisory committee or information council appointed under this Act is hereby exempted, with respect to such appointment, from the operation of sections 281, 283, 284, and 1914 of title 18 of the United States Code, and section 190 of the Revised Statutes (5 U. S. C. 99), except as otherwise specified in subsection (b) of this section.

(b) The exemption granted by subsection (a) shall not extend—

(1) to the receipt or payment of salary in connection with the appointee's Government service from any source other than the private employer of the appointee at the time of his appointment, or

(2) during the period of such appointment, and the further period of two years after the termination thereof, to the prosecution or participation in the prosecution, by any person so appointed, of any claim against the Government involving any matter concerning which the appointee had any responsibility arising out of his appointment during the period of such appointment.

ADMINISTRATION OF STATE PLANS

SEC. 1004. (a) No State plan submitted under one of the titles of this Act shall be approved by the Commissioner which does not—

(1) provide, in the case of a plan submitted under title III or under title V, or section 1009 of this title, that the State educational agency will be the sole agency for administering the plan;

(2) provide that such commission or agency will make such reports to the Commissioner, in such form and containing such information, as may be reasonably necessary to enable the Commissioner to perform his duties under such title or section; and

(3) provide for such fiscal control and fund accounting procedures as may be necessary to assure proper disbursement of and accounting for Federal funds paid to the State under such title or section.

(b) The Commissioner shall not finally disapprove any State plan submitted under this Act, or any modification thereof without first affording the agency administering the plan reasonable notice and opportunity for a hearing.

(c) Whenever the Commissioner, after reasonable notice and opportunity for hearing to the agency administering a State plan approved under one of the titles of this Act, finds that—

(1) the State plan has been so changed that it no longer complies with the provisions of this Act governing its original approval, or

(2) in the administration of the plan there is a failure to comply substantially with any such provision, the Commissioner shall notify such State agency, in the case of a plan submitted under title III or V or section 1009 of this title, that no further payments will be made to the State under such title or section (or, in his discretion, further payments to the State will be limited to programs under or portions of the State plan not affected by such failure), until he is satisfied that there will no longer be any failure to comply. Until he is so satisfied, the Commissioner shall make no further payments to such State under such title or section, as the case may be (or shall limit payments to programs under or portions of the State plan not affected by such failure).

JUDICIAL REVIEW

SEC. 1005. (a) If any State is dissatisfied with the Commissioner's final action with respect to the approval of its State plan submitted under this Act, or with respect to his final action under section 104 (c), such State may, within sixty days after notice of such action, file in the United States district court for the district in which the capital of the State is located, a petition to review such action. The petition for review shall (1) contain a concise statement of the facts upon which the appeal is based and (2) designate that part of the Commissioner's decision sought to be reviewed.

(b) Notification of the filing of the petition for review shall be given by the clerk of the court by mailing a copy of the petition to the Commissioner.

(c) No costs or docket fees shall be charged or imposed with respect to any judicial review proceedings, or appeal therefrom, taken under this Act.

(d) Upon receipt of the petition for review the Commissioner shall, within twenty days thereafter, certify and file in the court the record on review, consisting of the complete transcript of the proceedings before the Commissioner. No party to such review shall be required, by rule of court or otherwise, to print the contents of such record filed in the court.

(e) The court after review may dismiss the petition or deny the relief prayed for, or may suspend, modify, or set aside, in whole or in part, the action of the Commissioner, or may compel action unlawfully withheld. The judgment of the court shall be subject to review as provided in section 1291 and 1254 of title 28 of the United States Code.

METHOD OF PAYMENT

SEC. 1006. Payments under this Act to any individual or to any State or Federal agency, institution of higher education, or any other organization, pursuant to a grant, loan, or contract, may be made in installments, and in advance or by way of reimbursement, and, in the case of grants or loans, with necessary adjustments on account of overpayments or underpayments.

ADMINISTRATIVE APPROPRIATIONS AUTHORIZED

SEC. 1007. There are hereby authorized to be appropriated for the fiscal year ending June 30, 1959, and for each fiscal year thereafter, such sums as may be necessary for the cost of administering the provisions of this Act, including the administrative expenses of State commissions.

ALLOTMENTS TO TERRITORIES AND POSSESSIONS

SEC. 1008. The amounts reserved by the Commissioner under sections 302 and 502 shall be allotted by the Commissioner among Alaska, Hawaii, Puerto Rico, the Canal Zone, Guam, and the Virgin Islands, according to their respective needs for the type of assistance furnished under the part or title in which the section appears.

IMPROVEMENT OF STATISTICAL SERVICES OF STATE EDUCATIONAL AGENCIES

Sec. 1009. (a) For the purpose of assisting the States to improve and strengthen the adequacy and reliability of educational statistics provided by State and local reports and records and the methods and techniques for collecting and processing educational data and disseminating information about the condition and progress of education in the States, there are hereby authorized to be appropriated for the fiscal year ending June 30, 1959, and each of the three succeeding fiscal years, for grants to States under this section, such sums as the Congress may determine.

(b) Grants under this section by the Commissioner shall be equal to one-half of the cost of State educational agency programs to carry out the purposes of this section, including (1) improving the collection, analysis, and reporting of statistical data supplied by local educational units, (2) the development of accounting and reporting manuals to serve as guides for local educational units, (3) the conduct of conferences and training for personnel of local educational units and of periodic reviews and evaluation of the program for records and reports, (4) improving methods for obtaining, from other State agencies within the State, educational data not collected by the State educational agency, or (5) expediting the processing and reporting of statistical data through installation and operation of mechanical equipment. The total of the payments to any State under this section for any fiscal year may not exceed $50,000.

(c) Payments with respect to any program of a State educational agency under this section may be made (1) only to the extent it is a new program or an addition to or expansion of an existing program, and (2) only if the State plan approved under subsection (d) includes such program.

(d) The Commissioner shall approve any State plan for purposes of this section if such plan meets the requirements of section 1004 (a) and sets forth the programs proposed to be carried out under the plan and the general policies to be followed in doing so.

Approved September 2, 1958

Appendix C

ILLUSTRATIVE FORMS OF AID TO ADMINISTRATORS OF CATHOLIC SCHOOLS

Proposed Contract for Religious Teachers[1]

Made in _____(town)_____, county of _____, State of New York on the _____ day of _____, 19___ between _____, Pastor of _____ Church (to be designated hereafter as the Pastor) of the first part and _____ Superior of _____(community)_____ (to be designated hereafter as the Superior) of the second part.

1. The parties named above have agreed that the _____(name of community)_____ shall provide _____(number)_____ religious teachers to conduct the educational program in keeping with the requirements of the Archdiocese of New York in _____ School. It is agreed that these teachers must be competent for the classes to which they are assigned as determined by the standards of the Superintendent of Schools.

2. It is agreed that the Pastor shall provide a fitting residence, suitably situated, properly furnished (including linens) and adapted to the life of the _____(community)_____. This residence shall contain a chapel, a community room and shall be free of rent and taxes. It is agreed that the pastor shall make such improvements and repairs as may become necessary from time to time, and shall defray the cost of water, fuel and electricity.

3. It is agreed that the Pastor shall pay to the Principal and to each teacher the yearly salary specified by the regulations of the Archdiocese of New York. These salaries shall be made in monthly payments on the first day of every month for the twelve months of each year.

4. It is agreed that the pastor shall arrange to have the Holy Sacrifice of the Mass offered at least once every week in the chapel of the _____ residence.

5. It is agreed that the appointment or transfer of the religious teachers shall be the sole responsibility of the Superior or his representative.

6. It is further agreed that in case of the withdrawal of the _____(community)_____ from the school, written notice shall be given 6 months in advance by the Pastor or the _____(community)_____ respectively. It is understood that this may only take place at the end of the school year in June.

7. It is agreed that the Pastor shall provide to the Principal funds for the purchase of equipment, textbooks and other necessary supplies. It is further agreed that any monies realized by the sale of supplies and books to the pupils shall be presented to the Pastor.

The terms of this agreement shall begin on the _____ day of _____, 19___, and terminate on the _____ day of _____, 19___.

_____(Superior)

_____(Pastor)

[1] Source: *Administrative Manual for Elementary Schools,* Archdiocese of New York, 1956, p. 127.

Proposed Contract for Lay Teachers in Catholic Schools

ARTICLES OF AGREEMENT

This agreement made and entered into between _____,
Pastor of _____ Church, hereinafter referred to as
the party of the first part, and _____, residing at
_____, hereinafter referred to as the party of the
second part.

WITNESSETH

1. That the party of the first part agrees to employ the full-time services
of the party of the second part as a teacher in _____
School for the academic year of _____, beginning the _____
day of _____, 19___ and to pay therefore the sum of _____
_____ dollars payable monthly during the period of _____
_____ months.

2. The party of the second part accepts the position of teacher in _____
_____ School and agrees to devote his full time to teaching
and such other collateral activities including direction of students and administrative work as are usually associated with this position and may be
prescribed or agreed to by the party of the first part through the principal of
the school.

3. In the event the party of the second part is unable to perform all or a
substantial proportion of his duties for a period in excess of _____
(days or months) on account of ill-health or other reasons this agreement
may be suspended.

4. The party of the second part agrees to observe and enforce the rules
and regulations of _____ School as promulgated
by its principal, to conduct himself at all times in a manner which shall not
bring reproach or criticism upon himself or the school, and to promote the
principles and ideal for which the school stands. The party of the first part
shall at all times be the judge of the competence, conduct and fulfillment of
responsibility of the party of the second part and may terminate this agreement for grave failure in any of the foregoing.

5. If the party of the second part in his teaching shall have been guilty
of a grave offense against Catholic doctrine or morality, or if he shall have
been involved in a public crime or scandal, the party of the first part may
dismiss him summarily without notice.

Signed this _____ day of _____, 19___

By _____(Teacher)

By _____(Pastor)

FAMILY NAME FIRST MIDDLE PLACE OF BIRTH DATE

GRADE PROGRESS RECORD

YEAR	GRADE	NAME OF SCHOOL	TEACHER	YEAR	GRADE	NAME OF SCHOOL	TEACHER
	K						

SCHOOL ACHIEVEMENT RECORD

ACADEMIC PROGRESS

ACADEMIC PROGRESS	YEAR	19	19	19	19	19	19
	GRADE						
CHRISTIAN DOCTRINE							
READING							
ORAL READING ABILITY							
COMPREHENSION OF WHAT IS READ							
ENGLISH							
ORAL EXPRESSION OF IDEAS							
WRITTEN EXPRESSION OF IDEAS							
CORRECT USAGE							
SPELLING							
WEEKLY ASSIGNMENT							
TRANSFER OF SPELLING ABILITY TO WRITTEN WORK							
HANDWRITING							
NEATNESS AND LEGIBILITY							
APPLICATION OF PRINCIPLES TO WRITTEN WORK							
ARITHMETIC							
MASTERY OF SKILLS							
ABILITY TO SOLVE PROBLEMS							
HISTORY							
CIVICS							
GEOGRAPHY							
SCIENCE							
MUSIC							
ART							

MEANING OF MARKS

E – OUTSTANDING ACHIEVEMENT. A RARE MARK, INDICATES AN EXCEEDINGLY HIGH QUALITY OF WORK
VG – ABOVE AVERAGE ACHIEVEMENT, INDICATES VERY GOOD PROGRESS. WELL ABOVE THE USUAL.
G – AVERAGE ACHIEVEMENT, INDICATES GOOD PROGRESS FOR THIS GRADE
L – BELOW AVERAGE ACHIEVEMENT, INDICATES A GREATER NEED FOR EFFORT IF THE REQUIREMENTS FOR THIS GRADE ARE TO BE COMPLETED SATISFACTORILY
S – SATISFACTORY PROGRESS FOR THIS CHILD WHO IS INCAPABLE OF DOING THE WORK ON THIS GRADE LEVEL. BUT IS CONSIDERING HIS ABILITY, HIS WORK IS SATISFACTORY
U – UNSATISFACTORY PROGRESS, INDICATES FAILURE TO PRODUCE AN ACCEPTABLE QUALITY OF WORK

GROWTH IN DESIRABLE HABITS AND ATTITUDES

	YEAR	19	19	19	19	19	19
	GRADE						
GROWTH IN RELIGIOUS HABITS							
PARTICIPATES IN RELIGIOUS ACTIVITIES							
IS REVERENT AT PRAYER AND IN CHURCH							
PRACTICES SELF-CONTROL							
OBEYS PROMPTLY AND WILLINGLY							
GROWTH IN SOCIAL HABITS							
RESPECTS AUTHORITY							
WORKS AND PLAYS WELL WITH OTHERS							
CONFORMS TO SCHOOL REGULATIONS							
IS COURTEOUS IN SPEECH AND MANNER							
ACCEPTS RESPONSIBILITY							
KEEPS DESK AND MATERIALS NEAT							
RESPECTS PUBLIC AND PRIVATE PROPERTY							
GROWTH IN WORK AND STUDY HABITS							
BEGINS WORK PROMPTLY							
COMPLETES WORK ON TIME							
KEEPS PROFITABLY BUSY							
PRODUCES A QUALITY OF WORK THAT MEASURES UP TO ABILITY							
GROWTH IN HEALTH AND SAFETY HABITS							
IS CAREFUL OF PERSONAL APPEARANCE							
OBSERVES SIMPLE HEALTH RULES							
OBSERVES TRAFFIC AND SAFETY RULES							

E – PUPIL ALMOST ALWAYS PRACTICES THE TRAIT.
G – PUPIL ACTS IN THE MANNER INDICATED MOST OF THE TIME.
C – PUPIL ACTS IN THE MANNER INDICATED PART OF THE TIME.
U – PUPIL SELDOM ACTS IN THE MANNER INDICATED.

CHARACTER AND ATTITUDE TESTS

NAME OF TEST	GRADE	DATE	RATING

ATTENDANCE RECORD

YEAR	19___		
HALF DAYS ABSENT			
TARDY			

PRESENT ADDRESS

NUMBER	STREET OR AVENUE	ZONE	TELEPHONE

INTELLIGENCE TESTS

NAME OF TEST	FORM	C. A.	M. A.	I. Q.

STANDARDIZED ACHIEVEMENT TESTS

GRADE	DATE	NAME OF TEST	FORM	GRADE EQUIV	P. R.	NORM

NAME OF TEST	GRADE	DATE	FORM	GRADE EQUIV	P. R.	NORM

FAMILY RECORD

FATHER'S NAME   PLACE OF BIRTH   RELIGION   DECEASED ( )   SEPARATED ( )   REMARRIED ( )

MOTHER'S MAIDEN NAME   PLACE OF BIRTH   RELIGION   DECEASED ( )   SEPARATED ( )   REMARRIED ( )

FATHER'S OCCUPATION   MOTHER'S OCCUPATION   BROKEN HOME: YES ( )   NO ( )

BAPTISM DATE   CHURCH   PLACE   CERTIFICATE: YES ( )   NO ( )

FIRST COMMUNION DATE   CHURCH   PLACE   CERTIFICATE: YES ( )   NO ( )

CONFIRMATION DATE   CHURCH   PLACE   CERTIFICATE: YES ( )   NO ( )

RECOMMENDATIONS—OBSERVATIONS—SPECIAL ABILITIES AND INTERESTS

YEAR	GRADE	TEACHER

RECORD OF ENTRIES AND WITHDRAWALS

YEAR	NO.	DAY	CAUSE

GRADUATED: SATISFACTORILY ( )   UNSATISFACTORILY ( )   DATE:

HIGH SCHOOL ENTERED:

PERMANENT OFFICE RECORD, ELEMENTARY SCHOOLS, ARCHDIOCESE OF CHICAGO

Pupil Cumulative Record Form

Registration Form[2]

For each new pupil in school a completed registration form should be required. Following constitutes minimum information which should be secured from the parent on this form:

Date _____

Name _____ Age _____
          (Last)   (First)   (Middle)

Address _____ Phone _____

Father's Name _____ Place of Birth _____ Religion _____

Occupation (what and where) _____

Mother's Maiden Name _____ Place of Birth _____ Religion _____

Occupation (what and where) _____

Birthplace of Pupil _____ Date of Birth _____
                  (City)   (State)

Baptism: Date _____ Church _____ Place _____

First Communion: Date _____ Church _____ Place _____

Confirmation: Date _____ Church _____ Place _____

Number of Children in Family: ___ Boys ___ Girls   Rank in Family _____

Family Physician _____ Address _____ Phone _____

School Last Attended _____ Place _____ Grade _____

Other Schools Attended _____ Place _____ Grades _____

_____ Place _____ Grades _____

_____ Place _____ Grades _____

Resides with _____ Religion _____

[2] Source: *Handbook of School Policies and Practices,* Diocese of Belleville, Ill., 1952, p. 36.

ARCHDIOCESE OF CHICAGO SCHOOL BOARD

Elementary School Summary Form

INSTRUCTIONS TO PRINCIPAL:

1. This form is to be filled out and signed when a pupil transfers from your school to another school.
2. This form always should accompany the blue copy of the official transfer form sent to the principal of the school to which the pupil is transferred.
3. This form also may be used when a summary form is requested by the principals of Catholic high schools.
4. This form never should be given to the student, his parents or guardians.

Name of Pupil _____ Date of Birth _____
                 LAST   FIRST   MIDDLE   MO.   DAY   YEAR

Name of Parent or Guardian _____ _____
                             LAST   FIRST   MIDDLE   STREET ADDRESS   CITY

From_____ School _____
                                                STREET ADDRESS   CITY

To_____ School _____
                                                STREET ADDRESS   CITY

STANDARDIZED TEST RECORD (Record results of the last test administered)

INTELLIGENCE TEST

GRADE	DATE	NAME OF TEST	FORM	CA	MA	IQ

ACHIEVEMENT TEST

GR.	DATE	NAME OF TEST	FORM	GRADE EQUIVALENTS									
				PAR. MEAN.	WORD MEAN.	AVER. READ.	SPELL.	LANG.	ARITH. REAS.	ARITH. COMP.	ARITH.	MEDIAN	

PERSONAL RECORD (Indicate by placing X in the respective column)

Attendance:	Good _____	Average _____	Poor_____
Social Habits:	Good _____	Average _____	Poor_____
Study Habits:	Good _____	Average _____	Poor_____
Health:	Good _____	Average _____	Poor_____

COMMENTS:_____

_____

_____

Date _____ Signature _____
                                              PRINCIPAL

Summary of Record for Pupil Transfer

459

REPORT OF ACCIDENT

TYPE OF ACCIDENT
(Check X which)

SCHOOL BUILDINGS

1. Classrooms and auditorium............
2. Laboratories ....
3. Vocational shops ....
4. Domestic science dept.....................
5. Gymnasium—basketball ....
6. " —other ....
7. Swimming pool and showers.........
8. Dressing-rooms and lockers...........
9. Toilets and washrooms....................
10. Corridors ....
11. Stairs and stairways........................
12. Other building ....

SCHOOL GROUNDS

13. Apparatus—swings ....
14. " —slides ....
15. " —teeters ....
16. " —bars ....
17. " —other ....
18. Athletics—baseball ....
19. " —football ....
20. " —soccer ....
21. " —track events ....
22. Other organized games...................
23. [Running...................
24. Unorganized | Scuffling..................
25. Activities | Other falls................
26. [Other...............

GOING TO AND FROM SCHOOL

27. Motor vehicle—bicycle ....
28. Other motor vehicle........................
29. Other bicycle ....
30. Other ....

HOME*

31. Falls ....
32. Burns, scalds, explosions................
33. Cuts and scratches...........................
34. Other home ....

OTHER*

35. Motor vehicle—bicycle ....
36. Other motor vehicle........................
37. Other bicycle ....
38. Other street and sidewalk...............
39. Playground (not school)..................
40. Other places ....

1. Was pupil out of school one-half day or more on account of accident? ....
2. If so, how many days?...................
3. Was pupil under doctor's care because of accident?......................

Cat. No. 7818

Name of
School .... Date.................... 19........

Time .... o'clock   Place...

Name of   ┌ **Girl** ☐
Person Injured.. └ **Boy** ☐

Address.. Age.............. Grade...........

Kind of   ┌ **Serious** ☐
Injury... ┤ **Minor** ☐
                                                     └ **Slight** ☐

Disposition   Sent   Sent to   Remained
of Injured   Home.......... Hospital........ at School............. Other ....

Was Accident Due to (Check X which)

1. Apparatus, faulty ....   6. Playing in street................
2. " abuse of ....   7. Tools ....
3. Bicycles, Skates, Scooters, etc..............   8. Action of another person...............
4. "Hitching-on" ....   Name of
5. Machinery ....   such person ....

SAFETY PRECAUTIONS

1. Were all due measures taken to insure safety? Yes...........No........ ...
2. Was proper use of apparatus, machinery, etc., explained? Yes...........No...........
3. Was first aid given? Yes...........No...........By Whom?.......................
4. Was a physician called? Yes........No........ Time of arrival...........o'clock A.M.......P.M......
   Name of Physician...............................
5. Did accident occur during regular class period? Yes...........No...........
6. Was parent or guardian notified? Yes...........No.......How?....................

Detailed Account of Accident (be specific)

Name of Witness	Address
1.	
2.	
3.	
4.	

Teacher ....

Principal ....

*"Home" and "Other" accidents should be reported whenever a doctor's attention is required or whenever a pupil is required to remain out of school one-half day or more.

Report of Accident—Student

CINCINNATI PUBLIC SCHOOLS
REPORT OF ACCIDENT - EMPLOYEE

Report to be made in quadruplicate as follows:
1. Department of Administration (white)
2. Division of Health and Hygiene (green)
3. Division of Staff Personnel (pink)
4. Office of Principal or Supervisor (yellow)

1. Date of Report _____

2. Name of injured employee _____
   First Name   Middle Initial   Last Name

3. Address _____
   street address   city   zone   state

4. Date of injury _____ Last day worked _____

5. Detailed account of accident (be specific) _____
_____
_____
_____
_____
_____

6. When and where _____

7. Names of witnesses _____
_____
_____

8. Attending physician or hospital _____

9. Occupation of injured employee _____

10. Department or school of injured employee _____

11. Estimated length of disability, if any _____

12. Is Workman's Compensation form being requested? _____

Note: Use the reverse side for additional comments. We would also
appreciate any suggestions for steps to be taken for the
prevention of future accidents of this nature.

Signature of Employee _____

Signature of Principal
or Supervisor   _____

(Signature is verification that the Principal or Supervisor has
checked the validity and completeness of the above statement)

Report of Accident—Employee

461

Appendix D

ILLUSTRATIVE LISTS OF FORMS AND EQUIPMENT

School Equipment[1]

A. Standard Equipment for any Catholic School

1. Typewriter(s); letterheads and matching envelopes.
2. Mimeograph, hectograph, or ditto machine.
3. Paper cutter, stapling machine.
4. Filing cabinets.
5. Wire or tape recorder.

---

[1] Source: *A Handbook of Policies for the Catholic Schools of the Archdiocese of New Orleans,* New Orleans, 1951, pp. 68–70.

462

6. Public address system (preferably with radio attachment).
7. 16 mm projector.
8. Tri-purpose projector; for other audio-visual aids, cf. p. 49 of *Handbook*.
9. Strong-box or safe.
10. Key rack.
11. Bulletin board, trophy case.
12. Material for remedial and developmental reading program.
13. Centralized science equipment.
14. Standardized tests (intelligence, achievement, personality, placement, vocational).
15. Electric school bell; electric clock(s).
16. Fire bell.
17. Electric eraser cleaner.
18. Telephone(s). (Number properly indicated under name of school in body of phone book and in classified section under both "Schools" and "Convents.")
19. First Aid Room Equipment.
20. Centralized place for movable playground equipment.
21. Teachers' rest room.
22. Drinking fountains in school building.
23. Rubber stamp with name, address, zone, and phone of school.
24. Rubber stamp for principal's signature.
25. Rubber stamp for each teacher's signature.
26. Artistic pictures and statues.

B. Standard Equipment for any Class Room

1. Statue and crucifix (facing pupils if possible).
2. Holy water font.
3. Christmas crib (at Christmas time).
4. Artistic pictures (in moderate number and carefully selected).
5. Plants and flowers (in season).
6. American flag (properly installed).
7. Individual desk (not a table) with drawers for teacher. Chair for teacher.
8. Individual desk for each pupil (desk should be adjustable or at least fit the pupil comfortably). *Desks are not attached to the floor.* Low tables and chairs for kindergarten.
9. Clock (preferably in rear of room).
10. Thermometer.
11. Pencil sharpeners (at height of average pupil in class).
12. Waste paper basket.
13. Calendar (type of advertisement on calendar is important).
14. Official school calendar and class schedule.

15. Book case.
16. Reading table with chair(s).
17. Chalkboards; bulletin board.
18. One dozen erasers.
19. One box of colored and white or yellow chalk.
20. Tack board.
21. Pointer and yardstick.
22. Pencil rack or pencil container.
23. Adequate space for coats, hats, etc.
24. Ample natural and artificial light (20 foot candles uniformly distributed).
25. Window shades (double roller preferable—in good, clean condition) or Venetian blinds.
26. Visual aids suited to the level.
27. Phonograph or (better) combination phonograph-radio.
28. Library books (five to the pupil if there is no central library).
30. Poster and construction paper.
31. Oaktag sheets.
32. Cream manila.
33. Master key chromatic pitch pipe.
34. Staffliner, keyboard for music.
35. Scotch tape, thumb tacks, pins, paper fasteners.
37. Blackboard cleanser (neither water nor oil should be applied to chalkboards).
38. Kleenex.
39. First aid kit, unless there is a common health room.
40. Rubber bands.
41. Assorted envelopes.
42. Flower vases.

C. Standard Schoolyard Equipment for Elementary Schools
1. Chute-the-chute (slide) ⎫
2. See-saw   ⎪
                            ⎬ Not on hard-surfaced ground
3. Swings   ⎪
4. Trapeze bars   ⎭
5. Hard-surfaced ground marked for:
   volley ball   basketball   indoor baseball   shuffleboard
      Ample supply of sportgoods equipment for each.
6. Drinking fountains (properly installed and meeting health regulations).
7. Flagpole and flag (U.S. and U.N.)
8. Benches.
9. Bicycle racks.
10. Wire fence. A high brick or wooden fence is less desirable.

D. Standard Custodial Equipment
1. Brooms, mop, buckets, and wringer.
2. Detergent soap.
3. Disinfectants (preferably handled periodically by experts).
4. Chemical acids.
5. Wax.
6. Dusters.
7. Paper towels with dispenser (for pupils).
8. Toilet tissue; sanitary napkins for girls' room.
9. Liquid hand soap and dispenser.
10. Hot and cold water.
11. Waxing machine.
12. Exterminators (preferably handled periodically by experts).
13. Sweeping compound.
14. Waste paper container (in toilet rooms).
15. Window cleaners (cheesecloth, ammonia, chamois). (Windows should be washed on outside at least twice a year; on inside at least once a month.)
16. Janitor's storage service.
17. Incinerator.

E. A Suggestion

In order to inspire the pupils to keep their school neat, clean, and un-damaged, the following sign might be printed in large letters and placed strategically through the school, including the entrances to toilet rooms.

LEST YOU FORGET!

YOU ARE ON CHURCH PROPERTY BLESSED AND

DEDICATED TO ALMIGHTY GOD

BUILT AND MAINTAINED BY THE GENEROUS

CONTRIBUTIONS OF THE PEOPLE OF

———————————————————— PARISH

SHOW YOUR APPRECIATION. DO NOT MARK

THESE WALLS OR DAMAGE THESE BUILDINGS

OF WHICH WE ARE JUSTLY PROUD

Mimeographed Forms[2]

Order List

——————— Year

Form No.

201	ABC Report	_____
202	Absence and Tardiness—Pupil	_____
203	Accident Report	_____
204	Application for Exemption from Vaccination Policy	_____
205	Building Facilities Application	_____
206	Building Facilities Report	_____
207	Cafeteria Report for Clerk	_____
	Corporal Punishment:	
208a	Report by Teacher	_____
208b	Report by Principal	_____
209	Daily Lunchroom Report	_____
210	Employees Attendance Record	_____
211	Estimated Enrollment Classes Various Classes	_____
212	Estimate of Supplies on Hand	_____
213	Excessive Tardiness of Employee	_____
214	Excuse of Teacher at Close of School	_____
215	Extra Employee's Individual Hour and Wage Record Sheet	_____
216	School Patrol Permit	_____
217	Substitute Teachers' Payroll	_____
218	Teacher's Certificate of Personal Illness	_____
219	Time Schedule	_____
221	Referrals	_____
222	Report of Absence and Tardiness	_____
350	Application for Increments	_____
351	Attendance Cards—Boys	_____
352	Girls	_____
353	Book Labels	_____
354	Book Loan Cards	_____
355	Book Loan Sheets	_____
356	Change of Address	_____
357	Enrollment Blanks	_____
358	Grade Books	_____
359	Home Visit Cards	_____

[2] Source for order lists: Norwood, Ohio, Public Schools.

Printed Forms

Order List

Elementary Schools

_____ Year

Form No.

Monthly Attendance Report Forms:

360	Principal's Report for School Month Ending (% Attendance)	_____
361	Enrollment and Attendance of Room (green sheet)	_____
362	Pass Slips	_____
363	Permanent Record Cards	_____
364	Personnel Folders	_____
365	Post Cards—Requests for Personnel Folders	_____
366	Registers	_____
	Report Cards	
367	Green—Kindergarten	_____
368	Blue—Primary Grades, 1, 2, 3	_____
369	Salmon—Intermediate Grades, 4, 5, 6	_____
370	Yellow—7, 8	_____
371	Report Card Envelopes	_____
372	Room Seating Plans	_____
	Term End Reports	
373	Kindergarten	_____
374	Grades 1, 2, 3	_____
375	Grades 4, 5, 6, 7, 8	_____
376	Withdrawal Slips	_____

Forms Ordered by the School Nurse:

401	Physical Examination Record
402	Dental Cards
403	Vaccination Cards
404	Medical Attention Cards
405	I. Exclusions (Illness) Cards

Mimeographed Maps

Order List

_____ Year

The Superintendent's Office supplies stencil maps, 8½ x 11, as follows:

Africa	_____	New England	_____
Asia	_____	North America	_____

Australia	_____	Ohio	_____
British Isles	_____	Roman World	_____
Canada	_____	South America	_____
Central States	_____	Southern States	_____
Europe	_____	United States	_____
Grecian World	_____	U.S. Rainfall	_____
Italy	_____	Western States	_____
Mexico	_____	World	_____
Mid-Atlantic States	_____		

Appendix E

ILLUSTRATIVE FORM FOR BIDS ON A
NEW SCHOOL BUILDING

Proposal Form

Submitted by

_____ _____ 19___
                Name of Bidder

To the Board of Education of the City School District of the City of Cincinnati:

The undersigned, having carefully studied the local conditions affecting the cost of the work, and the Contract Documents, including Legal Notice, Instructions to Bidders, Proposal Form, Guaranty, Contract Form, Bond Form, General Conditions, Drawings and Specifications, and Addenda Nos. _____ issued and attached to the Specification on file in the office of the Business Manager, 511 W. Court St., Cincinnati, Ohio, hereby propose to perform everything required to be performed and to provide and furnish all of the labor, materials, necessary tools, expendable equipment, and all utility and transportation services necessary to perform and complete in a workmanlike manner all of the work, required for such branch or branches of work as are hereinafter designated, in the time hereinafter specified, in connection with the construction of

WASHINGTON PARK ELEMENTARY SCHOOL

14TH, RACE AND ELM STREETS

CINCINNATI, OHIO

project of the Board, all in accordance with the aforementioned Contract Documents, for the sum of money enumerated for said branch or branches.

469

the said amount or amounts constituting the Base Bid or Bids. Such Base Bid or Bids may be increased or decreased in accordance with such alternate and/or substitute proposals as may be selected by the Board.

	BASE BIDS Item 1. General Construction	*Labor*	*Material*	*Total*
Section II.	Excavation, Filling, Grading and Yard Paving	$__	$__	$__
III.	Concrete Work	__	__	__
IV.	Masonry Work	__	__	__
V.	Steel Joists	__	__	__
VI.	Miscellaneous Iron Work	__	__	__
VII.	Architectural Metal Work	__	__	__
VIII.	Gypsum Roof Deck	__	__	__
IX.	Metal Frames and Doors	__	__	__
X.	Roofing and Sheet Metal Work	__	__	__
XI.	Carpentry and Millwork	__	__	__
XII.	Exterior and Interior Aluminum Work	__	__	__
XIII.	Lathing and Plastering	__	__	__
XIV.	Terrazzo Floors and Tile Work	__	__	__
XV.	Resilient Floors	__	__	__
XVI.	Acoustical Tile Work	__	__	__
XVII.	Glass and Glazing	__	__	__
XVIII.	Miscellaneous Items	__	__	__
XIX.	Painting	__	__	__
XX.	Finishing Hardware	__	__	__

Item 1. Total General Construction, Sections II to XX inclusive. $__ $__ $__

Item 2. Kitchen Equipment, Section XXI $__ $__ $__

Item 3. Plumbing Work, Section XXII $__ $__ $__

Item 4. Heating and Ventilating Work, Section XXIII $__ $__ $__

Item 5. Electrical Work, Section XXIV $__ $__ $__

Item 6. Lump Sum Base Bid for any combination of Items 1 to 5 (State which items are being combined.) $__ $__ $__

Item 7. Unit price per cubic yard for Abandoned Cisterns and Like Items

$__

Item 8. Unit price per cubic yard for Lean Concrete Fill

$__

Item 9. Unit price per cubic yard for Sand and
Gravel Fill $_____

ALTERNATES

Item 10. *Alternate no. 1.* Amount to be *added*
to or *deducted* from Base Bid if natural alumi-
lite finish is used in lieu of brush finish for all
aluminum work specified under Exterior and
Interior Aluminum Work, Section XII
    Add $_____ $_____ $_____
    Deduct $_____ $_____ $_____

Item 11. *Alternate no. 2.* Amount to be *added*
to or *deducted* from Base Bid if natural alumi-
lite finish is used in lieu of brush finish for all
aluminum work specified under Exterior and
Interior Aluminum Work, Section XII, except
finish panels with Alcoa Architectural Colors
    Add $_____ $_____ $_____
    Deduct $_____ $_____ $_____

Item 12. *Alternate no. 3.* Amount to be *added*
to or *deducted* from Base Bid if natural alumi-
lite finish is used in lieu of brush finish for all
aluminum work specified under Exterior and
Interior Aluminum Work, Section XII, except
finish panels of aluminum surface with colored vitreous enamel matte finish
    Add $_____ $_____ $_____
    Deduct $_____ $_____ $_____

Item 13. *Alternate no. 4.* Amount to be *added* to
or *deducted* from Base Bid if natural alumi-
lite finish is used in lieu of brush finish for all
aluminum work specified under Exterior and
Interior Aluminum Work, Section XII, except
finish panels of steel surface with colored vitreous enamel matte finish
    Add $_____ $_____ $_____
    Deduct $_____ $_____ $_____

Item 14. *Alternate no. 5.* Amount to be *added* to
or *deducted* from Base Bid if Truscon Steel
Vision vent windows, frames and mullions
and porcelain enameled panels are used in
lieu of aluminum work specified under Exterior and Interior Aluminum Work, Section
XII

Add $_____ $_____ $_____
Deduct $_____ $_____ $_____

Item 15. *Alternate no. 6.* Amount to be *added*
to or *deducted* from Base Bid if ceramic glazed
structural tile is used in lieu of interior terrazzo face block construction
    Add $_____ $_____ $_____
    Deduct $_____ $_____ $_____

Item 16. *Alternate no. 7.* Amount to be *added*
to or *deducted* from Base Bid if manufactured
granite, "Granux" or equal, is used in lieu of
exterior terrazzo face block construction
    Add $_____ $_____ $_____
    Deduct $_____ $_____ $_____

Item 17. *Alternate no. 8.* Amount to be *added*
to Base Bid for waterproofing exterior brick
    Add $_____ $_____ $_____

Item 18. *Alternate no. 9.* Amount to be *added*
to Base Bid if vinyl plastic asbestos tile is used
in all areas where asphalt tile is called for
on the drawings
    Add $_____ $_____ $_____

Item 19. *Alternate no. 10.* Amount to be *deducted* from Base Bid if Alternate Stair Construction indicated on the drawings is used
    Deduct $_____ $_____ $_____

Item 20. *Alternate no. 11.* Amount to be *deducted* from Base Bid for omitting skylights
and jalousies and extending roof construction
over the areas affected
a) General construction
    Deduct $_____ $_____ $_____
b) Electrical work
    Deduct $_____ $_____ $_____

Item 21. *Alternate no. 12.* Amount to be *added*
to or *deducted* from Base Bid if vertically slid-
ing wardrobe doors are used in lieu of vertically pivoted doors
    Add $_____ $_____ $_____
    Deduct $_____ $_____ $_____

Item 22. *Alternate no. 13.* Amount to be *added*
to Base Bid if light diffusing glass, Factrolite,
or equal, is used in lieu of sheet glass in certain areas as listed for north elevation
    Add $_____ $_____ $_____

Item 23. *Alternate no. 14.* Amount to be *deducted* from Base Bid if low draft loss fly ash collector is used in lieu of high draft loss collector
    Deduct   \$_____ \$_____ \$_____

Item 24. *Alternate no. 15.* Amount to be *deducted* from Base Bid if mechanical soot blowers are omitted
    Deduct   \$_____ \$_____ \$_____

Item 25. *Alternate no. 16.* Amount to be *deducted* from Base Bid if coal conveyors are omitted
    a) Heating and ventilating work
        Deduct   \$_____ \$_____ \$_____
    b) Electrical work
        Deduct   \$_____ \$_____ \$_____

Item 26. *Alternate no. 17.* Amount to be *deducted* from Base Bid if mechanically operated ash hoist is furnished in lieu of hydraulically operated ash hoist
    Deduct   \$_____ \$_____ \$_____

Item 27. *Alternate no. 18.* Amount to be *deducted* from Base Bid if radiant heating is omitted in kindergarten rooms
    Deduct   \$_____ \$_____ \$_____

Item 28. *Alternate no. 19.* Amount to be *added* to Base Bid if permanent washable type filters are furnished in lieu of Fiberglas throw-away type filters
    Add   \$_____ \$_____ \$_____

Item 29. *Alternate no. 20.* Amount to be *deducted* from Base Bid if 1500 ampere feeder bus duct is used in lieu of 3000 ampere feeder
    Deduct   \$_____ \$_____ \$_____

Item 30. *Alternate no. 21.* Amount to be *added* to or *deducted* from Base Bid if Trane Company Model FBPE unit ventilators with air discharge in rear are furnished in lieu of Herman Nelson unit ventilators
    a) General construction
        Add   \$_____ \$_____ \$_____
        Deduct   \$_____ \$_____ \$_____
    b) Heating and ventilating work
        Add   \$_____ \$_____ \$_____
        Deduct   \$_____ \$_____ \$_____

Item 31. *Alternate no. 22.* Amount to be *added* to or *deducted* from Base Bid if Fiberglas built-up roofing is furnished in lieu of built-up felt paper roofing

Add   \$_____ \$_____ \$_____

Deduct   \$_____ \$_____ \$_____

Item 32. *Alternate no. 23.* Amount to be *added* to or *deducted* from Base Bid if Fiberglas insulation is furnished in lieu of wool felt insulation on cold water lines and magnesia insulation on hot water lines and hot water storage tank

Add   \$_____ \$_____ \$_____

Deduct   \$_____ \$_____ \$_____

Item 33. *Alternate no. 24.* Amount to be *added* to or *deducted* from Base Bid if Fiberglas insulation is furnished in lieu of asbestos insulation on heating supply and return piping

Add   \$_____ \$_____ \$_____

Deduct   \$_____ \$_____ \$_____

Item 34. *Alternate no. 25.* Amount to be *added* to or *deducted* from Base Bid if Fiberglas insulation is furnished in lieu of magnesia insulation on boilers and breeching

Add   \$_____ \$_____ \$_____

Deduct   \$_____ \$_____ \$_____

It is understood and agreed by the undersigned that the Board of Education reserves the unrestricted privilege to reject any or all of the foregoing unit prices which it may consider excessive or unreasonable, or to accept by including the same in the contract as unit prices applicable in the event of additions to or deductions from the work to be performed under the contract, any or all such unit prices which it may consider fair and reasonable.

It is hereby certified that the name of every person interested in this proposal is contained herein.

Time of Completion—(To be filled in by Bidders bidding on total branches of General Construction)

It is understood and agreed that all work covered by this proposal, together with the Alternates and any Additions thereto shall be completed on or before _____ 19__ unless for good reason, an extension of time is granted by the Board of Education.

"Standards-Substitutions"

All bids shall be based upon the "Standards" specified. Bidders desiring to make substitutions for "Standards" specified, shall list proposed substitutions on a separate form, together with the amount to be added to, or to be deducted from the amounts of their base bids. If no addition or deduction in amount is offered, it shall be so indicated by the bidder. This listing of substitutions shall be part of this proposal. The Board reserves the right to accept or reject substitutions.

It is understood that this proposal and all other proposals shall be publicly opened and read by the Clerk of the Board of Education, in the presence of the Board, which will convene at its usual meeting time after the time for filing such proposals has expired, at the Board Room of the Board of Education, 608 East McMillan Street, Cincinnati, Ohio, the usual place of meeting of the Board of Education, and this and all other proposals shall be tabulated and computed by the Business Manager of the Board, and a report thereof made to the Board at its next meeting. The Board will treat all bidders for this work alike in every respect, and it will take final action upon this and all other proposals for this work not later than sixty days after this and all other proposals are opened, as aforesaid. No proposal shall be considered as accepted, nor any obligation hereunder assumed by the Board of Education until such time as said board may deposit in the United States mail, written notice addressed to the successful bidder or bidders at the address given on the proposal, of acceptance of this proposal, or of award of a contract.

It is also understood and agreed by the undersigned that the right is reserved by the Board of Education to reject any and all bids.

In consideration of the above, it is hereby agreed that this proposal shall be irrevocable for a period of sixty days, after it is opened by said Clerk, and that if this proposal is accepted, the bidder will, within five days after receiving notice of the acceptance of said proposal, enter into contract, in writing, for said work, with surety to the satisfaction of the Board, faithfully to perform said contract according to its terms and according to said drawings and specifications and that _____ _____ will promptly pay all damages and expenses accruing to said Board by reason of the failure or refusal of the undersigned to enter into said contract.

Firm Name: _____
By _____
Title _____

Official Address

(Note: Bidders must not add any conditions or qualifying statements to their proposal as otherwise it may be declared irregular as being not responsible to the Legal Notice.)

Guaranty

We, the undersigned, are held firmly bound unto the Board of Education of the City School District of the City of Cincinnati, in the sum of _____
_____(Dollars) ($_____), for the payment of which we hereby jointly and severally bind ourselves and our legal representatives by these presents, signed and sealed by us, at Cincinnati, this _____ day of _____, 19__.

The condition of this obligation is such, that if the above proposal is accepted and contract awarded to

_____

(Name of Bidder)

_____

and said _____

(Name of Bidder)

_____

shall, within five days after the receipt of notice of such award, enter into the prescribed contract, in writing, with approved surety; or in case the said

_____

(Name of Bidder)

_____

shall fail or refuse to perfect said contract as aforesaid, and shall promptly pay all damages accruing to said Board by reason of such failure or refusal, then this obligation shall be null and void; otherwise it shall remain in full force and effect.

Index

477